The Papers of Samuel Marchbanks

By the same author

The Papers of Samuel Marchbanks

comprising the Diary, the
Table Talk and
a Garland of Miscellanea
by
Samuel Marchbanks

but enlarged (to include a
Biographical Introduction and
Copious Notes calculated to remove
all Difficulties caused by the
passing of Time and to offer the Wisdom,
not to speak of the Whimsicality,
of this astonishing man to the Modern Public,
in the most convenient form)
by his long-suffering friend,
ROBERTSON DAVIES

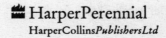
HarperPerennial
HarperCollins*Publishers*Ltd

A hardcover edition of this book was first published in 1985 by Irwin Publishing Inc.

First paperback edition published by Collins Publishers: 1987
First HarperPerennial edition published: 1991

Material in Parts One and Two of The Papers of Samuel Marchbanks is drawn from:

The Diary of Samuel Marchbanks, Clarke Irwin 1947

The Table Talk of Samuel Marchbanks, Clarke Irwin 1949

Marchbanks' Garland is drawn from material in Samuel Marchbanks' Almanac by Robertson Davies. Used by permission of The Canadian Publishers, McClelland and Stewart Limited, Toronto.

Canadian Cataloguing in Publication Data

Davies, Robertson, 1913
    The papers of Samuel Marchbanks

HarperPerennial ed.
ISBN 0-00-223168-9

I. Title.

PS8507.A67P37 1991   C818'.5407   C91-094474-1
PR9199.3.D3P37 1991

---

91 92 93 94 95 96 97 98 99 WEB 10 9 8 7 6 5 4 3 2 1

Design: Brant Cowie/Artplus Ltd.

Contents

Introduction

*T*HERE CAN BE no doubt that Samuel Marchbanks is one of the choice and master spirits of this age. If there were such a volume as *Who Really Ought To Be Who* his entry would require several pages. The author of the *Diary*, the *Table Talk* and the never-sufficiently-to-be-praised *Garland* has probably said more on a wider variety of topics than any other philosopher of the past forty years, and it has been the happy inspiration of the publisher to bring out these three books in a single volume.

It was clear, however, that some editorial work was needed. Who, under the age of forty-five, can say with accuracy what a coal-fired furnace was, or what people meant when they spoke of "sending telegrams"? It is not that Marchbanks is trapped in a past age; he is for all time. But inevitably in our sadly rushing world there have been social changes that need to be clarified for recent generations. The question was: who should edit Marchbanks?

When I was approached, I accepted with alacrity. I would, I promised, equip the works of Marchbanks with what is called "a scholarly apparatus," meaning that I would iron out all the difficulties, correct any errors of fact that might have crept into the original versions, explain the significance of any names that might be unfamiliar to modern readers, and generally act as a gentle headwaiter to Marchbanks' splendid banquet.

It proved not to be as easy as I thought. Although he is the most accessible of philosophers, economists, political theorists and *littérateurs* for his readers, Marchbanks presents special problems for his editor, and I had not realized how much our long friendship and close physical resemblance — though I am substantially the smaller — would complicate an apparently straightforward editorial task.

❀❀❀❀❀❀❀❀❀❀❀❀❀❀❀❀❀❀❀❀❀❀❀❀❀❀❀❀❀❀

*M*ARCHBANKS IS ONE of the last of a breed of Canadians whose racial strains and mental habits derive from those Loyalists who came north to this country after the American Revolution of 1776. They were a cantankerous, resolute breed, superficially loyal to old manners and old trains of thought, but in fact determinedly individualistic. To think of Marchbanks himself as a Tory is absurd. He said to me, not long ago: "Canada at present has three political parties whom I think of as Flopsy, Mopsy and Cottontail. Flopsy and Mopsy are devoted to the banks and the industries; Cottontail claims to speak for the Workers, by which it seems to mean unionized persons intent on working the shortest negotiable hours for the highest negotiable rates of pay; as a man who has for forty-five years worked hours definable only by As Long As It Takes, and for the kind of pay available to literary men, I feel no kinship with Cottontail. Politically I am the leader and entire membership of the Marchbanks Humanist Party to which, in forty-five years, I have not attracted a single adherent. Why this should be so I cannot guess, but it makes me grieve for my country."

Readers of the pages that follow will have no trouble in guessing why Marchbanks has no followers. He is a man of fiercely disputatious character and has few friends. Of these few I am the longest in duration and the most humble and submissive in nature. For these reasons — because I can put up with him — the publishers have asked me to edit Marchbanks, and I have consented. The result is in your hand.

I approached my task with misgiving. Marchbanks is an impetuous and inveterately inaccurate writer; correcting his innumerable errors and explaining his slapdash references and half-baked assumptions has been a tough job, even for one experienced in editorial work. Throughout his life Marchbanks has earned his living as a journalist and he has all the romantic disdain for fact that distinguishes his kind. He writes at full speed, never pausing for reflection or using one word when he can think of two. He is lucky to have me for an editor. But am I lucky to have him as a subject? Can you ask?

He is a man deeply resentful of criticism or restraint of any kind. If he needs a fact to support his argument, and cannot immediately find one, he makes it up. But—and this is what has made my task a burden—it is hard to be sure when he has given rein to his imagination. Time and again I have found his most improbable assertions strongly rooted in fact. The magpie mind reflected in his work is crammed with oddities which he can support by reference to some out-of-the-way book nobody else would think of reading, or some tattered yellow newspaper clipping that shows him to be right. He is an editor's nightmare.

Nevertheless, I have done the job. The Notes I have added to Marchbanks' text extend its interest very considerably. We editors are not the pallid hacks that Marchbanks thinks us.

❊❊❊❊❊❊❊❊❊❊❊❊❊❊❊❊❊❊❊❊❊❊❊❊❊❊❊❊

WHEN MY WORK was nearly completed I decided to approach Marchbanks himself, and discuss the project with him. This in itself is unscholarly. When you are preparing a critical edition of a man's work—a man who is not safely dead—it is unprofessional and dangerous to let him have any say in what you are doing, because he will want to put a finger in the pie. What you have made tidy, he will want to mess up. Nevertheless, knowing Marchbanks as I do, I was aware how dangerous it would be to let this book appear in print without his knowledge.

Perhaps I allowed vanity to guide me. I greatly admired that film *Dinner With André*, and I hoped I might provoke something similar, along the lines of *A Drink With Marchbanks*.

I sought him out, therefore. As I knew I would, I found him at five o'clock in the afternoon of a February day at one of his favourite ports of call, a tavern called The Crank and Schizoid, close by the Clarke Institute of Psychiatry in the city of Toronto. Marchbanks likes to go there to eavesdrop on the professional gossip of the psychiatrists who frequent the place when their work-day (nine fifty-minute hours) is over. "Nothing leaks like a full shrink," Marchbanks has often said, and he picks up a lot of information in the pub about persons highly placed in government and business.

There he was, in a dark corner, and before him on the table was a glass of his favourite tipple, a lukewarm gin-and-acid-rain.

"You do not surprise me in the least," he said, when I explained my visit. "I knew this would happen, and I knew the publishers would ask you to do the job. Not, as you presumptuously suppose, because of your reputation as a scholar, but because of the deep sympathy that has so long existed between us. You recall the old Victorian melodrama of *The Corsican Brothers*? No, of course you don't. You never know anything that is of real significance. In that play the brothers are united by a psychic bond, in spite of superficial differences of character. When one of them is kicked by an enemy, the other is unable to sit down for several days: if the other is attracted by a woman, the first is moved — he knows not why — to send her a bouquet of flowers. You and I are like that, Davies. We are *The Canadian Brothers*. You, the academic, pussyfooting brother and I the dashing, romantic brother. It is as simple as that."

I yearned to contradict him with passion. But no — I recognized the justice of what he had said. I did not glory in it, but I acknowledged it.

"Well — yes, Sam," I said; "I suppose that's about the size of it. But need you rub it in?"

"Who's rubbing anything in?" he demanded. Facts are facts, and psychological facts are indisputable. But reflect: you and I, between us, have lived a remarkable, fully-realized life. I free and you trammelled. I clear-eyed and you blinkered by commonplace opinions. I intolerant of popular nonsense and you hoodwinked by everything you hear from politicians and self-styled experts. I daring to call my soul my own, and you yielding squatter's rights in your soul to anybody who can brow-beat you. Singly, what are we? I have been called insufferable, and you are widely known to be self-destructively tolerant. But put us together, and what have you? Man, as Hamlet described him — noble in reason, infinite in faculty — the beauty of the world — the paragon of animals! We need one another, you and I. I can't say I like it, but I am prepared to put up with it."

"Are you saying that you are my *alter ego*?" said I, astonished at this generosity.

"No, I am not. I detest the term *alter ego*; it suggests some dreadful non-cholesterol cooking substance. We are, each to the other a *Doppelgänger*, if you know the term."

"Aha," said I, pleased to be on familiar ground, "then it might be said that, in Jungian terms, I am the real man, and you are my Shadow." I was delighted to have found a point of view from which I could write a really satisfactory introduction to this book. But—

"Intolerable presumption," shouted Marchbanks, thumping the table so loudly that several psychiatrists looked round. "I am the reality, the essential man, free, proud and undeluded by the hokum of the modern world; you are the Good Citizen, the Taxpayer, the Homebody, the Dupe and Donkey of Democracy, the creature who goes through life chained and blindfolded, to sink at last in his taxed coffin into his taxed grave, leaving his Reality—his Money, such as it is—to be devoured by the hyenas of the State. You move me to Biblical obloquy: I spurn you with my foot, I spew you out of my mouth, I blow you out of my nose, I—"

"Shut up, Sam," I begged; "people are looking!"

Indeed they were. The barkeeper was muttering, "Keep it down, eh, you guys."

"Of course people are looking," said Marchbanks. "In this country people always look in amazement when anyone is moved by passion or simply by righteous indignation. For you to suggest that I am *your* Shadow—therein scholarly impertinence has surely found its masterpiece."

"Then consider it this way," said I; "let us call ourselves two sides of a coin."

"Very well," said he; "let the coin be a Canadian five-cent piece. I am the *recto* side, bearing the Royal Countenance and the inscription, "Ruler By God's Grace"—the side that speaks of nobility of spirit and continuance of great traditions: you are the *verso* side, bearing the image of the beaver, symbolic of the Canadian Citizen—a dowdy rodent, most valuable to his country when skinned. That will do nicely."

I sighed. "You are so contradictory, Sam," I said. "You declare yourself to be the head of a one-man splinter party. What does that make you, if not an anarchist? Yet now you are equating yourself with royalty."

"Well, what about it?" said he. "I see no contradiction. Of course I am an anarchist. What is an anarchist but a defier of settled power, a protester against all rule, a detector of flaws in every system, an element in society necessary if we are not to be trampled under the feet of a few hundred people who have won a TV popularity contest they call an election, and their masters and hidden manipulators — the Civil Service? Royalty, on the other hand, is the single check left in a democratic state against factions and gangs and the puppets they call their leaders. When, in my anguish as an overburdened citizen, I fling myself at the foot of the Throne, I am appealing to the one person in the realm whose destiny, like my own, is determined by a power no government can reach. I am Marchbanks, by the Grace of God."

"I still don't see where anarchy comes in," said I.

"Oh, you are always whining for explanations! Have you no intuitive understanding of great issues? Can't you see that it is rules and laws that make most of the social problems? Flopsy, Mopsy and Cottontail are all competing to devise systems of law to make us perfect citizens of a perfect state. They cannot grasp that morality and freedom are interwined. Have you never read the manifesto of the Marchbanks Humanist Party?
How does it begin? —

> *The more taboos and prohibitions there are in the world*
> *The poorer the people will be.*
>
> *The more sharp weapons the people have*
> *The more troubled the state will be.*
>
> *The more cunning and skill man possesses*
> *The more vicious things will appear.*
>
> *The more laws and orders are made prominent*
> *The more thieves and robbers there will be.*

And who wrote that, do you suppose?"

"You, I imagine."

"No, you don't imagine. That's what's wrong with you, and your kind; you don't, and can't imagine. Those words were written by the Chinese sage Lao Tzu in the sixth century B.C. And upon

those principles, understood in modern terms, rests the program—
or I had better call it a non-program—of my Humanist Party."

❋❋❋❋❋❋❋❋❋❋❋❋❋❋❋❋❋❋❋❋❋❋❋❋❋❋❋❋❋❋

*S*IGHING, I CALLED the bartender and ordered another
large double straight malt. This encounter was going to
be even worse than I had supposed.

"Let's talk about your life," I said. "Readers of our selection will
expect some information about your life. Come on, Sam; were
you really born in a place called Skunk's Misery?"

"To doubt it is to doubt geography," said he. "You will find it
only on the largest maps, but if you enquire of the right people, in
the right place, they will tell you where it is. The old homestead
has sunk rather far into the swamp, I understand, but some relics
of it are still there. The weekly paper, *The Skunk's Misery Trombone*,
on which I learned my craft; the barbershop where as a boy I had
my ten-cent haircut, with the barber's stomach, warm and mater-
nal, lolled over me like a duvet. You behold in me the descendant
—unworthy perhaps, but probably not—of pioneers and Loyalists.
I am a WASP, and nothing of the derision that is nowadays directed
at that ethnic group touches me."

"But a WASP is a White Anglo-Saxon; you are always blowing
about the purity of your Celtic descent."

"You surely don't suggest that I describe myself as a WC, do
you? That would simply be playing into the hands of my detractors. No, no; for those loose thinkers who have no conception of a
Celt, I must appear as a WASP."

"Very well," said I, "but was there nothing picturesque about
your childhood. Surely you come from a broken home?"

"Not a crack to be found in it anywhere," said he. "I toast my
entire family and ancestry in this glass of gin-and-acid-rain, and if
we are to go on talking you had better order me another."

I motioned to the bartender. "Not coming from a broken home
is rather a poor start for a Canadian writer. Perhaps you were a
battered child? No? Well, we must do the best we can. Tell me
that you endured crippling poverty."

"Never missed a meal or wore a dirty shirt," said he. "Of course
I mingled a great deal with the poor. Still do. But you understand

that I speak of the Poor in Spirit, many of whom are well placed in the world and winter in the South. Nevertheless, poor as church mice. No, let me amend that: poor as Rationalist Mice — terrible cases of Rationalist Rickets among their children."

"Well, what about education? You had to struggle for it against uncomprehending elders? Lay on your stomach on cold winter nights, reading Homer by the dying fire on the cabin hearth?"

"All education is a struggle," said Marchbanks. "I had to struggle against schools and universities, of course, in order to get time to educate myself, which I did magnificently."

"Oh Sam," said I, "how can you say that when I have spent weeks and months going through your stuff, correcting stupid errors and rooting out unwarrantable assumptions, and suppressing downright lies. Your education was a mess."

"But a rich, fruity mess," said he with a leer of disgusting self-satisfaction.

"Your struggle to get a start — the pain of rejections, the hours of walking the streets in cold weather, hugging your tattered manuscripts, the oppressor's wrong, the proud man's contumely — surely you had plenty of that."

"Oh, plenty of the oppressor's wrong and the proud man's contumely, not to speak of the critic's sneer and the broadcaster's horse laugh. But I always had jobs. Employers fought over me. And I played fair with them, let me tell you. Worked like a dog — nay, a Trojan. Indeed on one occasion the Trojan government sent a deputation to study my methods, but they had to go home in defeat. The Trojans would never have stood for my concept of journalistic industry; they wanted a five-day week and statutory holidays, and I would have nothing to do with such shiftlessness. As for dogs — well, you know what I think about dogs."

"You are a great discouragement to a biographer," I said. "What about your private life? What about Sex?"

"Lower your voice," said Marchbanks; "those shrinks at the bar have very big ears when anybody is talking about Sex."

"You mean that at last I have struck pay-dirt? I am all agog."

"You may say so. You can have no idea of the social prestige I enjoyed during the years when my *Table Talk* was being talked at all the best tables. For one thing, I was considered powerfully attractive by what we must no longer call the Fair Sex. You remember that irresistible fellow in De Maupassant's story —"

"Do you mean Bel Ami? You mention him somewhere in your writings."

"That's the man. I was thought of as Bel Ami until the abrasive quality of my character changed it to Bon Ami. And of course hostesses wanted my opinion of their food. I was a celebrated gourmet. You understand what French perfume manufacturers mean by *un grand nez* — a chap who detects and judges the most delicate fragrances? In gourmet circles I was esteemed as *un grand estomac*. And it was during my Bel Ami period that I brought *pedalezza* to its finest perfection."

"*Pedalezza*!" said I, rolling the word like a rich morsel over my tongue. "*Pedalezza*! O divine *pedalezza* —"

"Shh! You're agog again," said Marchbanks. "The shrinks are looking, and I don't want to let them in on this yet. But when I choose to reveal everything, it will be discovered how generously I have benefited the profession of psychiatry, not to speak of the even greater profession of pornography. Yes, I devised a new form of Sex — not quite a perversion, but an elegant variation, which will go down in erotic history as Marchbanks' Caprice. Though I prefer the term *pedalezza*."

I sat down with my eyes fixed upon him, expectant. But Marchbanks was coy (a horrible sight) until I signalled to the bartender for refills. When the drinks came, he spoke.

"You have heard of *carezza*? Of course you have."

"Erotic stimulation by tickling?" said I.

"*Pedalezza* is a variant, deriving something from *frottage*, that other delight of the refined sensualist, but managed with the feet."

Even as he spoke I felt a very personal grasp upon my inner thigh, so unexpected that I leaped to my feet, looking fiercely around me for the offender.

"Calm down," said Marchbanks. "That was a touch of *pedalezza*, and you may imagine how it would work on the more delicate sensibility of a woman. It is to that I owe my unrivalled social popularity."

"Are you popular in society? I didn't know," said I, composing myself with the straight malt, for my nerves had been shaken.

"Society in the old sense is gone, utterly gone," said he. "But in the era when my *Table Talk* was collected and set down, I was the delight of the *Belle Époque*. In great demand for dinner parties, because whenever I was present fascinating things happened. Sometimes faces were slapped, or people ran from the table shrieking. But more often a totally unforeseen geniality spread through the party—an almost Viennese wistful gallantry—and wholly unpredictable romances blossomed. Hostesses never really knew how it came about, but they quite rightly associated it with my presence. 'Secure Marchbanks, and then build a table around him,' was the way they put it. During the Winter Season I had to refuse scores of invitations, because like all Advanced Sex, *pedalezza* is physically demanding."

"Come on," I said, "you have raised my expectations and you can't deny me now."

"You must understand that *pedalezza* is not for everyone. The arthritic and people with Lower Back Pain are debarred from its practice, as of course are those who lack the power of keeping up an interesting converstation above the waist while occupied otherwise from the waist down. While I fascinated the ladies on my left and right with the conversation recorded in my *Table Talk* I was having a high old time with *pedalezza* under the table."

"Come to the point," said I.

"The point?"

"The Climax, as Dr. Kinsey calls it."

"Ah, simplicity itself. I slipped off the elegant evening pump from my right or left foot—on a great night, I employed both —and stretching my silk-socked extremity beneath the table I would gently squeeze the thigh, or the sensitive area just above the knee, of a lady sitting on the other side of the table. This requires a prehensile quality of foot, which can be developed by picking up oranges from the floor for half an hour every day. The lady thus squeezed might squeak a little, but more often she blushed prettily and sometimes—if I were not quick—I would find that my foot was being given an answering squeeze. As a usual thing she showed a new warmth toward one or the other of her dinner partners, which pleasantly surprised him and gave me exquisite delight. I felt that I was playing the role of Fate in lives that needed a touch of fateful unpredictability."

"And that was *pedalezza?*"

"It was. I wish I might say that it still is, but you will have observed that I walk with a slight limp. A lady whose virtue I had underestimated stabbed me in the foot with a silver fork. It was all I could do not to scream with pain, but the laws of *pedalezza* are rigorous, and I forbore."

"But—allow me to ask—what was there in it for you, Sam?"

"I do not follow you."

"This *pedalezza*—the ladies never knew it was you?"

"But of course not! That was its ultimate refinement. *Exquisite enjoyment wholly divorced from any personal involvement.* What can Sex offer more?"

❋❋❋❋❋❋❋❋❋❋❋❋❋❋❋❋❋❋❋❋❋❋❋❋❋❋❋❋❋❋❋❋❋

TIME WAS PASSING and, although Marchbanks was in full command of himself, repeated doubles of straight malt were beginning to tell on me. "How do you manage it, Sam?" said I enviously.

"One hopes to learn a few things with the passing of time. Although there is some inevitable waning of the physical powers, one hopes to compensate by the acquired wisdom, physical and intellectual, of the years. *Geezerkraft*, I have named it, and those psychiatrists you see at the bar have adopted my term. It has an agreeable German ring in their ears, and German, as you know, is the language of psychiatry—German with a Viennese accent. You would do well to acquire a little *Geezerkraft* yourself."

I knew it, but I resented him knowing it. So I tried once more to assert the primacy of an editor over a mere author—to strike a blow in the age-old war of Critic and Creator.

"Jus' one more thing about your book, ol' man," said I. "Too damn many big words. Who knows 'em, eh? I mean—jus' for instance —that word Apophthegms. You see how hard it is to say—even I stumble over it. It's a puffy sort of word. Won't you change it?"

"Most certainly not. It is the fully appropriate word for some fully appropriate words. Indeed, that is what the word itself means. From Greek *apo*, meaning appropriate, and *phthegm*, meaning a gobbet neatly spat out. You should not try to restrict and shackle language, Davies. It is man's greatest achievement, and the principal thing that has raised him to his supremacy over the other animals. Without language there could be no abstract thought, no history, no consciousness of past, present, or future. Language, indeed, is the noblest of Man's inventions to meet the problem of Time. So don't restrict language: rejoice in it. I am proud to think I speak the tongue that Milton spake."

"You speak a tongue I don't think anybody ever spake," said I morosely. I was conscious of an imperative need. I rose and made my way to what I took to be the appropriate door and stumbled inside. What did I see but a lady psychiatrist whom I knew by sight, in a state of appropriate dishevelment! I was stricken, but she remained calm.

"If you wish to see me professionally, you should come to my office," said she. "If, on the other hand, you wish to see me personally, this is hardly the place to begin."

As I struggled to speak, Marchbanks, all *bonhomie*, burst through the door and seized my arm.

"Your pardon, doctor," said he. "My patient eluded my vigilance for a moment. As you see, a simple Peeping Tom. No harm in him, as anyone of your profession will be aware." He steered me back to neutral ground.

"And that will pay you out for that story I suppose you have printed about me," he said.

"It is in the book. It is now history, or at least biography. Everything I could glean about you, I have put in my book."

"You mean it is in *my* book," said he. "You may play your role of editorial Meddlesome Mattie as you please, but it remains *my* book."

"Ours?"

"*Mine!*"

✣✣✣✣✣✣✣✣✣✣✣✣✣✣✣✣✣✣✣✣✣✣✣✣✣✣✣✣✣✣✣✣✣

*A*nd so I suppose it must be. This is Marchbanks' book. But I have equipped it with copious notes that clarify certain difficulties, identify people Marchbanks assumed that everybody knows, and have dealt as best I can with problems arising in the memoirs of a man whose life has been flawed by ambiguity.

Here it is. I can do no more.

Robertson Davies

Saint David's Day
1985

The Diary of Samuel Marchbanks

edited, and with Notes by
ROBERTSON DAVIES

A WARNING TO THE READER

This is not a work of fiction, but of history—a record of the daily life of a Canadian during one of the early years of the Atomic Age. All the people mentioned in it are real; all the incidents described are actual happenings. Any suggestion to the contrary will be keenly resented.

S.M.

Winter

• SUNDAY & NEW YEAR'S DAY •

Laus Deo was the pious ejaculation with which the diarists of old began their year's entries, and I can do no less. Woke early this morning, and thanks to my discretion last night, my tongue was as red and shiny as a piece of Christmas ribbon, and my breath was like a zephyr from a May meadow. . . . Wasted no time on New Year's resolutions, for I outgrew such folly long ago. Any betterment in my character will be the outcome of prolonged meditation, and slow metabolic and metaphysical reform —a psychosomatic process, in other words. My only resolve is to keep this Diary faithfully for a year, without cant and—so far as in me lies (which may not be very far)—without exaggeration. There have been too few Canadian diarists ✒: however unfittingly, I have determined to fill the gap.

• MONDAY •

A holiday; sat by my fireplace most of the day, with the drawers of my various bureaux and desks gathered about me, and went through their contents, throwing away old letters and odds

---

Marchbanks was of course mistaken because in this, as in so much else, he regarded himself as the measure of mankind. There were diarists everywhere in Canada, scribbling away like mad, but in secret. One of the most voluminous was the Prime Minister, the Right Hon. W.L. Mackenzie King. Their diaries are now the Bread of Heaven to scores of editors and historians, as the Diaries of Marchbanks are to me. Ah, Sam, how little do you know of the avidity and hunger of posterity!

and ends, in one of my periodic strainings toward order and efficiency. Though the wrench is painful I can throw away old letters which were not interesting even when hot from the postman's hand, but there are some things which I can never bring myself to part with. I have old erasers, for instance, which have turned to stone and merely dirty and tear any paper upon which they are set to work, but they have associations for me which makes it impossible to throw them away. There are paper clips which have grown rusty with age, but I will not discard them for the excellent reason that I got them free and may some day get some use out of them. There are pipe-cleaners which are not very dirty, and although I have not smoked a pipe for some years, who can say when I shall begin again? ⸹ There are the keys of a flat in which I once lived, and which I preserve out of sheer sentimentality. There are old Christmas cards which are too pretty to put on the fire. There are three cigarette holders which have become plugged with immovable substances, but which may some day become unplugged (if I ever get a free hand with a compressed-air machine) and will then be as good as new. There is a box which is empty, but which bears the name of a very famous jeweller; I am keeping it in order that I may lend a factitious air of grandeur to a modest wedding-gift, some day. Therefore I cannot really reduce my drawers to order; I can only throw away some of the accumulation of years of tousled living. But even a little tidying gives me a righteous glow, and the rubbish made the fire burn brightly all day.

• TUESDAY •

Was talking to a man today who was bemoaning the dullness of his life; he wanted adventure, and it never came his way. His job gives him no outlet for the daring and resource which he is sure he possesses. I am never much impressed by such complaints;

Marchbanks always smokes a pipe—dirty, stinking things, many inherited from his forebears. He also smokes cigars of the vilest, cheapest varieties. When no more than a lad he acquired this socially objectionable habit, and is still in its loathsome toils.

it seems to me that most of us get all the adventure we are capable of digesting. Personally, I have never had to fight a dozen pirates single-handed, and I have never jumped from a moving express-train onto the back of a horse, and I have never been discovered in the harem of the Grand Turk. ∮ I am glad of all these things. They are too rich for my digestion, and I do not long for them. I have all the close shaves and narrow squeaks in my life that my constitution will stand, and my daily struggles with bureaucrats, tax-gatherers and uplifters are more exhausting than any encounters with mere buccaneers on the Spanish Main.

• WEDNESDAY •

Faced the fact with dull submission that the holiday season is now over and that a long, hard winter is before me. A man told me that he had always despised me because I confessed that I had trouble with my furnace; he never had any with his. But last week his "iron fireman" ∮ broke down, and he had to stoke his own machine for a day or two, and he had a new appreciation of my sufferings. . . . I am glad to hear it. What can a sybarite, a plutocrat with an automatic stoker know of the wretched tribulations of the proletariat? While I sweat and slave in my cellar, bursting my truss every time I heave a shovelful of coal, he lolls at ease in his arm-

---

Even in his private Diary, Marchbanks was never fully candid about his love-life, and the above statement is open to doubt. Careful research has enabled me to amplify this aspect of the story of Our Hero, and what I have discovered is included in the Introduction.

An "iron fireman" was a reputedly labour-saving device, basically a revolving metal worm which moved coal from the coal-pile to the maw of the furnace (of which more later). But the "iron fireman" frequently choked on stones, pieces of metal and other rubbish which had become mingled with the coal. When this happened it was not unusual for the contents of the worm to ignite, spreading backward to the coal supply, causing fires at worst, and, at best, dreadful stenches and effusions of coal gas.

chair, listening to the soothing hum of his mechanical stoker. . . . I am glad that he has been humbled and brought low. Now he will have sympathy with the deserving poor.

• THURSDAY •

Read an article in a Western newspaper, in which the writer rejoiced that the war had caused the railway dining cars to discard finger-bowls. He says that he has never liked finger-bowls, looking upon them as a useless and irksome frippery. . . . I scorn him. He is probably a poor wretch who has eaten off a corner of a kitchen table all his life, and who drank out of his finger-bowl the first time he was given one. Throw out the finger-bowl, and what goes next? The napkin. After the napkin, the table-cloth, and after the cloth, the knife and fork. My poor Western brother, if you want to eat with your hands you cannot do it at my table. I have always liked finger-bowls, and if possible, I like a few flower petals floating in them. I take my ceremonial lustrations as seriously as the Hebrews of old.

• FRIDAY •

Looked over some late Christmas cards today, including one with the words of *I Saw Three Ships* on it, and an elaborate background of music. But the music was not the music of the song; in fact, it was no music at all, but merely an artist's arrangement of notes, signifying nothing. ⨎ I like Christmas cards to have plenty of holly, and stage-coaches, and roaring fires, and stars, and Babes in a Manger and other such Christmassy pictures on them; I don't care much for the ultra-modern ones which try to get as far as possible from the season. . . . Was caught under the mistletoe today—at my age, too! I had forgotten that the stuff was

---

Marchbanks read music with ease, and played several instruments excruciatingly. He is the only pianist I have ever known who played with a stutter.

there. I am now in the time of life when only children lie in wait for me near the magic plant. There is something dispiriting about this. ✒

• SATURDAY AND OLD CHRISTMAS •

❀ Twelfth Night, and the official end of the Christmas celebrations, so I took down all the decorations and cards, and dutifully stuffed myself with mince pies and cheesecakes. There is a belief that one will have a happy month for every mince pie one eats today, and every year I gag myself trying to round out an entire year of bliss. I usually stick at June and have never passed August. Some day I must bake a particularly small batch of mince pies for this special purpose, so that I shall not need to short-circuit my epigastrium in pursuit of a fine old custom. . . . Those who do not eat twelve pies are supposed to be plagued by the Lubber Fiend — a goblin somewhat vaguely identified by folklore specialists. I know several people who might accurately be described as Lubber Fiends.

-II-

• SUNDAY •

❀ An amateur astrologer told me last night that I am overly critical, and should try to develop more benevolence toward mankind. Today, therefore, I went about beaming benevolently on everyone I met, and was greeted with scowls and rebuffs by most of them. The plain fact is that most Canadians dislike and mistrust any great show of cheerfulness. If a man were to sing in the

---

✒ As time passed more, and older, more toothsome girls kissed Marchbanks under the mistletoe, but as they frequently kissed him on the top of the head and were heard to murmur "Sweet old man!" the Erotic Quotient of these kisses might be graded as Minus Seven.

street he would probably end up in jail; if he sang at his work the efficiency expert would ask him to come to his office for a frank talk. The way to impress your boss is to look glum all the time. He may mistake this for intelligence and give you a raise. The same thing holds true in politics: he who laughs is lost.

• MONDAY •

Was chatting with a man who has been suffering from bad dreams, which he erroneously describes as nightmares. As I understand the matter the only genuine nightmare is the sort of dream in which you suffer from increasing dread and shortness of breath, accompanied by pressure on the chest, until it seems that you must either throw off the weight or be smothered. It is at this point that you find yourself sitting bolt upright, screaming blue murder. If you don't you are probably found in your bed in the morning, quite cold and stiff. I have only had nightmares once or twice in my life, and many people never have them at all. Bad dreams, however, are common with me, and I rather welcome them, as they break the monotony of the long hours of sluggish slumber. . . . A psychologist once tried to attach great significance to my bad dreams, but I did not play quite fair with him, for I withheld from him one relevant fact *i.e.*, that I never go to bed without having a bite to eat, and my digestion sometimes gives me bad dreams even when I am wide awake. Of course, my nightly snack may merely act as a porter who throws open the gates of my repulsive Unconscious, letting all the bugaboos and hobgoblins out for a frolic, but frankly I don't care. Better a bad dream than no dream at all.

See Dr. Ernest Jones' classic Freudian study On The Nightmare. *It is not sufficiently recognized that Dr. Jones wrote this remarkable book while resident on Brunswick Avenue in Toronto, while he was employed at Ontario's first psychiatric clinic, just before the First World War.*

• TUESDAY •

A child asked me to mend her doll today; it has broken up into a trunk, a head and four limbs, like a country with too many parties. / I gave her the usual speech about my inability to mend anything, and then set to work. It was a gruesome experience, reminiscent of the scene in Mrs. Shelley's romance where Frankenstein puts together his monster out of bits of slaughterhouse waste. But more by good luck than good management I outfitted the doll with new entrails made of strong string, and tightened these by winding one leg around for twenty-three revolutions. Now the doll is better than new, for it kicks, twists and squirms like a real infant.... This evening heard *Carmen* on the radio, and reflected how hard it was to vamp a man while singing at the top of one's voice. That is the operatic problem; the singer must keep up a big head of steam while trying to appear secretive, or seductive, or consumptive. Some ingenious composer should write an opera about a group of people who were condemned by a cruel god to scream all the time; it would be an instantaneous success, and a triumph of verisimilitude.

• WEDNESDAY •

As I want to get the remainder of my winter's coal in tomorrow, I had to shovel my drive today; it had not been touched since the first snowfall, and this was no task for a child; it was no task for a hypochondriacal diarist, either, but I tackled it with the valour of ignorance. In ten minutes I was sweating freely, in spite of a cutting wind. After twenty minutes I could think of nothing except a recent warning by a coroner that shovelling heavy snow

---

Marchbanks, a fine classical scholar, is doubtless alluding to Aesop's fable of The Belly and the Members. *The Belly, of course, is the Dominion Government, which gobbles up everything, and the Members are the constituent Provinces of Canada, who don't like it.*

was a good way to bring on a stroke. After half an hour I had what I am certain was a slight stroke, and went inside for a dose of a special stroke-medicine I keep. It did me a lot of good, and after that I took stroke-medicine every half hour regularly. As a result I finished my drive magnificently and did not have even a touch of stiffness from the unusual exercise. I know plenty of people who would have been as stiff as frozen mackerel if they had done what I did, the way I did it.

· THURSDAY ·

My coal came today, and went into the bin with the usual amount of banging and thumping. A fine black dust settled on everything in the house, and when I looked in a mirror inadvertently, I was startled to see that I had been metamorphosed into a blackamoor. . . . Then I went down into the cellar, and addressed my furnace in these words: "O Furnace (I always model my speeches to my furnace on Cicero's orations). . . . O Furnace, three winter months having now gone by and the Yuletide and New Year seasons having been completed I, Marcus Tullius Marchbanks, have purchased all the coal, wood, coke, charcoal and kindred combus-

---

As the furnace, in the form in which Marchbanks knew it, is now almost wholly unknown, some explanation is needed. It was a large metal cylinder, made of galvanized iron, usually placed in a part of the cellar difficult of access, and made even more so by huge pipes which extruded from it about four feet above the ground, so that it had to be approached in a crouching posture. With difficulty a fire of household trash might be made in its gizzard, or grate, and upon this coal was heaped by the hopeful householder. If the coal ignited (which depended on the proportion of it which was in fact brown stone) a feeble heat might in time mount to the upper floors, accompanied by a variety of toxic gases. The furnace had other attachments, called dampers and draughts, upon which the expert householder played as upon some mighty organ. Marchbanks never really got the hang of his furnace, and was much afflicted by it. His approach was anthropomorphological as the above entry amply testifies.

tibles that I intend (to purchase, understood). Look to it, Furnace, for I shall feed you justly, but not wastefully, and if it should so hap that when all these good things are gone the gods still send us inclement weather, I shall cram your maw with broken chairs and cardboard boxes, but not another morsel of coal will I buy. Witness, O ye gods of the household, and you, O Furnace, that M. Tullius Marchbanks will throw himself upon his poker and perish before he will spend another denarius on coal."... The furnace was impressed and roared politely, but there was a faint contemptuous smell of coal gas when I went to bed.

• FRIDAY •

✿ Read too long and too much today, resulting in a severe attack of the Miseries. Reading is a form of indulgence, like eating and smoking. Some men smoke heavily and some drink heavily; I read heavily, and sometimes I have the most awful hangovers. Tobacco manufacturers, I understand, hire men to make continual tests of their product, and these poor wretches get shaky hands and tobacco hearts, and when they take a bath nicotine comes out of their skins into the water. It is the same with whisky-testers. Well, I am a book-tester and I have an occupational disease, which is called the Miseries.... To make matters worse, I ate an apple and got hiccups, and was convulsed three times a minute for almost an hour. Hiccups are very funny to everyone but the man who has them. To have the Miseries and hiccups together is to drain a bitter cup. Bup!

• SATURDAY •

✿ This afternoon climbed out on the roof of my verandah and shovelled snow down into the garden; it had piled up to the point where I could hardly get my bedroom window open, and although I am no fanatic for fresh air it is convenient to be able to hurl slops into the road, or lean out and shout "Who's there?" at late callers. I become dizzy when standing on a soapbox; the roof of a verandah is as high as the Eiffel Tower to me. Consequently I did my shovelling with the utmost caution and paused now and then to cling to the wall with my eyes shut, recovering my balance. Knocked down several icicles and was interested to find how sharp they were. If ever I decide to murder somebody, I shall stab him with an icicle, which will melt, destroying my fingerprints and all traces of the weapon. The melted ice will mingle with the victim's blood, and I shall go to his funeral in that state of profound satisfaction which we all feel when we have done something dangerous and illegal without being caught.

-III-

• SUNDAY AND ST. FISTULA THE STALAGMITE •

Pursuing my policy of "See Your Home First" I investigated my heating system today, trying to find out why one room which I use a great deal never gets any heat. I took the face off the hot-air register, lay on my stomach and groped; soon I fished up a large mass of shredded paper, pencil shavings, old bridge tallies, saw-dust and other breakfast food, which some former occupant had used to block off that room. This impressed me as a very subtle way of starting a fire, and I determined to search further, so I inserted as much of myself as I could into the bathroom register, and salvaged thirty-two used razor blades, a large piece of stick, and a thimble in good condition. I was now aroused; it was a fore-bear of mine, Gaston l'Immerdue Marchbanks, who mapped the sewers of Paris for Napoleon; therefore I investigated a cold-air pipe near the telephone, and recovered a great gross of pencil stubs. Next spring I must dismantle my whole heating system, to see what I can find.

• MONDAY •

Drug addiction is horrible, addiction to drink is pitiable, but to be a slave of the salted-nut habit is to be lost indeed. Years ago I realized my weakness in this respect, and vowed never to set tooth to salted nut again as long as I lived. But tonight I visited the home of my friend X (a prominent prohibitionist, by the way) and turned as white as a blanched almond when I saw the nut-dish at his elbow. It was obvious from the dry, salty tone of his voice that he had been hitting the cashews pretty hard, and as we talked he ate bowl after bowl of the insidious dainties. His wife (in rags, and barefoot, for their home and fortune had been ruined by his vice) patiently filled the bowl whenever it was empty. Once, however, when she attempted to take a fat filbert from his hand, he struck her brutally across the mouth. I walked home sadly, determined to urge the government to take over the salted-nut industry — vile traffic! — not for profit, but for control. ∮

• TUESDAY •

❀ There are days when nothing seems to happen to me at all; I passed today in a coma. . . . But I did read the suggestion of a scientist that men over forty-five, with physical defects, should be made to fight the next war, in order that young men may be spared. This convinces me of something which I have suspected for a long time, namely that scientists are simpletons who happen to have a knack with test-tubes, but possess no real intelligence at all. The logical thing to do, when the next war comes, is to recruit an army from all those of whatever age or sex who are unable to pass certain basic intelligence tests. This would be a good way of getting rid of a lot of the stupid people who cumber the earth; probably there would be a high percentage of scientists, Civil Servants, uplifters and minor prophets in an armed force collected in such a way. But if every country adopted this method the country with the biggest population of boobs, yahoos and ninnies would win, and I

∮ Canada is ever mindful of her puritan heritage, and every government defends its monopoly of the liquor trade by saying that it seeks, not profit, but control of a loathsome traffic. Of course, the sale of booze brings profits that would make a pirate blush, but governments avouch that they spend this money on the poor and needy, and on such necessities as the airplanes in which politicians speed about the globe, bent upon their holy work.

am not entirely convinced that we have overall superiority in this respect, though we seem bound in that direction.

• WEDNESDAY •

Reflected today on the sinful luxury which is sapping the morale of our country. My brother Fairchild has just bought himself an "electronic janitor," a costly device which, I understand, keeps his house at an even temperature of 70 degrees without any effort on his part whatever. I don't know quite how it works, but it has something to do with molecules and the quantum theory. . . . Another man I know has a method of sprinkling his ashes with common household substances (salt and pepper, I think he said, and a dash of vinegar) and burning them again; in this way he never has any ashes to carry out, because last week's ash is this week's fuel. . . . The hardy pioneer virtues which made Canada what it is (a nation of ash-choked grouches) seem to have disappeared everywhere except in me. I still get up before dawn — which on these winter mornings means before 8:30 a.m. — and give myself an appetite for breakfast by wrestling with my Cellar Demon.

• THURSDAY •

Had to do some travelling today, so rose early and discovered that it was very cold; would gladly have stayed at home and hugged the fire, but duty called, and I obeyed. Made the first stage of my journey by car and was thoroughly chilled; as the conversation for several miles was about ghosts, I cannot blame it all on the weather. Sponged my lunch from some people I know who keep a very warm house, so I thawed out there, but I had to go at once to a meeting, the chairman of which was either a disciple of Bernarr McFadden ✒ or a wearer of long underwear, for he insisted

---

✒ *Bernarr McFadden (1868–1955), the Father of Physical Culture and one-time aspirant to the Presidency of the United States, was a*

on opening the window and letting merry little breezes creep up my trouser legs. I must remember to get some long underwear of my own. Then home again by train; my seat was by the door, and three news butchers kept bursting into the coach, letting the Arctic in with them. I got some valuable exercise jumping up to shut the door, but it was not enough to keep me warm. Made the final stage of my journey by bus, which really was well heated. Listened to a CWAC vamping a sailor in the seat behind. She had hair of a rusty mouse-colour, but she referred to herself as a "redhead" and hinted broadly that she was a specialist in the arts of love. I doubted if this were true, but I admired her self-confidence.

• FRIDAY •

Woke this morning to find that I had a chill, the result of yesterday's junketing. Managed to do some work in the morning, but by noon it had settled in the small of my back, and I was doubled up like a jack-knife. There is only one place in which this position can be maintained without severe pain, and that is bed, so to bed I went and passed several miserable hours wishing I were not a prey to so many foolish and humiliating ailments. I have the less desirable characteristics of a number of great men —the digestion of Napoleon, the eyesight of Dr. Johnson, the breathing apparatus of Daniel Webster, the lumbago of Disraeli, the neuralgia of De Quincey and the deafness of Herbert Spencer —but none of their genius. I am a walking textbook of pathology, and I would sell myself to any university medical school which would make a decent bid. But they all refuse to do so, because

---

zealot on behalf of the healthy life, urging cold baths, wearisome calisthenics and a meagre diet on everybody who would buy his books and magazines. He made a fortune, as the magazines offered pictures of healthy girls, lightly clad, doing extraordinary and thought-provoking things. Unhappily for his reputation, a book by his divorced wife called Dumbbells and Carrot Strips *(1953) revealed that McFadden was a miser, and liked health because it was cheap.*

they think that I will leave my cadaver to them, free, after my demise. But I shall cheat them: I shall be buried with all my invaluable diseases; no pinchpenny university is going to get me cheap.

• SATURDAY •

A slight improvement in my condition today. I was able to struggle downstairs and roast my back in front of an open fire. . . . Somebody told me a few days ago that they got the impression that I disliked children. Not at all: I love the little dears. But I have no patience with ill-mannered, noisy, destructive, rude, rampaging little yahoos and it is my misfortune, from time to time, to come in contact with herds of these, roaming wild in the streets; can anyone blame me if I drive them away with curses and blows? But I love to see children playing happily and quietly, while I watch from behind barbed wire, about 300 feet away. . . . Ah, the sweet innocence of childhood! What a delightful thing it is in the young; what a pain in the neck it is in those who are assumed to have reached maturity! No, Marchbanks unhesitatingly declares himself to be a Child-Lover, but that is no reason to expect him to dandle young baboons upon his knee, and he flatly refuses to do so.

-IV-

• SUNDAY •

Was out for a walk this afternoon, and was joined by a dog; it was unknown to me, and was obviously of mixed ancestry; it was not a Social Register dog. What there was about me which struck its fancy, I cannot say, but it romped under my feet, smelled me searchingly, licked my gloves and hindered my progress seriously. Its most irritating trick was to run just ahead of me, with its head turned back so that it could stare rudely into my face; naturally it fell down a lot because it did not look where it was going, and every time it fell down I had to dance an impromptu jig to keep from falling over it. . . . I like dogs, just as I like children. I like to think about them, and I like to read in the papers that dogs have been given medals for life-saving. But I do not particularly relish dogs in the flesh. When I meet a dog socially, with its owner, I am prepared to pat it once, and to allow it to smell me once, and then, so far as I am concerned, the matter is closed. Dogs who go beyond this limit are asking for a kick in the slats, and they usually get it.

• MONDAY •

Was looking through a catalogue of new recordings for player-pianos today and noticed a heading saying "Hymns and Religious Rolls," which included such sanctified ditties as *Come To The Church In The Wild Wood*; elsewhere I found another roll listed called *I Won't Give Nobody None Of My Jelly Roll*. The question which puzzles me is this: is the antithesis of a religious roll a jelly roll? . . . Why, by the way, is music written on religious or pseudo-religious themes called "sacred music"? And why, under that title, is it thought to be immune from the criticism which affects other music? Much of it is the most arrant tripe, but nobody ever says so. I once heard of a clergyman who said that he thought that "God must grow tired of this perpetual serenading"; I quite agree, particularly if God has a sensitive ear and a fine taste in lyric and panegyric verse. . . . This evening picked up an old volume of Hannah More's *Sacred Dramas* and took a quick look at *David and Goliath*. All the s's in the book were the 18th century kind which look like f's, and the opening spasm, as sung by David, ran thus:

> Great Lord of all thingf! Pow'r divine!
> Breathe on thif erring heart of mine
>   Thy grace ferene and pure;
> Defend my frail, my erring youth,
> And teach me thif important truth
>   The humble are fecure.

This lisping bit about the humble being fecure interested me, for it is the earliest reference to focial fecurity for the Common Man that I have feen. And fertainly Goliath, who waf rather an Uncommon Man, got a frightful fock in the jaw. /

❋ Prepared for a relaxed evening, and was sitting happily in my pyjamas and dressing gown (a pre-war creation of blue towelling) when some friends dropped in, but as they were pyjama friends, so to speak, this only added to my comfort. They told me that a passing reference to my truss in a recent conversation had encouraged them to wonder just what sort of truss I wear. As a matter of fact, that reference was mere pleasantry. Several years ago I read an advertisement which said "Throw Away Your Truss," and I did so; to be precise, I sent it to the Grenfell Mission, for the relief of some ruptured Eskimo. A week or two later I saw an ad which said "Throw Away Your Surgical Boot," so I did that, too, and got a wooden leg instead. It was only a few days until I saw another ad saying "Re-Shape Ugly Noses While You Sleep," which I did, changing my warty proboscis to an elegant Grecian model. At the same time, I invested in a hearing aid ("fits in the ear but cannot be seen") and gave my ear trumpet to a Boy Scout, who complained that he thrust it into his ear until it hurt, but was unable to produce the faintest toot. Now, when I go to bed, I pile all this salvage on the floor, with my false teeth and wig on top, and in the mornings it takes a female spot-welder half an hour to assemble me.

• WEDNESDAY AND EPICŒNIA •

❋ My eye was caught this morning by a statement in the paper that "76 per cent of adults have bad breath." I am always puzzled by such dogmatic observations. How are these conclusions

---

/ *No, no Marchbanks! David slew Goliath by hitting him in the forehead with a stone, and when the giant fell David cut off his head with his own sword, which was insulting. But David was a very insulting boy; he called Goliath "uncircumcised," which was discrimination, and against the Bill of Rights.*

reached? Do investigators scamper about the streets, sniffing? For many years I have maintained that the breath is an emanation of the soul, and that people who have disagreeable breaths are in poor spiritual health. Plenty of people with bad teeth and a dozen diseases have sweet breaths, because they are at peace with God and man. Conversely I have met many athletes, fresh-air fiends, uplifters, do-gooders and physical culture addicts whose breaths were a shocking revelation of their spiritual corruption and malnutrition. An unhealthy breath rises from an unhealthy soul, not from a disordered gizzard. For years I have fought shy of any business dealings with bad-breathed people, for experience has shown me that they are undependable, if not positive crooks. But I will trust any man, however unpleasing of aspect, if his breath whispers to me of April and May.

• THURSDAY •

A soft day, and I think it must be raining down the chimney, for I can't get my furnace to go. I have shaken, and poked, and tinkered with the drafts, and removed the accumulation of overshoes from the cold air intake, but to no avail. I have even (I blush to write this) tried a propitiatory offering: I built a little altar before the furnace door, and offered up a bowl of delicious turkey-giblet soup on it, but the Fire-God remained sulky, so I ate the soup myself and resumed my hopeless poking. . . . But I know what will happen; if I go to bed, leaving the drafts full on, I shall waken in the night semi-cooked, for the furnace will rage and roar at 4 a.m.; but if I check it ever so lightly it will congeal and go out, and in the morning I shall be faced with an immense clinker, like a piece of peanut-brittle. Sometimes I wonder why I don't jump into the furnace myself, and end it all.

• FRIDAY •

A man I know has been so broken by the restrictions on horse-racing that he has attempted to console himself by collecting calendars with pictures of horses on them: he has a very fine one with Man o' War on it just in sight as he works. I have heard of pin-up girls before, but this is my first experience of a pin-up horse.... Nevertheless, I know one Senator whose Ottawa office is entirely hung with photographs and portraits of Holstein cattle. "Look at those flanks," he will cry, as one enters the room, and as he goes on to even more startling intimacies, and as one looks eagerly for an art study of Lana Turner, the realization dawns that he is talking about Buttercup-Nestlerode-Springfilled III, queen of the dairy, whose butterfat production has never been equalled. Once a young divinity student visited this Senator, and as he knew nothing of his enthusiasm, and did not understand fully what was being said, he was convinced after twenty minutes of dairy-talk that he was in the presence either of an eminent woman's doctor or a libertine of Neronian abandonment.

• SATURDAY •

Tried to listen to the opera broadcast of *Rigoletto* this afternoon, but as a man in the cellar was doing something cruel to the furnace, and a horde of visitors descended upon me, I did not make much headway with it.... Went to bed early and read about Dr. Johnson, a man after my own heart, for he loved tea, conversation and pretty women, and had not much patience with fools. Rose at 11:30, ate a big plate of breakfast food and an orange, put the snaffle on the furnace, and retired to sleep the sweet sleep of the deserving poor.

-V-

• SUNDAY •

Met a little girl today who was wearing a pair of high rubber boots, which she referred to as her Wellingtons, and of which she was very proud. Have not heard high boots called Wellingtons for a long time, and it reminded me of my Uncle Hengist, who was a clergyman and a great hand at organizing strawberry socials, bazaars, bean suppers, local talent concerts and similar pious breaches of the peace. At all such affairs he set up a curtained booth, with a sign outside which said "See the Grand Historical Tableau — The Meeting of Wellington and Blucher at Waterloo. Admission Ten Cents. Proceeds for Missions" (or the Organ Fund, or the Abandoned Women, or whatever the good cause might be). Inside the booth was a table, on which a Wellington boot faced a Blucher boot. Uncle Hengist thought this very funny, and his parishioners put up with it for years, although they were all privy to the fraudulent nature of the exhibit. It was not until he became Bishop of Baffinland that he gave up obtaining money by this shady ruse.

• MONDAY •

Was talking today to a man and his wife who were groaning that their three children were boys; a girl, they thought, would be much easier to bring up, and a refining influence upon their young gorillas. This is a misconception about the nature of daughters which should be exploded. I think immediately of the Rev. Sabine Baring-Gould, *that* gentle man who had nine daughters, all beautiful and all possessed of the spirit of tigresses. The poor man would sit in his study at Lew Trenchard, trying to write *Onward, Christian Soldiers*, or some such ditty, when a servant would rush in, crying, "If you please, sir, Miss Angela has fallen off the roof, Miss Beatrice has fallen off her horse, Miss Cecilia has sprained her ankle (if you'll pardon the expression, sir), Miss Dorothea has

---

The Rev. Sabine Baring-Gould (1834–1924) summed up in himself much that is most fascinating about the Church of England. He was well-off, as every churchman should be, and he was squire of Lew Trenchard, in Devonshire, and was thus able to appoint himself vicar of the local church. He fell in love with an illiterate mill-girl, paid for her education, married her and lived happily with her from their marriage in 1868 until her death in 1916. They had five sons and nine daughters (all reputedly beauties). In addition to his clerical duties he wrote 159 books. A productive life indeed. He died in 1924 at the age of ninety. He is chiefly remembered as the writer of the militant hymn, Onward, Christian Soldiers.

shot a gamekeeper, Miss Emily is riding the bull, Miss Frances has climbed the steeple, Miss Gertrude has fallen into the pond, Miss Geraldine has bitten the dog, and Miss Harriet is pumping water on the curate!" Such were the trials of that Devon vicarage — and all caused by daughters!

· TUESDAY ·

Everyone I meet these days asks me how my furnace is getting on. As a matter of fact, it is behaving very well; cold weather seems to agree with it thoroughly. I have only to whisper my desire down one of the cold-air pipes and it obliges at once. . . . But I am having unusual trouble with ashes. Twice a week I fill all the cans, hoppers, baskets, cartons and old derby hats in the house, and drag them out to the curb, and even at that I am accumulating a little hoard of ashes in a corner of my cellar. . . . There is fireplace ash too. My fireplace has a trap door in its hearth which allows all the ashes to tumble down into a cave in the cellar wall. When I remove the door of the cave all the ashes gush forth into my face, covering me so thickly with ash that I look like Boris Karloff in one of his mummy roles. Of course I hold a basket under the deluge, but never in the right place. . . . Some months ago I went away for a few days and left a furnace man in charge of things. When I came back the cellar was full of ashes; "I couldn't find enough o' vessels to put 'em out in," said he, in the rich accents of Old Ireland. That has always been my trouble. Not enough o' vessels.

· WEDNESDAY ·

To the movies, to see a piece which exalted the virtues of country life; the chief incident was the burning of a barn which belonged to an elderly farmer, and the eagerness of his neighbours to give him livestock and produce with which to start farming again. But this is not a form of generosity exclusive to the country. I well recall when the Astor mansion in New York burned to the ground in 1896; all the rich city folk hastened to do what they could for the poor Astors, who had been burnt out. Old Mrs. Van Rensellaer threw a shawl over her head and ran over at once with a big tureen of real turtle soup. The Vanderbilts sent silk bed sheets and down pillows; the Van Courtlandts offered the Astors their ballroom to bed down in for the night; the Goulds insisted on sending them a full set of crested fish-knives, and a large salmon as well; the Rockefellers sent their butler with a big block of Standard Oil stock, and a dish of out-of-season fruit. It was a wonderful outburst of spontaneous kindness on the part of all the Astors' neighbours. It is simply foolish to think that only the humble have kind and generous instincts; many a great heart beats beneath a ruby and sapphire stomacher. ✒

• THURSDAY •

✹ Rain today, and frost coming out of the ground. A black day at Marchbanks Towers, which is so situated that water pours into the cellar every spring and during the January thaw. There is something about the sound of water pouring into one's cellar which cannot be ignored; I sat by the fire for a time, trying to distract my attention with a good book; this failed, so I tried a bad book, (the latest selection of the Bawdy Book Club, of which I am a member), but even that was useless, and at last my conscience drove me down into the depths to see what was happening. There was no doubt about it; the water was mounting. So I seized a broom and tried to sweep it toward the drain; I was alarmed that my furnace might get its feet wet, and develop one of its fits of sulks. My woodpile was soggy at the base; my window screens were beginning to shift in an uneasy way. For a mad moment I contemplated

---

✒ It is one of the most pleasing characteristics of Marchbanks that he is always ready—nay, eager—to say a word on behalf of those who are generally abused, such as Royalty, and the Rich. "Are they not also God's creatures?" he demands, trying to shout down the rising chorus of "No!"

scooping up all the water I could in a bucket and rushing upstairs to empty it out into the garden, but Reason regained her throne almost at once, and I rejected the notion as unworthy. Fortunately the rain stopped soon afterward, and I was able to go to bed with a fairly calm mind.

• FRIDAY •

Was talking to a friend of mine, and noticed that he had a strange smell. When I commented on this he blushed becomingly, and said that it was some shaving lotion which he had been given for Christmas. It was manufactured especially for masculine use, and was called (I think he said) "Horse." A number of scents for the male are now on the market and all of them guarantee to make the wearer smell of something wholesome and rugged like heather, or the harness-room in a livery stable. They have short, rugged, masculine names, like "Gym," "Running Shoes," "Barn," "Cheese," "Glue," and the like. I think that they have a definite place in modern society. A sedentary worker, like myself, has no characteristic smell; anybody who met me in the dark might think that I was a professional woman of some kind (not the oldest kind, of course). But if I sprinkle a few drops of "Corduroy Trousers" on my handkerchief, it is obvious for several yards around me that I am a man. Business women always use scents like "Riot," "Delinquency," "Turpitude," and the ever-popular "Beast-Goad."

• SATURDAY •

Listened to *Tales of Hoffman* broadcast from the Metropolitan Opera in New York, this afternoon; Hoffman was sung by Raoul Jobin, a Canadian, and Pierette Alarie, another Canadian, was the leading coloratura; the conductor was Wilfred Pelletier, also a Canadian. Reflected for the millionth time that it is a pity that Canadians with this sort of ability have so little chance or encouragement to use it for the advancement of their native land. Canada exports brains and talent with the utmost recklessness, as though we had a surfeit of them at home, instead of having one of the highest living standards, and one of the lowest artistic and æsthetic standards in the world. *f* . . . Going to bed, discovered that my tube of toothpaste was suffering from severe hernia, and gushed in the most unexpected places when squeezed. Tried to weld the ruptured place over the electric stove, with desperate results, and the odour of frizzling dentifrice spread nauseatingly through the house. Abandoned myself to despair for a few minutes, and then burned some brown paper to dispel the stench of failure.

-VI-

• SUNDAY AND SS. FIACRE & HANSOM •

Took a dish of tea this afternoon with some people who served the strongest mixture that I have ever swallowed under that name. It was the colour of a spaniel's eyes, and when I supped it my tongue was immediately numbed. I ventured to ask for a little hot water, but it was powerless against such tea; I estimate that a cup of it, poured into a wash-tub full of boiling water, might have made an endurable drink for me, but I will not guarantee it. . . . I ventured to remark to my hosts that they liked their tea very strong. "Oh yes," said they; "Tea is no good to us unless it will trot a mouse." I asked a few questions about the latter expression, and learned that what they meant was that they liked their tea so strong that a mouse could trot over the surface of the cup without sinking. . . . It occurred to me, in a horrible revelation, that they probably kept a mouse in their kitchen for testing purposes, and I lost all my thirst at once.

• MONDAY •

Was roused before seven this morning by a telegraph boy with a message. It read, "Am sending crocheted pillow shams today stop Auntie." I blenched, and the paper fell to the floor from

---

f This was written, of course, in 1947. How times have changed since the establishment of The Canada Council, so aptly called (quoting from the dear old hymn) "Help of the Helpless."

my nerveless fingers, for of course this was code, and it meant, "All discovered stop prepare to fly at once stop" and it was from my spymaster 𝄢 Serge Pantz. I immediately gathered all the incriminating papers in the house, and burnt them in the fireplace, and then ate the ashes; with a little milk and sugar they were not unpalatable. . . . Then I waited and waited and waited until another telegram came. "Send me your recipe for prune bumblepuppy at once stop delicious stop Auntie." This, when decoded, meant: "Destroy no records stop guard them with your life if necessary stop." I must confess that this depressed me, for I knew how testy Pantz would be when he discovered that I had eaten the ashes of the records. But Soviet Above Self has always been my motto, so I set about my day's work. Disguising myself as an old apple-woman, I stood on a curb until noon and sold my special cyanide apples to as many capitalists as I could persuade to buy them, and then went to a beverage room to poison the minds of the Workers. This is always hard, as they won't keep their heads still while I am squirting the poison into their ears. Anyway, a lot of them have pretty poisonous minds already. . . . I am getting sick of this spy business. I think I'll turn rat, and peach on Pantz to the R.C.M.P.

𝄢 *This was at the peak of Canada's great Spy Scare. I cannot believe that Marchbanks' role in it was quite as he represents it here. The flat refusal of the Soviet Embassy to afford me access to their Code Book for 1947 makes it impossible for me to check. Was this the notorious* Joy of Cooking Code *of which rumours may still be heard? . . . Espionage in Canada has long had literary connotation. It is noteworthy that in 1954 Canada's highest literary award, the Governor-General's Medal, was awarded to a writer, not otherwise known, calling himself Igor Gouzenko, for a novel called* The Titan. *As it seems most unlikely that Canada would make such an award to a non-Canadian, writing in Russian, the titillating suspicion arises—was "Igor Gouzenko" one of Marchbanks' innumerable pen-names?*

• TUESDAY •

The spy-scare is mounting, and I hear that some nosy garbage-man has reported to the City Council that I always put my garbage out wrapped in *Pravda*. To offset any suspicion this may have aroused I put on my Rotary button, my Kiwanis button, my Lion button, my Hi-Y button, my Teen-club button, my Soroptimist button, my W.C.T.U. button, my B'nai B'rith and Hadassah buttons, and all my ritual jewels from Beta Sigma Phi and walked around town, thus heavily disguised as a Good Citizen. I patted several children, and gave bones to every dog I met, and upon the whole I think I made a favourable impression. I may get out of this mess with my skin whole if I play my cards properly.

• WEDNESDAY •

My mail this morning included some information about this season's Valentines, though why I should be interested in them I do not know. But I was tickled to read in choice advertising agency English that "thoughtful creators of Valentine varieties have not overlooked the emotional needs of the bachelor girl who doesn't 'go steady' but sports the odd gentleman friend. . . . If she's still uncertain of her boy-friend's intentions and emotions, a Valentine could be found which might provide either an encouragement to the shy swain, or 'no thorough-fare' to the wolf, without in any way compromising the young lady's dignity or affections." . . . In my younger days it was easy to short-circuit a wolf by sending him a one-cent comic Valentine entitled "The Masher," the verse on the latter being:

> You think you're a Masher, and all hearts do please,
> But you might as well know you're a Big Hunk of Cheese.

It may be argued, of course, that this type of Valentine compromised the sender's dignity, though not half as badly as it compromised that of the receiver. . . . I see no mention of a Valentine suitable for a dyspeptic diarist whose emotions have been cauterized by a rebellious and evilly-disposed furnace.

• THURSDAY •

❋ Another note from the Income Tax people this morning. A while ago they presented me with a bill for the whole of my 1941 tax, insisting that I had not paid it. By great good luck and contrary to my usual unbusinesslike procedure, I had my receipts, which I brandished angrily in their faces. Gradually the whole sordid story leaked out: they had taxed me both as Samuel Marchbanks and as Fortunatus S. Marchbanks, in spite of the fact that nobody has called me Fortunatus since 1897; having billed Sam they were out to skin Fortunatus, but I am not quite such a dual personality as that. When their error was pointed out to them, they did not even apologize for their threat to take proceedings against me, but managed to dig up an item of a few dollars which they said I ought to pay, plus interest. . . . The churlishness of tax-gatherers is phenomenal. I wonder if there is a case on record in which a private citizen has extracted an apology from a tax-gatherer? I wonder if their work makes them curmudgeons, or if curmudgeonliness is a qualification for the job? I have received a stack of letters about this affair, all written from the standpoint of a government official addressing a hardened and evasive criminal. The insolence of these herdsmen of The Golden Calf is past all bearing. ✑

• FRIDAY •

❋ The papers tell me that the sports world has been shaken by a horrible basketball scandal, which surprises me more than I can express. I have for years been under the impression that basketball is a gentle game played by fat little girls who trundle up and down a gymnasium floor with jellying thighs and bobbing

---

✑ Never in his lifetime did Marchbanks or any of his contemporaries ever receive in a pay envelope the full sum designated as his salary by his employer; the fell hand of the tax-gatherer had always dipped into it before he got it. This is a modern adaptation of the hateful medieval droit de seigneur, *which ensured the local boss first crack at every bride. The modern taxpayer is, in a very real sense, the Cuckold of the State.*

bosoms, trying to toss an old soccer ball into a hoop, squealing and giggling the while. But apparently the real basketball players are big hairy fellows who chew tobacco and occasionally accept bribes. . . . Not long ago I discovered that I was similarly out-of-date on the subject of lacrosse. My idea of lacrosse is genuine Indian baggataway, with twenty-four of the most murderous ruffians in town clashing and hacking at each other with hickory clubs and pieces of fish-net. An old lacrosse player once pulled up his trousers and showed me his shins, and they looked like raw hamburger even after twenty-five years. But now it seems that lacrosse really is a girl's game, refereed by prim females who cry, "Ah, ah there, Lucy," and "Tut, Tut Marjorie," and "Now girls, remember your Guide honour" when hair-pulling seems imminent.

• SATURDAY •

The spy-hunt has made me as jumpy as a hen on a hot griddle all week, and today was a climax. Telegram from Serge Pantz — "Sending you half-a-dozen tatted doilies stop love stop Auntie." This, decoded, meant "You have failed, pig of a dog; prepare to die." This was going too far, so I wired back (collect) "Expecting little stranger next week what do you mean to do about it? Gladys"; this, decoded by Pantz, means "Pish, dog of a pig, I flatly refuse to die." However, knowing Pantz, I put on my bullet-proof combinations at once, disguised myself as a woman, and went out and hid in the powder room of a Ladies' Beverage Room (No Men Allowed). I am counting on the R.C.M.P. finding Pantz before he finds me; indeed, I sent them a little anonymous note about him last Monday.

-VII-

• SUNDAY •

Had a heated argument this afternoon with one of those well-meaning people whose democracy is a burning faith rather than a belief based on reason; a majority, he roared, while his eyes brimmed with sentimental tears, must always be right and must always have its way; he talked feelingly about the wisdom of the Common Man. "But," I protested, "why should you assume that a group of people, all of mediocre ability and restricted information, possesses more wisdom than the same people as individuals? For instance, if I told a group of fifty average people that the cube root of 100 is 1,000,000 it is most unlikely that anyone would dispute my word, because they do not think; but in actual fact the cube root of 100 is 4.641." He was nonplussed, and I saw that he had fallen for my bit of sophistry himself. . . . I am a democrat, but the idea that a gang of anybodies may override the opinion of one expert is preposterous nonsense. Only individuals think; gangs merely throb.

• MONDAY •

Quite a number of people, I notice, have taken to calling me by my first name: I was hailed as "Sam" this morning by a young fellow whose name I do not even know. This does not distress me; if he thinks that he makes the world a cheerier place by calling everyone by a first name or a nickname, I am content that he should do so. But I wonder if people do not attach too much importance to the first-name habit? Every man and woman is a mystery, built like those Chinese puzzles which consist of one box inside another, so that ten or twelve boxes have to be opened before the final solution is found. Not more than two or three people have ever penetrated beyond my outside box, and there are not many people whom I have explored further; if anyone imagines that being on first-name terms with somebody magically strips away all the boxes and reveals the inner treasure he still has a great deal to learn about human nature. There are people, of course, who consist only of one box, and that a cardboard carton, containing nothing at all.

• TUESDAY AND ST. VALENTINE'S DAY •

It was warmer today than it has been for many weeks. The snow sagged, and I sagged with it. My overcoat, which has seemed like a wisp of cheesecloth in bitter weather, felt like the coat of a shepherd dog. . . . Nobody sent me any Valentines which seems a little shabby, considering that I sent out more than a dozen, including a few anonymous insulting ones to the leaders of the principal political parties and high-ranking churchmen. . . . Rereading Dickens' *Dombey and Son*. What an easy life children have nowadays! A century ago a child expected to be beaten, pinched, shaken, cuffed, locked in dark cupboards, bastinadoed and told it would go to Hell all day and every day, even in the happiest homes. And with what result? They grew up to be the Gladstones, Huxleys, Darwins, Tennysons, and other Great Victorians whom we all admire. Nowadays, with our weak-kneed kindness, we are raising a generation of nincompoops and clodhoppers. The revulsion against progressive education may be expected any time now. Eminent child psychologists are already beginning to advocate cruelty as a theory of training. Is your child disobedient, saucy and self-willed? Shove red-hot gramophone needles under its nails, and be a pioneer in the new movement!

• WEDNESDAY •

A fellow who is very much in the know at Ottawa tells me that there will be no relief of the stocking shortage until after the Opening of Parliament. All the best stockings are being held for the Prime Minister, the Supreme Court Justices, the Senate and Common Speakers, and the Black Rod and Sergeant-at-Arms. The Prime Minister refuses to wear anything but the best of silk, though the Supreme Court is rather advanced in its views and favours nylons. . . . There is an ugly story of a Senate Speaker a few years ago who turned up at the Opening wearing an old pair of gun-metal lisles of his wife's: he got what-for from the Governor-General's aide, this man said.

This was at a time when ceremonial dress was more common than it now is, and the Rt. Hon. Mackenzie King looked especially fetching in a gold-laced Windsor uniform. Marchbanks has frequently advocated

• THURSDAY •

To Toronto on business. The Royal York was the scene of a Better Roads corroboree, and in the Gentleman's Powder Room, I was accosted by a young rustic who had apparently been attending a committee-meeting in a beverage room. ⸙ He was wandering about, trying to find the exit, but the multiplicity of doors confused him. When I met him, he had just finished an unsuccessful tour of a row of doors which, as they did not come to the floor, may have looked to him like the entrances to further saloons. He was hanging on to the soiled towel bin, lost in admiration of the wonders of the great city. Perhaps I reminded him of someone from home, for he hailed me. "Say, this here's certainly one swell toilet," he cried. I nodded. I did not want him to think that I was fully accustomed—indeed indifferent—to such splendours.... Toronto is a depressing place. Riding up Yonge Street in the trolley, past all those postage stamp stores, dress-suit renters, used car bazaars, pants-pressing ateliers, bathtub entrepreneurs and antique shops specializing in leering china dogs, my heart was heavy. This, I thought, is Canada's answer to Bond St., to Fifth Avenue, to the Rue de la Paix. ⸙

• FRIDAY •

Home tonight on a local train. Was interested in its electrical apparatus: when the train stopped the light was so poor that the filaments in the bulbs could be clearly seen, but when we worked

---

that Canada dress all its Civil Servants in uniforms, of a splendour indicating their rank and salary, so that humbler folk may recognize them, revel in their number, and applaud them at baseball games and other public functions. The call for gold braid alone would support a large industry, and re-open some of our quiescent mines.

⸙ *This quaint name was formerly used to identify a pub.*

⸙ *The area so described is now called The Strip, and its transvestite population alone rouses the envy of Hamburg, Copenhagen and other foreign sin centres.*

up a good speed it was reasonably bright. How was it produced? By the friction of the wheels on the axles? Or more romantically, by the beautiful wife of the engineer, standing in the tender, brushing her thick auburn locks, the electricity so generated supplying our own light? At each station she stopped brushing (to lean down and whisper some delicious secret into the hairy ear of the station agent, her teeth flashing the while like pearls imbedded in a pomegranate) and our light failed. . . . Whatever the cause, the light was too poor to read by, and I shall write and tell the president of the line that the axles must grind harder, or the engineer's wife must brush more vigorously, or I shall see that ugly questions are asked at the next session of Parliament.

• SATURDAY •

✳ Have received many letters relating to my recent fearless attack on the Salted Nut Traffic — that spawning-ground of juvenile delinquency and broken homes. A typical missive today from an apologist for the nut-growers: "Surely you are intolerant in your desire to take salted nuts from us all; the moderate nut-eaters far out-number the nut abusers." This is merely specious. Another writes: "My father, as good a man as ever lived, always kept nuts on the sideboard, and we children saw him eat them, though I never saw him debauch. When I was twenty-one, he took me into the dining room, and said, 'Jasper, you're a man now; there they are — cashews, brazils, filberts, everything; use nuts, but don't abuse them; the nut is a good servant, but a bad master'. I consider your nut-prohibition plans fanatical." But I am not to be deterred in my war on salted nuts by such letters as these, or the insidious propaganda of the nut-gorged press. I shall not sheathe my sword until we have a nut-free Canada.

-VIII-

• MOTHERING SUNDAY •

✳ It is at this time of year that I begin to think seriously about suicide. My interest in the matter is not practical; I never reach for the bread-knife or the poison bottle. But I begin to understand what it is that people see in suicide, and why they do it. They have seen too many Februaries; they have lugged too many cans of ashes; they have shivered on too many bus stops. Rather than face the remaining two months of official winter, and the likelihood of a bitter May, they commit the Happy Despatch. The rest of us, the cowards, live on and see the summer come once more.... Snow and ice have backed up somewhere on my roof and water has begun to leak down an inside wall, to the serious detriment of the wallpaper. Shall I send a man up there, and pay his widow $50 a week for life if he falls and breaks his neck, shall I risk my own neck, or shall I pretend that it is not happening until the strain becomes too great and I go crazy? Canada's high rate of insanity is caused by just such problems. Meanwhile water comes down my stairs like the rapids of the Saguenay, and I shall not be surprised to see a salmon leaping upward from step to step.

• SMOTHERING MONDAY •

Yesterday's suicidal mood persists. Contemplated throwing myself from my office window, as so many despairing men did during the Great Depression. But it is only one storey above ground, and at worst I would break a leg, and look foolish. Anyway there are storm windows, and I can't be bothered to remove one of them. What Canadians need in February is a painless, simple, and definitely retractable method of suicide.... At one time I used to see a man every day who had tried to cut his throat several years before; it had left him with a wry neck and a livid, weeping scar. After making such a mess of himself it was clearly his æsthetic duty to finish himself off, and get himself out of the way, for he was a public eyesore. Failure to succeed in suicide is the ultimate ignominy, but criminologists tell us that hundreds of people try to shoot themselves every year, and miss; inability to concentrate their energies, which brings them to the verge of death, inadvertently yanks them away from it.

• BOTHERING TUESDAY •

Was chatting with a man who knows a lot about the coal situation. He tells me that things are now so bad that people are asked to come and cart away their own supplies. This frightens me. I do not drive a car myself, and I am quite certain that nobody would lend me one if he thought that I was going to put half a ton of coal in the back seat. I doubt if I could get a taxi to help me with a few hundredweight of coal, even if I did it all up in brown paper packages and held it in my lap, pretending it was bananas.... I crept down into my cellar, and viewed my dwindling bin with new eyes; I looked at my furnace, which seemed to wear a malignant leer on its ugly iron face; I did futile sums in my head about cubic footage divided by square shovelage, multiplied by backward springage. I wildly contemplated pulling up the floor of my cellar, on the off-chance of discovering a private peat-bog. I tried to recall something I had heard about tightly wrapped newspapers, dipped in molasses, making excellent fuel. By this time my teeth were chattering, and I went to look at my indoor thermometer; it said 70, and I felt better at once.

• WEDNESDAY •

To the movies this evening, and saw yet another of those films in which a young married couple, for no reason which would impress anyone outside Hollywood, see fit to behave as though they were an unmarried couple. By this feeble device it is possible to slip scenes past the Censors' Office — scenes in bedrooms, bathrooms and hotel rooms — which would otherwise be deemed salacious. Why the spectacle of a young unmarried woman brushing her teeth should be considered inflammatory and lewd, whereas the same scene is merely cosy and chummy when she is married, I cannot understand, but such is the power of the wedding ring to anæsthetize and insulate the passions according to the Censors.... The mess concerned a young couple who met, married and laid the foundation for a posterity in four days, after which the husband went to war and faced the foe for a year and a half. He returned to find his wife a stranger, with a baby which looked, and talked, like Charles Laughton. This dreary incident, which was unfolded at a turtle's pace, failed to grip my attention, and my right knee got a cramp; my right knee is an infallible critic. /

• THURSDAY •

Travelling again today, but not toward the fleshpots of Toronto this time. Instead I travelled upon a line which, if it does not already hold the title, I nominate for the worst in Ontario. Ancient and smelly rolling-stock, a roadbed laid out by a drunken manufacturer of roller-coasters, an engine with the disposition of a love-crossed billy-goat—it has all these and lesser iniquities which I shall not enumerate. Worse, there was a train-sick child aboard, for whom I was very sorry, for she was plainly in great distress. But her mother, like many other mothers, had got hold of a wrong idea and would not use her common sense, if she had any. "There's only one thing to do," she kept on saying, "and that's to keep washing her stomach out." So she poured the child full of water, orange juice, and soft drinks at five-minute intervals, and the child promptly threw it up again, noisily and agonizingly. I wondered how long it would be before I followed suit, but they got out somewhere in the wilderness, and the trainman threw a few old copies of the *Globe and Mail* over the shambles.

Marchbanks has lived to see the whole world of sexual activity revealed in the movies, the goatishness of which frequently appals him. His delicate mind shrinks from the thought of the day-long rehearsals that must lie behind these depictions of what appears to Hollywood as the Chief End of Man. He has lived to see Sex replaced by Fat as the Ultimate Sin, and at the annual shows of the Ontario Society of Water-colourists pictures of Christ Forgiving the Woman Taken in Adultery have given way to a new theme—Christ Forgiving the Woman Suprised in Laura Secord's.

• FRIDAY •

Talked for a couple of hours to a group of young people today, and enjoyed myself very much. But I was amazed to find them so solemn; they approached every subject, however trifling, with knit brows and a high moral attitude; they obviously thought that seriousness and solemnity were the same thing. I made a few little jokes in an attempt to cajole them into happier mood, but they looked at me with pain, and pretended not to notice these excesses of ribald eld. . . . Met some of them tonight at a party, where jelly-doughnuts made up a part of the fare. It takes a high degree of social accomplishment to hold a cup of coffee in one hand, and eat a jelly-doughnut ⫻ from the other, and this cannot be done by anyone who wants to indulge in deeply serious conversation at the same time. In consequence many of my heavy-minded young friends squirted doughnut-blood on themselves because they did not approach their food in a realistic frame of mind. A jelly-doughnut is deadlier than a grapefruit in the hands of an unwary eater.

• SATURDAY •

Was talking today to a man quite High in the Civil Service about the censorship of books and put my question to him: What do the censors know about literature and, specifically, how can they decide whether a book is fit for me to read or not? I expected him to confess that the censors knew nothing, but instead he told me that the censors have a long and special training: first of all they attend a series of lectures on Sin, delivered by unfrocked clergy of all denominations, then they pursue a course of reading which comprises most of what is to be found on the Reserved Shelves of university libraries (the books you can't get unless you know the librarian or his secretary); then they travel widely, taking in the spicier entertainments of Naples, Port Said and Bombay; then they are brought back to Canada, and if they still wear

---

See? These innocent young folk had not yet learned that confectionery is bad, Bad, BAD!

bedsocks, and blush deeply whenever they pass a cabbage patch or a stork, in mixed company, and are able to tame unicorns, they are decorated with the Order of the Driven Snow and given jobs in the censorship department.

-IX-

• SUNDAY •

I meant to get up early this morning and cleanse my soul with hard work and godly reflection but a profound torpor settled upon me and I did not waken until a crash outside put me in dread that the chimney had fallen off the house. But it was no such thing; several large chunks of ice had dislodged themselves from the roof and had fallen to the ground. Dare I take this as the first hint of Spring?

• MONDAY •

A day of dissolution and thaw, and very welcome to me, for if all this winter's snow were to melt at once, my cellar would be flooded, and my furnace might get wet feet, and a cold in the head, and be even uglier than it is.... During lunch the phone rang, and I galloped to it, chewing vigorously; it was a wrong number.... Mentioned my passion for bathtub reading to a lady of my acquaintance, who told me of an ingenious scheme devised by an aunt of hers, who hung a framed chart of Kings of England, from Egbert, son of Ealhmund (827–839) down to Victoria (1837–1901) in the bathroom in full view of the obligatory seat, with the result that all her children and visitors, over a period of years, gained a fine knowledge of the skeleton of British history, and were even certain of where such obscure kings as Stephen and Henry II came in. The shortest reigns, she informed me, were those of Ethelbald, Hardicanute, Harold II and Edward V; the longest, of course, was that of Queen Victoria with George III hot on her trail.... Phone rang at 7:30 and at 9:25; wrong number both times.

• TUESDAY •

❀ Was asked today to look over a large manuscript volume of poetry by a lady who suffers from a poetical seizure two or three times a week. In a life almost entirely devoted to embarrassing situations, I have found that nothing is more embarrassing and difficult than complying with such requests. The best of poets are touchy; the worst are basilisks and scorpions. As long as that book of verse stays in my possession I shall feel like the sailor who had an unexploded shell in his thigh; one false move and I am a goner. . . . Two more false alarms on the phone today. This is getting past a joke. . . .

• WEDNESDAY •

❀ Decided to take a firm line with wrong numbers today; in the past I have feebly said, "I'm afraid you have the wrong number," though in actual fact I am not in the least afraid; usually the boob at the other end of the line, who dialled the wrong number in the first place, grunts nastily as though it were my fault. So when my first call came today, it was, as I had expected, a wrong number, and a voice said, "Is Mrs. Blank at home?" "Not to the likes of you!" I roared in a feigned Irish accent. My next chance came in the afternoon; "Can you send me out a dozen fresh eggs?" asked a voice; "Sure thing; right away, lady," I promised. At 7:30 the phone rang again; "Is Effie there?" inquired a mouse-like voice, "She is," said I, assuming the tones of a schoolgirl, "but she's too drunk to come to the phone; shall I ask her to call you when she can stand up?" . . . Altogether it was a most successful day, and I shall adopt this procedure in future with all wrong numbers.

• THURSDAY •

❀ Observed a young lady of my acquaintance using a man's handkerchief to stanch her cold. This seems to be the final and decisive piece of evidence that women have emancipated themselves from the superstitions which have surrounded them for centuries. A generation ago no woman, whatever her needs, ever carried a handkerchief larger than four inches square, with nose-abrading lace at the edges. This was tucked in her bosom, from which insecure rest it usually descended inside her clothes to the region of her stomach, so that she could not get at it without unseemly self-exploration. If she had a cold and really wanted to blow her nose, she had to retire to a private place and blow on a duster, or a torn-up piece of nightdress; sometimes, in moments of extreme stress, petticoats were thus violated.

• FRIDAY •

To the movies tonight and saw yet another picture about a girl who marries a soldier on short acquaintance. In this particular Hollywood nugacity the girl was a multimillionairess, who tested her suitor by pretending to be a secretary, to discover whether he loved her for herself alone; of course, he did so, and I think this was a fault in the plot, for money, especially in very large quantities, is so much more desirable than the average young woman that no man of real wisdom would hesitate for an instant between the two. Of course, money will not bring happiness to a man who has no capacity for happiness, but neither will the possession of a woman who has no more brains than himself. But money will greatly increase the happiness of a man who is already happy (like me). Wisdom is the greatest possession in the world; money comes next; the intimate caresses of Hollywood stars come a long way down the list.... The hero of this movie was noticeably fat; he was greasy, too. Is the fat, greasy man to be the Adonis of the future?

• SATURDAY AND SEPTICÆMIA •

Took advantage of the thaw this afternoon to dig a few drains; every spring I am seized by the idea that I would have made an excellent engineer, and I construct an elaborate system of drains to prove it. The effect is not always what I intend, but *bona fide* engineers have told me that my schemes are far ahead of the times; my attempts to make water run uphill have been particularly admired.

-X-

• SUNDAY •

Did some tidying in my cellar this morning; it has been my custom to do some work of this kind on the seventh day, meditating meanwhile on the beauties of humility and simplicity. The occupational disease of people in my line of work is infallibility, complicated by loquacity and carbonic acid gas in the blood. The proper corrective for the mental ills of the man who deals primarily in words is a brief spell of dealing with things; the contrariness and obduracy of such things as dirt, boxes and old potato bags, which he cannot charm into subjection with his honeyed tongue, bring humility to the writer's heart.... Contrariwise, of course, men who spend their lives dealing with things ought to try to clarify their thoughts on Sundays; the fault is as great on one side as on the other. The impotent man of thought; the bonehead man of action — what is there to choose between them? ... Then wrote some letters. I am one of the few people who uses sealing wax on private correspondence; I like it, for it makes the letter gay and gives it a decidedly personal air. I have a couple of very pretty seals; the one I use most frequently is a goddess (or a nymph or a dryad or some such young woman) *in puris naturalibus* kneeling by a stream. Postmen love it; it feasts their eyes, they tell me. I have never thought highly of the modern custom of sealing letters with horse-hoof glue and spit.

Marchbanks was compelled to give up sealing-wax when the Post Office introduced the Atomic and Computerised Letter-Sorter, which chokes on wax and cannot bear an envelope of any unusual size. For younger readers some explanation must be offered of Marchbanks' use of the word "gay"; to him it meant light-hearted, carefree, sportive or offhand. His letters were often gay, in this now outmoded sense.

• MONDAY •

A man I know happened to mention on the bus this morning that he was suffering from a trifling complaint — an ingrowing hair. Immediately he was bombarded with tales of horror about ingrowing hairs; one man had known a case in which such a hair grew three feet into the flesh, and was removed only after major surgery; another knew of a case in which an ingrowing hair developed a hard ball of gristle on its root and left a crater when extirpated; a third had heard tell of an ingrowing hair which, when removed, proved to be a continuation of the patient's spine, so that he was left with nothing to connect his vertebrae.... I was reminded of the stories women tell any other woman who is going to have a baby.... To a meeting tonight, and reflected upon the excessive hardness, smallness and shakiness of folding chairs which, combined with speechmaking, always reduce me to the lowest depths of melancholy. Why are all good causes inextricably bound-up with folding chairs? Is there no virtue in springs and cushions?

• TUESDAY •

To the movies tonight to see a film dedicated to the exposition of one of the Thirty-Nine Articles of the Hollywood Faith, to wit, that a fellow who chews gum, wears his hat in the house, and rapes the English language every time he opens his mouth is a better matrimonial choice for a nice girl than a suave fellow who has lots of money and has been successfully exposed to education. The Apotheosis of the Yahoo is one of the primary objects of Hollywood.

• WEDNESDAY •

The movies last night — an organ recital tonight! It seems to me that I just stagger from one hotspot to another, wallowing in the pleasures of the senses.... To a party afterwards, where I met several ladies called Mrs. Mumbledemum; this Mumbledemum family must be very large, for I am introduced to members of it everywhere. The name is hard to hear, and not too easy to pro-nounce, and it seems to fit almost anyone, so there must be a lot of people who were born Mumbledemums, or who have become Mumbledemums by marriage. Nowadays when anyone smiles at me whose name I don't know, I just smile in return, and say, "How do you do, Mrs. Mumbledemum?" in a low, indistinct voice, and they always reply. On occasion I have been addressed as Mr. Mumbledemum myself, and I always grin and pretend that I am a member of that fine old family.

• THURSDAY •

An Indian I know (a chief of the great Swivel Chair tribe) was pointing out sun-dogs in the sky to me tonight, and prophe-sying stormy weather from them. I had never heard of sun-dogs before, but it appears that they are the roots of a rainbow, of which the arch is invisible. It is an impressive sight to see a Swivel Chair Chief, sitting as straight as an arrow on the back of his Buick, gazing into the setting sun and forecasting the weather. . . . But this evening I happened to be with this same Indian (we had been sitting around the campfire with a friend, a medicine man of the Long Bill tribe, chewing the pemmican) and on our way back to our tepees we met a third Indian of the Bifocal tribe, who looked up at the sky and said, "By the look of the stars we should have fine weather," and my Swivel Chair Chief agreed heartily! I never know what to make of these Indians when they start looking into the future. Stars, sun-dogs, stray dogs, dog-catchers — everything they see has a deep meaning for them, but I have to take the weather as it comes.

• FRIDAY •

Today I found myself in the peculiar position of having to restrain my furnace: it was in high spirits, chewing up the coal and spitting out the cinders, and outside the thermometer was pushing upward toward 60 degrees Fahrenheit, birds were twittering, drains were gurgling, and snow was yielding up the smell of rich brown earth, subtly mixed with cat and dog. When I opened the furnace door gusts of heat and flame belched forth, shrivelling my cheap celluloid wastecoat buttons. I toyed with the idea of raking out the fire and throwing pails of water on it, as I once saw a railroad fireman do, but I wanted the fire again, and I knew that it would never forgive such an insult.... As the snow melts, leaves which I should have raked last year come into view, looking discouraged and sad, like soggy breakfast cereals. My lawn, which I left reasonably tidy in the autumn, looks like a garbage dump, and I know why. The jolly dogs (man's best friend) who live round about, have thrown their old bones and chocolate bar wrappings there all winter. A pox on man's dumb chum! If I behaved like that, around their doghouses, they would bite me.

• SATURDAY •

This afternoon slept soundly through the first act of a broadcast of Beethoven's *Fidelio*, but I heard enough of it to discover that all of the all-American cast spoke English with thick foreign accents, and in that too-rich, fruity speaking voice which opera singers don't seem able to help.... Went out and chopped some ice off a walk, which was hot work, and was amazed to find that crocus, iris, thrombosis and early haemophilia are all coming up on my borders, thereby making work and ruining my Saturday afternoons for weeks to come.... To a meeting to choose artists for a concert series. How glorious it must be to rise from the miserable status of a $500 artist to the altitude of a $2500 one! But how bitter, as old age advanced and one's fingers stiffened, or corns appeared on one's vocal cords, to slip from the $2500 eminence back to $500 a night, and from that to entertaining at political rallies and lodge benefits for a measly $5 and all one could eat in doughnuts and coffee! Congratulated myself that I am a writer, a job in which advancing senility is rarely detectable.

Marchbanks was at this time a member of the committee of his local Community Concert Association, a body which undertook to provide four heavy injections of musical culture every winter, rather like chemotherapy. The concerts took place in a school hall that smelled in

-XI-

• SUNDAY •

Confined to my bed with a desperate and unspecified internal malady, which my friends interpret in the light of their own experience. Those who have had gallstones say that I have all the symptoms of a rock-bound gall; appendix martyrs assure me that I shall know no peace until I have my appendix snipped out; the man who came on an emergency call to look at the plumbing tells me that I must have what he calls "an ulster." I reply that it can't be an ulster as I haven't even a coated tongue, and the joke is so bad that it makes me feel much worse. However, any sort of joke is praiseworthy from a man in my condition. I hug a hotwater bottle to my breast (or a little lower down) and groan.

• MONDAY •

I feel no better today. Reflect that Mind is the lord of Matter, and that if I were a Yogi I should dispel my ailment with a few breathing exercises and repetitions of the mystic syllable "Om." But I am not a Yogi and the only syllable I feel like uttering with any regularity is "Ow." The boredom of this ailment is becoming intense.

• TUESDAY •

The doctor tells me that I must have a test tomorrow to discover what is going on inside me. This throws me into a frenzy of apprehension. Respectful and even reverential as I am toward

---

equal proportions of Education (chalk) and Youth (feet). Much of the fun of these concerts was to see how the artists compared with their publicity photographs, Grobian Smout the bassoonist looking decidedly the worse for wear and somewhat green about the dress suit, whereas Lanugo Pott who played the neutered piano and could be got cheap because he was young, seemed to be wearing a tail coat inherited from a larger and much older relative.

the medical fraternity, I wish upon occasions like this that I could escape to some desert island where no doctor had ever set foot. Such dreadful things happen when doctors begin their tests. I think about the Blue Baby which has been so much in the press of late. Could it possibly be that I am a Blue Adult, and that all the tests will be for nothing? I roll and toss in my bed (which has become as hot as a blast furnace) and wish that I had lived a better life, and given more to the poor. I resolve that if I survive the test I shall become a holy hermit and live in a cave, giving good advice to all who visit me. The only thing which deters me is the reflection that the standard of cooking in hermitages is notoriously low, and most hermits have ulsters.

• WEDNESDAY •

The Test: I am forced to swallow about a pint of liquid cement, flavoured with chocolate; this stuff is apparently impervious to X-rays, and a giant X-ray lamp is placed behind me; a doctor who looks like a scientist in a Boris Karloff film puts on a large pair of red goggles and stares right through me; I have even less concealment than a movie star in one of those new bare-bosom evening dresses. He watches the cement on its odyssey through my gizzard; every once in a while he murmurs with pleasure as my digestive system does something particularly clever; I wish that I, too, could have a peek, but it is impracticable. . . . This process goes on for some time, and I begin to wonder if it is a deep plot to turn me into a living statue by stuffing me with cement, so that I may be stood outside the clinic with a lamp in my hand, as a sort of advertisement. I begin to wriggle slightly just to make sure that I retain the power of movement. . . . At last it is over, and I can go home. The Test is finished. But what did it reveal? Shall I ever know?

• THURSDAY •

Spent the day recovering from The Test. Fortunately quite a number of people dropped in to see me, and I was able to describe it to them in juicy detail. But all my friends are amateur doctors, and insisted on diagnosing me themselves. Those who had gallstones were morally convinced that I was also a mass of limestone, and should be quarried immediately. The appendix veterans, on the contrary, maintained that I showed every symptom of appendicitis in the last and most horrifying stages, and urged me to be separated from my appendix within twenty-four hours or never to speak to them again. The ulster man came to put a washer on a tap and looked through the door to ask after my ulster. I denied that I was harbouring an ulster. He said that his brother-in-law had taken the same pigheaded attitude, and had eventually been seized with something resembling spontaneous combustion, and had been taken to the hospital, screaming for a drink out of a fire extinguisher. Upon the whole it was a lively day.

• FRIDAY •

A woman whom I know slightly, and who knows me, sent me the following clipping from a Toronto daily: "Bristol, England, March 14. Five pints of beer, leeks, figs and liquid paraffin have been given recently to Alfred, the Bristol zoo's 15-year-old gorilla, who has been suffering from stomach trouble. Keepers said what finally cured him, however, was a pint of cider." I suppose this is meant to be a jocose reference to my indisposition. Humph! I reflect cynically upon Cornelius Whurr's deathless couplet:

> What lasting joys that man attend
> Who has a polished female friend!

She does not realize what I have been going through; she has not heard about The Test; probably if I told her about ulsters she would interrupt with some irrelevancy about the time she had a baby. The idea that women are sympathetic is grossly overdone. Fifteen-year-old gorilla indeed!

• SATURDAY •

Received a letter today, which promised me good luck in four days if I would only copy it and send it to four other people. Gracie Fields is alleged to have won $40,000 after receiving it, and David Van Brooks (whoever he may be) is said to have lost $20,000 after breaking the chain. . . . I am joining David Van Brooks' party, although I have no $20,000 to lose. I am capable of many varieties of idiocy, but sending chain-letters is not one of them. . . .

-XII-

• SUNDAY •

Was delighted this morning to receive a tribute from the other inhabitants of my tenement on the able manner in which I have coped with the furnace this winter; it had never been cold, they said, the fire had never gone out, the ashes had not penetrated too searchingly into the living rooms, and the cries of anguish and the profanity and execrations from the furnace room had not too far transgressed the bounds of reverence and decency. I mumbled my thanks from a full heart, and dived into the cellar, to look at my old enemy. The thermometer outside registered 62, and he looked sick and beaten; I gave him a malignant kick in the lower draught and left him.

• MONDAY •

Had an opportunity this afternoon to examine the finest two-headed calf I have ever seen; it was no monstrosity, but a calf with two perfect Durham heads on one pair of shoulders; it lived for a week in this interesting condition, and when I saw it, it was well preserved in ice and on its way to the taxidermist's. It is destined to become a macabre little ornament on somebody's dining-room wall, and probably a nasty shock to anyone who has been too free with the dandelion wine. . . . I am sure that I would not make a good taxidermist; the temptation to improve upon nature would certainly be too strong for me. Think how easy it would be, when stuffing somebody's pet terrier, to slip a couple of human glass eyes into the sockets, instead of the usual buttons. Then the owner would really be justified in saying that his pet looked almost human. If I were stuffing this two-headed calf, for instance, I could not resist making one head smile and the other one frown, so that they looked like masks of Comedy and Tragedy. But such irreverent antics would ruin a taxidermy business, in which self-restraint is the first requirement.

• TUESDAY •

Was passing some time in a barbershop, turning over the pages of that sterling periodical *The Police Gazette*, when I came upon a page of pictures of lightly-clad girls who were described in the letterpress as "beauties." To prove that they were beautiful, their measurements of ankle, calf, thigh, hip, waist, bosom and neck were given. But I maintain that this mechanical, mathematical symmetry has nothing whatever to do with beauty. Beauty in a woman is largely made up of mystery, charm, and aloofness; these girls were about as mysterious, charming and aloof as those paper cups which are supplied with water-coolers. . . . Musing thus I laid aside *The Police Gazette* and took up *The Gospel Witness* and permitted my mind to heave and roll upon the troubled seas of its passionate prose.

• WEDNESDAY •

If I were a burglar, I should choose the houses I would rob by a careful inspection of their garbage cans. High livers, whose houses are sure to be stuffed with valuables, have large garbage cans from which pheasant carcasses and the rinds of costly fruits protrude. Less favoured mortals have small cans, smelling of old tripe and onions. As it is the quaint custom in Eastern Ontario to expose the garbage cans to the public several times a week, this handy credit index is always available, and peeking under the lids is quicker than wiring Dun and Bradstreet. I offer this suggestion, gratis, to book agents, magazine salesmen, and such needy riff-raff.

• THURSDAY •

Every day I learn something new. Today I read of a movement among artists of the Left Wing to destroy art altogether. The leader of this jihad is a fellow called Julian Symons, who writes: "The arts are disintegrating; the objective of art today is to divert attention from the class struggle. The intelligentsia who try to nurture the coy bloom of art as we know it are tending a dying flower. . . . The transition from the bourgeois art of the last three hundred years to any possible Socialist art of the future will not be made without . . . sacrifices." Ha, Ha, Symons old boy! You should come to Canada, where the great mass of the public hasn't even found out about the bourgeois art of the last three hundred years, let alone this new Socialist art of which you speak in such trenchant terms. Get wise to yourself, Julian, you old red carnation, you!

• FRIDAY •

How I abhor candid people! Today a candid friend told me that this Diary was drivel. What is the diary of any man likely to be but drivel? How many of us are able to record a deed of daring every day, or a ponderous reflection on the nature of the universe? How many of us are able to record that we have been reasonably honest, that we have kept our hands from picking and stealing, and that Lust and Covetousness have been strangers to our hearts? In my time I have read many diaries, published and in manuscript, and the noble and uplifting ones were invariably the work of men whom I knew to be engine-turned, copper-bottomed self-lubricating liars and hypocrites. . . . One of the most irritating diaries I ever read was written by a fellow I know who used to pinch all the best remarks I made and attribute them to himself. Hell gapes for such villainy.

• SATURDAY •

Raked and rolled my lawn this afternoon; some of my neighbours are gardeners born and bred, and thoroughly enjoy an afternoon of back-breaking labour in the great outdoors; but to me it is nothing but toil and a concession to popular opinion. I am afraid that people will look down on me if my lawn is a hayfield, and I would rather work myself into a decline than have them think that I am lazy (which is the real truth of the matter). . . . As a result of this unwonted activity my spine shrank a couple of inches and I was forced to walk in an uneasy posture, and when I sat down invisible daggers assailed me in the small of the back. Some of us are built for physical toil, and some for mental toil; every time I lift a rake I get a pain, but I have not had a headache in twenty years. But alas, most of us have to spend many hours a week at work for which we are unsuited.

-XIII-

• SUNDAY •

Had lunch out-of-doors for the first time this year, and further welcomed the fine weather by getting a touch of sunburn. Went for a stroll in the afternoon and admired babies; I find that the most successful approach to the subject of babies is to discuss them as though they were hams; the firmness of the flesh, the pinkness of the flesh, the even distribution of fat, the sweetness and tenderness of the whole, and the placing of bone are the things to praise. Carrying on the ham approach, you may safely say that the baby makes your mouth water, and you may pinch it appraisingly, but if your enthusiasm gets the better of you, and you stick a fork in it, you had better prepare to sell your life dearly.

• MONDAY •

Magnificent spring day, recalling to my mind those lovely lines of Keats:

> Oh, how sweet the morning air,
> Oh, how sweet the morning air,
>   When the zephyrs,
>   And the heifers,
> Odoriferous breaths compare!

Met a man who must have been deeply affected by spring, for he wanted to talk about love, a subject on which he had no particularly novel or interesting views. But he gave me a description of how he proposed to his wife, and of his nervousness upon that occasion. He asked me if I thought most men were nervous when proposing? I replied that I thought that formal proposals were rather uncommon, and that couples usually arrived at an understanding without ceremonious palaver, kneeling on the drawing-room carpet, blushing, fainting, bursting a corset-string, and the like; I have never heard of a formal proposal between people of reasonably equal age, and I have given more advice to the lovelorn than Dorothy Dix, ∮ in my time.

• TUESDAY •

❊ Some people I know were telling me of a curious experience which they had recently; they put a collection of old and rejected household articles in their car and drove to a dump to dispose of them. While busy at the dump, they were accosted by a strange figure, a woman of tall and stately presence, wearing a paper crown and carrying a staff in her hand, who strode majestically through the avenues of ashes, tin cans, dishonoured washboilers and superannuated bathtubs, attended by a rabble of admiring children. This apparition hailed my friends in a strange, incoherent, but musical language, and her breath was richly per-

---

∮ Dorothy Dix was the pen-name of Elizabeth Meriwether Gilmer (1870-1951) whose advice column in innumerable newspapers was one of the wonders of the age and was carried on after her death by competent ghosts (not hers). If the U.S.A. had had any gumption it would have elected this moderate, decent, common-sensical lady as its President, and spared modern history many a convulsion.

fumed with bay-rum, or it may have been lilac lotion; she was in fact as high as a kite and as mimsy as a borogrove. Having said her say, she strode off in queenly style, and she and her raffish crew were soon lost in the mazes of the dump.... My theory is that this was Titania, the fairy queen, fallen upon evil days, but magnificent in ruin; or it may simply have been some rumdumb old bag with a sense of humour. In either case the matter is worth investigating.

• WEDNESDAY •

Received news today that a friend of mine, a scientist of highly complex mentality, is about to marry a lady who is also a scientist of equally daedal intellect. This impresses me as an excellent scheme; then when they are tired of love they can always talk about science, and if love grows cold, science will keep them together, until it warms up again. I have long held the opinion that community of interest is more important to a marriage than scalding passion. People who mean to marry should make sure that there is something more than love between them. In the words of the old song:

> Will the love that you're so rich in
> Light the fire in the kitchen
> And the little god of Love turn the spit, spit, spit?

Love, like ice-cream, is a beautiful thing, but nobody should regard it as adequate provision for a long and adventurous journey.

• THURSDAY •

Had to do some motoring today. I have two characters, my Pedestrian Character, in which I am all for the Common Man, the freedom of the roads, and the dignity of Shank's Mare; and also my Motorist Character, in which I am contemptuous of the rights of walkers, violent in my passion for speed, and arrogant in my desire to kill anybody who gets in my way. Although not a driver myself I am a tireless adviser of the person who drives me and assist her in shouting insults at the other users of the roads. As I have never ridden a bicycle, I am the enemy of cyclists in both characters. If I am walking, they sneak up behind me, and slice the calves off my legs with their wheels; if I am driving, they wobble all over the road, never signal, and seem to be deaf, blind and utterly idiotic. In spite of their stupidity, cyclists rarely get themselves killed; the roads are slippery with defunct cats, squashed skunks and groundhogs, and hens who have been gathered to Abraham's bosom, but I have never seen a mass of steel, leather windbreaker and hamburger which was identifiable as the cadaver of a cyclist.

• FRIDAY •

Went today to view the X-rays which were taken of my inside some weeks ago. They were hung up on a rack and lighted from behind. I saw what was wrong at once; a long, thin, jagged monster was gnawing at my vitals; it was at least two feet in length, and on every joint there was a cruel hook. The doctor was very kind. He showed me my pylorus, and commented pleasantly on the nice appearance my spine made in the picture. But I could not take my eyes off the monster. Was it a tapeworm? Or was it something infinitely worse — something hitherto unknown to science? How long could I last with a thing like that in my vitals? As the doctor drew attention to the wonders of my inner world I grew more and more apprehensive, for I knew that he was saving the worst for the last. But the time came when he seemed to have finished. Summoning up all my courage, I asked the fatal question. "And that, doctor," I said; "what is that?" He lowered his voice, in case one of the nurses might overhear. "That is your zipper, Mr. Marchbanks," said he.

Marchbanks' adventures with the medical profession were many and often disquieting. It was this same doctor (a man of unimpeachable personal and professional character) who once said to him, while conducting a rectal examination, "Have you ever given any thought to joining the Masons, Mr. Marchbanks?" Marchbanks knew, of course,

• SATURDAY •

✻ Was in a bookshop today, reading a magazine on the sly, when a man and a woman came in and bought a school-book for their child. Neither one had the look of a reader (this is understatement) and as they left the man said, "Jeez if they were onto their job they'd put all this school stuff in one book, and then I wouldn't be all the time wastin' money." This seemed to me to sum up much of the popular attitude toward books and education. There was a time when reformers thought that if education were available to the masses, the masses would love it, and every humble cottage would be bursting at the seams with cheap reprints of the world's classics. In this supposition, as in many another, the reformers were somewhat optimistic. A real dictatorship of the proletariat — if such a thing existed — would quickly result in a bookless world.

that modern fraternal orders—Masons, Oddfellows, Moose, Bison etc. —all trace their antecedents back to the mystery religions of Ancient Greece, but he had not supposed the Greek influence went quite so far as this collocation of question-and-action suggested.

Spring

-XIV-

· GAMMOCKING SUNDAY ·

✺ One of those fine bright days upon which communion with Nature is all but obligatory, so I obediently made my way into the country and tried it. But fine as the phrase "communion with Nature" sounds, it is anything but easy in practice. Observed that the pussywillows were well advanced, but what of it? I never cared much for pussywillows. The roads were muddy, and the air smelled pleasantly of spring, except when I passed a swamp, where it smelled powerfully of drains. Investigated an old churchyard and read some old tombstones, and admired the carving on them, which was really very skilful, though not particularly tasteful. Nature seemed to have no special message for me, so I went home and resumed the combat with my furnace, which is trying to roast me alive.

· MONDAY ·

✺ A cold, wet, foggy day — a sort of Indian winter; people who have gone about during the fine weather gloating that we should pay for it later are in the seventh heaven of delight because of the fulfilment of their prophecy. Business took me to Toronto, the Ontario Babylon, and in an odd moment, I tried to buy a copy of Edmund Wilson's latest book, *ƒ* but was told it had been banned

---

ƒ This was Memoirs of Hecate County *(1946). Marchbanks succeeded in obtaining a copy from a venal bookseller and found that the book, though indecent by Ontario standards, was also dull, and it*

from sale in Canada. Why? And by whom? Why is it that my government, which takes anything up to eighteen months to check and return my Income Tax form, can tell me what I may not read within a fortnight of the book's publication? I should like to know whether the official who banned this book read it through? I should like to know whether he knows anything about Edmund Wilson and his work? I should like to know what, specifically, he objected to in the book which he banned? Is this official a critic? What education has he had? I imagine him as a little man with thin lips and rimless spectacles who does not read himself (his real job is checking invoices for the Customs) but who acts on suggestions from professional sin-sniffers — a class abounding in our fair land.

• TUESDAY •

Train-travel tonight, and I sat up in a daycoach, reading. Everyone else, however, was disposed to sleep, and curled up in astonishing contortions on the seats; they looked as though they had all eaten toadstools, and died in agony. A young airman across the aisle from me took off his tunic, his tie and his boots, scratched himself as thoroughly as decency allowed, and laid himself down with his feet under my nose; I tapped the feet with my book; and he moved them a little nearer to himself, but they were still plainly visible out of the corner of my eye. A soldier nearby stuck his clenched fist into his mouth, which gave his snores a hollow bassoon-like quality. The women, for the most part, tucked their heads out of sight and elevated their hind-quarters, like Mohammedans praying. The air was heavy with the frowsy, dead stench of sleeping humanity. I sat bolt upright, feeling like the only reveller at a wake, and read the night through, starting nervously whenever the owner of the socks kicked in his sleep, or when the fist-sucker seemed in danger of strangulation, or when one of the

was necessary to wade through much tedious matter before one came to a spicy bit. Nevertheless he read it through, to defy the Censor, whom he later discovered was not a little man with thin lips and rimless spectacles, but a fat slob with thin lips and rimless spectacles.

women groaned. Toward morning they all looked greenish-gray, which added nothing to the charm of the scene.

• WEDNESDAY •

As I was slicing some bread this morning there was a ring at my door, and I opened it to find an ugly-faced ruffian with a heavy paunch standing on the mat. "D'yuh own this house or rent it?" he demanded. "Who wants to know?" I asked. "I do," said Pauncho; "this house had oughta be insulated, and if yuh don't own it there's no good my wastin' time talkin' to yuh." I disembowelled him neatly with the breadknife, and called the Sanitation Department to come and clear away the mess. . . . I am often amazed that reputable firms, anxious to sell their products, will permit underbred, impudent, discreditable, rascally slubberdegullions to go from house to house, losing friends and alienating people from them. Nowadays, when there are so many government snoops and stool-pigeons asking questions everywhere, mere hawkers of potato-peelers, loose-leaf encyclopaedias, and patent jam-jar rings think that they may adopt the same insulting tone. Consumption, cancer and the pox are all said to be on the increase in this country, but in my opinion the disease of bad manners is outstripping them all.

• THURSDAY •

Visited the dentist today, and as I was a few minutes early I had a chance to look around his waiting-room and make a few Holmes-like deductions from what I saw. Like all dentists, he is apparently a slow reader, for magazines which other people discarded in the 1942 salvage drive are just beginning to find their way to his table. Examined his diplomas carefully. Why do all the boss-dentists who sign these things write so illegibly? A man who cannot control a pen any better than that is surely a dangerous fellow to be poking around in one's mouth with the nut-picks and tiny power-driven grindstones which dentists use. Lying on the table was a parcel which obviously contained a pound box of a popular brand of candy, left there by the patient who was at that moment in the monster's clutch. "Aha," I thought; "a woman, obviously, and a self-indulgent woman at that; probably fat." But when the door opened the candy was claimed by a big bruiser in a leathern jerkin, who had been getting his snappers put in condition for a delicious feast of nougat, chocolate creams, fudge, and caramels. There are times when I think that Sherlock Holmes was a fraud.

• FRIDAY •

My furnace passed peacefully away in its sleep last night; I could have prolonged its life with a transfusion of coke, but I thought it better not to do so; its temperature had risen to 82 degrees and I was sweltering, so I let nature take its course. The obsequies will be celebrated very quietly by the ash-man.... Thus ends another winter's epic struggle, and as I watched my old enemy grow colder and colder this morning, I was able to think of him with the magnanimity of a victor. He did all he could to outwit me, but science, skill, experience, and superior brainpower were on my side. When I hung up my long poker and my clinkerhook, my scraper and my shaker, and put the shovel in the corner, there was triumph in my heart, but a little sadness too.... My furnace now being extinct, and invalid as a source of grief and irritation to me, I masochistically turn my attention to my garden. I am learning about gardening in the only practical way—by experience. Last year I planted $3.45 worth of flower seeds, all in five-cent packages, and not one single bloom rewarded my efforts. Maybe my method was wrong. My desire was to have a garden which might be described as "a riot of bloom," and so I mixed all my sixty-nine packets of seeds in a big bowl and sowed them broadcast through the flower beds; all I got was the usual riot of weeds. But once

---

In the Fahrenheit scale, in which water freezes at 32 degrees and Marchbanks boils at 75 degrees. It has been abandoned in Canada in favour of the Celsius scale in which water boils at zero and Marchbanks swoons at 20—or is it 10? He has never mastered this new-fangled reckoning.

again I am filled with hope for my garden. Upon the pleasures of the past the sun never sets, and over its horrors the iniquity of oblivion blindly scattereth her poppy.

• SATURDAY •

Was trying to explain about Hitler to some children today; he was, I said, a very bad man. "Was he the kind that wanted his custard before he'd eaten up all his meat and vegetables?" one of them asked. I said that his sins had been even more scarlet than that, but was unable to abridge the iniquities of the Third Reich to nursery terms, for fear of putting ideas into their heads. . . . It turned cold tonight, and as my fireplace was inadequate for my wants, I had to relight my furnace. I make no bones about it; this was an humiliation which I found hard to swallow. The furnace giggled and sniggered and made thumping noises all evening, just to let me know that it was there, and had not finished with me yet.

-XV-

• SUNDAY •

The press of the times forced me to work today, just as though it were any Monday or Tuesday, which afflicted me abominably. I hate work, regarding it as the curse of Adam, and am fully in sympathy with the medieval view that work is an ignoble way of passing the time, beneath the dignity of anyone of fine feelings or intelligence. However, as there was no escape, I pushed my pen and punched my typewriter all day, and all evening till bedtime, taking time off only for a short walk. When I returned, my furnace had gone out. Tired of being checked, it yielded up the ghost, leaving only a mass of clinkers in the firepot. Addressed myself to the task of relighting it, and at last, when I was worn to a nubbin and hysterical with exasperation, the new fire was ready, and in time a gentle warmth stole through the house.

• MONDAY •

Tonight to the movies to see a Noel Coward film ✒ of which I had heard and read a variety of conflicting criticisms. I enjoyed it very much, but I can understand that many Canadians would not care for it because it dealt with a kind of English life which is unfamiliar to most people here. So far as acting, directing and humour were concerned, I thought it far beyond all but the best Hollywood products. . . . Right behind me was a fellow who had brought his deaf and blind fiancée to the films, and he explained every piece of action to her in detail, and repeated all the dialogue as well. I thought the girl was dumb, too, but whenever anything particularly moving came on the screen, she said "Jeeznitawful," which I interpreted as an expression of emotion. . . . When this picture was shown in Ottawa, there was a newspaper controversy about the accent in which the characters spoke, which refined Bytowners thought common. It is interesting that most Ontario people suffer from the delusion that they speak without an accent of any kind, and that corruption of the King's English exists only outside the confines of this blessed spot, this earth, this Ontario.

• TUESDAY •

Looked out of an upstairs window this morning and saw a squirrel apparently fast asleep on the roof of my woodshed; when I returned five minutes later it was still dozing peacefully in the sun. I did not know that squirrels ever rested in this lazy way; I thought that only the more highly developed mammals, like man, had enough sense to keep still for long periods when the weather was fine. . . . A friend who wants to save my soul has sent me three tracts, which I have added to my collection of works of edification. One of them tells of a "devoted Christian businessman" who was knocked down by a truck, and called his family about him for a deathbed orgy; to all of them he said "Good-night" except Char-

---

✒ This Happy Breed, *a tale of humble life.*

lie, the Black Sheep; to Charlie he said "Good-bye" in such a significant manner that Charlie was soon brought to his knees, "crying
out in agony of soul" and repenting. "Charlie is now a preacher of
the Gospel," says the tract, triumphantly.... Another is about a
wicked sea-captain who repented on his deathbed in time to be
saved; a cabin-boy with a Bible completed the job just in the nick
of time. The eventual profession of this boy is not mentioned.

• WEDNESDAY •

Woke early this morning, looked out my window, and saw
snow descending in large wet flakes; later, when I had summoned up the energy to get out of bed, the sun was shining brightly;
as I sat down to breakfast, the skies clouded and it began to rain.
This reminded me of Sir William Watson's painful lines:

> April, April,
> Laugh thy girlish laughter;
> Then, the moment after,
> Weep thy girlish tears.

I have long thought that these displays of meteorological hysterics
might better be described thus:

> Idiot April,
> You dribble and grin;
> Calm yourself, April,
> Wipe off your chin.

This in turn reminded me of the girl in Schubert's song who laughed
and wept by turns, and didn't know why, but coyly suspected that
she must be in love. I have known plenty of girls who were in
love, in my time, and I never saw one yet who behaved in this
uncertain manner; they all looked like the cat who had just swallowed the canary.

• THURSDAY •

Attacks on my peace of mind are unpleasantly common this
week. Today a man presented me with a volume called *Seven*

Years Street Preaching in San Francisco, California, Embracing Triumphant Death Scenes. He said that he thought I needed it more than anybody.... It has its lively side: I am particularly impressed with the author's observations on an auctioneer whom he saw in San Francisco: "If we could get ministers to cry aloud as earnestly over living immortal souls as this man does over spoiled cheese at two cents a pound, what a waking up they would produce among the sleeping thousands of this land!" ... The triumphant death scenes are very choice, particularly those of Orlando Gale and Romeo Darwin, both of Ohio, and I am amazed that dying women and men should be able to find breath to make such long and involved speeches. I notice that the author has little hope for those who died outside the Methodist faith, and is particularly scathing about the Church of Rome. Upon the whole I judged that the writer of this book has never been exceeded in zeal, even by auctioneers selling spoiled cheese.

• FRIDAY •

Paid a visit today to the liquor store, that mighty democratic institution, where I hobnobbed with high and low, rich and poor, clergy and laity for twenty minutes or so, while waiting my turn. Was not pleased to see a little girl there with her mother; the child could not have been more than four years old. Now was it her mother's fault, that desire for a bottle of Ontario wine caused her to bring her child into that crowd, or the fault of our fatherly government, which makes the purchase of liquor so complex an undertaking? How long will it be before they learn to treat liquor sensibly in this country?

• SATURDAY •

Meant to do some gardening this afternoon, but as a heavy snowfall made it impossible, I enjoyed a pleasant swoon on a sofa for a couple of hours, and arose much refreshed.... Then to a party, where I showed my prowess at those games where you have to fill out forms saying who Cain's wife was, and whether it was Lincoln or Petrillo who said "We must save the Union at all costs." I like games of that sort; the games I hate are those where somebody comes into the room and says that his first is in coffee but not in tea, and his second is in India but not in Canada, and so forth, until he has told you everything except what you want to know, namely, when the refreshments are going to appear.

-XVI-

• SUNDAY AND METABOLISM OF ST. PANCREAS •

To the zoo this afternoon, and watched some boys who were busy trying to goad the bear into a display of temper. Reflected that their bravery depended entirely upon the strength of the wire around the bear-pen, and wished that the prophet Elisha would suddenly appear and repeat his vindictive trick as described in *2 Kings ii;* of all created creatures, there is surely none capable of such bone-headed, thoughtless cruelty as a healthy growing boy. ... Looked at some owls which sat blinking and solemn in the daylight; a friend who was with me turned to me and said, "If you put that big one in an expensive suit and sat him behind a desk he could do as well as the manager of any business in the country."

• MONDAY •

Saw seeds for sale in a shop today, and was sorely tempted. Every spring I have to fight the desire to go on a seed-buying spree; it has been my lifelong habit to plant three seeds where one would do, and I usually buy several packages of everything, including watermelon and century plant. I love the gay pictures on the little envelopes, and the brave, boastful directions on the back of

---

James Caesar Petrillo (1892–1984) czar of the Musicians' Union, who did so much to advance that profession by his insistence on frequent cessations of rehearsal, so that spittle might be emptied from horns, the chin-rests of violins wiped, and racy tales of marital infidelity exchanged.

each package. "Sow in open soil when all danger of frost is past"; "plant in a cold frame and set out in June"; "separate until plants are one-sixteenth of an inch apart"—I know all the directions, and could write a gardening-book myself. The only trouble is that I am rarely able to grow any flowers, because I always forget what I have planted, and when the time comes to thin the flowers, I never can tell them from the weeds.

• TUESDAY •

Sent a telegram today containing the word "critic." Had a hard time convincing the girl who took my message that such a word existed, and that I did not mean "cricket." Later on I went into a bookshop and asked for Leacock's *Sunshine Sketches of A Little Town*. And—so help me, Jimmy Johnson—the girl in the shop had never heard of it! One of the finest, if not the finest, book ever written about Canadian life, read all over the world and translated into several foreign languages, and she had never heard of it! What do these people learn at school? What occupies the chamber in their minds where miscellaneous information should be stored? How do they manage to get through life without finding out anything? And how do these intellectual shut-ins ever get jobs?

• WEDNESDAY •

I may not be able to grow flowers, but my garden produces just as many dead leaves, old overshoes, pieces of rope and bushels of dead grass as anybody's and today I bought a wheelbarrow to help in clearing it up. I have always loved and respected the wheelbarrow; it is one wheeled vehicle of which I am perfect master. I cannot drive a car, I fall off bicycles, and the only time I tried to get into a wheelchair it tipped forward and threw me out. But with a wheelbarrow I am any man's equal.

• THURSDAY •

Several of my friends who are zealous in the temperance cause are back from Toronto today with sore throats—the result of their impromptu serenade of the Premier at Queen's Park yesterday. They tell me that they sang the four verses of *Fight the Good Fight* at least seventeen times, while the depraved, rum-loving M.P.P.s sat in their velvet chairs roaring, "Fifteen men on a dead man's chest," and "They took the ice right off the corpse and put it in the beer," and other gems of pot-house psalmody. . . . A dog-breeder tells me that the Mexican Chihuahua is given gin in puppyhood to stunt its growth. I knew that Hollywood child actors were given gin for this purpose, but I never before heard of a dog being shrunk with gin. Perhaps that accounts for the permanently sozzled expression of the Chihuahua, and its peculiar bark, which sounds so much like a hiccup.

• FRIDAY •

A conference which is going on now has caused the papers to be filled with cartoonists' ideas of what personified Peace looks like; she is either an iron-jawed, gimlet-eyed female with a bust like the prow of a destroyer, or she is a droopy, big-eyed miss with no bosom at all, who looks as though she lived entirely on marshmallows; in both cases she wears a garment equally suggestive of a modest girl's nightie, and the glory that was Greece. Why should Peace be such a pill? . . . I am going to import one of those pretty little owls from Greece; they are about a foot high, and extremely fetching in appearance. They are the true owls of Minerva, and very intelligent; they say "Whoo!" *ƒ* in Greek. . . . I get a good deal of mail, but little of it is personal, and none of it is interesting. The strangest people and institutions choose to send me letters. The railways, for example, keep sending me messages boasting about how much money they have made, which I think dreadfully bad taste. What would they think of me if I sent them letters saying, "Last year, after paying all bills and charges, Marchbanks had $7.68 to spend as he liked." They would be disgusted; so am I.

ƒ In Greek, "Whoo!" is o. Whether you prefer it in English or Greek is simply a matter of Whose Whoo!

• SATURDAY •

✸ Discerned symptoms of a cold deep in my inner being today, and immediately set to work to circumvent it. For twenty-four hours before a cold breaks out in its unmistakable symptoms of salt rheum, cough and *tædium vitæ* I suffer from tremblings of the spirit and a sense of impending doom; during this period I consume glass after glass of sodium bicarbonate in hot water; sometimes it does the trick and sometimes it does not. I got the idea that it would stave off a cold from a man who subsequently died of pneumonia, so I may be on the wrong track. But the results, whether healthful or not, are certainly violent. My frail form is racked by horrendous belchings, like the roars of a lion. The Chinese are said to frighten away evil spirits by beating gongs; I have my own not wholly dissimilar method.

-XVII-

• SUNDAY •

✸ A cold, the like of which has never before confronted medical science, has me in its grip, and my head feels as though it had been roughy scooped out with a tin spoon, and stuffed with soiled laundry. My sense of taste has completely gone; I cleaned my teeth with a widely-advertised drain-opener tonight and did not even notice until it ate the bristles off my toothbrush. Went to bed, propped up on many pillows, so that I should not strangle in the night. Had a chest-rub, a hot drink, and crunched up a mouthful of aspirin before going to sleep. Woke, some hours later, having dreamed that I was in the grip of a big dog, which was tossing me from side to side and barking furiously. Was alarmed to find that in truth I was being thrown all over the bed by some mysterious agency, and the sound of deep, angry barking was deafening. As consciousness returned, I realized that I was having a Coughing Fit. As the old song has it:

I attempt from love's sickness
　　To fly, in vain;
For I am myself
　　My own fever and pain.

I was myself my own dog, bark and all; each paroxysm raised me at least two feet above the bed, and then as I emitted a frightful roar it flung me down again. This went on for some time — long after I had begun to ask of Death where was its sting? But everything passes in this world, and at last I fell asleep, and dreamed that I was being suffocated.

· MONDAY ·

❈ Today I live in the gray, muffled, smelless, puffy, tasteless half-world of those who have colds.

· TUESDAY ·

❈ Made the acquaintance of a rum-drinking budgerigar this evening. Was chatting with some people who offered me a glass of rum, and after I had been convinced that they were not joking and not crazy, ✒ I settled down in the cosy beatitude which comes over a man who has unexpectedly been given a drink. At this moment their budgerigar broke out of his cage, whizzed across the room and settled on my shoulder. I thought it was my simple

---

✒ *Although this happened after the supposed cessation of the War of 1939–45, liquor was still rationed in Canada, and hospitality was cautious. At the outbreak of war the Rt. Hon. Mackenzie King declared that Canada must "don the full armour of God" and of course this meant liquor rationing. The armour stayed on for quite a while after the fighting stopped, but the watering of the nation's booze has persisted to this day, and something in excess of 80 per cent of the cost of a bottle of liquor, which is 75 per cent as strong as it used to be, is tax. This is why a Canadian, tasting his first Martini on a visit to New York, is often seen to gasp and clutch his throat. He is unaccustomed to the Real Thing.*

and child-like nature which had fascinated him, but I was wrong. He cake-walked along my sleeve, suddenly dipped his beak into my glass and took a hefty swig; luckily Nature has not equipped budgerigars with much in the way of a gullet, so he didn't get more than his share. He had a few more gulps, and then flew off to a mirror, in which he kissed his own reflection several times, with evident satisfaction. It has been years since I had enough rum to provoke any such ecstasy; there are advantages in a limited capacity.

• WEDNESDAY •

A man who had been poking his nose into the MS. of this Diary told me he didn't think it was very funny. This is the sort of comment which makes me secrete adrenalin by the bucketful. First of all, how did the ridiculous assumption spring up that my Diary was meant to be funny? What record of man's life, shot through and through with toil and anguish, disappointment and shame, frustration and denial is ever funny? When Tolstoy gave up wealth and rank and, in an agony of pity and idealism, tilled the land with his peasants, was it funny? When Gauguin left a secure life in Paris and went to paint the beauties of Tahiti, casting his lot with savages, lepers and degenerates, was it funny? And when Marchbanks, furnace-fried and garden-torn, commits his reflections to his Diary, is that funny? No, baboon! No, donkey! Tragic, mystic, sublime, perhaps. But only a coarse and warty soul could find food for laughter here.

• THURSDAY •

My coal bin is empty at last. For weeks I have been feeding my furnace a mixture of coke, slack, wood-shavings, cannel coal and odds and ends of rope and raffia from the floor of my coal bin, and now it is all gone. I shall not buy any more. I am, I think, a tolerant, easy-going fellow, but when it is suggested that I should spend any more money on that accursed furnace this year, everything goes black before my eyes, and I fall on the floor, foaming at the mouth and uttering animal cries. Of course, I cannot freeze. I have a woodpile, and I shall keep my furnace burning with that. If, when it is all done, the weather is still cold, I shall move to an hotel. My furnace does not like wood, and makes horrid stinks when given wood to burn. It shoots smoke up its heating pipes, and heats up its chimney, and keeps my whole house at the temperature and atmosphere of an Indian tepee. But I do not care. I can endure anything better than spending money for another load of coal—half of which (the big half) will be coke. Anyhow, other big expenses loom before me. My lawn-mower simply must be sharpened; I avoided having this done during the war years (to avoid taking several men from more vitally necessary jobs) and now a large machine shop has undertaken the work, on a cost-plus basis.

• FRIDAY •

Nothing happened to me today which was not routine; my life grows duller and duller. Sometimes I think that I should take up a hobby, but the problem always is, which one? I could breed budgerigars, but I'm not sufficiently interested in budgerigars. I could become an authority on the history of something-or-other, but that would be so much like my ordinary work, that it would not recreate me. I once worked up a small enthusiasm for wood-carving, but when I found that it meant investing $100 or so in chisels and gouges, and haunting lumber yards in search of fine pieces of Spanish mahogany and sandalwood my enthusiasm waned. The trouble is that I don't really like doing anything; I just like to sit, and when I sit I become bored. It's a vicious circle, and I suppose I am what the psychologists call maladjusted. . . . I once knew a man whose hobby was making jewellery. He had a few stones and a few chunks of gold and silver, and he made rings and brooches which he gave to his friends. They were so horrible that nobody would wear them, but that was his fulfilment. I also knew a chap who did rotten bookbinding; his system was to take a book you really liked, and bind it in suede leather which made your teeth grate. I finally got so I didn't care whether he was fulfilled or not.

· SATURDAY ·

✿ Having averted my face from it for several weeks, I tackled the problem of Income Tax today. People of a mathematical turn of mind tell me that the forms are very simple if you attack them logically, but I am incapable of attacking an Income Tax form logically, or even coolly. Whatever my Better Self may say about citizenship and duty, my Worser Self remains convinced that it is a wicked shame that the government should take a big chunk of my earnings away from me, without so much as telling me what the money is to be used for. I know about the Baby Bonus, of course, but whose baby, specifically, am I bonussing with my money? Probably a damp, sour-smelling baby which I should hate if I met it face to face. Whose Old Age Pensions am I paying? Probably those of some lifelong prohibitionists, if the truth were known! People to whom I would not give a used paper handkerchief if I met them in the street are picking my pockets by means of this iniquitous Income Tax! The whole thing puts me into such a passion that I am incapable of adding and subtracting correctly. Clutching hands seem to snatch at me out of the paper until I scream and scream and scream.

-XVIII-

· SUNDAY AND MAY DAY ·

✿ A man who spent part of the winter up in the Kapuskasing district told me that the best-dressed people in Canada live there. They haven't much to spend their money on beside personal adornment, and they go in for rich and colourful raiment of a

Marchbanks has himself been an Old Age Pensioner for many years, and a recipient of the publication Especially For Seniors *(circulation 810,980) distributed free by the Government of Ontario. Lifelong journalist that he is, Marchbanks attempted to contribute to this magazine, but after the rejection of two deeply-pondered articles —* Make Friends With Your Bladder, *and* Rocking-Chair Sex For The Over-Eighties *he gave up in discouragement.*

kind never seen in the city. Manufacturers prepare special lines of Babylonian parkas and Tyrian windbreakers for the northland which are unknown in the cities of Ontario, where men dress in gray and blue sacking and allow their wives to choose their ties for them. In the north, this man told me, the trappers and loggers are great patrons of the beauty shops, and like to have their hair and beards arranged in crinkly marcels. I was not surprised to hear this, for man in a natural state is a vainglorious creature; it is only when he puts on the shackles of civilization that he becomes colourless, shamefaced, and slinking. . . . May Day today, which I celebrated by organizing a dance round the May Pole for some children, after which I treated them to chunks of May Pole sugar, which is scarce this season.

• MONDAY •

Today at lunchtime I saw a girl's hat blow off into the street; she was a pretty girl (well—fairly pretty—not fat, anyhow), nicely dressed, and her distress was pitiable to see. The hat was a small round gray felt gourd, and after rolling about in the dirt for a while, it came to rest under a parked car. With the alertness of an old campaigner in the Sex War, I at once took cover in a shop door, for I knew that that girl would immediately be on the lookout for a man to get her hat for her, and I had no mind to crawl on my ulcers in the street, under somebody else's oily old jalopy. Sure enough, she had her victim within three minutes; simpering pathetically he fished out the hat, and his reward was a smile—not nearly enough in these days of trouser shortage. . . . But at five o'clock I saw a young workman lose his cap in the street, and what happened? His companions jeered coarsely, young women sniggered and sharpened their fingers at him, and a big fat capitalist in a blue car rode right over his hat just as he was snatching for it. This typical display of the inequalities under which men struggle in the modern world saddened me so much that I hardly had strength to resist a young Jehovah's Witness who tried to sell me a magazine on my way home.

• TUESDAY •

My cold is not better; it is worse, and I am confronted by one of those vexing problems for which there is no wholly satisfactory solution. Shall I stay at home, and enjoy the delights of mild invalidism, or shall I do my day's work, and enjoy the gloomy pleasures of martyrdom? . . . To lie in bed, cosseted with hot-water bags and flannel chest-warmers, supping gruel, syllabubs, and tansy tea — that is the ideal state on a vile, rainy, soggy day like this. But again, to snuffle at my work, to throw paper handkerchiefs into the waste basket in monotonous rhythm, to cough pitifully and roll my rheumy eyes toward Heaven whenever anyone reproaches me — this too, is bliss. . . . Then again a man with a cold is a privileged snarler; he can be as abrupt as he likes with his colleagues, and they are forced to believe that it is his illness which speaks through his lips, and not his habitual sweet spirit. Lying in bed, there is no one to snarl at, for if one snarls at one's nurse she may retaliate with a mustard plaster — which is, of course, for one's own good, and has nothing whatever to do with revenge. . . . I eventually decided in favour of work, and developed a cough which sounds like coal pouring down a chute.

• WEDNESDAY •

I listen to the radio a good deal these days, for my ears are enchanted by the wonders of the newscasts, though occasionally I shed a tear for the ignorance of the announcers. Today I heard Connecticut with the second "c" sounded — an inexcusable solecism, and yesterday I heard Count Bernadotte called "Bernadotty." I am often told that radio announcers cannot be faultless; I know that, but I insist that they should speak like educated people and not like yahoos. After all, they are paid to talk, and if they cannot speak well they are bad workmen, and deserve criticism like other bad workmen. If man has conquered the air merely to fill it with bombs and illiteracy, we might as well discount this civilization, and try a new one.

· THURSDAY ·

Word reached me today that I am shortly to possess a handsome kitten; I have been on the track of a kitten of just the right sort for quite a time. Immediately turn my attention to suitable names. Nicholas is a fine name for a cat, and so is Solomon. Dr. Johnson called his cat Hodge, which convinces me that it must have been a rustic, bumpkin cat, with a miaow like a creaking door. All sorts of famous men have been cat-lovers, but unfortunately they have not left a record of their cats' names. I should like to call my cat Bubastis, after the Cat Goddess of ancient Egypt, but my neighbours are very conservative, and would give me oblique glances if I crept about my garden calling "Bubastis, Bubastis" in a high, soft, cat-attracting voice. Cardinal Richelieu gave his white cat seven names, after seven different Popes, but my motives might be misunderstood if I followed his example (not being a Cardinal). The ideal name eludes me, but I shall find it at last.

· FRIDAY ·

To the bank today, and stood in a queue right behind a man who appeared to be paying off the National Debt in pennies; he and the clerk counted them all several times with intense concentration, and after a while I began to count them too, to combat my boredom. . . . When at last the Golden Boy moved away, and I confronted the wicket, I was intimidated to find that the young lady behind it was several inches taller than I was, and looked down at me as though she thought I had not come honestly by the few dirty bills which I poked at her through the bars. By the time my trifling business was finished, I was cringing pitifully before this goddess. . . . But when I went to another wicket to get my book, I saw the true state of affairs. She was really a little girl, about the size I am accustomed to dandle on my knee, and she was standing on a box! It is this sort of misrepresentation on the part of banks which drives simple people to socialism. In the socialist state everybody will have to keep his feet flat on the floor, his head in the clouds, his shoulder to the wheel, his back to the wall, his ear to the ground, and his nose to the grindstone. And short girls will be made to stand under tables at the banquets of state officials, and retrieve the dropped napkins of the gorging *Parteigenossen*.

• SATURDAY •

Kitten arrived today—a tortoiseshell inclining toward tiger stripes; its milk-name was "Tiger," and it may stick unless I can think of something better. It is a female, so Nicholas and Solomon must be abandoned. Cats marked in this way reveal Chinese ancestry, so I am told, but so far Tiger has shown none of the much-advertised Chinese calm. She has climbed the curtains, skated on the lid of the piano and displayed an utterly anti-Confucian passion for fish scraps, bits of chicken, custard, junket, bread-and-milk and similar flesh-pots. A stickler for tradition, I wanted to butter her paws to accustom her to her new home, but the butter price will not permit it. Engaged in a lively discussion as to whether olive-oil was a permissible substitute. Made a punching-bag for Tiger out of a ball of paper and some string, and watched her box; kittens and babies are always able to reduce us to the last extreme of drooling fatuity; at last Tiger was settled for the night in a box containing an old sweater and a hot-water bottle, the latter being a substitute for her mother. I hope she doesn't get a shock in the morning, when she finds her mother has turned cold, bald and a disagreeable shade of red.

- XIX -

• SUNDAY •

Went cheerfully through the whole day without realizing that the usual haphazard tinkering with the clocks was in progress, and that I should have been enjoying the benefits of Daylight Saving Time. I don't really care how time is reckoned so long as there is some agreement about it, but I object to being told that I am saving daylight when my reason tells me that I am doing nothing of the kind. I even object to the implication that I am wasting something valuable if I stay in bed after the sun has risen. As an admirer of moonlight I resent the bossy insistence of those who want to reduce my time for enjoying it. At the back of the Daylight Saving scheme I detect the bony, blue-fingered hand of Puritanism, eager to push people into bed earlier, and get them up earlier, to make them healthy, wealthy and wise in spite of themselves. ∥

• MONDAY •

An extremely attractive young woman of my acquaintance told me of an amatory adventure she had today. While at the grocer's she noticed that she was an object of deep interest to a dark, passionate young man behind the counter. Wherever she went he followed her with a burning eye: his heavy breathing was audible at a considerable distance; when at last he caught her eye, he gave her a glance charged with 25,000 volts of tender meaning. As she is quite accustomed to these tributes she paid no attention and forgot about him entirely until her groceries were delivered. But then she found his name, address and telephone number, neatly written in black crayon on one of her bananas! The use of a banana

---

As the year 2000 approaches, and with it the end of the Aeon of Pisces, it might be a good idea for U. N. to consider some better way of determining historical dates than by counting backwards and forwards from the Year One of the Christian Era, thus giving Time a kind of Push-Me-Pull-You air. Time ought to move forward gently, without these convulsions. But let us have no suggestions that we reckon time from the Destruction of the Temple at Jerusalem, nor yet the Founding of Rome by Rhomboid and Rumpus (who were suckled by a werewolf); these are events too recent to fit in with the latest discoveries of archaeology, which have revealed a tooth in a cave in North Wales, belonging to a boy, presumably Welsh, which is 75,000,000 years old. Why not date from the year this boy (whose name appears to have been John Jenkin Jones) lost his tooth, and call the Age of Man the Age of Jones? Thus all dates in future would be After Jones, or A.J., as in "The Second World War was fought A.J. 74,008,061–74,008,067."

as a *billet doux* would have interested the late Havelock Ellis. I suggested that the next time she should casually drop a lemon, as a sign that his suit is hopeless.

• TUESDAY •

As I sat outside the main dining room of the Royal York this evening, a large black dog appeared from nowhere and began to lick my hand, sit on my feet, wipe its nose on my trousers, and give other evidence of its esteem and regard. At the best of times I have a low opinion of Man's Dumb Chum, and as I could see a headwaiter eyeing me balefully, as though about to call the hotel detective and the bouncer, I gave the creature a couple of sharp kicks in the slats and urged it to go elsewhere. But dogs love me just as inveterately as I hate them, and the creature took my abuse the way screen heroines take the soft cooings of Charles Boyer. This rattled me so much that I got up and moved to another chair, but the dog followed me, leaping up and down and wagging a tail like a wagon-tongue. Drastic action was called for, and so, with a Judas smile, I fed it a particularly ferocious coughdrop which I had in my pocket — a coughdrop of atomic strength ╱ — and that did the trick. It gave me a look of reproach which would have done

---

╱ I have identified this coughdrop as a Woof-Nix, a drop of Marchbanks' own invention, and associated with a black passage in his usually blameless career. For many years he held the position of Coughdrop Critic for The New England Journal of Medicine, and devised a ranking scheme, based on the Best Seller Lists, to show the comparative sales of the most popular coughdrops. For eighteen months without a break a drop called Woof-Nix held the proud position of Top O' The Drops, until a jealous rival revealed that Marchbanks was himself the inventor and manufacturer of Woof-Nix, which he made from road tar and raw turpentine, with a slight hint of garlic as a flavouring. Its nastiness had been its great merit for millions of masochistic coughers. The scandal, of course, meant that Marchbanks had to retire from the medical world. Sorry to bring this up, but truth is great, and will prevail.

credit to Beautiful Joe, and rushed away howling. When I last saw it, it was trying to get a drink out of an ornamental spittoon which was, however, filled with sand.

• WEDNESDAY •

Went to see an entertainment describing itself as Russian Ballet tonight. But it had sacrificed all the grace and carefully concealed art of Russian Ballet for a kind of athletic joyousness which was about as amusing as a high school gym exhibition. In the art of ballet, inspiration is most decidedly not ninety-five per cent perspiration.

• THURSDAY •

If the purchase of costly, foolish little gadgets will do it, I should have a magnificent garden this year. Today I bought a hose-reel, a charming toy with a lot of green paint on it, for rolling up my hose and trundling it around the garden. The fact of the matter is that since the purchase of my wheelbarrow, I have lost all sense of values, and am ready to buy anything which looks like a garden tool. Although the wowsers pretend that men come to ruin through drink and women, the real truth of the matter is that more men are ruined by the purchase of expensive domestic junk than in any other way. Drink imposes its own limit, and women soon become a weariness of the flesh, but the passion for saucy little garden gadgets, bedizened with green paint and ballbearings, is never stilled. It gnaweth like a serpent and wasteth like a fever.

• FRIDAY •

In the morning paper, I see some pictures of flower arrangements done by Toronto interior decorators. In one of them some Arum lilies had been painted blue! Such tricks are not in the great Japanese tradition of flower arrangement. Indeed, when I studied the arrangement of flowers with the Hon. Miss Morning Mouth at the Imperial Greenhouses at Tokyo, we were forbidden even to bend the stem of a flower or strengthen it with wire. I recall that one student (a pretty little creature called the Hon. Miss Bursting Cocoon) was caught by the Hon. Miss M. M. pressing the stem of a calceolaria with a warm iron, to make it straight, and she was in danger of expulsion. However, she made amends by writing one of those moving Japanese poems. It went like this:

> I pressed a stem;
> Ahem!
> Now, when the moonlight falls on the jade
>   roof of the Imperial Brewery,
> I am desolate.

• SATURDAY •

Had an inaugural use of my hose-reel today. It was not a success, being designed for hose of the type which some people attach (for reasons unknown to me) to their hot-water bottles. My hose was too strong for it, and the pretty little barrel kept unwinding just at the moment when I most wanted it to remain firm. The green paint came off on my hands in gobs, and the little hook which was supposed to keep the whole thing in a beautiful, ship-shape roll, came off at once, and had to be replaced with a piece of string. What is more, when the machine is loaded with hose, the little wheels won't revolve. Some day, perhaps, I may learn to resist the soft appeal of garden appurtenances which belong strictly in the category of toys.

-XX-

• SUNDAY •

Dirty weather today, culminating in hail later this afternoon. When I read about other people's hailstorms in the papers, the hailstones are always described as being as big as pigeons' eggs, and sometimes as big as baseballs; my hailstones were no bigger than grains of tapioca, and melted as soon as they reached the ground. It was a disappointing performance. Frankly, I think that there is a tendency deep in the human soul to exaggerate the size of hailstones. To combat the cold I relit my furnace, using some odds and ends of coal, coke, dust and semi-liquid black goo from the corners of my cellar. The fire gave off a strangling black smoke, but no heat whatever, and deposited something like coal tar on all my furniture, upholsteries, and even on my person. I was noticeably swarthy when I went to bed.

• MONDAY •

I see that the movie magnates think of reviving *The Sign Of The Cross*, with Charles Laughton having his feet tickled, Elissa Landi being eaten by lions, and Claudette Colbert bouncing up and down prettily in a bath of asses' milk. It was one of those films in which Christianity and Romantic Love were inextricably confused; Christianity and Pure Love were equated with marrying the girl and restraining premarital caresses to an occasional light kiss on the lips; Paganism and Impure Love meant not marrying the girl, and occasionally joining her in her asses' milk bathtub. But the most fascinatingly repulsive confusion of Christianity and Hollywood Mush that I have ever seen was in *Ben Hur* in which lovers were shown in the foreground of the scene of the Crucifixion, with the caption, "He died, but Love goes on forever."

• TUESDAY •

Heard about the engagement of two people known to me. Immediately the old question sprang into my mind; "What can they see in each other?" Pondered on this and decided that it was a stupid question. After all, I suppose everybody is lovable to some degree, if you approach them in the right way. Very often when I am introduced to women, I think, "What is she really like behind the disguise which she wears?" And very often I discover that she is pleasant enough, and probably would expand and glow if she received enough affection. . . . This habit of mine is not unlike that of the wicked villains of French novels, who were frequently described as "stripping women with their eyes"; when I was younger I used to do that, but as my eyesight grew worse, I had to depend more and more on guesswork, and finally gave it up altogether. Nowadays I never even take off a woman's overcoat with my eyes. I am far more interested in the detection of wigs and false teeth than in conjectural revelations of a beauty which rarely exists.

• WEDNESDAY •

My kitten Tiger is making the acquaintance of the whole world out-of-doors, and her amazement at such things as grass, plants and flower beds is pretty to watch; give her a border full of iris, and she thinks that she is in a jungle, and prowls realistically. Perhaps God made cats so that man might have the pleasure of fondling the tiger. . . . The kitten has a luxurious, Bohemian, unpuritanical nature. It eats six meals a day, plays furiously with a toy mouse and a piece of rope, and suddenly falls into a deep sleep whenever the fit takes it. It never feels the necessity to do anything to justify its existence; it does not want to be a Good Citizen; it has never heard of Service. It knows that it is beautiful and delightful, and it considers that a sufficient contribution to the general good. And in return for its beauty and charm it expects fish, meat, and vegetables, a comfortable bed, a chair by the grate fire, and endless petting. The people who yelp so persistently for social security should take a lesson from kittens; they have only to be beautiful and charming, and they will get it without asking.

• THURSDAY •

Was not pleased this morning to receive a circular from an insurance company, addressed "To The Householder Or Roomer." It is not the implication that I take roomers which annoys me; I have nothing against boarding houses or boarders and have indeed filled the role of Roger the Lodger myself in many homes. No; it is the word "Roomer" itself which I dislike. The English language contains excellent and honourable words to meet all cases; a man who eats and sleeps in a house kept by somebody else is a boarder (unless he is an in-law, of course); a man who merely lives there and eats elsewhere is a lodger. If we accept the nasty word "roomer" into the language, we must accept its beastly counterpart "mealer." "Do you room at Mrs. Murphy's?" "No, but I meal there." . . . What is more, I hate letters addressed to "The House-holder Or Roomer," because they try to cover altogether too much ground with a miserable circular and a one-cent stamp. Furthermore, I loathe and condemn all circulars printed in type which tries to look like the print of a typewriter; I regard them as even baser than letters signed with a rubber-stamp of a signature. I have never bought a cent's worth of insurance from any company dealing in such nasty deceits, and I never will. *✒*

• FRIDAY •

Long letter today from a friend who loves cats, who calls me an "ailurophile," which I realize, after a little thought, is Greek for cat-lover. "Glad you have a cat," he says; "I don't know how you managed so long without one. Every writer needs a cat. But you are wrong in saying that the names of the cats of great men are not on record. The earliest known cat was Bouhaki, who belonged to King Hana of the eleventh Egyptian dynasty; and you must have heard of Mahomet's cat Abuhareira. What about Mark Twain's four cats, Apollinaris, Blatherskite, Sourmash and Zoroaster? What about Victor Hugo's two—Chanoine and Mouche? What about Carlyle's cat Columbine? What about Rossetti's cat Zoe? What about Matthew Arnold's cats Blacky and Atossa, and Horace Walpole's two cats Fatima and Selima, and Theophile Gautier's two, Seraphita and Zizi, and Swinburne's Atossa, and Dickens' cat Williamina (first called William, by mistake) to name only a few? Dr. Johnson owned not only Hodge, whom you mention, but also

---

✒ This was, of course, before the invention of the computerized address machine, which scorns anyone whose name contains more than twelve letters. This affair has reduced him to Samuel Marchb, who sounds like the kind of Middle European poet who gets the Nobel Prize because the Russians (probably quite rightly) can't stand him.

a kitten called Lily. I am surprised that you could write without a cat; no other writer of the least consequence has been without one."

• SATURDAY •

✾ Have been thinking about what my correspondent said yesterday; maybe the trouble with modern literature is that too many writers have deserted cats and gone over to dogs; a dog is a physical, not an intellectual companion. Perhaps, after all, the Indians had a good idea in their system of totems; certainly some people seem to be Dog-men, whereas others are died-in-the-wool Cat-men; I have known quite a few Bird-women, and once I met a Monkey-woman, who was never happy unless accompanied by a small monkey which appeared to have had its trousers patched on the seat with bright green. It's a strange world, and we are all more in the grip of primitive ideas than we care to acknowledge. The other day I saw a little girl trying to walk on a hardwood floor without touching the cracks. "The cracks are poison," she explained, "and if you walk on them you'll die." Children invent magic; later in life we are still subject to this sway, but we invent "scientific" theories, and "philosophies" to make it intellectually respectable.

-XXI-

• SUNDAY •

✾ The first picnic of the season, somewhat complicated by the difficulty of finding a piece of ground dry enough to sit on without receiving the impression that one had put one's hindquarters in cold storage. At last found a charming dingle (or gully, if you insist) and spread the refreshments; after all, a picnic is essentially a meal in the open air and there is no point in disguising the fact with attempts to appreciate the over-rated beauties of nature. There are two kinds of picnic which I hope to enjoy before I die; the first is the kind exalted in so many French paintings, in which the men lie on the grass and play mandolins and drink wine, while the ladies remove their clothes and paddle in a nearby river (see *Le déjeuner sur l'herbe* by Manet); the second is an English Victorian picnic, with plenty of fine silver, a wine-cooler, a footman and a maid to serve the grub, and everybody dressed to the nines in sporting costume. The modern picnic, with peanut butter sandwiches and coffee, is good in its way, but lacks breadth and richness.

• MONDAY •

One of the candidates for the Prime Ministership *❦* is advertising that he was born in a log cabin, and apparently has a movie of the event to prove it. Why do so many people think it admirable to be born in a log cabin? To be born in a log cabin, during the past sixty or seventy years, merely indicates that one's parents were shiftless; all the best people, whose parents were up-to-date in their views, were born in hospitals. A log cabin, with a dirt floor, wind whistling through the chinks in the walls, rain falling, snow drifting, and wolves howling outside the door, is no place to usher a child into the world; it is likely to pick up all kinds of nasty ailments right away. To the truly progressive mind, being born in a log cabin is a shameful circumstance, to be concealed from political opponents, who may insist that a child so born is likely to break out, even in middle age, with croup, or thrush, or diaper rash, or some other humiliating and unstatesmanlike disease, right in the middle of a peace conference.

• TUESDAY •

Without either effort or invitation on my part, politics has begun to colour my whole life. In Canada this is inevitable;

❦ The Rt. Hon. John Diefenbaker (1895–1979); his opponent countered by letting it be known that in his youth he had been a professional baseball player. It was not from such pits as these that Richelieu, the Younger Pitt, or even Disraeli or Gladstone, were dug. But the richer Canada grows, the more its politics lurches toward the folksy. Instances are known of M.P.s having their finger-nails artificially dirtied by the manicurist at the Chateau Laurier before meeting with deputations of their constituents.

what horse-racing is to Irishmen, or singing-contests to Welshmen, politics is to the Canadian. It is his absorbing passion, bred in the bone and coursing through his blood. It weighs upon him like atmospheric pressure, sixteen pounds to the square inch. There are Canadians who take no interest in politics, but they are chiefly drawn from the class which converses in sign-language, eats with its hands, and cannot count above ten. The true Canadian can be brought back from the grave, lured from his treasure-chest or beguiled from his mistress' bower by two things — an argument about religion or an argument about politics. I have seen elderly ladies who looked like waxwork advertisements for Mother's Day become raging tigresses when politics has been mentioned, and babes scarcely weaned bash babes of uncongenial opinion with their dollies, as election day draws near. Indeed, as a babe I swung a mean Teddy Bear myself in defence of my party prejudices.

• WEDNESDAY •

Because I have let my furnace out I have to make grate fires every night, to dry out my armchair; otherwise its boggy embrace threatens me with sciatica and swimmer's cramp. Making a grate fire means splitting kindling and lugging wood, and by the time I have finished these jobs, I am too hot to want a fire. There is a saying, attributed to Lincoln, that "he who splits his own wood, warms himself twice." Frankly I don't believe that Lincoln said any such thing; he split lots of wood himself, and knew what a bore it is. But when great men die, preachers and schoolteachers, and others who are in constant need of support in their battle against human nature, invent sayings of this kind and attribute them to the dead, who are unable to talk back. Probably when I am gone I shall be represented to posterity as a man who always ate all his spinach, advocated hard physical exercise, and never left undone what he could do today. These will be gross untruths, of course, and no child who bases his life upon them will ever be anything like me; it is thus that mentors of the young hornswoggle their little pupils and prevent them from becoming wise and great.

• THURSDAY •

A holiday, which I observed by getting back to the land. That is to say, I cut my lawn for the first time this year. The pleasure-grounds at Marchbanks Towers present an interesting example of optical illusion applied to landscape gardening; they do not look particularly extensive, but when you begin to pace out their dimensions, behind a decrepit lawn-mower, then they take on the proportions of Versailles.

• FRIDAY •

I see that some of his political supporters are telling President Truman that it will do him no good to be known throughout the Land of the Free and the Home of the Brave as a fellow who plays the piano for relaxation; this, the politicos fear, may give the impression that Harry is a "longhair," and not a "regular guy." Here is a quaint sidelight on democracy, as interpreted by politicians. . . . I fear that I have a reactionary mind; I like to think of my leaders as wiser, more cultivated and more intelligent than myself; if they are not, God help us all! But the proper democratic attitude seems to be that a national leader should be the intellectual peer of a barbershop loafer, and as illiterate and undistinguished as possible.

• SATURDAY •

Painted some verandah furniture this afternoon, so that when summer comes I shall be ready to enjoy all four hours of it. Decided on a rather delicate and refined design — red and green on a white background — and paid twenty cents for a special brush to accomplish this work; I have never been one to skimp money on materials; a workman is as good as his tools, I have always maintained, and if I have to blow twenty cents on a paintbrush, I do it without a murmur. . . . Completed my work, and, as I was admiring the effect, it began to rain; this means that my paint will probably not dry for several days, and will be tacky for years. Unwary visitors, sitting on my verandah furniture, will carry away impres-

sions of my red and green arabesques which I never intended. . . .
I already have a green screen door, painted at enormous expense
by a professional housepainter, which leaves every visitor with a
green thumb. I can make a mess of my own house, without paying
a professional painter to do so.

-XXII-

• SUNDAY •

❊ Read an article in an American Sunday paper about the proper
way to treat British war brides. This was a tidbit; "Kidding is
hard to get used to, but you have to learn; it may consist of mimicking, to see if you can take it. . . . Later you may learn to kid
back. . . ." I pondered this, and my advice to war brides, in Canada,
at least, is not to kid back; Canadians don't like to be kidded or
mimicked, though they are extremely fond of kidding and mimicking others. Stains on many a drawing-room carpet are all that
remain of war brides who imitated the Ontario accent, or spoke
slightingly of our folk-festivals, such as Mother's Day. Kidding or
mimicking is best done in your native land, with plenty of your
compatriots around to see that the unfortunate foreigner takes it
in the proper sporting spirit.

• MONDAY •

❊ To a political rally tonight, a form of entertainment in which,
like all Canadians, I take endless delight. Every country has
its distinctive art form; in Spain the bullfight; in France the treading of the grapes; in Italy the battle of the flowers; in England the
cricket-match; in Scotland tossing the telegraph pole and squeezing the bawbee; in Wales the Eisteddfod; and in Canada the political rally. The sight of six or seven serious-minded men in unpressed
pants sitting on a platform on kitchen chairs throws us into an
ecstasy; if their mild remarks are translated into hoarse roars by a
public-address system, our joy knows no bounds; if the microphone is so cunningly adjusted that the stumpy have to strain to
reach it and the lanky crouch to get near it, we are transported

with delight. If we ourselves are sitting on chairs which squeal and complain when we move, we are happy; if a heckler is thrown out, we cheer; if the jamboree ends with the National Anthem three tones too high for our voices, we squeak like patriotic mice. O huzza for the political rally! Wow! Bam!! Powie!!

• TUESDAY •

Seriously disappointed in my kitten Tiger today. During the evening a mouse climbed up through a cold-air grating near my chair and surveyed the room with satisfaction. Aha, I thought, and fetched Tiger, who was sleeping elsewhere. I put her down by the grating, but she immediately climbed up on a sofa and went back to sleep. The mouse appeared again, but I made such a noise waking Tiger up that I frightened it away. But Tiger was now disposed to play, so I exercised her with her personal punch-bag for twenty minutes or so. Then the mouse came back. Anticipating a splendid display of jungle ferocity and agility I pointed it out to Tiger, who sat down and looked at it philosophically. Sensing the situation the mouse began to make free of the room and ran about happily, while Tiger watched, and I tore out my hair in double-handfuls. At last, however, this unnatural cat decided to chase the mouse, and bumped her nose on a door just as the mouse dashed under it. . . . I wonder if Tiger's glands work properly?

• WEDNESDAY •

Was talking today with a man who collects antiques, and he showed me some of his treasures. Among them was a beer mug made of pottery which had a life-like pottery frog attached to the bottom of it. The purpose of this pretty thing was to scare the liver and lights out of the drinker as he finished his pint. I think poorly of this sort of humour, smacking as it does of itching-powder, fake bedbugs, rude noisemakers, dribble glasses, and the detestable like. The frog-mug was reputed to be about 150 years old, and I was surprised to find that such a comparatively mild joke was appreciated in the eighteenth century. My delving in history had led me to believe that no joke was admired in those days which did not result at least in a broken leg or the loss of an eye. Merely making a man's stomach heave with a fake frog must have seemed very poor sport to our rude forefathers, and was probably left to the ladies.

• THURSDAY •

To another political rally tonight; my thirst for politics is not to be slaked by mere epicene listening to the radio. And speaking of radio, the radio boys nearly broke up this rally by tapping the microphones, pulling wires, climbing over the speakers, and hooting into the amplifiers during the first twenty minutes of its progress. This made clear to me what I have long suspected, which is that the average radio man doesn't know what makes radio work, and when it won't work he is the embarrassed victim of his own gadget—Man at the mercy of the Machine. While all this was going on, some poor fellow was trying to make a speech, but nobody paid any attention to him; they were hoping one of the radio boys would be electrocuted before their very eyes, and expire in agony with forked lightning coming out of his boot-heels. But the Leader arrived in the nick of time, and the radio decided to settle down and enjoy the fun. *. . .* The Leader performed the amazing feat of speaking for seventy-five minutes without once taking a drink from the two glasses and the full jug on the table before him; I

Marchbanks has lived to see radio's successor, television, make even greater fritters of public occasions. When the TV people are at work the spectators are treated to the vision of the cameraman's butt-end, thrust toward them as he trains his instrument upon his victim. When the TV people have had enough they pack up their traps noisily and leave the room, sneering at the audience, as if to say "We have grabbed the cream; lap up the skim if you will." Marchbanks once investigated the question of the dress worn by TV crews, who greet Popes and Emperors alike in rags and tatters, unshaven and unshorn. He was unable to arrive at any reasonable explanation except that it is some strong assertion of democracy in its negative aspect.

have seen lesser men consume a hogshead of water in the course of a fifteen minute speech. But a real statesman has something of the endurance of a camel; he fills up with raspberry vinegar in the morning, and speaks all day without further need for refreshment.

• FRIDAY •

❀ Read a criticism of Canadians which says that we are great brooders, and attributes this in part to the fact that our winter lasts for seven months. This is nonsense; our winter lasts for nine months, in a lucky year. Of course, we let our fires out, and peck at the frosty ground in our gardens, and huddle into any patch of white, watery sunshine which breaks through the clouds during April and May, but we pay for our haste in colds and lumbago. In June, July and August, Canadians may do without a fire, but September and May are not to be trusted. Is it any wonder then that we brood? Is it surprising that our incidence of insanity is so great that it is a shame and a scandal to our country? I am just an ordinary brooder myself; I make no claim to being a Big League brooder; but I brood about my furnace several hours each day, even when it is out for the brief summer season. And I do well to brood, let me tell you!

• SATURDAY •

❀ Much mail for me today, from fellows anxious that I should vote for them on Monday; the newspapers, too, say that they do not care how I vote, so long as I vote. This constant harping on the subject reminds me that the word "vote" actually means "prayer," and this in turn recalls the remark of a very wise man that when the gods wish to punish us they answer our prayers.... I am glad that we do not have automatic voting machines here, as they do in the U.S.A. Like all machines, they exist primarily to go wrong, and when the late F. D. Roosevelt cast his last vote for himself the machine stuck and he swore at it, and then had to waste much valuable time apologizing for his ribaldry to women's lodges, preachers' unions and similar groups.... I have been listening to the radio hysterics of all three parties for a full week, and now I feel that the fate of the nation lies in my hands.

-XXIII-

• SUNDAY •

Admitted defeat today, and re-lit my furnace. A stickler for tradition, I let it out on the fifteenth of May, arguing that if spring had not come it could not be far away. But Nature, always ready with a nasty surprise for those who take her for granted, asserted herself and an Ice Age set in at Marchbanks Towers; nothing would dry that was wet; nothing that was dry would stay dry; outside it was cold, wet and raw; inside it was cold, wet and stuffy. There was nothing else for it; I went downstairs and faced the Monster. As I shoved kindling into his maw it seemed to me that he leered. . . . The life of Man is a struggle with Nature and a struggle with the Machine; when Nature and the Machine link forces against him, Man hasn't a chance.

• MONDAY AND ELECTION DAY •

An election today, and everyone I met had a slightly woozy look, as though he had been sniffing ether on the sly. The streets were filled with cars, lugging voters to the polls; sometimes I wonder if that haulage business really pays; what guarantee does the free passenger give that he will vote for the man who provides him with a car? A really astute politician would send cars to pick up his known opponents, and would then carry them off, twenty-five miles or so into the country, and jettison them. Few of them would be able to walk home before the polls closed. . . . After the results were announced I was interested to see the wonderful unanimity of feeling which prevailed: the winning side was disposed to be generous, and told the losers that they wished they had done better; the losers, on the contrary, assured the winners that they had foreseen what would happen, and were in no way cast down by it; the socialists, who had been telling the world that they would win, proceeded forthwith to explain that they never dreamed of winning, and expressed delight that they had received any votes at all. Every one was so anxious to show complete satisfaction and good fellowship that a stranger, dropped by parachute, would have assumed that they were all on the winning side.... The losers' hangover will begin tomorrow, when the ether wears off.

• TUESDAY •

✸ To a circus tonight. A circus is the only entertainment which can follow an election without appearing to be anticlimax. The analogy between a circus and an election, indeed, could hardly be more complete: the tightrope walkers, the acrobats, the contortionists, the trained seals, the mangy old lions with no teeth and the clowns! the clowns!! the clowns!!!

• WEDNESDAY •

✸ The coming of sunshine and warm weather has aggravated a tendency which I have observed for some time; I mean the custom of girls walking about the streets hand-in-hand. If I see a young man and a girl walking hand-in-hand I regard them as a little soft, but not beyond reclaim; but when I see girls walking thus, gazing into each others' eyes, and laughing with laughter which is like the shattering of electric light bulbs in a tin biscuit-box, I wonder what's afoot. This afternoon I saw a girl got up like Huckleberry Finn (blue trousers rolled up, an open shirt, and a rag round her head) squiring a smaller girl in a skirt across a street, and they were so lost in Love's Young Ersatz Dream that they were almost run over by a car.... In my experience, limited and monastic though it has been, women do not greatly like other women; they prefer men as conversationalists, walking partners, and hand-holders; they refer to gatherings of their own sex as "hen-parties," and regard them as dull. ⸙ ... I have always considered hero-worship in school-

---

⸙ *This was, of course, before the dawn of Gay Lib which Marchbanks, as a disciple of the late Dr. C. G. Jung of Zurich regards as clever old Mother Nature's counteraction against excessive growth of population. All the fun of the fair and none of its problems—unless, of course, you count AIDS.*

boys, and heroine-worship in schoolgirls, as the most humiliating of adolescent diseases, worse even than pimples and damp hands.

• THURSDAY •

The circus flavour lasts. Everywhere I go these days I see little girls trying to make their dogs skip, little girls trying to balance themselves on rolling barrels, little boys trying to walk along fence-tops and little boys trying to evolve a "cod fight," like clowns. The technique of the "cod fight," is simple; while the fighters seem to be hitting each other the most resounding blows, they are slapping their free hands together at about waist level; when they do this with enormous loose gloves, the effect is superb; but when two small boys try to do it with their bare hands, they usually hurt themselves, and discover that being a clown is a somewhat more specialized profession than they thought. This is an important discovery in anyone's life.

• FRIDAY •

The humidity today was intense, and I was talking to a man who told me (not without a note of pride in his voice) that he had taken four baths since morning. It occurred to me to warn him that he would wash away all his natural oils and develop a nasty, mealy skin, but I refrained; if you warn people against too much bathing they tend to jump to the conclusion that you never bathe yourself, and begin sniffing at you unpleasantly whenever the mercury rises. . . . As a confirmed movie-goer, I am in a position to assure the public that the average Canadian does not bathe too much, and that his or her natural oils are in a splendid state of conservation.

• SATURDAY •

Was talking to a man today who advanced the theory that the violence of the recent election was attributable to the bad weather; wet, cold politicians, he said, were markedly more vicious than warm, sun-drenched ones. Politicians, he continued, are like grapes; when they are allowed to ripen long upon the vine, they achieve a sweet, rich flavour, and give off a delightful aroma of wisdom and urbanity; but when they get too much rain and frost they are small, sour, thick-skinned and inclined to seediness. . . . Parliament he said (by now intoxicated with the insidious liquor of metaphor) was a wine, composed of all these diverse political grapes, and sometimes we got fine old fruity Parliaments, full flavoured and of exquisite bouquet, and sometimes we got little, sour Parliaments, provocative of bellyache; it all depended on the grapes. . . . Fascinated by his eloquence, I suggested that we should throw a few newly-elected members into a vat, and trample them with our bare feet, singing merry vintage songs the while, in order to see how the new brew would turn out; O for a beaker full of the Twentieth Parliament, Full of the true, the blushful Hippocrene!

-XXIV-

• SUNDAY •

Had some notion of a picnic today, but it rained. A man I know who lives in the woods tells me that the mosquitoes this year will be as big as sparrows, and may be expected to last until well into December. He bases this prediction on the way the beavers are building their dams. As everyone knows, beavers eat a lot of insects, and particularly mosquitoes (for the formic acid which the latter contain, and which assists the beaver in seeing under water) and a beaver's burrow contains a special chamber for the storage of the insects caught during the summer season. Apparently the beavers this year are making these chambers unusually big, and from this my friend deduces that they expect a bumper crop of mosquitoes, of particularly large size. . . . I have always wished that I were better versed in nature lore of this kind.

• MONDAY •

To a picnic this afternoon on the shores of a lake which contained many islands; because of the soft dampness of the air and some tricks of light, the scene was strongly reminiscent of the Hebrides. Saw a garter snake, the first in a long time, and observed its beautiful squirmings and dartings from a prudent distance. I am told by my naturalist friends that these creatures are about a foot long and completely harmless, but in the matter of snakes I suffer from telescopic vision; if I stand too near a garter snake it assumes the proportions of a boa constrictor. . . . Fear of snakes seems unrelated to other kinds of physical courage. I have seen large, tough men jump and squeak like school-girls at the sight of a grass snake, and I have known two girls who thoroughly enjoyed a romp with any snake they met. Personally I have developed a suave but distant politeness toward reptiles of all sorts, and I prefer to see them in zoos, if at all.

• TUESDAY •

Noticed a mixed group of dogs playing today, and wondered whether they had any consciousness of breed, as we have of race; I can see no sign of it. The lordly Afghan seems willing to play tag with a terrier, and a spaniel plays with a St. Bernard without any apparent consciousness of the difference in size between them. There seems to be no Master Race, no Jewish Problem, and no Quebec and Ontario feeling among dogs. . . . Tonight to the movies — one of those dreary pieces about a musical genius who has fits and kills people. Why is it that genius on the screen is so frequently represented as a form of idiocy? Is it to comfort the mediocrities who have paid the price of admission to sit and think, "O how lucky we are not to be geniuses; how fortunate we are to be happily dumb and imperturbably numb!"

• WEDNESDAY •

The recurrent Canadian Flag controversy concerns no class of society more deeply than elocutionists, as one of them was explaining to me today. For years they have made a specialty

of a rousing poem by the late E. Pauline Johnson ("Tonakela") /
called *Canadian Born*, every verse of which ends with some such
assertion as:

> But each has one credential
> Which entitles him to brag
> That he was born in Canada,
> Beneath the British Flag!

Canadian Born is what elocutionists call, in the parlance of their
trade, "a ring-tailed peeler," containing such noble and rampageous
lines as:

> The Dutch may have their Holland,
> The Spaniard have his Spain;
> The Yankee to the south of us
> Must south of us remain!

—these latter words being delivered in a loud, quarrel-picking voice.
I have heard it recited often (sometimes even in Indian costume)
at church socials, political picnics, Dominion Day Celebrations,
and kindred uproars, and it never fails to rouse the audience to
blood-thirsty fury—sometimes directed toward the foes of their
country, and sometimes toward the elocutionist herself (for it is
generally assumed to be a piece for a lady to speak). Tonakela has
gone to the Happy Hunting Ground, and the chances that any of
our icebound modern Canadian poets will write another such patriotic bobby-dazzler are slight indeed.

---

*Marchbanks, sometimes a careless scholar, is wrong; Tekahionwake
was the Indian name of Emily Pauline Johnson (1862–1918) who
was the daughter of G. H. M. Johnson, chief of the Six Nations Indians.
A poetess from birth, Tekahionwake wrote copiously, and gave recitals,
clad in Indian dress, in which she presented a fine figure. She recited on
one occasion to Queen Victoria, who was much amused and gave the
poetess a handsome brooch.*

• THURSDAY •

✸ Hot all day, and hot tonight—too hot to do any work, though I had plenty to do. . . . Thunder storm in the night, which meant that I had to rise from my bed and flit about the house, like a wraith, shutting windows and falling over things people had left on the floor.

• FRIDAY •

✸ Since I got a cat of my own, my life has been full of cats. Visited a lady today who has two beautiful black and white cats named Inky and Pinky. I hear news occasionally of my brother Fairchild's Persian, named Button Boots. I see cats on the streets and by the roadside, where I never saw a cat before. A few days ago, making my way toward the In and Out shop, I was almost knocked over by a black Persian, as big as a spaniel, dashing past me, pursued by a man carrying a wrapped bottle. Whether it was a jinni which had escaped from the liquor I did not have time to enquire. As for my own kitten Tiger, I am learning things from her that I never knew before. First of all, I never knew that a kitten could burp, which Tiger does with all the abandon of an old mariner. Second, I never realized that a kitten could be completely and infallibly house-trained, and suddenly forget all it had been taught, reverting to intolerable Bohemianism. Also, why does she like to hide in the piano, plucking ghostly music from the strings with her claws? Is she a sphinx, or merely a humorist of a somewhat earthy sort?

• SATURDAY •

✸ Worked in my garden this afternoon, until rain drove me indoors. Fed the kitten and observed that she ate from the front of her plate toward the back, thereby keeping all her food under her chin, in case an enemy should try to snatch a morsel from her. I have noticed many human beings who eat in precisely the same way, and I deduce that it is a continuance of jungle behaviour. Next time I see a man who crouches over his plate and scoops all his food from the outside edge, I shall let out a howl like a pterodactyl, and watch him give a primordial, prehistoric jump.

-XXV-

• SUNDAY •

As it was a fine day I sat on my verandah and permitted passers-by to stare at me. Staring is the great Sunday-afternoon pastime. People who go walking on the seventh day seem convinced that anyone who sits on a verandah is blind, deaf and silly. They wander along the streets, gaping like egg-bound pullets, and making remarks in voices which carry perfectly for a quarter of a mile in all directions. "That house needs a good coat of paint," says one, and another replies, "If that were my lawn, I'd rip the whole thing up and re-sod it." "Look at those vines," someone cries indignantly; "they just ruin the brickwork and harbour vermin." "You'd think those people would weed their beds once in a while, wouldn't you?" counters his companion, while I sit upright and glare like a basilisk. But no passer-by ever pays any attention to me; they think I am a cigar-store Indian, or a stuffed souvenir of a hunting trip, probably. Some day I shall shout back. "Why don't you wipe that child's nose?" I shall scream, or "Did you buy that hat at a fire-sale?"

• MONDAY •

I am told that the strawberry crop this year will be a failure. I cannot remember a year in which this rumour has not been circulated. Probably it is like the rumours which fly about during the early part of December that Santa Claus has committed suicide. . . . However, I bought a few sour, green, imported berries, and ate them, just to make sure that I experienced some approximation of that most delicious of all flavours this year.

• TUESDAY •

To a movie tonight. It was a farce, and as often happens in farce, the actors thought that everything they said was much funnier if they shouted it at the top of their voices. The ladies also wore those peculiar lace negligees which are never seen anywhere but on actresses in farces. Women wear all sorts of garments when they want to be comfortable—magnificently cut housecoats, kimonos, flannel dressing gowns, and even old bathrobes which their husbands have discarded as unfit for further service—but they never wear those tight-fitting things with lace skirts split up the front, for the good reason that it is impossible to sit down in one, much less perform any of the feats appropriate to negligée.

• WEDNESDAY •

Listened to a broadcast of Shakespeare's *Richard III* this afternoon, done by the Old Vic Theatre Company, which is in New York at present. Decided that Shakespeare would never be able to get a job writing scripts for the C.B.C. because he insists on dealing with controversial topics, and uses language which would bring a flood of complaining letters from the Holy Name Society of St. Jean de Crabtree Mills (P. Q.) and the Ladies' Art, Culture, Poker-Work and China-Painting Club of Pelvis (Sask.). . . . Enjoyed the broadcast greatly, though I wondered why all the ghosts in the Dream Scene sounded as though they were speaking to Richard over the long-distance telephone. But that is the only way in which radio can suggest the supernatural, I suppose.

• THURSDAY •

Was roused this morning by a loud cawing, and looked out of my window to see a large crow sitting on a branch with its mouth full of bread, making daybreak hideous with its cries. This recalled to me Aesop's fable about the crow which was flattered into singing by a fox, and dropped its piece of cheese as a result. It was obvious that this crow could sing and hold on to a huge piece of food at the same time. So much for that old scoundrel Aesop, whom I have long suspected of being better as a puritan moralist than as an accurate observer of nature. Read Aesop's Fables in the light of everyday adult experience, and what do we find? We find that the man who gives up the substance for the shadow is often richly rewarded, and admired by posterity for his vision. We find that the dog in the manger can always get a well-paid job as a union leader, and the more difficult he is to appease, the greater is his success. We find that the lion who assists a mouse usually has to listen to a lot of saucy talk from the mouse about Imperialism. It is my belief that Aesop was a simpleton who took good care never to look about him, for fear of finding that the world did not agree with his theories.

• FRIDAY •

I see by the papers that Scotland (or, more accurately, the Scottish Nationalist Party) is going to submit a brief to the United Nations on the unjust oppression of Scotland by England. Personally, I don't think that England would ever give up Scotland without establishing a state of Pakistan for the protection of the Irishmen and Welshmen who contribute so much to the cultural and intellectual life in Glasgow, and the Englishmen and Jews who have won for the universities of St. Andrews and Edinburgh the reputation for brilliance which they now enjoy. My own ancestors descended upon England from Scotland a century or more ago, pausing at the border only long enough to change their name from Marjoribanks to its present form. I don't imagine that their descendants would want to be herded back to the bleak hillsides from which they escaped after the Great Capercailzie Famine of 1745. Nowadays you won't find a Marchbanks in Scotland even during the grouse season; most of us just do our grousing wherever we happen to be. "A tussock wowsie's nae doitit," as Robbie Burns said, putting the whole thing in a nutshell.

Burns spoke, of course, in the Scottish Vernacular, which is apt to be gnomic. I asked a Scots gnome for an explanation, but all he would say was:

> *A speirin' gowk and a toom wame*
> *Are aye gruttin' an' aye the same.*

This gets us nowhere, and as I have better things to do than question gnomes I abandon the matter.

• SATURDAY •

While I was cutting grass and weeding this afternoon I was greatly troubled by mosquitoes, flies and other nuisances, and in this way my attention was drawn toward the benevolent insects —bees, grasshoppers and the like. I recall reading in a book about insects that they evolve their own economic laws, and abide by them. Thus ants go in for full employment, while bees consider it worth while to support a monarchy and an aristocracy; grasshoppers are definite *laissez-faire* liberals, and dung-beetles are bourgeois capitalists. But what about accidents, I pondered? Ants are socialists, possessing a complete, nasty, compact little socialist state of their own; but what happens to their economic laws when I run my lawn-mower over their anthill? They didn't foresee that. And the bees get an unexpected handout from me when I put out honey boxes for them to clean; that boosts their economy unfairly. I am convinced that no insect sees me, except the mosquito, and yet in my garden I play Providence to the insect world without giving the matter a moment's thought. I am the Unknown Factor, the *Parcae* in the lives of thousands of creatures with whom I am not even on nodding terms. A sweetly solemn thought.

-XXVI-

• SUNDAY •

Put out my hanging baskets yesterday, and woke this morning to find that the temperature had dropped to 42 degrees. Just the sort of shabby trick that our Canadian summers are always playing. I well recall going for a picnic on the 24th of May in 1932, and returning home because it suddenly began to snow! It is this uncertainty of the weather which makes Canadians the morose, haunted, apprehensive people they are.

• MONDAY •

A magnificent day, and I passed a considerable part of it wishing I did not have to work. The more complex our civilization becomes, the less fun there is in it and the more work there is to do. The ultimate in civilizations is that of the ants, who work ceaselessly, and have no fun at all. And what do they get out of it? Well—did you ever look at an ant's face under a microscope? It looks exactly like a composite photograph of Henry Ford / and John L. Lewis, / with just a suggestion of the characteristic frozen mug of the Nazi High Command. . . . To the movies tonight and saw a very dull film which tried to make out that missionaries have a lot of fun. Well—did you ever look at a missionary's face under a microscope? That is the result of trying to persuade the heathen that it is wrong to get stinko on the fermented juice of the banyan, without using profanity, police or physical violence. The fact that many missionaries are married also makes it hard to interest the heathen in the Christian institution of monogamy, which they confuse with monotony.

• TUESDAY •

Upon the advice of my physician (a distinguished man who has a perfect understanding of my case) I take a little rest each day after lunch. But recently my repose has been shattered by a bird which imitates the sound of a telephone-bell perfectly. I compose myself for slumber, than br-r-r-ring goes this accursed bird, and up I jump and rush indoors to the phone, to find that there is nothing stirring at the other end of the wire. Naturalists deny the existence of any such bird, but it lives in a maple tree just

---

Henry Ford (1863–1947) was an American automobile manufacturer, revered as the Father of the Tin Lizzie. Also famous for being able to do the dirtiest engineering repair work without getting his collar dirty, and for declaring that history is bunk. Not esteemed for his beauty.

John L. Lewis (1880–1969) was a mighty figure in the miners' union but was chiefly noted for his immense eyebrows. Much of his authority was thought to originate in these growths with which he could both beetle and beat. Marchbanks' seminal study, The Eyebrow, Secret of Charisma *is much admired in political economy departments in the more advanced universities.*

by my verandah, and I have seen it; it is about the size of a jay, and has a black and green plumage. If I can catch it there will be telephone-bird pie on the menu at Château Marchbanks.

• WEDNESDAY •

✿ A very hot day, and owing to some lack of caution I had committed myself a week ago to do some heavy gardening today— to clean out a wilderness, in fact. The wilderness was a mosquito headquarters, and they were holding an œcumenical conference, which I broke up with a great display of personal bravery. There were times however when I debated whether it would not be easier to lie down and die on the spot than to go on with the job. I was forcibly reminded of a poem which I read years ago in Second or Third Book about a negro slave who collapsed in the field with his sickle in his hand, and died while thinking of his days of glory in Africa, where "the lordly Niger flowed"; ∮ he was too far gone to feel the heat of the sun, or the cruel overseer's whip, or the indignity of his present position. That was just the way I felt. "Better death than work!" I cried, throwing myself into the jaws of my lawnmower, but it spat me out contemptuously. It is too dull to cut grass, let alone serve as an instrument of suicide.

• THURSDAY •

✿ Was chatting today with a man who has just had a baby; that is to say, his wife actually had the baby, but as any one knows who has experienced it, the work of the superintendent in such processes is often as exhausting as that of the mother. He was weak and run down, and subject to dizzy spells, as the people who have just had babies always are in the advertisements, so I urged him to get himself a good nerve tonic, and did what I could to revive him with strawberries.... As men will, when they get

---

∮ *This poem is* The Slave's Dream *by Henry Wadsworth Longfellow (1807–82), whose popularity has dimmed, owing to his being wholly comprehensible. Aspiring poets, take note.*

together, we discussed the curious fact that, whenever it becomes known that you are going to have a baby, everybody hastens to tell you their favourite Horrible Tale about the Baby With Two Heads, or the Baby that Vanished, or the Baby that Got Mixed Up In The Hospital, and never knew whether it was a boy or a girl. Everybody likes to scare the wits out of an expectant father. I am going to write a book some day, called *Radiant Fatherhood*, which will make the whole thing seem beautiful and natural, and an experience to be cherished for a lifetime (which is, indeed, as long as one can cherish anything).

• FRIDAY •

The morning paper contains yet another repetition of the claim that the Bible is the best-selling book in the world, and that *Pilgrim's Progress* comes next. I see this assertion in some form or other about once a month, but I have never seen any figures to prove it, and I suspect that it is merely something which a number of devout people would like to believe. Of course many Bibles are sold; I have seven Bibles myself, three of which I bought, and four of which I was given. But for *Pilgrim's Progress* — does anybody ever finish it? As a child my gorge rose at the lugubriousness of Pilgrim, and I had a wicked hankering for Vanity Fair; after I grew up I tried to read it again, and failed. Bunyan was a notable stylist, but his mind was the mind of a sanctimonious tinker.

• SATURDAY •

I see that the Dominion Bureau of Agriculture is urging us to keep goats; the bureau writes about goats with tenderness and affection. Once it was my duty to look after a family of goats — a nanny, a billy and a kid — for a week during an outdoor production of *As You Like It*, and in that time I grew to like them, and even to

---

At the present time Marchbanks has eleven Bibles, some of which include the Apocrypha, *the books puritan scholars decided to omit, as being more fun than is proper. Very saucy stuff!*

trust them. They had some nasty ways, but were really much more intelligent and friendly than cows. It is a lie to say that they eat tin cans and underwear; they like glue, and esteem the label from a tin can as a great delicacy, but they do not eat the tin, and they simply turn their noses up at an old undershirt. Nor do they butt you if you treat them kindly. My only complaint was that they stank—not a dirty or unwholesome smell, but a powerful animal emanation—and after I tended the goats I had to change my clothes before I was acceptable in fastidious circles.... Goats have a lively sense of humour. They like to push and shove you to see if they can make you angry, and if you resent it, they jump up and down and laugh. But if you shove them back again, and hurl genial insults at them, they know that you are a good fellow, and accept you as a sort of honorary goat. I have had some high old times with goats.

Summer

• HEYDEGUISE SUNDAY •

Off on my annual holiday today, to the United States for the first time since 1938. Crossed the St. Lawrence on a ferry, in company with fifteen million fuzzy insects; asked a man with a glass eye what they were; "Sand fleas," he replied laconically. Did not believe him. . . . Stayed tonight in a hotel in the Adirondacks, which is famous because Theodore Roosevelt once changed horses there. Many relics of him were on display, including his raincoat, rucksack, and a horseshoe which was wittily labelled as "not from one of his horses." Reflected that I have many such relics at Marchbanks Towers, including a bed in which Queen Elizabeth never slept, a pen which was not used to sign the Treaty of Versailles, and a cake which was not burned by King Alfred. Take this negative attitude towards antiques, and we all are richer than we ever imagined.

• MONDAY •

On the road all day, with pauses for refreshment and to look at dubious antiques. Visited the New York State Capitol at Albany, and saw a drum displayed in its entrance-hall which had been seized from the British in the Revolutionary War. Was filled with a wild impulse to break the glass, snatch it back again, and run like hell for the Canadian border, but as I had just finished lunch I decided that it would not really be a practicable plan. Pressed onward, and gaped in amaze at the magnificent palaces which line the Hudson River. Stopped for dinner at Tarrytown, and in the Florence Hotel there had an adventure so frightful that I shall not even confide it to the private pages of this Diary. Never, since Mr. Pickwick found himself trapped in the bedchamber of the Lady with Curl Papers, has a traveller suffered so acutely and so undeservingly. ⸙

• TUESDAY •

✻ Entered New York this morning; it cost me ten cents at the Hendrick Hudson toll-bridge, which I thought rather expensive; I am used to getting into cities for nothing. However, when one is travelling, one must expect to spend a certain amount of money foolishly. . . . Had lunch in the garden of the Museum of Modern Art, which was about as pleasant as anything could be, for in addition to serving a top-notch lunch these enlightened Americans permit one to have a bottle of their own California wine at meals. In spite of this freedom I did not see anyone who was even slightly drunk, much less in a condition to swoon upon the ground, or hack at the modern statuary. . . . Afterward rode in Central Park in an open carriage (I am essentially a barouche man, and have never really accepted the motor car) and the driver attempted to cheat me out of a dollar, but was foiled. After some argument I drew myself up: "Shall we submit this to the arbitrament of a con-

---

⸙ *But, in this permissive age, it may be revealed. Enquiring of the lady with whom he was travelling—an incorrigible romp—as to the whereabouts of the lavatories, he was directed upstairs, and there secreted himself in one of the booths which were the only accommodation— which would have warned a more worldly man. Hardly had he relaxed than the room was invaded by a group of middle-aged women, a female club that was about to carouse downstairs. Sequestering themselves in the booths all around him, they began to shriek female intimacies to their friends, while Our Hero, swooning with modest alarm, tucked his feet up on the seat, dreading that he might be discovered, and denounced as a Peeping Tom, or bent upon Female Harassment. When at last he escaped he was white with terror, to the delight of his cruel companion.*

stable?" said I. "Aw Cheest!" he said, and drove away. New York, I perceive, contains almost as many rogues as Toronto.

• WEDNESDAY •

Having heard many travellers' tales of the dreadful deceptions practised upon strangers in New York, I walked about the city today expecting to be accosted by men who wanted to sell me gold bricks, or possibly the controlling interest in Brooklyn Bridge. However, nothing of the sort happened. Decided that perhaps my appearance was too urbane, so this afternoon I tried chewing a straw and saying, "Wal I swan to thunderation!" every time I looked at a high building. Still no rush of confidence men. Perhaps the perils of New York are exaggerated. . . . The shops are full of things to buy—possibly too full. At any rate I suffer from a sensation of surfeit, when faced with so much merchandise, and don't want to buy anything. I am content to stroll about the streets and admire the beauty of the women, which is somewhat standardized, but breathtaking none the less. Strawberry shortcake is standardized, but nobody ever gets too much of it. . . . And the charm of this city is that when one is tired it is possible to get a glass of beer without resorting to a stinking pest-hole called a Beverage Room.

• THURSDAY •

Wandered about the streets, enjoying whatever sights came my way. Looked into the Temple Emanu-El, the principal synagogue, and thought it vastly more beautiful than St. Patrick's, which, by the way, is having its face washed, and nothing can be seen of the outside of it but scaffolding and irritable, plethoric pigeons. . . . Saw also a man in sackcloth, with unkempt beard and hair, bearing a sign which read "Indict Senator Bilbo; UNO and World Government." Recollecting J. S. Mill's warning that a country where eccentricity is a matter for reproach is in peril, I tried not to stare at him too curiously, though his lacklustre eye and general appearance of madness fascinated me. Was talking to a lady this afternoon who said, "Have you been to the theatre yet,

Mr. Marchbanks?" I replied, as politely as I could: "Madam, when I am in a city which possesses a theatre I am on hand whenever it is open to the public. I consider the theatre to be the most rational, enspiriting, rewarding and ecstatic of human entertainments, greatly superior to music and painting. Does that answer your question?" She fled in dismay, poor witling.

• FRIDAY •

Henceforth, when anyone asks me "Were you in 'Twenty-One' when you were in New York?" I shall say that I was, but my answer will be disingenuous. This evening a New Yorker took me to dinner, and as we discovered a mutual passion for Chinese food he whisked me to 21 Mott Street, an unimpressive establishment in Chinatown where I ate such food as only the gods and a few particularly favoured mortals are privileged to taste. After a careful inspection of the menu we decided to order the Wedding Banquet For Eighteen, and eat it all ourselves. This we did, augmenting it with many bowls of rice and uncounted cups of delicious Chinese tea. (At least, I stopped counting after my tenth cup.) Together, this congenial soul and I waded through such a mass of fried shrimps, chicken, pork, almonds, bean shoots, bamboo sprouts, ginger, soybean and crisp noodles as I never saw before in my life, while our female companions picked away daintily (in the way of women) at a few poor trifles provided for them. After this we went for a ride on the Staten Island ferry, to enjoy the air and contemplate our inward bliss.

• SATURDAY •

Left New York today. Passed through a ghost town called Piercefield, which contained more derelict houses than inhabited ones. I suppose young ghosts go there to get a little preliminary experience in haunting. I don't know why they complain of a housing shortage in the U.S.A. when Piercefield is wide open. . . . On into the Adirondacks for the night and slept amid scenery that would delight a Welshman or a Scot. ∬ Mountains, like the sea, are in the blood.

-XXVIII-

• SUNDAY •

❀ Some important atomic bomb tests were held today, but no consequences were observable in my part of the world. Half-consciously I had been expecting the end of everything, and had made preparations accordingly. I burned a few letters which I did not wish to have vaporized; when we are all reduced to atoms, who can tell what atoms will read other private atoms, as they hurtle through space? I put a few of my more prized possessions in prominent places so that they would be vaporized as prominently and showily as possible. I threw a few bricks and rocks into my furnace, so that its vaporization might be painful. Then I spent as much time as I could manage lying on a sofa so that if necessary, I might enter Eternity in a relaxed posture. But nothing happened.

• MONDAY •

❀ Cut my grass today. I neglected it over the weekend, thinking that the atomic bomb might settle all such problems forever. As I plodded back and forth I reflected miserably upon my own political rootlessness, in a world where politics is so important. When I am with Tories I am a violent advocate of reform; when I am with reformers I hold forth on the value of tradition and stability. When I am with communists I become a royalist—almost a Jacobite; when I am with socialists I am an advocate of free trade, private enterprise and *laissez-faire*. The presence of a person who has strong political convictions always sends me flying off in a con-

---

∬ Marchbanks, of course, is both, without a drop of English blood. The exact proportions have never been determined, but both strains assert themselves when appropriate: now the bardic, then the granitic— that's Sam.

trary direction. Inevitably, in the world of today, this will bring me
before a firing squad sooner or later. Maybe the fascists will shoot
me, and maybe the proletariat, but political contrariness will be
the end of me; I feel it in my bones.... Tiger, my kitten has wandered away.

• TUESDAY •

Tiger not back for breakfast; that cat treats its home like an
hotel... No mail this morning. It is a constant source of
surprise and indignation to me that, although half my life is spent
in writing letters, nobody ever writes to me. Of course I got mail;
there were the usual government handouts, addressed to me by
chairwarmers at Ottawa and Toronto; there were the usual printed
appeals urging me to hasten to Palestine and give my life in the
cause of Jewish freedom; there were the usual people who wanted
to give me a course in short-story writing, or convert me to the
cult of colonic irrigation; there were thick reprints of speeches
delivered by the presidents of insurance companies; there was a
letter from a woman urging me to take up in this Diary the unsat-
isfactoriness of modern underpants, in which (she says) electri-
cian's tape is used instead of elastic. But not a word addressed to
me personally—not even a postcard. Disheartening.

• WEDNESDAY •

Still no Tiger; worried about her. Enquired of some children
if they had seen her. "Perhaps she has wandered off with the
Toms; two of our kittens did," said they. This alarmed me greatly.
Wandered off with the Toms! What an appalling thought! What a
revelation of feline delinquency! Do the Toms engage in a hid-

---

*Observe that Marchbanks writes "an hotel." He also pronounces the
word "herb" without the "h," which makes Englishmen smirk behind
their lace hankies, for they pride themselves on their aitches. But Our
Hero's style is the aristocratic style, to be observed in the speech of, for
instance, Winston Churchill.*

eous traffic in young cats—White Slavery in the cat world? At night, when all is still and the human world lies wrapped in sleep, do raffish crews of roystering Toms rush through the streets, curling their silky moustaches and luring innocent little pussies to a Fate Worse Than Death? Is Tiger at this very moment living in Guilty Splendour in some underground Haunt? Surrounded by every luxury—fish-skeletons galore, Jersey cream in kegs, catnip unlimited—does she ever think of her simple home and the toads she used to play with in the back garden? I shall advertise for her.

• THURSDAY AND THE DELICATIZING OF ST. AUDREY •

✾ Answer to my advertisement for Tiger. "Did youse lose a cat?" said a voice over the phone. "What kind of cat have you got?" I countered. "Kind of a yalla cat," said the voice. "My cat was not yellow," I replied indignantly, and hung up.

• FRIDAY •

✾ A man said today that he supposed I got a lot of free meals on my press-card when I was in New York; apparently he believes that legend that a newspaper writer has only to go into an expensive restaurant, eat himself out of shape, drink the bar dry, and then present his press-card in order to have the proprietor fall on his neck in gratitude. It is not true. When in New York I did have a sandwich in a modest grill, and did present my press-card when the bill arrived, but I had to pay all the same. It was not until I was outside that I realized that I had presented, not my current press-card, but an old one which I had preserved for sentimental reasons from the days when I was the entire editorial staff on the Skunk's Misery *Trombone*, a lively little paper with a rather limited circulation. I suppose the restaurant proprietor had never heard of it; he was an uncultivated type, and addressed all his customers familiarly as "Joe." I did not think that anything would be gained by arguing with him; people who call other people "Joe" are not usually strong in logic.

• SATURDAY •

Tiger is home again! She had not run off with the Toms but had, I suppose, lost her way in one of her tree-climbing expeditions and had passed a comfortable few days with people who fed her and (if I can judge by the condition of her coat) brushed her, as well. Reproached her bitterly for all the anguish of spirit she had caused. . . . Passed the afternoon cleaning my cellar. Hercules, cleaning the Augean stables, had an easy task in comparison. Ran to and fro with driblets of coal; piled wood which had been lying under coal; resurrected and viewed with dismay bits of linoleum which had lain under coal. Wretched though present-day coal is as a heater, it has one undeniable characteristic—it is dirtier, and gets into more obscure corners, than any coal ever previously sold. Finished the afternoon looking like Old Black Joe, and with a dismaying collection of rubbish which the garbage man will be too haughty to remove. I suppose I shall have to bury it by stealth in the flower beds.

-XXIX-

• SUNDAY •

Tiger, my kitten, is suffering from an ailment which is not uncommon among animals and children in hot weather. This is an intolerable nuisance, for when she ran away she was beautifully housebroken, and now she has forgotten her good manners. When a child has this trouble it is able to give a warning shriek when the demon seizes it, and one can then rush it to the proper quarter, strengthening its moral fibre with threats and entreaties as one runs; but Tiger is crafty, and watch her as I will, she always evades me at the critical moment, leaving her little surprise in a corner, or under a chair. I think she likes to see me on my knees, in a prayerful posture, plying the floor-cleaner and disinfectant, and soliloquizing in Old Testament language.

• MONDAY •

❊ To visit some friends at their summer cottage, and had a very fine ride on the river in a power boat. When speaking to the owners of boats I become tongue-tied, for there are some of them who resent having their property called anything but "craft," and turn green if one speaks of a "boat-ride." I am not the ideal passenger, either, for I am no good at shoving the boat away from the shore, or snatching at ropes when we return to the dock. True, I come of a sea-going race, but not very recently; when Caesar approached the shores of Britain several members of the Marchbanks family painted themselves blue and set out in their coracles to drive him away; owing to some miscalculation they failed to do it. But a coracle is a round affair, more like a soup-plate than a boat, and since the introduction of banana-shaped craft no Marchbanks has ever been anything but a land-lubber.

• TUESDAY •

❊ To the movies tonight to see a film in which Ingrid Bergman and Gregory Peck played the parts of a female psychiatrist and an amnesia patient respectively. I can feast my eyes on Miss Bergman's beauty without paying too much attention to what she says or does, but Master Peck is another matter. His notion of acting is directly contrary to that of such exponents of the art as Irving, Coquelin and Stanislavsky; he does not use his head, but casts the full burden upon his face, which he works furiously, breathing meanwhile through his mouth. His resemblance to Buster Keaton is disturbing to me also; I am always expecting him to be hit with a pie, or to fall into a tub of cement.

• WEDNESDAY •

❊ Tiger is not better, so I took her to the veterinary this evening. He diagnosed her case as one of garbage-eating; when she ran away she must have treated herself to a bit of over-ripe fish. He gave me some pills for her, and also demonstrated the proper way to give pills to a cat; you suddenly draw the cat's head backward, pry open its mouth, shove the pill down into its stomach with a pair of forceps, and whisk the pill briskly around in its insides. Then you let go, and the cat uses language that scorches its whiskers. I decided that I would use the alternative method, which is to powder the pill and slip it slyly into the cat's food. A man who is accustomed to going right to the seat of the trouble with a sick cow, and giving pills like baseballs to Percheron stallions, may safely take liberties with Tiger, but I am not in his class as a beast-tamer, and I know it. "A cat is no fool, and she may resent this," he said: I knew that, too.

• THURSDAY •

A man came to me today in a state of great agitation because he thought that there should be more streetlights, and that they should be turned on earlier. "Young people park in cars in those dark places and The Dear knows what goes on," he said, trembling at the thought. I tried to calm him, telling him about Chastity, and how she that has that is clothed in complete steel, but he did not seem to put as much faith in Chastity as in Electricity.... I wonder why people always think that dreadful things happen in the dark? When I look back over my own past, and examine my police record and my conscience, I find that the peak-hours of Sin in my wild youth were between 11 a.m. and 2:30 p.m. If I were a Puritan, I would not worry about parked cars, where nothing much happens beyond the conventional slap-and-tickle which is virtually obligatory in youth; ⫻ but I would creep abroad at mid-

---

⫻ *Ah, happy, far-off days of innocence! Marchbanks was once present, as a spectator only, at a divorce trial in which a deaf judge demanded of the erring wife where "intimacy" had taken place. "In the back of a car," she replied. "Eh?" demanded the beak, his hand to his ear. "IN THE BACK OF A CAR!" she bellowed, angrily. The judge, plainly long a stranger to the gentle promptings of Venus, pondered for a moment, obviously summoning up the back of a car in his head. Then — "How?" he enquired. In such circumstances the tragedy of divorce suffers a severe wrenching.*

day, peeping behind the lace curtains of sober houses on quiet, tree-lined streets. It is there that I would find things to make my mouth go dry and my eyes pop.

• FRIDAY •

To the movies to see Charles Laughton as Captain Kidd. Although the period of the film was supposed to be the reign of William and Mary (1694–1702) we were treated to a panorama of London, in which the principal feature was Tower Bridge, which was built in 1894; Hollywood is particularly prone to such bone-headed errors, even though it does spend large sums on experts and historical research.

• SATURDAY •

I see that a girl who was in the Hamilton beauty contest is complaining that twelve of the sixty-two contestants wore "falsies" to give greater impressiveness to their pectoral development. This reminded me of the fact that before the war the cadets at the Royal Military College wore "falsies" also, concealed in their scarlet tunics, in order to add a few inches to their chests. I have seen many a convex cadet remove his tunic, only to reveal that he was concave. This was standard military practice until the red tunic went out, about the time of the South African War, and many a dashing cavalry officer was saved from death because the Zulu assegai, or hill-tribesman's snickersnee, had become imbedded in his "falsies." But now, alas, anything might lurk beneath the blouse of a battledress and the military "falsy" has fallen into disuse. Chest-wigs for the pectorally bald are still sold by the principal military outfitters, I am told.

-XXX-

• SUNDAY •

Was reading a sermon by an eminent Montreal divine on the subject of frivolity, of which the divine disapproved. Pleasure, he said, was a legitimate indulgence; he would even go so far as to say that people needed pleasure in their lives; but he warned most seriously against frivolity. This interested me so much that I looked up the word in my dictionary, and found that it meant more than I had thought — "trivial, empty, paltry, lacking in character and depth of concentration" were only a few of the scathing comments in the definition. . . . Sighed heavily, for my schoolmasters used to accuse me of frivolousness; my inclination toward untimely levity annoyed them. And it has grown with the years. If I tended toward frivolity as a boy, I am incorrigibly settled in it now.

• MONDAY •

Watched a group of children playing school today; it seemed to me to be a depressing game for the holidays, but they enjoyed it hugely. Not many lessons were taught, but there was a great deal of spanking, asking permission to leave the room, and being sent to the principal. The most prized role was that of Teacher; the largest child got that by sheer physical prowess and the smaller ones were reduced to submission by violent threats. . . . I recall playing school when a child with a group of Roman Catholic children; the oldest was given the prized role of Sister Mary Somebody, who must have been an uncommonly severe disciplinarian. As a mere Protestant, I was only allowed to be the janitor; from time to time I was permitted to say "Is it warm enough for you, Sister?" whereupon Sister Mary Somebody would give me a stately nod of the head. I soon tired of the limited possibilities of the janitor's part and went off to play by myself, while Sister Mary Somebody went on happily spanking, cuffing and scolding.

• TUESDAY •

Business took me to Toronto today, and I was amazed at the number of dead animals I passed on the highway. Most of them were skunks, though from time to time one saw a defunct rabbit, a squashed squirrel or a jellied groundhog. Why are skunks more prone to die on the highway than other animals? Is it because skunks, for thousands of years, have been used to stopping everything by sheer force of personality, and have not yet accustomed themselves to the automobile age? Certainly it is a lesson in the mutability of all earthly things to see a skunk, once nobly menacing and vainglorious, lying—a poor rag of grizzled fur—by the roadside. But it cannot be said of skunks, as it is of men, that they all smell alike in death. . . . And speaking of skunks, was it on purpose that the City of Toronto arranged that symphony of vile effluvia which assaults the nostrils on Fleet Street? Gas works, tannery, glue atelier and soap-rendering emporium all unite in a ferocious stench compared with which the bazaars of Calcutta are as morning roses washed with dew.

• WEDNESDAY •

My garden is a failure again this year. My morning-glory is not more than an inch above ground; my castorbeans (which should be like trees by now) are sickly shoots; a cow appears to have nested in the remains of my peony bed. The only things that are doing well are my runner beans, and some gourds, which are growing like Jack's beanstalk and seem likely to push down a wall. . . . And do I care? No! If Nature doesn't want to co-operate with me she knows what she can do.

• THURSDAY •

Because there is to be an Orange Walk ⫻ tomorrow, I was drawn into a discussion of the Battle of the Boyne by two

---

⫻ *The Orange Walk was a procession organized by the Loyal Orange Lodge to take place on the 12th of July, or as near as possible, every year. The participants were adult male Orangemen, adult female Orangewomen, and adolescent youths, known as 'Prentice Boys, who formed fife-and-drum bands, and the pervading spirit of the occasion was ultra-Protestant. Canada, having few indigenous prejudices, has been compelled to import them from elsewhere, duty-free, and it is the rare Canadian who is not shaken, at some time in the year, by "old, unhappy, far-off things/And battles long ago", like Wordsworth's solitary reaper. We are a nation of immigrants, and not happy in our minds.*

men who regarded it as a matter of the utmost contemporary importance. But I soon found that the Battle of the Boyne they were talking about was not the one I learned about in school; my Boyne was merely one in a series of small battles, and it was fought on July 1, and not on the Glorious Twelfth; and in my battle King William's forces were principally composed of Dutch, French, Danish and English troops, and not of valiant Ulstermen; and in my battle the victory of King William was thought to have something to do with the fact that he had 35,000 men to his opponent's 25,000, causing King James to run away, which was wise if not precisely valiant.... But my friends seemed to be talking about an entirely different fight. I quoted them Bernard Shaw's wise dictum: "Peter the Fisherman did not know everything; neither did Martin Luther." But they would pay no attention. If we were all robbed of our wrong convictions, how empty our lives would be.

• FRIDAY •

The Orange Walk today. I had to go to Toronto again and missed it, but all the way along the road I passed Orangemen gorgeously arrayed and wearing the set, determined expression of men who might have to fight for their convictions and rather hoped they would. Some of them carried bottles of fife-oil; this is a special lubricator which you drink yourself and then blow into the fife.... Arrived in Toronto, which is the Rome of the Orange Order, too late to see the parade there, though I kept meeting Orangemen and Orangewomen all day long, and even saw an Orangeinfant, so covered in rosettes and ribbons that it could hardly breathe.... It was a hot, exhausting day, and during the afternoon I was forced to refresh myself with a pot of Orange Pekoe tea.

• SATURDAY •

Should have worked in my garden, but lay in a deck-chair and read Damon Runyon instead. It is about this time of year that my gardening enthusiasm, so hot in the Spring, fails me, and I make my annual discovery that a weed is just as pretty as a flower if you look at it the right way.... Sometimes I think I got too much gardening when I was a boy, and I know that many people suffered in the same way. Indeed, a friend of mine tells me that his father won a prize for the finest garden in his home town for two years in succession, and that this triumph was based firmly upon the back-breaking labour of my friend and his brothers and sisters. Thus it is in many families; the father is the planner and overseer; the children are the toilers and fieldhands; and from this uneven division of labour a fine garden springs. Gardening is an undemocratic pursuit. Somebody crawls through the flowerbeds, weeding and grovelling like the beasts that perish; somebody else strolls in the cool of the evening, smelling the flowers. There is the garden-lord and the garden-serf. When we are all socialists gardens will vanish from the earth.

-XXXI-

• SUNDAY •

❋ Agog today, preparing for the second instalment of my annual holiday. This year I had difficulty in finding a place to stay; for some reason no place where I have once been is ever able to give me a reservation again, and I had to do a lot of writing and wiring before I finally got a favourable answer from a place called Camp Laffalot, at Skeleton in Muskoka. I have packed my sola topi, my butterfly net, and—as I know Muskoka—my fur coat for wear after sundown. I can hardly contain my impatience until tomorrow. Yo-ho for Camp Laffalot!

• MONDAY •

❋ On the road at dawn this morning. Stopped at Orillia to see Stephen Leacock's manuscripts in the Public Library, but the Library was closed for all but a few hours a day; the Little Town is still a Little Town, apparently. Looked at the Champlain Monument in Couchiching Park, which is magnificent; another monument, called Somebody's Mother, and flanked by four drinking fountains, assaults the vision as one enters and leaves the Park.... Drove on until I came to a sign — "You Are Now Entering Lovely Skeleton." Appropriately enough this village consists entirely of frame houses. Without difficulty I found Camp Laffalot, and at once my nostrils were assailed by that pleasant and characteristic smell of damp woodwork which is peculiar to summer hotels. Three young females with legs of vivid scarlet and peeling noses mounted the stairs ahead of me; the custom of the burnt human sacrifice still persists in Muskoka, I observe.... This place has tolerable inside plumbing; all will be well.

• TUESDAY •

Woke at 4 a.m. to find that I was freezing; looked from my windows at Drowned Skeleton Lake, over which lay a heavy mist; pulled the bedside rug over me and shivered till morning.... A bell rang at 7:30, and the first thing I saw from my window as I crawled out of bed was two ample ladies, well advanced in middle life, hiking down to the lake in their bathing suits. Appalled by such hardihood, I huddled into a heavy suit and two sweaters, and went to breakfast; felt better after fruit, porridge, two eggs, a heap of toast, and an imperial gallon of hot coffee. By ten o'clock I was roasting, and had to discard everything that decency would permit; soon I shall be as half-baked as the girls I saw yesterday.... The name Laffalot, which I assumed to be Indian, is a droll contraction of Laugh A Lot, I find, and the invention of the proprietor, who hopes to put his guests in a good mood with it. He explained this to me himself. Ha ha, I thought; and later, after more reflection, tee hee.

Marchbanks was a lifelong enemy of the outdoor privy. He was convinced that such places are the breeding-grounds of snakes, and that the unwary visitor might be fatally stung, or hideously invaded, while contemplating.

• WEDNESDAY •

✺ Have scraped acquaintance with some of the other denizens of Camp Laffalot. We sat on the lawn this morning, and in the fashion of guests at summer hotels, lied about our importance in our hometowns and hinted that we were richer than we looked. The only reason we were not at the Royal Muskoka or Bigwin Inn, we implied, was that we could not stand the stuffy crowd there, preferring the genial company at Camp Laffalot. We agreed that Drowned Skeleton Lake was the gem of the Muskokas, and that Laffalot had distinction and exclusiveness not granted to other summer hotels. These things settled, some of us went for a drive, to enjoy the scenery. Personally I get all the scenery I can conveniently hold in half an hour; and after a four-hour drive I estimated that I had said, "magnificent!" 422 times, "astounding!" 146 times, and "lovely!" 1066 times. These are the only words I know which apply to scenery, except "redundant," which I use only in my thoughts.

• THURSDAY •

✺ There is always a good deal of romance at a summer hotel. Was talking today to a pretty girl who told me that a young man was going to canoe twenty miles, portage five miles, and motor sixty miles to take her to a dance that night. I said that I wasn't a bit surprised, and she would have flushed prettily if she had not already been cooked to the colour of underdone beef by the sun. She then pointed out islands in the lake to me, saying that there was a home on this one which cost $20,000, and that a nasty old miser who lived on another had a yacht for which he had had the effrontery to pay a mere $25,000. I was glad that somebody else was taking her to the dance; I am never comfortable with girls who can think higher than $3.50 at one time.

• FRIDAY •

✺ Was talking this evening to a maiden lady of uncertain age who was thrown into a fantod when she discerned that I was a writer. "Don't you dare to put me in a book, you naughty man," she trilled. I toyed with the idea of saying that it would be a rare pleasure to press her between the sheets, but decided that there was a hint of indelicacy about such a remark which might be misconstrued. I then thought of saying that it would be a privilege to embalm her in prose, but that was worse. So I kept my mouth shut and tried to look mysterious, which gave me eyestrain. She did not know that I was a very base sort of writer; she probably thought I wrote novels, or perfume advertisements for *Vogue*.

• SATURDAY •

Left Laffalot today; it would be effective, but untrue, to say that my going caused a pall to fall over Skeleton; the emotion, such as it was, was all on my side. In the course of a short week, I had learned to cope with the tropic days and Arctic nights of Drowned Skeleton Lake; I had learned to listen to the astounding tales of personal prowess told by the other guests, and to counter them with a few choice untruths of my own; I had learned to say, "Gad, what a beauty; I never saw such a big fellow" whenever I saw another guest come in from the lake with a fish the size of a minnow. I had learned to eat enormous meals with an appearance of merely picking at my plate. But the time had come to leave, and I left.... Motored to Toronto, and put up at my club, the Junior Deipnosophists, for the night. As usual, I forgot my toothbrush, and may have to go back to Skeleton to get it. I have had it for years, and it has sentimental value which no new, luxuriantly-bristled, hard toothbrush could equal.

A deipnosophist is one who makes an art of dining, as distinguished from a gourmet, who makes an unholy fuss about it. The deipnosophist delights in literary conversation, and takes immense pleasure in quite simple dishes, like rice-pudding and vanilla shape. The deipnosophist likes friendly but skilled service, and deplores the tendency growing among waiters and waitresses to plunk down a dish in front of the diner, snarling "There y'go!"

-XXXII-

• SUNDAY •

✾ Not long ago a friend of mine opened the door of the garage at her summer cottage, and found a man inside who had hanged himself about two months before; what is more he had been cut down. She is deeply anxious to know (a) why he hanged himself; (b) if he hanged himself or was hanged; (c) who cut him down; (d) what it was about her garage that appealed to his morbid fancy. She will probably never know any of these things. It is thus that life falls short of the movies; in a film she would immediately have been accepted by the detective in the case as a full partner and would have shared his risks of life and limb until the criminal was in the hoosegow, and the full story in the newspapers. But the real-life detective never even asked her to sit all night in the haunted garage and shoot on sight anyone who came down the ladder from the loft. We deplore this lack of imagination on the part of detectives, who never seem to catch anybody, anyway.

• MONDAY •

✾ Visited some people today who had just moved into a new house. They were leading a circumscribed life, not walking where the varnish was tacky, not leaning where the paint was wet, and not falling too often into buckets of decorators' paste. They had moved in, driven by necessity, before the workmen had finished, and the workmen resented it, as they always do. There is nothing a party of painters and decorators likes better than a large house, all to themselves, in which they can lead an ample and gracious life, occasionally doing a little work. The only way to oust them is to move in on top of them, and let the children play with all their more valuable tools after they have gone home at night.

• TUESDAY •

Received a letter written on Reform School stationery from a little girl who takes me to task because I spoke slightingly of Gregory Peck; she tells me that *Photoplay Magazine* esteems this Peck highly. I do not care a fig for *Photoplay Magazine*; I write for a highly exclusive public, subtle and pernickety in its tastes, and they are not to be bamboozled by any such pretentious tripe, nor by the antics of Master Peck, either. She concludes, "you better apologize." The day I apologize to you, you contumacious mammothrept, ∮ there will be two moons in the sky.

• WEDNESDAY •

To the movies tonight to see *The Song of Bernadette*, which opened with these words: "To those who believe, no explanation is necessary; to those who do not believe, no explanation is possible." This seemed a very fair statement of the case, calculated to please all the Catholics, Orangemen and nullifidians present. The audience seemed to find Bernadette amusing at times. Up in the gallery something stirred; was it a bird, was it a bird? . . . I wonder what the Church of Rome thinks of Hollywood, its new ally? With so many Catholic films appearing, and a firm hold on the Hays Office, things are looking up for the *Propaganda Fide*. But I warn the hierarchy that Hollywood is fickle; five years ago it was whooping it up for the Jews; any time I expect a series of films extolling the spiritual grace and mystical fervour of the Continuing Presbyterians, in which Gregory Peck, Bing Crosby, and Jennifer Jones will all be pressed into service as pawky Scots, hooting and skirling the granite pieties of the Auld Lichts.

∮ This was a favourite term of objurgation with Marchbanks and there were people who insisted that he had made it up. But no: innovative in so much, he was no neologist. The word is of Greek derivation and suggests that someone has been brought up by his or her grandmother, and is therefore a peevish, self-willed, obstinate, pasty-faced brat of hell.

• THURSDAY •

Circumstances have made a movie fan out of me this week. Tonight was haled to see Gypsy Rose Lee in a drama which told of the reclamation of a crook by a tavern entertainer who held him in lubricious thrall; this palsied theme, handled with pleasant irony, made good entertainment. . . . I was especially impressed by Gypsy Rose Lee, and hereby publicly announce that she is my movie queen and, in my view, the most lovely and accomplished of all Hollywood's lallapaloozas. She has elegance, wit and a charming voice, and if I were a younger man I should write to Hollywood and offer her a half-interest in my chicken farm. . . . It was a similar upsurge of emotion which led my uncle, the Rev. Hengist Marchbanks (author of the popular theological work *Scatology and Eschatology*) to offer marriage to Miss Lottie Gilson, known professionally as "The Little Magnet" in 1888. Needless to say she refused him, but he kept a picture of her (in red silk tights) pasted in the front of his copy of *Cruden's Concordance* until he was called to his long rest in 1902.

• FRIDAY •

Conversation today with a young man of eleven who confides to me that a girl at his school loves him. Ask how he can be sure. "She gobbed on me yesterday," he replies. I ask for an explanation and he tells me that in the young unmarried set in which he moves, it is a sure sign of affection if the male or female party hawks up a substantial quantity of spit and ejects it upon — or 'gobs' — the loved one while lining up to enter school, where the presence of a teacher makes reprisal difficult. Astonished at this new gambit in the sex-life of the nation and as I walk home espy a girl of considerable charm just in front of me. Shall I gob on her? For a few enchanted moments I toy with this notion, but reject it as she might be old-fashioned in her ideas and fail to understand.

• SATURDAY •

Painted a fence today. Passersby greeted me with remarks like, "Doing a little painting, eh?" or "Well, I see you are painting your fence." A short-tempered man might have replied, "Oh, you're quite mistaken; I'm making a fretwork watch-cosy for my Aunt Minnie," but I am not short-tempered. Such remarks, stressing what is obvious, are not meant to be taken literally. They are what psychologists call "phatic communion"—that is to say, talk intended to establish a sense of fellowship rather than to convey any intelligent meaning. . . . There are a lot of people whose entire conversation is composed of phatic communion; carried to excess it earns them a reputation for phatheadedness.

-XXXIII-

• SUNDAY •

A sticky dull day; I awoke with the bedclothes sticking to me, my clothes stuck to me, and whenever I arose from a varnished chair there was an audible sound as my trousers tore themselves from the seat. Bathing and fanning were futile; the only thing to do was to keep still and suffer, but this palled during the afternoon and I climbed a hill and looked down over the town; steam rose from it and here and there church spires and factories rose shadow-like above the vapour bath. . . . What I always say about the Canadian climate is that it saves us millions of dollars in travel; we can freeze with the Eskimo, or sweat with the Zulu, or parch with the Arab, or drench with the Briton, and all in our own front gardens. Sometimes we even have some really beautiful weather, but not often enough to spoil us.

• MONDAY •

To the movies this evening and saw a double feature—the first part of which was good, and the second part so bad as to be hugely entertaining. It contained, among other things, the briefest conversion ever witnessed on stage or screen; a priestess of the Sky Goddess (who performed her religious duties by wriggling her caboose in a provocative manner and tossing gardenias to handsome strangers) was told about the Fatherhood of God by an aged beachcomber in thirty seconds; she immediately rushed to her co-religionists, who were preparing to roast the hero, and shouted "Big Ju-Ju him say no kill", and at once all the amateur cooks knelt, while a shower of rain fell and put out the sacrificial fire. I laughed myself into a serious state of debility during this exhibition, which involved the services of some of the worst actors to be seen anywhere, even on the screen.

• TUESDAY •

A man was asking me for information about Dr. Guillotin. I know little about him, except that he was a physician; that he was fifty-one when he came into prominence in 1789, and that he persuaded the French Constituent Assembly to adopt the killing-machine which we connect with the Revolution. "My machine will take off a head in a twinkling, and the victim will feel nothing but a sense of refreshing coolness," he said to that body. Contrast the humanity of Guillotin with the malignity of the inventor of the electric chair, who causes his victim a sudden sense of intolerable heat; rightly is the chair called "the hot squat.". . . Death by the guillotine was not immediate, by the way; several of the bodies struggled and attempted to rise after the knife had fallen, and there is a horrifying and well-authenticated account of the head of one nobleman which was seen to wink as it lay in the basket.

• WEDNESDAY AND ST. EMMA THE STEATOPYGITE •

A day of intense heat and demanding work coincided, reducing me to a condition of dripping exhaustion, and furious rebellion against the clothes the male is expected to wear under such circumstances. I am forced to the conclusion that ours is a Lost Age, a period of transition between one great historical epoch and another, and that one of the surest proofs of our moral, spiritual and aesthetic inadequacy is the sartorial thralldom in which men are held. Women—the fattest, oldest and most repulsive—strip for the heat; men—however emancipated they may be in other ways—continue to wear a collection of hot, foolish and ugly garments, designed to bind and chafe at every possible point. These are mad, bad, degenerate days, and no good will come of them, mark my words.

• THURSDAY •

Hullabaloo today about the results of the British General Election, which is interpreted in some circles as a mighty triumph for the Common Man. I suppose it is, for it has turned out of office Winston Churchill, who certainly ranked high among the Uncommon Men of our times. I confess that I find the modern enthusiasm for the Common Man rather hard to follow. I know a lot of Common Men myself, and as works of God they are admittedly wonderful; their hearts beat, their digestions turn pie and beef into blood and bone, and they defy gravity by walking upright instead of going on all fours: these are marvels in themselves, but I have not found that they imply any genius for government or any wisdom which is not given to Uncommon Men. . . . In fact, I suspect that the talk about the Common Man is popular cant; in order to get anywhere or be anything a man must still possess some qualities above the ordinary. But talk about the Common Man gives the yahoo element in the population a mighty conceit of itself, which may or may not be a good thing for democracy which, by the way, was the result of some uncommon thinking by some very uncommon men.

• FRIDAY •

Papers full of the British election. For the first time, so far as I know, mention is made of Mr. Attlee's "attractive, blue-eyed, youthful wife." It is a continual source of astonishment to me that prominent men always seem to be married to exceptional and attractive women. I recall how attractive Mrs. Baldwin seemed to be to the press when Honest Stan went to Downing Street; Mrs. Chamberlain, also, was a woman in a thousand. The charitable conclusion, of course, is that these wonderful women make their husbands great, and keep in the background while the simpleminded fellow enjoys all the fun. . . . I wonder if the day will ever come when the wife of a new prime minister or president is described thus: "Mrs. Blank is a dumpy, unattractive woman, who dresses in the worst possible taste, and has frequently embarrassed her husband by her inept remarks in public places; it is generally recognized that he would have achieved office years ago if she had not put her foot in it on so many important occasions." ∮ ... But no: it is a cherished legend that the wives of eminent men are composed of equal parts of Venus and Juno.

• SATURDAY •

To a picnic this afternoon, and had a lot of fun with an echo. There is nothing to compare with an echo for making a man feel god-like; he shouts to the skies, and a great voice returns from the distant hills. But do men ever shout god-like remarks at echoes? No! They shout "Phooey!" and "Boob!" and such-like vulgarities. Once, when I was a mere youth, I belonged to a choral society which rendered an echo-song by Orlando di Lasso, dating from the 16th century, and which consisted wholly of one part of the choir shouting Italian equivalents of Phooey and Boob at the other, with an occasional Ha Ha thrown in to give an air of gaiety. Man's treatment of echoes is continued in his treatment of radio; having conquered the air to a point where the precepts of the great prophets, and the music of the supreme musicians, might flow over the whole earth, man devotes his invention to elaborations upon the Phooey and Boob theme, with an occasional mention of breakfast food and soap. I dread the day when the First Cause, disgusted with man, will Itself shout Phooey and Boob, and throw our whole Universe down some cosmic drain.

∮ Marchbanks has indeed lived to see this day, and welcomes the new frankness in journalism. But it is not wives only, but the husbands of female politicians who now distinguish themselves by displays of indiscretion or oafishness. Should the achievement of high office automatically bring about the dissolution of any existing marriage? Who can say that such a law might not coax a better class of person into public life.

-XXXIV-

• SUNDAY •

✳ Visited some people at a summer cottage today and, as often happens on these occasions, arrived just as there was a lot of hard work to be done. This time it was shifting a bathing float from the beach to the water, and we did it by the method used to build the Pyramids—slave power. After an hour of heaving and straining the accursed thing was in the water and I escaped with nothing more than a cut thumb and a great deal of mud on my person; some of the other guests were in far worse condition. We had earned our tea many times over, and the obvious jubilance of our host did little to cheer us. . . . A summer cottage can be a lovesome thing, God wot! but not unless it has proper plumbing. I am no lover of those old and picturesque privies which have assumed the gravity-defying obliquity of the Leaning Tower of Pisa. Employing a special form of Yoga I transcend the physical side of my nature and avoid them utterly.

• MONDAY •

✳ An extremely hot day, which I spent on the train surrounded by fractious children, prostrate old ladies and all the usual victims of a temperature of 92 degrees. . . . Had a two-hour wait at a small junctional point, so I strolled about, viewing the town, and musing idly on the architectural hideousness of Ontario. This town had tried to smarten itself by hacking down most of its trees, giving an indescribable impression of ravagement, like the skull of a woman who has gone bald through a fever.

• TUESDAY •

✳ Even hotter today, a fact which was drawn to my attention by several boobs who asked me if it was hot enough for me. I enjoyed the heat, and took three tepid baths; sometimes I think that I might do well to move to a semi-tropical country; people who do so are said to become lackadaisical, losing their initiative;

but I lose my initiative in cold weather, so perhaps it would work the other way for me, and I would become a demon of energy.

• WEDNESDAY •

Bruce Hutchison, I see, hotly denies the charge which someone has made that Canadians have no sense of humour. Canada, says he, invented the story about the little boy who got his head stuck in a chamber-pot and had to be taken to a tinsmith to get it off. I wonder what makes him think so. I have a book which quotes the story, at great length, from an English work published in the 1860's and I have seen it in at least one American collection. . . . But Hutchison may be right about our national sense of humour, for when once we take up a joke, we never let it go. Old, crippled jokes, worn out in the Barren Lands and the outermost stretches of the Antipodes come to Canada at last, sure that they will have a happy home here for at least a century, and will raise a laugh from affectionate familiarity, if for no other reason. "Not Original, But Faithful To Death" is our motto in matters of humour. We like a joke to go off in our faces, like an exploding cigar, and then we can laugh heartily and get back to glum platitudes again. This characteristic is particularly noticeable in Parliament.

• THURSDAY •

Did some painting this afternoon; this is one household chore which I really do well. Ability as a housepainter and a passion

---

In 1984, when H.M. the Queen visited Canada the baser element in the British press (approximately four-fifths) pitied Her Majesty elaborately for having to spend time among such dull, miserable, slab-sided oafs as Canadians. This is a disguise we assume to delude strangers, but it is a disguise that some citizens cannot persuade to come off, and they are like Hallowe'en maskers whose false-faces have stuck, or people caught by a change of the wind while making an ugly face. But those who can doff the mask do so in private, and are dashing examples of esprit, and sometimes even of espièglerie.

for musical comedy are two characteristics which I share with the late Adolf Hitler — the only two, I believe. . . . What is more, I can paint without drinking milk; most professional housepainters seem to live entirely on milk; and I believe that they regard it as a potent charm against painter's colic. I once painted a whole building (a two-storey henhouse) without consuming any liquid beyond a glass or two of water. But last time I had professional decorators in my house they left eighteen milk bottles in it. They were especially fond of chocolate milk and every now and then, in hot weather, a bubble in my paintwork breaks, and emits a long-imprisoned belch of chocolate.

• FRIDAY •

This evening a friend of mine, who has recently become a keen amateur of astrology, attempted to cast my horoscope. According to his calculations, I have missed my vocation; I should either have been a postman or a real-estate agent. He also told me that in order to be in tune with my astrological influence, I should dress in pinks, pale blues and yellows; he warned me against over-indulgence in food and drink and a tendency toward diseases of the digestive machinery; he told me my lucky gem and my lucky flower; he told me that if I worked hard (either as a postman or a real-estate agent) I should eventually enjoy a measure of success. I treated him with the derision he deserved. . . . Although I have no use for people who try to draw up astrological charts with a little knowledge gained from popular books on the subject, I cannot see why astrology should not be given a measure of credence. To believe in it demands an act of faith, but think of all the other things, no less improbable, we believe on acts of faith! If we believe in the findings of astronomers and theologians and physicists, who are always proving each other wrong, I don't see why we should not believe astrologers, who are quite often right. *

Later in life Marchbanks became an astrologer of substantial attainment.

• SATURDAY •

As I was cutting my grass today, a passer-by said, "Hullo; are you cleaning up your yard?" By this I knew him to be a Canadian of at least three generations' standing, for no other English-speaking race uses the word "yard" to describe a lawn, surrounded by flower beds. To me a yard is a small enclosed area, perhaps paved, in which clothes are lined. I looked the word up in my dictionary, and found that the use of yard to describe a garden was labelled as dialect. Presumably it came to Canada many years ago, and took root here. The true Canadian would describe the gardens of Versailles as "Louis XIV's front yard," without any sense of insufficiency. . . . The exact opposite of our national habit may be observed in England where any grassless, desolate, junk-filled bit of vacant ground is called "the garden." . . . Another word which persists in Canada and the U.S. is "stoep" for a sitting-out place, although most of us now use the elegant Portuguese word "veran-dah." Thus a Canadian of the uncompromising old stock sits on his stoep and looks at his yard, whereas his more cosmopolitan children sit on the verandah and look at the garden. If the verandah roof leaks, it may also be called a "loggia."

-XXXV-

• SUNDAY •

Attended a small gathering this evening where one of the guests went frankly and unashamedly to sleep and put in a good two hours on a sofa; I hasten to add that this was not alcoholic stupor, but fatigue, caused by giving aid and comfort at a children's party earlier in the day. The incident reminded me of a shameful evening in my own life when I went sound asleep while Prof. Ralph Flenley was explaining some obscure aspects of the Napoleonic wars. To contradict a professor is enough to make him hate you, but to go to sleep while he is talking curdles the milk of human kindness in his breast.

• MONDAY •

✿ Since the war the mortality among animals, domestic and wild, has surely doubled. Last Friday and Saturday I passed a dead hen, two dead cats, a groundhog which had been called home, and a spaniel which was noisily engaged in making its way toward Abraham's bosom. Today I spied a brown shape on the road which I could not identify, and I asked the lady who was driving me to stop; she did so, and I found that it was a porcupine. I pointed out to her that the animal showed no sign of having died a violent death, and might have had heart-disease; she replied that it looked somewhat run-down to her. I ignored this cheap raillery, and examined the corpse; the porcupine is not a lovely object, and lacks dignity in death.

• TUESDAY •

✿ Was talking to a man tonight who had seen service with the R.A.F. in Africa, in Sierra Leone. He tells me that in that part of the world a young woman's dowry is likely to be reckoned in sewing-machines, which she buys with the pay which she received in return for special services rendered to the white troops. A girl with six or seven sewing-machines can afford to pick and choose among the eligible young men of her own race. The custom of the dowry has virtually died out among all except the most wealthy, in our Anglo-American civilization. A young man who takes a wife must choose her for her beauty of character, or of figure, alone. He stands to get nothing else with her except the expenses inseparable from housekeeping and raising a family. The average Canadian bridegroom cannot even count on six sewing-machines. It's the man who pays, and pays, and pays.

• WEDNESDAY •

✿ A hullabaloo has arisen because a Cabinet Minister told some union representatives to get the hell out of his club, where they were pestering him as he tried to eat a sandwich. The heart of many an industrialist has warmed to this man as they have longed to say the same thing themselves on many occasions, but feeling in labour circles is intense.... As a politician myself (leader, secretary and permanent executive of Marchbanks' Humanist Party) I understand the Minister's action perfectly. There comes a time in every man's life when he wants to tell somebody who is pestering him to go to hell, and if he does not indulge the whim he is likely to get psychic strabismus, which, in its turn, leads to spiritual impotence. And spiritual impotence is the curse of our country as it is.

• THURSDAY •

I see that Alfred Hitchcock intends to make a film version of *Hamlet*, only he will change it about considerably, and will leave out the poetry; Cary Grant is to star in this masterpiece. I can just see it; Hamlet will no longer be a Prince, but a truck-driver in a small American town; he will be ultra-democratic, and everybody will call him "Ham.".... Of course the Hays Office could never permit a film version of the Shakespearean *Hamlet*, because its theme is too closely bound up with incest to be tolerable to the pure minds of moviegoers. The movies insist that a good boy must love his dear old Mom, but wisely, and not too well.

• FRIDAY •

This is the time of year when households are shaken to their foundations by the annual Pickle War. There was a time when the only limit on the amount of pickles "done down" each year was that imposed by the physical endurance of the sweating squaws. When women began to faint and fall into the seething cauldrons of Chili Sauce, the time had come to call a halt (unless you happened to like Chile Con Carne, and hired girls happened to be cheap). But with sugar rationed, the problem is now how much of each pickle is to be made? Personally, I favour Marchbanks' Peach Pickle, which is made thus: put half a fine peach in the bottom of a brandy glass, add two fingers of brandy, two teaspoonfuls of sugar, and fill up with cream; drink at once. A simpler version is this: sugar a peach lightly, put it in a brandy glass, add two fingers of cream and fill up with brandy; drink at once. Or here is a quick recipe for lazy cooks; eat a peach, and immediately drink a tumblerful of brandy. The last has the advantage of conserving the sugar, and is highly recommended for this reason, I understand. Marchbanks' Peach Pickle is guaranteed to add zest to the simplest meal; it is also the quickest pickle you ever had.

• SATURDAY •

To the movies tonight, and was given a seat next to a woman who brought a baby, which was certainly not more than eight months old. It was suffering with gas on its stomach, so she had laid it upside down over her knees, and was rolling it to and fro as she watched the picture. . . . So I moved to a seat next to an elderly woman who was enjoying the film in her bare feet; she had a pair of shoes, but she held them in her lap — to save them, I suppose. These incidents made me thankful for Rita Hayworth who was young, beautiful, clothed, right side up, and apparently in excellent health.

-XXXVI-

• SUNDAY •

Passed a large part of the day eating grapes. There are people who say that our Canadian blue grapes are harsh and prick the mouth with tiny barbs. To me, they seem matchless in flavour and colour, and I consume them by the basket, picking, chomping and spitting in a golden autumnal dream. . . . Once, years ago, I watched a chimpanzee in the London Zoo; the Latin name over his cage was *Simia Satyrus*, and truly he seemed like some bawdy, happy old satyr from the Golden Age when the world was young, and Rights, and Duties, and Social Problems were still maggots in the womb of time. He lay on his back with his arms folded under his head, and bit great mouthfuls of grapes from a bunch which he held in his toes. Every now and then he looked out at me, spat seeds, and shook with silent laughter, as though to say, "If you had any sense, old boy, you'd join me; this is the life." I have often regretted that I did not accept his invitation. A nice private cage and plenty of grapes — what more can life offer?

• MONDAY •

✺ I see an advertisement in the papers for "Pre-Arranged Funerals." If you want to, you can arrange your own funeral, and pay for it before you die. This scheme combines forethought with a special form of insurance, and I think I shall make arrangements for my own funeral this afternoon. Death has no terrors for me, but sometimes I break out in a cold sweat when I think what a preacher might say about me when I was no longer able to contradict him and check his facts. I shall write my own funeral oration, and I shall also decide what music shall lull my mourners. If strains of Maunder or Stainer were played at my defunctive orgies I should certainly rise from the dead and strangle those responsible. . . . If I can raise the money to cover expenses I think I shall arrange to have a sin-eater at my funeral, in the manner of my Celtic ancestors, and also a feast for the mourners, with cold meats, Stilton cheese, fruitcake, and plenty of sherry and port. I feel that nothing would make up for my absence so well as a sufficient quantity of good dry sherry. ✒

Marchbanks is devoted to sherry, and is amused by the advertisement designed to persuade oafs that it is not a simple tipple for old ladies. But he deplores the tendency to put ice in it, and to serve noxious domestic beverages (domestic, that is, to South Africa, Australia or Canada) under the name of the true wine of Jerez de la Frontera; he is also hostile to sweet syrups served at high prices under such brand names as Dry Sack, Wet Sack and Potato Sack.

• TUESDAY •

I see that an English film studio is going to make a film of the life of Karl Marx. Now how will they do that, I wonder? The real life of Marx would not do for the movies: he was an incorrigible borrower, an indifferent father and lived his whole life in the extreme of bourgeois dullness. What is there here to engage the talents of a handsome star, or even Paul Muni, whose special line is playing great men? . . . But I suppose it will emerge that Karl's father was a miner, greatly oppressed, and that Karl's mother is the hired help in the mine-owner's palatial residence, and the mine-owner's son lusts after Karl's sister and wants to put her in a Boudoir, instead of qualifying as a teacher and organizing the sweated teachers. In the culminating scene Karl will lead The Workers to burn down the mine-owner's mansion, as Bernard Shaw (played by Shirley Temple) stands on one side, urging caution, but wittily. In the last sequence Karl, now entirely overgrown with whiskers, will be seen in the British Museum, writing *Das Kapital.* The whole thing will be in Technicolor, inclining toward the redder shades of the spectrum. Oh, and at some point Karl must express fawning admiration for George Washington, or the film will never export.

• WEDNESDAY •

A lecturer on health was somewhat embarrassed recently when a member of his audience rose and said: "What will become of the health of Canada with the coming generation of mothers drinking and smoking as they do?" Dipping into my immense knowledge of social history, I cannot recall any generation of mothers which has not had its own deleterious indulgences. The mothers of yester-year did not smoke and drink rye, but they consumed dangerous quantities of strong tea, and sought oblivion by imbibing freely of Peruna, a nerve tonic which contained about as much alcohol as a bottle of imported Scotch. And their mothers smoked clay pipes and drank the liquor from the bottoms of silos, just to keep off germs. In spite of these things, they lived to ripe ages, and were often very merry and entertaining old parties. We can overdo the health business. Remember the old song—"A little of what you fancy does you good." A very sound philosophy, clearly expressed.

• THURSDAY •

✸ To the movies tonight to see a highly coloured piece about some people called Frédéric Chopin and George Sand, though any resemblance between them and the historical characters so named was coincidental, and had been avoided pretty carefully. The voluptuous Lady Korda played George Sand, and when she appeared in masculine dress she looked far more like the historical Chopin than the young bruiser who had been given that part. The historical George Sand was so lacking in attraction of the physical kind that Alfred de Musset once described her as a cow, quite dispassionately. . . . The film had been constructed along the approved lines of Hollywood history: Chopin was insulted and oppressed by the rich (whereas in actual fact he was fawned upon by the nobility and gentry almost from birth); he was a revolutionary, and a great whooper-up for the Common Man (though in fact he never met any common men except occasional piano movers and preferred the company of the most brilliant group of his time); he let George Sand bamboozle him (though in fact they nagged each other tirelessly, and he could not stand the racket made by her swarm of children); he dearly loved his native Poland (though he was actually half-French and took care never to go near Poland once he got away from it). A strange film, brightly coloured, sweet and gassy, like a fruit salad.

• FRIDAY •

✸ I am getting a cold. At present it is in what we medical men call "the period of incubation." This means that there is nothing specifically wrong with me, but I am conscious of uneasiness in my throat, and my head feels as though somebody had pumped soda water (with pinpoint carbonation, of course) into my brains, causing them to go bubble-bubble-bubble in a ticklish way every now and again. My ears, too, have not their accustomed sharpness, and everybody who talks to me seems to have a mouthful of mashed potatoes.... To me the annoying thing about the cold germ is that it has such a poor sense of timing; when I am in perfect health, but would welcome a chance to stay in bed for two or three days, I could not catch a cold if I slept in a freezing locker; but when I am too busy to fuss over trifles I catch colds with the greatest ease, and have to go on working in spite of them. I know that physicians advise against this, but I have yet to see a physician take a few days in bed because of a cold. They generally keep going as long as they can be carried from patient to patient. ⸙

· SATURDAY ·

In the night my cold passed from the stage of incubation to the stage of exasperation, and I woke up with weeping eyes, a streaming nose, no sense of taste, and very little sense of hearing. Went to work, kicking dogs, swearing at children, and pushing old women under buses. There is a misanthrope in every man, and the cold germ usually brings him well to the fore.... In the afternoon visited some people, all of whom had colds, and we passed an agreeable hour or so exchanging symptoms.... Later at an informal birthday party, and had a slice of cake with real icing on it, a rarity in these times. I haven't any sympathy with people who do not celebrate their birthdays; I like to see the utmost done in the way of cakes, gifts, and jollifications. To a philosopher the passing of another year is not a melancholy incident; he may be a year older, but if he is worth his salt he is also a year wiser.

Nowadays, of course, owing to the Doctors' Lib Movement, patients are carried to the sick doctor. This is convenient, as undertakers may pick up the dead directly at the office, without making a house-call.

-XXXVII-

• SUNDAY •

✱ Took some photographs today, as I was lucky enough to get a reel of film yesterday. Amateur photography bears the same relation to the real thing that amateur theatricals bear to the productions of London or Broadway. When I take a photograph I usually manage to get at least one object into the picture which taste and delicacy would exclude from it; if I take a baby there is certain to be a puddle under it; if I take a dewy damsel in a winsome pose, she is sure to have a bottle of hair restorer or eradicator protruding from her pocket; let me train my camera upon a fragrant old lady in her lavender gown, and an ill-timed eructation will cause her to come out on the film looking like a bar-fly; nobody ever seems to be properly tucked in, buttoned up, or combed and washed when I take them. There are people who believe that Nature always provides a reverse, or opposite, of everything she creates. I am obviously the opposite of Yousuf Karsh; if I had photographed Churchill it would certainly have been just after a bottle had broken in his pocket.

• MONDAY •

✱ A letter today from a gentleman who is in hospital with a broken leg; he has been reading some of my reviews and wants to know if I have many readers of his own age (twenty-eight). I don't know, to be truthful, though I understand that I am widely read in Old Folks Homes, orphanages, asylums for alcoholics, and Refuges for Gentlewomen in Reduced Circumstances; in poorhouses, too, I am a general favourite. This is because I am always compassionate toward the weak and lowly, and scornful toward the rich, the book-learned and the privileged. Years ago, when I was a mere lad, I discovered that the way to win the hearts of the lowly was to tell them that they were the salt of the earth; this is a lie, but they loved it.

• TUESDAY •

🏵 In the paper I see a picture of Shirley Temple buying her trousseau. Deary me, how time flies! Surely 'twas but yesterday that this lovable mite held all the world in chubby thrall. Even the Dionne Quintuplets, five to one, could not get the better of her in the great battle of publicity. And now she is a grown woman, trying to find a few pairs of step-ins with real elastic in the top. . . . A Hollywood tycoon once explained to me that the whole of Shirley's grip on the film public began and ended with the way in which she said "Oh my goodness!" This line appeared in all her films, and where the ordinary moppet would say "Oh my goodness!" with perfect, if nasal, articulation, Shirley said "Oh my gooness!" This bit of delicious juvenility reduced strong men to doting tears, and caused fond mothers to smack their children whenever the aforesaid young dared to sound the "d" in "goodness." When Shirley said "Oh my gooness!" and flashed dimples like Neon signs, she aroused the essential jellyfish in us all; we were at her mercy, even when she sang *The Good Ship Lollipop* and clumped laboriously through a tap-dance. But Ichabod, Ichabod, the gooness is departed from Shirley.

• WEDNESDAY •

🏵 There are times when I wonder, calmly and dispassionately, whether life is really worth living. Every Autumn there comes a period during which it is impossible to keep warm, though the lighting of the furnace would be rash folly. I have just enough black jellybeans in my cellar to feed my Monster from October 15 until May 5. Light up now, and I shall freeze in the Spring. . . . I see that somebody is advertising for a "Boy's Commode." In my young days those things were Great Levellers, making no distinction of sex.

• THURSDAY •

🏵 These are the days when lukewarm gardeners like myself debate earnestly whether they should cut the grass just once more, or not. There is a school of thought which maintains that it is bad for a lawn to be closely cropped when the first frost comes; there is an opposing school which says that a lawn which is left shaggy in the autumn will be slow and spotty next spring. . . . Frankly, I have exhausted any pleasure that mowing lawns ever held for me, and I wish I could get a boy to take over the job for a reasonable price. . . . When I was a lad I mowed an enormous lawn every week for years on end, and was thankful for a dry crust and a glass of polluted water when the job was done. I attribute my present rocklike character to this stern early training.

• FRIDAY •

The world was scheduled to end today, but something must have gone wrong. The Rev. Charles Long of Pasadena, California, said it, and I made a note of it on my memorandum pad. Deciding that Oblivion might as well overtake me when I was busy, I went about my accustomed tasks all day, keeping an eye peeled for any untoward happenings. At about 11:35 a.m. I heard a shrill sound which I thought might be the Trump of Doom, but it proved to be a child outside in the street, who had swallowed his gum and was bewailing the loss. As night drew on I wondered if it were worth while making a fire, but again I reflected that I might as well die warm, and it was well that I did so, for the world did not end at all. . . . This makes the eighth prediction of general doom that I have survived without harm, and every single one has been made by the shaman, fakir or medicine man of some sect in the U.S.A. I am beginning to question the Divine Inspiration of these creatures.

• SATURDAY •

Went out this afternoon to see if there were any autumn tints yet visible, and had a very good time, sweetened by the knowledge that I should have stayed at home to do a dozen pressing household jobs. . . . Home, and made a fire and sat by it, eating grapes, and thinking what a fine season autumn is. Chose an apple, and was just about to bite into it when a solemn thought struck me that apples are now seventy-five cents a basket, and this in turn fathered the sober reflection that some autumns are better than others. Put the apple back in its basket, only slightly tooth-pocked. . . . Passed the evening looking out clothes for the Europeans, and found that I had more than I imagined, including a great many pairs of socks. Handed these over to an experienced sock-rehabilitator of my acquaintance, who made them as good as new. The thought that some Greek or Dutchman will be wearing my socks this winter gives me a new sense of the brotherhood of man.

-XXXVIII-

• SUNDAY •

In bed, and feel very low; no Calvinist ever approached the Sabbath with a heavier heart or a greater contempt for the flesh than I do today. A neglected cold is wreaking its revenge upon me. I pick up a novel to beguile the leaden-footed hours: in the first chapter is an account of how a man died through neglecting a cold. Oh! . . . Have just devoured the bread and milk which is all of my dinner. My entrails are now a prehistoric swamp where reptiles and horned monsters romp.

• MONDAY •

Thought a good deal about death today, and particularly about my own Last Words if I should expire of this grievous malady. The fashion for Last Words has declined during the last century. The most interesting case of Disputed Last Words that I know of concerns William Pitt, the Great Commoner; there are those who say he died exclaiming, "Oh my country! How I leave my country!" though an opposed school of historians claims that what he really said was, "I think I could eat one of Bellamy's veal pies." . . . However, I was unable to concoct a satisfactory dying speech for myself; I am too ill for the strenuous intellectual labour involved. And this gives me a clue to the genesis of many famous Last Words: they are carefully composed, polished and memorized years before death, and then, when the Grim Reaper seems near, they can be spoken with full effect. . . . But in these degenerate days too many people die in hospitals, and as it is a well-known fact that no nurse ever lets a patient get a word in edgewise, Last Words are an impossibility. *ƒ*

• TUESDAY •

Visited the doctor today at his office; he has a machine there which he wants to use on me. While waiting for him took close cognizance of the picture on his wall. Most doctors content themselves with Sir Luke Fildes' touching masterwork *The Doctor*, in which a bearded physician leans over the bed of a sick child, trying to look as though he knew what ailed it. . . . But this picture showed a young soldier lying on a rough bed, covered with his jacket; his eyes are closed and it is plain that he has gone to that land where "nor physician troubleth nor enema grieveth," as the Good Book says. At a table by his side sits his superior officer, his eyes moist, looking at the contents of the young man's wallet; another officer, gazing out of the window, has succumbed to manly tears. . . . Of course, it may be that I interpret this picture wrongly; maybe the young fellow on the bed is drunk, and his two superior officers are crying because he hasn't enough money on him to be worth robbing. I don't know, and, by the time the doctor had finished with me, I didn't care.

• WEDNESDAY •

My physician has given me a sedative, swearing by Aesculapius, Panacea and Pharmacopoeia that it will do me good. I read *The Great Gatsby* until the drug renders me insensible, after which I am a victim of evil dreams, in which I am continually being shot at by ill-disposed persons. I struggle to escape; I try to call for

---

ƒ For many years Marchbanks has providently kept his Last Words neatly typed in an envelope tucked into the breast pocket of his pyjamas, so that he can produce them at the last moment, for release to the waiting Press.

help, but I am powerless. At last I am able to arouse myself, and wonder whether the cure is not worse than the disease. The only perceptible effect of the sedative on me was to parade the *disjecta membra* of my scrambled ego before my mind's eye.

• THURSDAY •

Felt better today, and made a mighty effort to get out of bed; could only endure this for half an hour. Retired ungracefully, and passed the time by reading a book about famous murders. I suppose there are dozens of murders done every year which are never discovered; so far as I can judge, the types of murderers who are captured are two: (a) ignoramuses who kill in hot blood, with plenty of witnesses and a profusion of bloody axes, initialled handkerchiefs and whatnot as clues; (b) people who try to be too clever, and who invent subtle schemes of murder, and alibis for themselves. But the woman who pushes her aged husband downstairs, or the man who feeds his wife lobsters and whiskey, is rarely charged with murder, because the method is direct and simple. The best murder, of course, is achieved by driving our victim to murder himself, and this is by no means as difficult as it might seem; indeed, it was done often during the market crash of 1929, when the rain of stockbrokers jumping from upstairs windows made a walk down Bay Street quite dangerous.

• FRIDAY •

Got up this afternoon with great success, and this has altered my whole attitude toward life. No wonder invalids are crochety, crabby people. There are, in fact, two approaches to invalidism: (a) You can be a Sickbed Hitler, and insist on running everything and everybody from your Bedroom Chancellery; (b) You can be an Uncomplaining Sufferer, which means that you must tell everybody you had a bad night when you really slept like a horse, and you must do all you can to indicate that you are in continual pain, which you endure with nobility. Both these plans are great fun, but I think the Uncomplaining Sufferer has the best racket of all. He can make his relatives sacrifice to him for years, and feel cheap as they do it. If I ever become chronically ill I shall see what can be done to combine the two methods, producing a monster of valetudinarianism to be known to science as the *Tyrannosaurus Marchbankensis*, or Nurses' Nightmare.

• SATURDAY •

During my stay in bed I have done my best to keep up with my work as a book-reviewer, and have waded through a mountain of muck. Every day in every way I agree more and more with the anonymous reviewer who wrote:

> And much though each new book keeps lit my light,
> Defrauding me of sleep by dubious sleight,
>   I often wonder what the authors read
> One half so rotten as the stuff they write.

Tomorrow I go back into the great world, which has managed to do admirably without me for a week: the strikers have struck just as noisily without me; the international politicians have arranged several deadlocks and disagreements although I was unable to help them; that Mighty Mendicant, the Government, has stretched out its beggar's claw, whining piteously for a few hundred millions, although I was not by to encourage it. The world does so well without me, that I am moved to wish that I could do equally well without the world.

Autumn

-XXXIX-

• SUNDAY AND CINDERMAS •

My annual duel with my furnace has begun. Perhaps "duel" is not the right word, for it suggests a contest of lightninglike thrust and parry, and my fight with the furnace is much more like medieval jousting—a slow but hideously powerful and destructive combat. At present my aim is to keep a fire low enough to warm my house without dehydrating me and all my possessions; this I do by throttling the furnace, keeping all air from it, and treating it with ostentatious contempt, as though I did not care whether it went out or not. It retorts by belching its hot breath all through the house, cracking the surface of the furniture, and making the floors groan and pop in the night. There is a tank in my furnace into which I pour water every day, and the superstition is that this water mingles with the hot air and produces a balmy climate all through my house. But in actual fact gremlins drink this water, and the mice in my cellar commit the Happy Despatch in it, and the air from the furnace is like the parching simoom of the East Indies. Frankly I hate furnaces, and would far rather have a big Quebec heater, upon which I could spit when I was disgusted with it. Spit on a furnace, and it doesn't even hiss.

The great terror of the furnace-owner at the time of which Marchbanks writes was Coal Gas, which spread through houses and killed many Canadians every year. It resembled the ordinary gas of indigestion and was caused by the same thing—faulty combustion. Working on this principle Marchbanks sought to alleviate the distress of his furnace by flinging a dozen or so packages of Cow Brand Baking Soda into his furnace

• MONDAY •

❋ Whenever I win a bout with my furnace, it always retorts by producing a particularly large and dirty supply of ash. In twenty years, I suppose, furnaces like the one which I now harbour in my cellar will be antiques, and we shall look back laughingly at the era of the bi-weekly ash collection. But at present it is a stern reality. The ashes have to be taken out of the entrails of the furnace, sifted by hand, and then conveyed in tubs and buckets to the street. After I have done this, I look as though I had been working in a flour mill, and smell as though I had been travelling from Montreal to Toronto in a smoking car. It is enough to put me in a bad temper for a whole evening. . . . Some day I am going to have a house heated by the rays of the sun in the most modern manner. Or perhaps I shall enjoy the luxury of a furnace man, and while he struggles and fights with the furnace, I shall sit upstairs dressed like Mr. Capitalistic Interests in a socialist cartoon, laughing and drinking cherry bounce, and shouting "More heat, more heat!" in a tyrannous voice. I have always thought that I should like to be a tyrant, but it costs money.

• TUESDAY •

❋ My furnace had its first ugly fit of the season today. When I opened its front door this morning for the usual health inspection, I noticed that it had a bad breath and a nasty, coated backdraft. However, it took its food without much complaint and I thought no more about it. By this evening, however, it had dyspepsia, and the usual cures did no good at all. So for the first time in the Furnace Season I sat up with it, coaxing its appetite from time to time with tiny shovelfuls of coke, a dainty which it much enjoys.

---

whenever it was indisposed. With a wet towel tied over his mouth and nose, and the bicarbonate offering in a basket on his arm, he would creep toward the Monster, cringing beneath its outstretched pipes, murmuring "There, there!" and "Wazzums a poor bloated baby, then?" There was no sign that the furnace responded—not by so much as a belch.

• WEDNESDAY EVE OF ST. LEGER •

This afternoon I tried to rake my lawn clear of leaves, but felt like Hercules cleaning the Augean stables, and soon gave it up. It would be easier to climb the trees in September and pick the leaves than to try to scrape them up from the ground, and I think that I shall do so next year. "What are you doing in that tree, Mr. Marchbanks?" the neighbours will cry, their suspicions aroused. "I am harvesting my leaves," I shall reply, with pardonable superiority. After that, of course, everyone will take it up.

• THURSDAY •

A lady suggested a scheme to me this evening for improving the standard of education in Canada, and all Canadian standards with it. The plan is beautiful in its simplicity: (1) quadruple the present salaries of the teaching profession; (2) insist that all teachers be worth what they are paid; (3) make the teaching profession the hardest to enter of all professions. Another lady had another suggestion, which was that all teachers be paid the same high salary; obviously a teacher should be as skilful and as learned to teach beginners as advanced students. But I fear that Canada cares too little about real education for either of these schemes to gain acceptance.... A gentleman then joined me in a prolonged complaint about Canada's high tax on books; it is precisely the same, he said, as putting a tax on a university education.

All governments, everywhere, insist that they do not tax books, but in Canada there is always a mysterious spread between the price clearly printed on a British or American book and what Canadians have to pay. Booksellers, queried about this, look furtive and murmur about demurrage, high cost of transport, shrinkage in the crate and other mysteries. It costs more to be well-read in Canada than anywhere else in the world.

• FRIDAY •

A friend who was interested in my observations on famous Last Words draws my attention to this passage in George Santayana's *Persons And Places*: "On one of the many occasions when he (Santayana's father) thought, or dreaded, that he might be on his deathbed, he felt a sudden desire for some boiled chicken, without in the least giving up his asseveration that he was dying; and as his deafness prevented him from properly modulating his voice, he cried out with a shout that resounded through the whole house: 'La Uncion y la gallina!'. . . . which is to say 'Extreme Unction and a Chicken'." Undoubtedly these are noble Last Words, combining as they do a prudent regard for both worlds, but as the elder Santayana did not die on this occasion, they are not Last Words in the true sense. . . . Very irritating Last Words would be, "I forgive you all," which would leave one's relatives in a condition of baffled and angry stupefaction. . . . Charles I had a brilliant inspiration when, on the scaffold, he turned to the attendant bishop and said, "Remember, Juxon." Since then hundreds of people have puzzled their brains as to what it was that Juxon was to remember. If it was an adjuration (very natural under the circumstances) to put Rough on Rats in Cromwell's soup, it is obvious that Juxon forgot, unforgivably.

• SATURDAY •

More furnace martyrdom; cold today, and the fire which I have nursed so lovingly was inadequate. I have kept it low, yet not dangerously low, and it refused to burn up when the need arose. So, in an unwise fit of temper, I gave it a severe poking, and went out for a couple of hours. When I came home again the thermometer was just at 90 degrees F. . . . Set to work to bring the monster under control, opening all checks and even shovelling ashes through the fire door to quench the flames. I was afraid that the furnace would be consumed by its own heat, and suddenly subside in a mass of molten metal. . . . I have deceived myself about my furnace; I thought that I had the upper hand of it, and that its proud spirit was broken. But no! The Old Nick is as active in its iron bosom as ever. Some day I shall destroy that furnace or it will destroy me.

-XL-

• SUNDAY •

Was talking today to an irate father whose little boy had recently joined the temperance movement. It appears that an agent of the temperance interests (it is known that they have all kinds of money at their command, because they are heavily subsidized by the soft drink cartel) had attracted a number of children into a church hall after school and had shown them movies of the inside of a drunkard's stomach in Technicolor; this impressed the tots greatly, and after the temperance agent had plied them with chocolate milk, they all signed a pledge to taste not, touch not, nor yet smell of the cork, and received certificates establishing their memberships in the Wee Wowsers' Total Abstinence Fraternity.... What annoyed this man was that his particular Wee Wowser had come home armed with the sword of the spirit, and had lectured him on the evils of beer; I gather that the Wee Wowser was told that what looked like soul-saving to him looked much like infant impudence to his father, and his membership in the Wee Wowsers terminated at that instant.

• MONDAY •

A friend of mine lost confidence in himself today because he discovered that he had put the garbage can carefully in the luggage compartment of his car, and had stood his wife's dressing-case on the curb to await the offal officer. I assured him that I had been doing things like that for years, and attributed it to abstraction of the kind from which Professor Einstein suffers.

· TUESDAY ·

My brother Fairchild paid me one of his infrequent visits today, and asked to watch while I stoked my furnace. This was unfortunate, for Fairchild is a bigoted Back-to-Fronter, while I am a determined Middler. That is to say, Fairchild stokes his furnace by raking the live coal from the back to the front, and putting his new coal in the resulting trough, whereas I make a bed of coals with the poker, and put my new coal in a heap in the middle. I was brought up a Back-to-Fronter, but I changed to Middleism when I married my furnace. The feeling which Back-to-Fronters have for Middlers is comparable to that which Roman Catholics cherish for adherents of the Greek Orthodox Church. . . . However, while Fairchild stood by I stoked the furnace in my usual way, and I noticed his jaw tighten and his temples throb. In a low voice, he asked me whether I expected to make a good fire that way? I said that I did, and to spare him embarrassment, I leaned toward the firedoor at that moment. I think it was the big poker he used when he struck, but luckily I caught the blow on my shoulder, and was able to push his head in an ash-bucket while I screamed for help. When the police came we were locked in a deathgrip on the cellar floor. . . . We parted fairly good friends, but my furnace went out in the night. The slightest thing upsets it.

· WEDNESDAY ·

Tonight on the radio Maggie Teyte sang *Oft In The Stilly Night* better than I ever expect to hear it sung again. Beauty of tone, intelligence and poetic feeling—all were there. I must have heard the song murdered a score of times by male quartettes, female vocalizers and other assassins. And of course I recall it from schooldays when it was usually rendered thus:

> Oft in a stilly *NIGHT*
> Ere Slummer's chainuz *BOWN* me
> Fon memry bringza *LIGHT*
> Uvuther dayza *ROWN* me.

I often wonder if school teachers know what a crime they commit by giving children fine verse ✒ to murder. Children are savages, and do not like any verse except gems of their own composition, such as:

> Julius Caesar
> Was an old geezer
> Who froze his feet
> In an ice-cream freezer.

True poetry should be left to adults; school lessons kill whatever taste for poetry the average child may have.

• THURSDAY •

❀ Thought I would go to the movies tonight, but when I arrived at the place I found a long queue, and neither Greer Garson nor Gregory Peck is a person whom I will stand in line to see. So I went for a country walk instead, and as it was a fine moonlight night, I enjoyed myself very much.

• FRIDAY •

❀ For a brief drive in the country today; was amazed by the number of farm dogs who seem anxious to quit this life and join their ancestors in whatever future existence a discerning Providence has provided for dogs. They rush at every car, attempting to hurl themselves under the wheels, and when they fail (which they do quite often, being slow and stupid) they bite at the tires,

---

✒ Yes, flying in the face of the best Academic Opinion, Marchbanks insisted that Tom Moore (1759–1852) was as fine a poet as many before whose shrines the Academic Community grovels. Moore had the ear of a musician, and of a lyricist, and the large, flat, hairy ears of Wordsworth and Coleridge may have been the ears of poets, but so far as true lyricism went, they were fashioned of tin.

hoping to cause a puncture. In the World of Tomorrow dogs who want to commit the Happy Despatch will present themselves before a Government Board, explain their reasons for wishing to die, and if successful, will receive a cyanide bone, coated with synthetic beef gravy. The expense of this service will, of course, be borne by the taxpayers. Dogs who fail to make a case for themselves will receive the Order of Mother Hubbard (first class).

• SATURDAY •

It was so warm today that I let my furnace go out; it thinks it went out of its own accord, but I know better; I starved it, and it expired. . . . Bought a new rake, and seized the opportunity to sharpen my penknife, free, on the various stones in the hardware store. Then set about tasks of raking leaves, emptying flowerpots, cutting back bushes, and preparing Marchbanks Towers for its long winter's nap.

-XLI-

• SUNDAY •

To a christening this afternoon, a ceremony in which I always take a large measure of innocent delight. At best it is a race between the parson and the infant, both gathering steam and momentum as the moment of immersion approaches; if the parson is still audible above the outraged screams of the child after this point, I award the victor's palm to him. The shrieking of the child, of course, is merely the Old Adam protesting against an invasion of his property. . . . I understand that in most churches a first-aid box is kept in the vestry for the use of parsons who have suffered damage during a christening; I have seen men of God horribly clawed by infants who possessed extraordinary resistance to Grace. . . . Sometimes I have doubted the efficacy of the baptismal rite; so many children seem to be in full possession of the Old Adam, or, more accurately, the Old Nick is in full possession of them.

• MONDAY •

To the bank this afternoon, and was once again amazed by the nonchalance with which the young women behind the bars treat my balance. To me it is a matter of the most profound significance; to them it is a mere sum in addition and subtraction. Without being in the least aware of it, they can drive their cruel pens deep into my heart. That is, they are not aware of it unless I sink upon the floor with a despairing cry and attempt to disembowel myself with my pen-knife; then they call the assistant manager to throw me out. Banks hate suicides on the premises—looks bad.

• TUESDAY •

To the movies tonight to see a piece written by Sir Arthur Pinero and produced with complete and humiliating failure on the stage in 1922, and now served up by Hollywood as something new and dainty. Its theme (which is the old and laughably untrue one that Love Conquers All) might have been handled acceptably by Barrie, but Pinero, who had all the delicate appreciation of human nature that one expects in police court lawyers and auctioneers, made a mess of it, and Hollywood has piled its own mess on top of the original. A pilot who has been injured and disfigured in the war marries a girl of remarkable ugliness, and in the throes of the Tender Passion they are transformed, and seem beautiful to one another; but they do not seem beautiful to anyone else, and this is supposed to be tragic, though it appears entirely normal and explicable to me.

This was, of course, written B.C. (Before Computers) when employees of banks were expected to have some knowledge of the cruder forms of arithmetic. Nowadays it is all done by computer, when the computer is in good health, but these fragile creatures suffer at least once a day from Intestinal Stasis, or Plugged Gut, and then all the bank employees rush about like Chicken Licken, crying "The Computer is Down!" and the economy comes to a complete stop.

• WEDNESDAY •

Saw some posters today, adjuring hunters to make sure that their cigarette stubs were doused before they threw them away; the solemn assurance was given that one carelessly thrown match might start a forest fire. I wish that the government officials who dream up these posters would come and light my furnace for me some time with one of their carelessly thrown matches, or a cigarette stub. Tonight I laboured fifty minutes cleaning out my furnace (which had passed quietly away at 8:30 a.m.) and putting paper and kindling in its maw, preparatory to re-lighting; then I put a few carefully lighted matches inside and awaited results. There were none. Remembering the posters, I threw a lighted match carelessly into the firedoor; it went out at once. Next I tried a cigarette stub; it went out too. So at last I made a torch of twisted paper, and that worked. I can only conclude that it is easier to start a forest fire than it is to light my furnace.

• THURSDAY •

Suffered an acute attack of the humdudgeon today; the symptoms of this illness are a sense of failure, self-contempt and mental fatigue; there is no cure for it; application to the bottle merely brings on a crying-jag; a walk in the park suggests ideas of suicide; while the fit lasts all seems dross; sufferers from the humdudgeon should be left alone, though if they can be persuaded to lie down, with a pillow under the knees, it helps.... It was during a fit of the humdudgeon, on a Sunday afternoon in London, that De Quincey made his first experiment at opium-eating, to allay the pains of toothache. He never completely abandoned the habit, and lived to the ripe old age of seventy-five, coked *f* to the gills a lot of the time.

---

f Marchbanks, great, generous soul that he is, has none of the qualities of the exact scholar. De Quincey was not "coked"; his indulgence was in laudanum, a tincture of opium, which is taken from a spoon

• FRIDAY •

Everything is relative, I suppose, but I wish that the law, or a Chamber of Commerce, or somebody, would define the word "lifetime" as it is used by merchants. Fourteen months ago I bought a suit which was made of a cloth which I was assured would not —could not—wear out; the tailor jabbed pencils through it to show me how tough the fabric was. I have given it good care, and the sleeves and the cuffs are undeniably worn through; the lifetime fabric is just wartime shoddy. A few years ago I was sold a Harris tweed suit, which I was assured would last my lifetime; I wore both elbows through in just over three years. And I have never had a pen with a lifetime guarantee which lasted five years. Yet the days of our years are three-score years and ten.

• SATURDAY •

Long discussion this evening with a man who wants to revise our system of funerals and burial. The Vikings, he points out, lived in their ships and loved them, and when they died their bodies were laid out in their ships and sent off to sea. Ours, he points out, is an automobile civilization, and if we had any real respect for the dead, we would sit them at the wheel of the car in which they spent so much of life, and which they loved so dearly, and we would then allow the machine to dash along a special funeral speedway and eventually over a cliff. There is a poetic sweep about this notion which appeals to me strongly. For non-drivers like myself, of course, the plan might prove somewhat humiliating, but perhaps an arrangement could be made to whisk me into oblivion on castors, cunningly let into the heels of my burial boots.

(or in advanced cases by the tumblerful) and in De Quincey's day could be bought at any chemist's, quite cheaply, as it was the common remedy for toothache. It was for this reason that De Quincey's famous autobiography is called Confessions of an English Opium Eater *(1822) and even the book has been known to induce slumber.*

-XLII-

• SUNDAY •

Was reading some of the letters of Edgar Allan Poe today, and they confirmed me in my belief that a man's private correspondence should never be published. He does not write his letters with a horde of snoopy strangers in mind, and he says things which he would never say for publication. Poe was a great literary artist, and we have all the poems and stories which he wanted the public to see; why publish letters in which he makes a fool of himself, drooling weakly to his child wife, and tearfully addressing his mother-in-law as "Dearest Muddy"?

• MONDAY •

Was talking to a most unusual physician tonight — a man who scorns vitamins and laughs uproariously at talk of allergies. Medicine, he said, was an art and not a science, and could only be usefully practised after deep study of human nature and of each individual patient. This attitude, he said, was commonplace among the great physicians of the past, but was out of favour with the modern school of pill-peddlers, who like to do their diagnosis by machine as much as possible, and prefer not to see the patient if they can possibly manage with a piece of him. Too many doctors are deeply interested in disease, but don't care much for people, he said.

• TUESDAY •

To Toronto on some business, and found it noisier and dirtier than ever. Of course, visitors see Toronto at its worst. I had to fly around the business section, meeting this one here, and phoning that one there, and my impression was all of tiresome noise, stench and rush. But native Torontonians rarely encounter this; they sit in their luxurious offices, with their feet on desks, smoking big cigars and wondering how long it will be before they can run around the corner for their hourly cup of coffee. At home their wives and children live in the pastoral surroundings of Bayview, where grass grows in the streets, in Forest Hill, where the wild matzo blooms luxuriantly all year round, or in Lawrence Park, where cows and sheep graze peacefully on the lawns. The calm, white, expressionless face of a real Torontonian is never creased with care, and his collar is never soiled with smuts from the chimneys. Those frantic, feverish, sweating wretches who run about the downtown area are all visitors from the country, rushing madly to do a week's business in a few hours.

• WEDNESDAY •

This afternoon bent to the task of carving a pumpkin face as a Hallowe'en surprise for some children I know; this is a neglected branch of art which I have made peculiarly my own. I scorn the mediocre pumpkin face with triangular eyes and nose, and a gash of a mouth: mine has a noble nose, a mouth full of teeth, eyes which search your soul when the pumpkin is illuminated, and a leer which sums up the whole spirit of Hallowe'en. The only proper way to illuminate a pumpkin head is with the stub of a candle; electric light is harsh and lacking in mystery.

• THURSDAY AND ALL HALLOW'S EVE •

Hallowe'en, and a fine windy night. There was a ring at my door, and when I opened it a frightful ghost, about three feet high, confronted me. "Who are you?" I demanded in a voice which trembled with fright. "I'm Charles," whispered the spirit, and whisked my proffered orange into the folds of its ectoplasm. . . . Not long after the ghost of Charles had disappeared, I heard a groan, and went outside just in time to see a gang of hooligans running up the street, having ripped my gate off its hinges. I cursed them with a slow, lingering, horrible curse imparted to me by my grandmother, who was a witch. They will not feel the full effect of this curse for a week or so, but then parts of them will begin to turn black, and drop off, and they will be regarded as undesirable even in the circles of society in which they now move. . . . There was a good deal of writing on windows with soap, too, mostly confined to such comments as "Ha ha" and "Boo." The world is so constituted that people who feel like writing on windows can never think of anything funny to write, while those who can think of funny things have too much brains to want to write them on windows.

• FRIDAY AND ALL HALLOWMAS •

The folk-spirit in poetry is not dead. Today I heard some children singing *Sing A Song O' Sixpence*, the last verse of which runs:

> The maid was in the garden
> Lining out the clothes;
> Along came a blackbird
> And snapped off her nose.

But to this a youthful poet in the group had added a delightful sequel:

> She went to the doctor
> To get a wooden nose,
> And when she came home,
> She couldn't blow her nose.

I hope to see this addition incorporated in the next edition of *Mother Goose*.

• SATURDAY •

People make their livings in the oddest ways. I heard today about a man who has become wealthy through the manufacture of "slumber slippers"—soft little slippers like ballet shoes which are placed on the feet of corpses. All God's chillun got special shoes.... And a man in Winnipeg has become well-off through the cultivation and sale of sunflower seeds, for the chewing trade. It seems that great numbers of immigrants from Middle Europe like to chew sunflower seeds, spitting out the husks and eating the tiny, oily kernel, which tastes like a nut.... I should like to get into one of these queer trades, and make my fortune: I wonder how neon false teeth would be, so that lovers could smile at one another in the dark? Or pipe-cleaners with blunted ends, so that they could safely be used as ear-reamers? Or a pair of stays that rings a bell when the occupant has eaten enough, for fat women on diets? The possibilities are infinite.

-XLIII-

• SUNDAY •

For years I have been known to a large circle of sports enthu-siasts as the Nimrod of the Fly-Swatter; I take no interest in other blood-sports, but when it comes to swatting flies I admit few equals and no superiors. I prefer a swatter with a rubber flapper to the ordinary wire affair; the wire mashes the game, but the rubber slaps it into oblivion and leaves the carcass unmutilated, and suitable for stuffing or table use.... It is not generally realized that when a fly rises from a standing position, it jumps backward; it is necessary to allow for this jump when swatting. I have also noticed that amateurs, particularly women, swat at flies as though they were driving spikes; this causes a noticeable breeze, and the fly is warned. The way to swat a fly is this: grip the swatter firmly but not tensely, hold it six inches over the quarry, and then swat with a decisive but not vindictive motion. If the fly escapes, do not pursue it with yells and wild swipes of the swatter; wait until it lights again, and swat like a gentleman and a sportsman. With my rubber swatter, I can often stun a fly while it is in the air, but you had better not try this; only an Annie Oakley like myself has the finesse for such refinements.

• MONDAY •

Business called me to Toronto, where I found the lobby of the Royal York thronged with men in handsome blue uni-forms which were richly ornamented with gold lace, gold rope and gold insignia; many of them wore impressive medals and ribbons, and I heard one of them address another as "General." All of them carried swords, the scabbards of which appeared to be composed of gold and ivory, and one of them was accompanied by a lady of dominating appearance who wore a purple cloak of military cut, and a hat with a prodigious ostrich plume in it. I assumed that they must be foreign grandees, perhaps a government-in-exile, until I noticed that fighting men in ordinary khaki and blue did not salute them, but seemed indeed to look upon them with ill-concealed amusement; I saw one airman point them out to his dinner partner with what I can only describe as a contumelious gesture. . . . I made discreet enquiries, and learned that the gorgeous creatures were attending a convention of a fraternal order—the Ancient and Honourable Order of Poltergeists, I believe. There is a corroboree of some sort at the Royal York every week. /

• TUESDAY •

Every day I pass a beverage room in the course of my duties, and at least every second day an habitué of the place pursues me for a hundred yards or so, telling me in a low, compelling voice how badly he needs twenty-five cents. I have given him money several times, chiefly from a fear that he will fall dead at my feet if I refuse, but I am beginning to be indifferent to his fate. What is more, an uncharitable suspicion dawns in my mind that he uses my money to buy beer. Now if he spends all his daily income, which is my twenty-five cents, on drink, he is obviously an improvi-

---

This was written in the days when Toronto's airport was simply a rough field with a farmhouse on it; now it is a large affair, and many huge hotels have appeared on its perimeter. It is in these that business meetings and fraternal love-feasts now take place, for in the U.S. Toronto enjoys the reputation of a "safe" city, with a low rate of crime. The conventioneers scamper (often underground) from airport to hotel, and meet over the weekend, never setting foot outside, where The Baddies may lurk. Irrational dread is the scourge of our time.

dent oaf, and the despair of economists, and the next time he appears trembling and muttering at my side I shall tell him so. If he were a true Canadian he would spend five cents of my quarter on food and drink, he would save five cents, and he would pay the other fifteen for Income Tax and the Baby Bonus. That is what I have to do. Why should he live a life of pleasure, spending his whole income on drink, when I have to slave and pinch to keep him and several thousand civil servants in luxury? This is the sort of social injustice which makes communists of white-collar workers like me.

• WEDNESDAY •

When I was born good fairies clustered round my cradle, showering me with wit, beauty, grace, freedom from dandruff, natural piety and other great gifts, but the Wicked Fairy Carabosse (who had not been invited to the party) crept to my side and screamed, "Let him be cursed with Inability To Do Little Jobs Around The House," and so it has always been. I cannot drive a nail straight, or mend an electric iron, or make a door stop sticking, or change a fuse. I do not glory in my inefficiency; I suffer under it. Whenever anything goes wrong with my household arrangements, I have to get a man in to mend it — no small task in these days — and I know that he despises me as he does the fiddling little job and takes away a dollar of my money. ∦ People who are good at odd jobs are blessed above common mortals; I have some trifling skill in swatting flies and shining shoes, but otherwise I am a nuisance in the house. If I were ever shipwrecked on a desert island with several thousand feet of lumber, a complete set

---

O tempora, o mores, *as Cicero exclaimed, meaning* My God, what prices! *It is such revelations as this that make* Marchbanks' Diary *a treasure to the student of history. At the time of writing a repairman's house-call runs at about $32.50 even before he discovers that he has not brought the right tools, and in our Fallen World, the only direction is up, so low are we.*

of carpenter's tools, and one hundred cases of assorted foods, I should die in a week of exposure and starvation.

• THURSDAY •

Attended a concert in the line of duty, and suffered agonies with my cough. There are coughers at every concert, but none like me; I am to ordinary coughers what the late Chaliapin was to a schoolgirl singing in her mother's drawing-room; I am a vituoso cougher, and when I cough at a concert it is like the trumpets of Joshua outside the walls of Jericho. Artists have been known to stop in mid-song, and stare into the auditorium in horrified amazement; a circus man I once knew said it put him in mind of an elephant trumpeting. I cannot help it; it is my cross, and I must bear it as best I may. Hardly had the concert begun, until I felt horrid ticklings and heavings in my throat, and I knew at once that I was a goner. I hastily ate a Smith Bros. cough drop, but it was powerless against the rising fury of my cough; I held in by sheer power of will until the first song was over, and then I allowed my cough to drown the generous applause. This went on until the interval, when I was able to get a drink of water. Every song, for me, was a struggle with a cough which raged to escape. I heard the artist telling the head usher to find that dog and put it out, and I trembled in fear. But later in the evening the demon within me relented, and I was able to enjoy the music, though exhausted by my struggle.

• FRIDAY •

Received a telephone call from a friend of mine, who wanted to know who invented the water-closet; he has had one in his house for years, but has only recently become curious about it. The answer is that it was first devised by the Elizabethan nobleman, Sir John Harington, who in 1596 described his invention, which he was certain would mitigate the plague, and what did the world do? It condemned him as a man whose mind dwelt on filth. Thus the very name of this great benefactor of mankind is known to about one person in 5,000,000 whereas the inventor of the zip-fastener was given an LL.D. by the University of Uppsala. What a world!

• SATURDAY •

✳ Undertook to bathe a small child and put it to bed, in the absence of its mother; this is not a fitting pursuit for a man whose temperament is philosophical and whose habits are sedentary. Several times I underestimated the elusiveness of a small creature covered from head to foot in soapsuds, and almost fell into the tub myself. The child took this for frolicsomeness on my part, and began to throw water on me; I toyed with the idea of stripping, in order to meet this situation on fair terms, but rejected the plan as undignified. When at last I had landed my fish and begun to dry it, the unforeseen problem of ticklishness obtruded itself, and then hair-brushing created a great hullabaloo. When at last it was in bed, and had had all the drinks of water and Kleenex it demanded, I was a nervous and physical wreck.

-XLIV-

• SUNDAY •

✳ To the zoo this afternoon, just to see how the animals liked the cold weather. The bear looked restless and banged his cage resoundingly from time to time; the raccoon and the skunk had retired for the winter; the foxes looked as though the cement floor gave them cold feet. But the ducks were very hearty, and nipped at the toes of my boots in a spirited manner; a duck nipping at one's boot is a good joke, but a duck nipping at one's nether regions when one is in a bathing suit is something entirely different. The pheasants were moulting—a process which is chronic with them, though the Ringneck Cock was in his finest plumage and a glorious sight. Two owls had been added to the collection, and were resenting it; I know of no animal which has a capacity for dignified outrage equal to that of an owl.

• MONDAY •

✳ A correspondence school has written to me, inviting me to take a course in writing; this is a type of criticism which I resent. "You do not have to be a genius to become a successful writer," they say, in what is meant to be a reassuring manner. Then they go on to urge me to look in my own neighbourhood for subjects. "Dig below the surface of your home town," they say; frankly I am afraid that this method would not win me "a big income and interesting friends," as they promise, but merely a pack of lawsuits. . . . People who have taken the course write eagerly, "Last week I hit *The Country Gentleman*; this week I hit *Mademoiselle*; next week I hope to hit the *American Mother*!" Frankly I don't think this course would suit me; I don't want to hit any of those people, though I might toss a pie at the American Mother, just for fun. . . . But I like the promise the people make that they will teach me how to create tense moments, and how to play on the heart-strings; I have never been any good at either of those things. And I particularly like their offer to teach me how to be funny; any school which can make a man funny by correspondence must possess a secret which has been hidden from the rest of mankind for some thousands of generations. It would be nice to be unfailingly, perpetually, remorselessly funny, day in and day out, year in and year out until somebody murdered you, now wouldn't it?

• TUESDAY •

✳ Walked home this evening in the dusk, and passed a surprising number of couples of High School age conversing in low, tense voices as they leaned over bicycles or huddled under trees. Poets insist that Spring is the time of mating, but personal observation convinces me that the austere, bright nights of late Autumn are equally favourable to romance. The interesting thing about these lovers' conversations are the pauses. The lad asks some question which (to my ears, at least) has no amorous significance, and the girl then casts down her eyes, fingers her Latin Grammar in an agitated manner, and after a breathless interval (during which I try to keep on walking without getting out of earshot) replies, "Oh, I guess so," or "Oh, I'd just as lief," causing her swain to breathe hard and gulp.... Why doesn't he throw himself on the ground, saying, "You are my Soul, my Better Self, be mine or I stab myself with this pair of protractors"; then she could reply, "Nay, press me not, I am Another's." In that way they could really have some romantic fun and store up things to tell their grandchildren. No style, no breadth, that's the trouble with the modern High School set.

• WEDNESDAY •

An unseasonable warm spell forces me to reverse my tactics with my furnace; instead of begging the thing to give me a little heat, I am now imploring it to relax its efforts. Perverse as always, it huffs and puffs and frizzles me with its breath.

• THURSDAY •

Was talking to a woman who has just had a baby, and who passed her period of recovery in a public ward in a Great Canadian City. There were nine other women in the room with her, and she said that they talked all the time — mostly about names for babies and the peculiar behaviour of their husbands. When these husbands came visiting one piece of dialogue was invariable:

HUSBAND: "Do you want anything to read?"

WIFE: (patting her bedside table) "No, no; I have MY BOOK.

... My informant was burned up with curiosity to know what these books were which were spoken of in such a portentous manner; she was able to discover that in all nine cases the "book" was a magazine of true love stories, or of confessions. This is an interesting sidelight on Canadian reading habits. Furthermore, she said that she never saw one of her nine companions open her "book" upon any occasion.... My informant read several books during her recovery, to the amazement and ill-concealed indignation of her room-mates. It was their opinion that too much reading was a sign of being stuck-up, and furthermore liable to harm the baby's eyes—by sympathetic magic, I suppose. /

• FRIDAY •

Was in a music store, buying more gramophone records, when a man came in and asked for a ditty called *Just a Rose From My Mother's Grave*. He expressed great admiration for this lugubrious piece. It led my thoughts to an even more affecting ballad, called *They're Moving Father's Grave To Build a Sewer*, which I last heard rendered with the most moving pathos and delicacy of expression by a high official of the National Film Board.

• SATURDAY •

This afternoon hove wood into my cellar and piled it; the heaving was a wild, brutal ecstasy, but the piling was a weary penance. It was necessary for me to grab up as much wood as I could hold, and scuttle under the rafters and furnace-pipes in a crouching position, rather as an ape rushes through the forest with a stolen bunch of bananas. After an hour or two of this my back began to hurt, and my philosophy took a violent turn toward pessimism. It was at this time also that my woodpile began to slip and slide, and drop on my feet. After some very delicate engineering I got it to stay in place, and decided not to tempt fate by putting any more on it, so I retired to an upstairs room and settled down with a book and a foaming glass of burdock blood-bitters....

The city was Ottawa, and the lady told Marchbanks another detail of life in the Maternity Ward which he suppressed from motives of delicacy. At specified hours of the day the Head Nurse (described as a butch, or sergeant-major type) appeared in the door and screamed B·R·E·A·S·T·S at the top of her lungs, and the imprisoned mothers obediently bared Nature's Fonts for the ravening infants, who were rolled in on a metal trolley, mad for nurture.

During the night a mouse tramped rather heavily on the cellar floor, and I heard a thunderous roll as my woodpile sank into ruin.

-XLV-

• SUNDAY •

Woke with an aching head and a vile taste in my mouth — the consequence of piling wood yesterday; the pursuit of pleasure always leaves me in splendid condition (a fact which puzzles and irritates the Moral Element among my friends) but hard work gives me the most intolerable hangovers. Obviously Nature is evolving a new type of man, geared for a life of pleasure, and I am the first model.... But on the principle of "a hair of the dog" I went out and heaved and piled the rest of my wood, having reconstructed the woodpile which fell down yesterday. By the time I was finished, I was on the verge of physical and mental breakdown. Though thousands of people indulge themselves in it regularly, and even develop a taste for it, there is no doubt in my mind (and that of scientists whom I employ to prove it) that Work is a dangerous and destructive drug, and should be called by its right name, which is Fatigue.

• MONDAY •

Attended a concert in a collegiate auditorium tonight, and sat in the front row in order to have room for my legs; in the ordinary concert-hall seat (designed by and for dwarfs) I have to sit side-saddle, while numbness seizes first one haunch and then the other. But being in the front row I had a fine view of the empty orchestra pit, and during a rowdy rendition of Chopin's Scherzo in B Minor a tiny mouse crept from under the piano in the pit and began to dance, lightly, elegantly and charmingly. When the music twiddled, the mouse twiddled; when the music bounced, the mouse bounced; there was no arabesque of sound which the mouse was not able to transmute into an arabesque of movement. When it was all over I applauded the mouse vigorously, assuming that it was a protégé of the Board of Education. I learned later, however, that the concert committee had been put out by the fact that the mouse got in, somehow, without a ticket. . . . Why are school mice always so fat and sleek? Is it because they have access to unlimited floor-oil?

• TUESDAY •

There is a special grubby joylessness about life these days which oppresses the spirit. As I look out of my window there is not a green leaf or a flowering plant to be seen; dust blows everywhere; a woman passes, and pulling at her arm is a little boy dressed in a snow suit, in which he is hot and fretful; a man with a paunch stalks by, looking as though all his meals in the last fifteen years had soured his stomach; a girl goes by wearing an elaborate hairdo, a pea-jacket and a pair of short slacks, from which her dirty legs emerge; she is pigeon-toed, but she holds her head proudly; an elderly woman in an ill-chosen hat waits for a bus; she breathes through her mouth and stares at the passers-by. Is there any hope in these people? Could immortal souls inhabit such frames without showing some spark through the eyes, or in a smile? November is a month to breed pessimists.

• WEDNESDAY •

Was discussing wart-cures with a physician this evening. He says that in his experience the best one is this: rub the wart with a slice of bacon, then go outdoors on a night when the moon is full, throw the bacon over your left shoulder and then, as the bacon rots, the wart will vanish. "But what if a cat eats the bacon?" I asked; "The wart will vanish that much sooner," said he. . . . Naturally this led to talk of magic, and a lady present spoke of an old woman known to her grandmother, whose custom it was (when her luck was bad) to bind her churn with willow-withes, and beat it with a stick; then whoever it was that was wishing her ill would come to the door and beg forgiveness. This was in Canada, about 1850-60. Our pioneer ancestors had a lot of simple fun that we miss.

• THURSDAY •

✿ Life, for a man of my temperament, is an endless procession of vexing domestic problems. Shall I have my storm-windows put on, or not? At present the weather is warmer than it was most of last May, and it is only by the most rigorous repression of my furnace that I keep my house livable. But I know that Winter will come upon me like a thief in the night, blowing its raw breath through every chink, ruffling the carpets on the floors and whipping the pictures off the walls. My indecision will be the ruin of me, I know it. But oh, the heat of storm windows in warm weather! I will.... I won't.... I will.... I WON'T. Come then, Boreas, and be damned! It is better to tarry than to burn.

• FRIDAY •

✿ Waiting for a bus today, I listened to the conversation of two women who were waiting also; they were exchanging symptoms. Such tales of nervous breakdown, bad dreams, uncontrollable crying, pain in the legs, bladder weakness and a general debility I have never heard: although they stood side by side they shouted as though they were conversing in a hurricane; as their symptoms grew worse and worse, their voices grew louder and shriller. They talked so loudly that I had no need of my formidable powers of eavesdropping. To my unskilled eye they looked healthy, though unwholesome and glum.... Most people like to be ill, and ask nothing more than a chance to rehearse their ailments. In some dark corner of their minds (I use the word loosely) there lurks the notion that if they ever admit that they feel quite well the gods will at once punish them with some direful malady.

• SATURDAY •

✿ Rain all day. What can a man do on a rainy day which is also his half-holiday? I am never at a loss for an answer to that question. Immediately after lunch, I went to bed, and bade farewell to the world for a few hours. The telephone rang. "It can't be anyone of any consequence," I thought: "every sane man is in bed this afternoon." After a while the ringing ceased. . . . Later there was a knock at the door. "Nobody is up to any good this afternoon," I said to myself; "that is doubtless someone wanting to sell me a ticket on a sanctified raffle, or a dozen repulsive Christmas cards, or a copy of the Christmas *War Whoop*, or a pillow stuffed with pine needles. — A pox upon them." The knocker went away. . . . "If everybody spent one half-day in bed," I reflected, "there would be no need of a United Nations Organization; world peace would come as a matter of course, the divorce rate would be cut in two, and even grim-visaged labour leaders would become creatures of light and spirit." At this point Oblivion claimed me.

-XLVI-

• SUNDAY •

Was looking through a book today which had a good deal to say about prayer as a mental exercise. Prayer, it said, was not a formal thing, and could be indulged in anywhere; pray on the bus, while eating your dinner, or while taking a bath, it said; it was particularly scornful of the notion that prayer should be done on the knees; much better to say one's prayers lying in bed. . . . Now this may be all right as mental exercise, but it entirely neglects the function of prayer as physical exercise. Most people, if they don't kneel to pray, never kneel at all, and kneeling is good for you. The Moslems understand the value of prayer as exercise, and several times a day they prostrate themselves with their heads toward Mecca; I once knew a Moslem who said that this kept the most sedentary of his sect in good physical trim. The Chinese, before the revolution, made a great point of the kotow, in which you kneel gracefully and touch your forehead to the ground when in the presence of your superiors, or in temples; this kept them admirably supple and healthy, and when the revolution put an end to the kotow the Chinese went straight to the bad. The present decline of Christianity may be traced to this habit of praying in bed, which is bad for the Christian liver. ∥

• MONDAY •

A doctor tells me that he has observed a number of cases of poultry diseases among middle-aged women in the last few weeks; apparently the women are regular attendants at Bingo games, where they absentmindedly consume large quantities of the corn which is used for counters; then they go home and drink several cups of tea, and the trouble begins. Sometimes, he says, it is simple distension of the crop, and can be cured by purchasing a set of celluloid Bingo counters, but often the disease has gone too far for anything but severe measures. He mentioned one patient of his (whom he referred to as a White Wyandotte type) whose wattles had turned greyish and whose eyes had filmed over simply from a prolonged surfeit of Bingo corn. Another woman he mentioned (a table Plymouth Rock) showed every symptom of pip, and waddled about his office uttering pitiful squawks and occasionally falling over on her side. Still another was far gone in fowl-convulsions, and he did not think she would last for the Christmas trade.... I tried to cheer him up by pointing out the sturdy character which the Scotch ∥ built on a diet of oats; he said that he was afraid that Bingo corn would turn Canada into a nation of sick hens.

Marchbanks once called my attention to the longevity and excellent health enjoyed by priests of the sacramental churches—Roman Catholic and Anglican—which he attributed to the great amount of bobbing up and down, kneeling and bowing involved in their ritual tasks. The clergy of the Reformed sects, on the contrary, age earlier, owing to their professional uprightness which may lead—especially in Presbyterians—to stiffness of neck.

Readers who think that Marchbanks should write "Scots" are referred to the discussion of this vexed question in the Oxford English Dictionary. For literary use, he has preferred the form employed by Burns and Walter Scott.

• TUESDAY •

The Russians are acclaiming Robbie Burns as a genius — a sort of primeval, pre-Marx Communist. This proves only that the Russians are not reading Burns' works complete. His dislike of aristocracy pleases them, no doubt, but his hatred of orthodoxy and bureaucracy cannot go down very well. Probably the Russian editions of his works are carefully expurgated, and such verses as *The De'il's Awa Wi' The Exciseman* are omitted. By judicious expurgation I could prepare a Shakespeare which would be an eloquent plea for Communism, and I daresay that I could prepare a cipher which would show that Shakespeare's plays were written by Joe Stalin. . . . My advice to the Russians is that they should give thanks that Burns is dead, and not alive in Russia today. He would be a great bother to the commissars of literature and popular thought, before they decided to kill him.

• WEDNESDAY •

Was introduced to an elderly lady today who offered me two fingers to shake; they were cold, damp and blue, like uncooked sausages. Her conduct in this matter did not please me greatly, for I would much have preferred to have no hand at all, rather than half a hand. It was the custom in the last century to give a few fingers — three, two, or in extreme cases, one — to people whom one regarded as social inferiors, or in some way undesirable. I only know one man who still does it, and as he does it to everybody I assume that he has a high regard for himself. The story is told that the late Arthur Balfour once offered a man one finger to shake, and the man vindictively shook it to such a degree that Balfour was unable to write for a week. Moderation in the handshake is highly desirable; neither the blacksmith grip, which crushes the hand into the semblance of hamburger, nor the chilly extension of two or three fingers. I think handshaking is overdone, in any case; why do we not compliment our friends by shaking hands with ourselves, like Chinamen, or boxers who have won a match?

• Thursday •

Was talking to a woman today who kept giving out strange squeaks and groans, as though she had mice in her corsage; I soon diagnosed her trouble; her corsets were creaking, and whenever she moved the stresses and strains of her underpinning were audible. This reminded me of one of my earliest business ventures, when I patented and attempted to sell Marchbanks' Patent Stay Oil, a scented unguent which was rubbed well into the corsets before putting them on. There are still a few women who need my Stay Oil, and I am thinking of getting one of the big cosmetic houses to try it on the public again.

• Friday •

Was talking to a young woman today who informed me that she had no soul. I think she hoped to shock me by this declaration, but it was old stuff to me. The world is full of bright young things and cynical old things who think they have no souls. They appear to regard the soul as a part of their personalities upon which the Christian Church has established squatters' rights, and they very properly resent such intrusion. As to defining the soul, they never attempt it, though I gather that they regard it as a sort of vapour floating about the heart — not unlike gas on the stomach. For a belief in the soul, and the deity of which the soul is a reflection, they substitute belief in such chimaeras as Progress, General Education, Single Tax, cold baths, colonic irrigation, free love, women's rights, vegetarianism, the Century of the Common Man, the infallibility of radio commentators, social security, and their laughable congeners and equivalents. As a result, their souls become anaemic and debilitated, and their faces have the unlit look of vacant houses.

Marchbanks was keenly interested in the souls of his acquaintances, and it was his custom to establish their size on the principle applied to shoes. The soul of the average man or woman, he said, was between a five and a seven, with the usual allowance for narrow or wide fittings. A

• SATURDAY •

Quite a heavy snowfall today, and I decided that it was time to prune my hedge for the winter; there is no sense in being hasty about these things. Pruned, and got thorns in my hands; then put on a storm door. Exhausted by these labours, retired to bed and read a book which the critics insist is very funny, but which impressed me as a melancholy affair. . . . One of the great lacks of our time is a body of really comic literature; when I want a good laugh, I am forced to turn to the writings of Dorothy Dix. . . . Lay at ease, thinking how nice it would be if I were to receive a telegram saying that I had been left a million dollars, free of tax; then reflected that there is really nothing that I want, which I could buy with a million dollars. I should like to travel and see the world, but no millionaire can do so today. Decided that what I really ought to do is to give away the $37.72 which I have in the bank, and declare myself destitute; then governments and benevolent societies would vie with each other to give me money and assure me of "social security." The day has arrived at last when the poor are going to inherit the earth.

-XLVII-

• SUNDAY •

Impossible to postpone any longer the tidying of some attic closets, so faced the task with a heavy heart. Under the debris of the years discovered an astonishing quantity of old wallpaper. I have never seen an attic yet which did not contain a lot of old wallpaper, and this makes me wonder why it is that a paperhanger doesn't feel safe unless he has a lot more material than he really needs. I learned how to calculate the amount of paper needed for

---

philosopher might run to a nine soul, and a saint to a broad eleven. When I questioned him about his own soul, he admitted bashfully to a ten. Later the same evening he revised his estimate, saying that a ten pinched a little, and it would be better to call it an eleven.

a room when I was at school: you multiply the square footage of the walls by the cubic contents of the floor and ceiling combined, and double it; you then allow half the total for openings such as windows and doors; then you allow the other half for matching the pattern; then you double the whole thing again to give a margin for error, and then you order the paper. Result: every attic contains enough extra wallpaper to print a complete Sunday edition of the New York *Times*.

• MONDAY •

Peeped nervously from behind my lace curtains today to see if the Offal Officer would really take away all the assorted junk which I banished from my attic yesterday; he did, and he even wore some of it as he drove down the street. . . . Christmas draws near, with its desperate challenge to every man to buy presents for people whose taste he does not know, or who have no discernible taste of any kind. I buy a few Christmas cards as a beginning, knowing full well that they will not be enough for my needs. The Christmas spirit has not yet taken possession of me.

• TUESDAY •

In the course of a conversation about drinks this evening, a man told me that I am wrong in supposing that no joy goes into the making of Ontario wines. Vintage time in the Niagara Peninsula, he says, is a season of Bacchic revel and riot; the merry Niagara farmers and their plump, rosy-cheeked wives roll up their blue jeans and tread out the grapes in an elaborate ritual dance, singing this song the while:

> Io, Father Bacchus, Io, Io!
> And hurrah for the Chairman of the L.C.B.O.!
> Merrily we sing
> As we dance in a ring,
> Banishing our troubles
> With gulps of gas and bubbles!
> Io, Father Bacchus, Io, Io,
> And hurrah for the Chairman of the L.C.B.O.!

When night falls, they all drape exquisite garlands of flowers about the priapic statues of the Chairman of the Liquor Control Board of Ontario which stand in every vineyard, and then depart into the woods in pairs. It is very dangerous to follow them.

• WEDNESDAY •

A year ago today I was in a motor accident — not a large one, but big enough to make me nervous of cars even yet. Without wishing to do so I still press hard on the dashboard of any car I am riding in, mumble warnings to the driver under my breath, and cringe and scrunch whenever another car comes within spitting distance. For peace of mind I should really ride with my back to the engine, and sometimes I do, but on a long drive I get tired of kneeling on the back seat, and besides it gives people in other cars a wrong impression.

• THURSDAY •

To Toronto, the Ontario Babylon, on business. In a restaurant a notice asks me not to whine for more sugar or butter "to spare the staff embarrassment"; later I am in a shop where a sign urges me to show all my parcels at the desk "to avoid possible embarrassment!" People must embarrass awfully easily in Toronto. . . . Passed hastily through Toyland, and saw children being introduced to Santa Claus. Two or three harassed men were busy shooing the tots away from S.C. down a ramp; they all wanted to turn around and barge back into the crowd whence they had come, disarranging the queue. This is an instinct deep in the childish heart. What does Omar Khayyam say? —

> Myself when young did eagerly frequent
> A Santa Claus to Toyland yearly sent —
> Then turned, and vainly tried to butt my way
> Outward by the same path as in I went.

Saw also a toy train big enough to pull children and a few adults. Would fain have had a ride on it, but I had no child with me, and feared that I might excite remark and even rebuke if I tried to pass myself off as a nursery-school type. The train had an excellent whistle which sent me, just as Sinatra sends the bobby-sockers. Whoo! it went, mellowly and invitingly: Whoo! Whoo!

• FRIDAY •

Toronto is already in the toils of Christmas, and from several windows the hollow Ho Ho! of a mechanical Santa Claus may be heard. Children watch these creatures with hard, calculating eyes, wondering if the old man is really crazy, or only pretending to be, like Hamlet. . . . Everywhere I went Christmas preparations were going on, but they all seemed to be of a secular nature. Gnomes, elves, giants and Disney oddities abounded, and there were a few angels, but even they had been Disneyized, and made cute, rather than spiritual. A Man from Mars would never know that Christmas was a religious festival from what he sees here. Is it the final triumph of Protestantism that it has pushed the sacred origin of Christmas so far into the background that most people are able to ignore it?

• SATURDAY •

Dashed out this morning to get some more Christmas cards; I am not what could be called a greeting-card type, but at Christmas I bow to the general custom. Saw a great many which inspired me with nausea, being depictions of jolly doggies hanging up their stockings, or pretty pussies doing the same thing; several cards were in what is called "the semi-sacred manner," showing the Holy Family with figures and postures strongly recalling the kewpies who used to appear in the advertisements of a famous tomato soup. St. Nicholas, too, appeared on many cards as a frowsy old drunk in a red ski suit, fingering his bulbous nose. In short, everything possible had been done to rob Christmas of its beauty, dignity and significance. It was not in this spirit that Dickens wrote *A Christmas Carol*, and it is not in this spirit that I, personally, shall celebrate Christmas. I can stand almost anything except vulgar infantilism, and against that I shall war as long as there is breath in my body. ✒

-XLVIII-

• SUNDAY •

❀ My brother Fairchild is my guest today, and as there is always something of an unusual nature going on in Fairchild's vicinity, I kept a close watch on him, and soon surprised him in the act of shaving himself with a little electric machine which he kept in a leather case. It was, he said, a razor, and not a miniature sheepshearer, as I thought; held close to the face, it chewed the whiskers off with tiny teeth; he passed it over the rugosities of his countenance with a great air of virtuosity, and I must admit that the little machine seemed to work. I asked him if it did not excite his face too much to have electricity applied to it? Was there no tendency for the skin to loosen and hang in folds? He denied this with more heat than was really necessary, for my question was purely academic. I have a fear of new-fangled contrivances. Fairchild is the daring member of the family.

• MONDAY •

❀ This Christmas shopping leads a man into the most alarming situations. Decided today to get a bottle of toilet water for my Great-Aunt Lettice, and sought out a shop which had a big display of unguents, balms, lotions, electuaries and the like. Asked for a bottle of scent, and a young woman with more curves than

---

✒ *During recent years the increasing venerability of Marchbanks'*
appearance leads various Noel Cowards of the Bourgeois World to
hail him with "Hey, are you Sanny Claws?" To this he is apt to make tart
rejoinders, such as "No, I am his older brother, Sharp Claws. Are you
Simple Simon?"—or Mother Goose, according to the sex of the witling
addressed. Or also, "No I am the musical member of the family, Sonata
Claus"—which astonishes the unsophisticated.

the Burma Road brought out two or three, and poured drops from them on her wrist and arm. Then to my horror she invited me to sniff them! I did so, tentatively. She rippled her muscles like a wrestler. "Young woman, have you any idea where this may lead?" I cried, but she smiled in an oblique manner and said that it was impossible to tell anything about perfume if it were not applied to flesh. . . . At last, after what seemed ages, she sold me a bottle of something at four dollars an ounce, which I fear Aunt Lettice will have to wear in the privacy of her own chamber, for if she ventured into a drawing room with it on she would immediately become the object of embarrassing attentions, and might have to make a run for shelter. I really wanted some lavender water, but this stuff is called *Très Ooomph*, and is guaranteed to rouse the dead.

· TUESDAY ·

Addressed Christmas cards tonight. There was a time when I used to hunt for the most suitable card for everyone on my list. I chose cards covered with lambs and reindeer for children, snow-scenes for friends who were wintering in Florida, High Church cards for friends of a ritualistic tendency, Low Church cards for evangelicals, Thick Church cards for those whose religion impressed me as a bit thick, cards with coaches and jolly drunken Englishmen on them for my jolly drunken American friends, and so forth. It was a lot of work, and I gave it up long ago. Now I buy my cards in large inexpensive bundles, and send them out in whatever order they happen to come. . . . Like everybody else I am sending cards this year to people who sent me cards last year, but whom I forgot last year, and who will not send me cards this year. This desperate game goes on for decades, and there seems to be no way of stopping it. . . . On several cards I put messages such as, "Why don't you write?" or "Am writing soon," which is a lie. I have no intention of writing them, but in an excess of Christmas spirit I pretend that serious illness, or the press of affairs, is the only thing which keeps me from sending them a long letter every week.

· WEDNESDAY ·

Was driving with a motorist today who nearly ran down several pedestrians who persisted in crossing streets against the traffic lights; he thought they did it on purpose, and I really think they were trying to commit suicide; some had a hopeless O-god-let-me-die look on their faces, while others wore the fixed grin of idiocy. It seems to me that when people dearly want to die, motorists should be encouraged to assist them. . . . This evening read in Nellie McClung's autobiography that a properly licensed dog has the same right to use the street as a citizen. I am glad that citizens do not exercise their rights as freely as dogs do, however. . . . Not long ago a clergyman said to me, *apropos* a scruffy dog he had with him, "Wouldn't it be a wonderful world if there were nothing but dogs? No wars, no racial discrimination, all friends." Was so stunned by this idea that I said "Yes, indeed" before I knew what I was about. Hurried home and washed my mouth out with soap.

· THURSDAY ·

To the government liquor store today, to lay in a Christmas stock. Wartime shortages turn the celebration of Christmas into a matter of makeshifts. Still no Chinese Rice Wine, which I like to burn on the top of my Christmas pudding, in the real old English style; will have to do the best I can with brandy, but it will not be the same.

· FRIDAY ·

My Chinese laundryman, hearing that I have been unable to get any Rice Wine to burn on my Christmas pudding, turned up in my office today with a flagon of the precious distillment. "Oh brilliant-hued chrysanthemum of Eastern Ontario," he said, kotowing deeply, "this utterly contemptible one entreats you to accept his laughably inadequate tribute to your sublime genius; drink, O Marchbanks, and gladden the heart of your washworm."

I uncorked the bottle, and the room was filled with the heady bouquet of dragon's bones. "This ineffectual trifler with the written word is choked by the copiousness of his thanks, O magical rehabilitator of world-weary underpants," I replied, bowing graciously and pouring out a couple of glasses of the liquor; we drank, ceremoniously, and exchanged a few more polite observations. Before he left I reached into the bottom of my desk, and presented him with a pound of opium which I happened to have; he bit off a quid and chewed it with evident satisfaction as he put on three sweaters, two suits of pyjamas, a buffalo robe and a rain-cape, before leaving. It was what we Sinologues call "A three-coat cold day."

• SATURDAY •

A few friends in this evening. Wanted to give them mint julep, though this is the wrong season for mint. But the scientific knowledge of a Marchbanks laughs at such trifling difficulties. Prepared the other ingredients, then brought down a bottle of Oil of Peppermint, which I sometimes take for indigestion: on the label it said "Adult dose: five to thirty drops," so I put thirty drops in each glass, never having been one to skimp on hospitality. . . . Guests looked rather strange, and showed a tendency to suck in air through their teeth. One, standing by the fire, belched suddenly with such force that his toupée fell into the grate and was badly scorched; his wife remarked sourly that at least it helped to kill the smell of humbugs. . . . I drank my julep to the dregs, just to show them that it could be done. The only trouble with me is, I'm ahead of my time.

-XLIX-

• SUNDAY •

A small girl of my acquaintance sang me a Christmas carol which she had learned in school. It was the familiar one which begins:

> Good King Wenceslas looked out
> On the Feast of Stephen —

and I expressed my appreciation of her performance warmly. This was a mistake on my part, for she began to cross-examine me about the words. Why was Stephen feasting outside in the snow? If Stephen had enough food for a feast why didn't he give some of it to the poor man who was gathering winter fuel, instead of leaving it all to King Wenceslas? I tried to explain that a Feast did not really mean a feast, and that Stephen was not really there, but I saw disbelief and scorn rising in her eyes. No wonder children think that all adults are crazy. ✍

• MONDAY •

❀ Woke this morning with a sense of sick shock, realizing that Christmas is near at hand and I have not done any shopping. Worried about this until at last I rushed out and made a tour of the shops, and was depressed to find how much stuff there was for sale which I would not give to a relative, let alone a friend.... There stole into my mind Coleridge's poignant lines:

> Ah, God! It is fell Christmas-tide
> So to the shops I hie;
> And my shopping-list, like the Albatross,
> About my neck doth lie.

This was to be included in *The Rime of the Ancient Mariner* but was dropped to please Wordsworth, who secretly held shares in a large toy-shop and was afraid it might hurt business.

• TUESDAY •

❀ Alack the day! Christmas gifts are not what they were. Was looking through the diary of my uncle, the Rt. Rev. Hengist Marchbanks (who lived to be ninety-six and was Bishop of Baffinland when he died) and discovered that in December, 1845, when he was a lad of thirteen, he made his own presents. This is what

---

✒ *Marchbanks did not know at this time that Wenceslas (1361–1419) was never a King, but a Bohemian Duke.*

he says: "Made dear Mama a trunk today, for I know that she wants one sorely. Cut down a sturdy oak this morning, and hollowed out the body of it with my adze; hewed the solid block into a charming lady's travelling trunk. Slew and skinned a Shorthorn bull, which showed symptoms of mumps, and stretched the skin tightly over the wooden casing; it makes a truly handsome covering. Tomorrow I shall line the case with clean copies of *The Christian Guardian*, and my surprise for Mama will be complete. Am giving Papa the usual jug of corn whisky, which I drained from the bottom of the silo this evening. Tested it to make sure it was good, and fell into a profound swoon. Popped a few prunes into the jug, to give the liquor body." Those were the days of really thoughtful, personal gifts.

• WEDNESDAY •

Met a small boy today—a sinister child with a stern jaw and a brooding hot eye—who had just mailed his letter to Santa Claus. "I told him what my minimum demands were," he said, "and I'm giving him till the 25th to come across—or else—" I blinked, and asked him to explain. He continued: "Claus has been in the driver's seat too long; everybody has always lickspittled to him and made him think he's a big-shot; well, the time has come for Organization; he thinks we can't get along without him, but we'll show him that he can't get along without us; he expects a year's good conduct for a few gew-gaws at Christmas; from now on there'll have to be a Christmas every month, and an eight-hour day for good conduct, with all statutory holidays and two weeks vacation in the summer; Claus has been exploiting us." He marched off, and as he turned to give me a knowing leer he inadvertently fell down an open manhole. I watched it for a few minutes, but he did not reappear. Walked home slowly, thinking about Fate.

• THURSDAY •

I see that a rich fellow in the U.S.A. has bought a fine tapestry as a Christmas present for his wife. I like tapestries, and have thought of weaving a few myself, in the grand manner, but with modern subjects. For instance, Dr. Brock Chisholm, ∮ with his foot on the recumbent body of Santa Claus, holding aloft a volume of *The American Journal of Psychiatry*, from which streams forth a golden light, would make a very pretty tapestry, suitable for a dentist's waiting room. Or a large piece depicting the inventor of the fountain pen meeting the inventor of the typewriter, and each of them scowling horribly at the other, would be suitable for a tycoon's office, as would also a depiction of the inventor of the rubber hotwater bottle, shielding himself from the onslaught of the inventor of the electric pad, while plunging a dagger into the breast of the inventor of the china hotwater bottle (or "stone pig"). Or how would it be if I did a really immense tapestry, showing industrialists and union leaders dancing on the prone form of a Consumer, while in the background Inflation snatched them up to the skies, by the hair? It could be hung in the Union Station at Toronto, to take away that bare look it has.

• FRIDAY •

A man asked me today if I had heard of the theory that the North American Indians are of partial Welsh descent, stemming from a pre-Leif-Erickson Cymric explorer? I have gone farther; I think I have proved the theory to be correct. About two years ago I chanced to meet an Indian in a woodland walk, and I facetiously addressed him thus:

∮ *George Brock Chisholm, M.D., (1896-1971) was Deputy Minister of National Health from 1942 to 1946, and it was during this period that he raised a ruckus by declaring that belief in Santa Claus was harmful to the mental health of children, as it led to the discovery that their parents were liars. This was silly, because all children and all parents know that children and parents who are not liars will not last a week in the hurly-burly of domestic life. Dr. Chisholm was no Jungian, or he would have known that Santa Claus is an archetypal figure, albeit a degraded one, and you cannot kill him with an axe. But as very few Canadians are Jungians either, this questioning of the existence of Santa Claus almost cost him his position with the Canadian Government.*

MARCHBANKS: "Dyna gapel y Bedyddwyr, onid e?" (*Translation*: "Look you, are you not the son of Mrs. Jones the Gas?")

INDIAN: "Nage, nage; dyna gapel y Methodistiad Calfinaidd." (*Translation*: "Indeed to goodness no! I am the love-child of Rev. Hopkin Hopkins.")

MARCHBANKS: "Ple mae'r Ficerdy?" (*Translation*: "Pless my soul, whateffer! do you understand me?")

INDIAN: "Dyna fe; dyna'r Ficer hefyd." (*Translation*: "Yes indeed, whateffer.")

MARCHBANKS: "Dyna deulu'r gof yn cerdded gyda mama modryba chwaer y crydd." (*Translation*: "Then let us sit down here and refresh ourselves with elegant conversation.")

INDIAN: (*Speaking Indian for a change*) "Golliwogagog, hoganogagog egganoggagog." (*Translation*: "I am all agog.")

• SATURDAY •

✳ Visited a friend this evening who had procured a bottle of a very special tonic called *Noilly Prat*; in the interest of temperance, we experimented to see how much of the tonic it was necessary to put with a jigger of gin in order to kill the horrid taste. After several tries we got the measurements exactly right.... Driving home, passed through a small town where Saturday Night was in full swing. Farmers shouted conversation from buggy to buggy; their wives stood in the general store, gossiping and criticizing the goods; girls walked up and down the street, arm in arm, pretending not to notice the young men who leaned on doorposts, haw-hawing and passing remarks. It was all rather idyllic and rural, and reminded me of my far-off youth in Skunk's Misery, before I was tarnished by the fetid breath of city life. I suppose everybody has these softheaded spells, when they think it would be fun to live in a small town. They pass quickly, of course.

-L-

• SUNDAY •

✳ A man was lecturing me on the benefits of deep breathing this evening. "Fresh air cleanses the bloodstream and keeps the mind alert," he said, sucking in deep draughts of cigar smoke which undoubtedly polluted his bloodstream and fogged his brain. "When you've got pneumonia — gasping for breath — you pay a pretty penny for oxygen out of a tank; but all day, every day, the precious stuff is everywhere around you, begging to be breathed, and do you breathe it?" He puffed in my face, ferociously. "No, you don't. You're a shallow breather, a thorax-man, like millions of others. Well, don't say I didn't tell you." I promised that I would never say he didn't tell me, and felt rather guilty about the whole matter. Walking home, I breathed as deeply as I could for several blocks. It made me dizzy. I am a poor creature unworthy of the fresh air which Providence has lavished upon me.

• MONDAY •

My brother Fairchild has been having rather a difficult time with magic. Hoping to ingratiate himself with his children, he bought them some magic tricks, with which he thought that they might mystify their little friends. Having made this false step, he was soon involved in the appalling task of teaching the children to perform the tricks. Teaching a child to do even the simplest sleight-of-hand is like teaching a hippopotamus to embroider pillow-slips. The result of the whole mad scheme was tears, bad temper, and frustration for Fairchild. . . . I sympathize with him. Once, in the bleak past, I cherished a desire to be a magician; I would have been quite content if I could have achieved the modest skill of say, Dante or Blackstone. ✒ I laboured before a mirror with coins, cards, eggs, handkerchiefs and billiard balls for weeks, my arms aching, until one bitter day when I came to my senses and admitted that nothing short of psycho-analysis and blood transfusions could make a conjuror of me. For the same

---

Two notable illusionists during Marchbanks' formative years. Dante, a genial Dane whose real name was Harry August Jansen (1883-1955) was a splendid conjuror, but perhaps his most popular trick was to take several feet of fine white cord, snip it into short lengths with scissors, and then — while the audience waited for it to be miraculously re-united — to throw it away murmuring "Pooh, what do I care for some scraps of

reasons that I cannot carpenter shelves, fix leaky taps or tend a furnace, I was unable to pluck fifty quarters out of the air or pull a rabbit out of a hat.

• TUESDAY •

✳ Passed a bank this evening which was being re-modelled. Workmen were taking down the iron cages in which the tellers used to be kept. If anything marks the decline of belief in private property, it is this. Not so long ago, putting a teller into his cage was a solemn ceremony; the manager locked him in, and there he stayed until the manager let him out; while he was in the cage he spoke in a hushed voice, like a man who had swallowed a bomb, and he handled money with a kind of religious awe. But the modern teller is a carefree soul, able to run all over the bank if he likes, and ready to hobnob with Tom, Dick and Harry. It is all part of the breakdown of the monetary system.

• WEDNESDAY •

✳ Two different manifestations of the same attitude toward women forced themselves on my notice this afternoon. On the street I passed a young couple just as the boy wrenched the girl toward him by the shoulder. "Aw, yuh little nincompoop, yuh!" he said, as he gave her a shake; she replied with a spirited, but uncultured, reflection on his legitimacy. Five minutes later I opened a magazine at a luridly coloured advertisement for perfume. In it another young man, in evening dress, was gazing at the shoulder of his female companion with glowing eyes, like a vegetarian about

---

old rope!". . . Harry Blackstone (Henri Bouton, 1885-1965) of Canadian descent, was brilliant with cards and coins. He travelled with two handsome Afghan dogs, and not less than a dozen beautiful girls, but the dogs never appeared in his show. Dogs have no turn for magic, and won't keep quiet when concealed in somebody's sleeve. Girls, on the contrary. . .

to bite into an onion; his hands hovered in the air behind her, as though he might suddenly snatch her, just as the boy in the street had snatched. The caption of the picture was "Potent Essence of Desire to Touch".... I shall never understand life, but I suppose the lesson of this is that if young men do not grab you and call you a little nincompoop, you need a perfume which will force them to do so. The girl in the advertisement was cool, exquisite and beautiful; the girl in the street was tousled, and had been barking her shins on rocking-chairs for weeks, I should judge. But both of them, apparently, were able to rouse men to wild flights of shouldermadness.

• THURSDAY •

Heard a lady greeting her physician this afternoon.... "Well, doctor," she said, breezily, "I hope you've been keeping well?" He gulped a couple of times and staggered a little, but his presence of mind did not desert him, for he immediately turned the conversation to a less ticklish subject. Of course it is terribly bad form to ask a doctor how he feels; it is almost the same thing as giving him a dig with a surgical scalpel, or telling him that he would not puff so much if he got more exercise. Doctors like to give the impression that they have no fluctuations of health, and are always in the absolute pink of condition.

• FRIDAY •

Did some more odds and ends of Christmas shopping today. Bought fifteen dozen handkerchiefs for female relatives. I don't know what women do with their handkerchiefs; every year I give away a car-load of them, but I have never known a woman who had a handkerchief on her person at any time when she needed one. Older women always keep their handkerchiefs upstairs so that they can send their younger relatives after them. And why are women's handkerchiefs so small? What a woman really needs is a handkerchief as big as a tablecloth, pinned to her bosom with a blanket-pin.

• SATURDAY •

The pest who was nagging me last week about deep-breathing was at me this evening on the subject of water-drinking. "How much water do you drink a day?" he asked, finishing a glass of my beer. "About half a paper cupful," I replied, knowing that it was not a satisfactory answer. He made a great show of disgust. "Four gallons a day is the minimum — the bare minimum," he said, when he could speak. "That would be about two pails," I said mildly. . . . Later he phoned me. "By the way," he said, trying to be casual, "I made a slight mistake. Should have said four quarts — not four gallons." He is reading a health book, and giving all his acquaintances the benefit. It is one of the mistakes of democracy that it teaches such people to read.

-LI-

• SUNDAY •

Rummaging in some of my personal debris today I found two Christmas cards which I bought in 1939 and forgot to send out. They will be very handy this year if I can find envelopes to fit them. . . . I was really searching for pen nibs, of which I have a large but unsatisfactory store. In these days when people write with ballbearings and solid ink, and at the bottom of the lake while swimming, and otherwise miraculously, I am an embittered reactionary scraping away with a wooden pen which I dip after every eighth word. I do this because I like a particular sort of flexible nib which cannot be obtained in any fountain pen that I have ever owned or tried. But alas! such nibs are now very hard to find, and in despair I buy every nib I see, hoping to find a substitute for my unobtainable favourites. Consequently I have enough nibs to open a stationery store, none of which really pleases me. I know that I am at anchor in the stream of progress, but I don't care. It has pleased God to make me a dipper man, and who am I to struggle against the Divine Will?

• MONDAY •

✸ I get the strangest stuff in the mail. A letter turned up this morning which began "Dear God—," but what followed was so confused that I could not make out whether this was a cry from the writer's heart, or a somewhat elaborate compliment to myself. The same post brought an invitation from the Book-of-the-Month Club, asking me to bestow the benediction of my presence upon its membership. The pamphlet by which this invitation was conveyed was beautifully printed and ornamented with finely reproduced illustrations from *Alice In Wonderland*. The richness of the printing, however, was not balanced by the literary quality of the matter printed, which was, for a book club, rather poorly expressed.

• TUESDAY •

✸ This afternoon a little girl demanded that I do something miraculous, so I swallowed a fork, and, after feigning indigestion very laughably, I produced it from the sole of my boot. She was impressed, but not completely satisfied. "There's no blood on it," said she. . . . Children have disgustingly literal minds and hearts of stone.

• WEDNESDAY •

✸ Thought a good deal today about games for a Christmas party. There are plenty of dull games, of course, in which one is given a piece of paper and put off in a corner to write the names of all the rivers one can think of beginning with "G", and there are embarrassing games in which one is tied back to back with a total stranger of the opposite sex and instructed to get free without breaking the strings. But between boredom and ribald lunacy there are some excellent games; the kind I particularly like are those in which one runs all over the house, hiding in the bathtubs and the coalpile, and jumping at people in the dark; the nearer a game approximates to the plot of a Boris Karloff film, the better I like it. There are also games in which the whole company passes judgment on the intelligence, charm and youth of each player in turn; the delight of such amusements is the narrow path they tread between good humour and malignance; many a beautiful friendship has been ruptured by such shenanigans.

• THURSDAY •

At last it seems that I have a Christmas gift for everybody who has a right to expect one from me, and for a few who have none. I see no signs whatever that anyone has a gift for me, but I am used to that; I have always found it more pleasant to give than to receive. (Advt.). . . . A man was complaining to me today about the agonies he goes through with Athlete's Foot; apparently his wife and his daughter suffer from this ailment also. He seemed to think that there was something rather distinguished about having Athlete's Foot as badly as he had it; he ranked it with such noble maladies as *Coronary Thrombosis* and *Paralysis Agitans*. I was not impressed. At one time in my life I mixed a good deal with shepherds and sheep-breeders, and a lot of their sheep suffered from Athlete's Foot, only they called it foot-rot, pronounced "fut-rot." The sheep got it by standing around in damp grass, staring at one another. Futrot was treated with a nasty substance called Stockholm Tar; if it brought no relief, the sheep was knocked over the head with a club. I think I shall suggest to my friend that he and his wife and daughter try Stockholm Tar for a few weeks, and if they do not improve, the next step is obvious.

One of these games of which Marchbanks was very fond was called Russian Sledge. The company was bidden to imagine that it was in a sledge, racing in the darkness over the steppes of Russia. Who should be thrown to the pursuing pack of wolves? One by one the players made their choices and gave their reasons, and one by one the victims dropped out of the game. As the party was reduced to three or four, matters became tense. What Marchbanks liked was to observe the decisions of married couples under this particular form of stress.

• FRIDAY AND PARCELMAS •

✸ Frantic wrapping of parcels. Through some idiosyncracy of character, I always seem to give people things which are hard to wrap. I refuse to put my gifts under the Christmas tree unwrapped, for part of the pleasure of Christmas is watching the faces of the recipients of one's gifts as they tear off the concealing folds. Sometimes the objects of my benevolence have been moved to tears; often they are so thunderstruck that they cannot speak.

• SATURDAY AND CHRISTMAS EVE •

✸ Christmas Eve, and a great deal of scurrying hither and yon, and lending one's forefinger to people who want to use it in tying knots. Having wrapped my gifts in the attic, I have to carry them down to the foot of the Christmas tree. As I did all my Christmas shopping in a hardware store this is no easy task, and a couple of adzes and some axe-helves slipped out of my arms and tumbled down the stairs with deafening crashes at every step.... When the others had gone to bed, crept down to the Christmas tree and read all the tags on the parcels, by the light of a candle-end: very few for me. Heard a thumping in the fireplace and thought for a wild moment that it was Santa Claus, but it was my brother Fairchild, covered with soot; he too had been peeping and had taken refuge up the chimney when he heard me coming. We retired to the kitchen, and ate pieces of cold plum pudding.

- LII -

• SUNDAY AND CHRISTMAS •

✸ Christmas Day: hurry-scurry, hamper-scamper, *tohu-bohu* and *brouhaha*. The happy excited voices of children sounding like the laughter of angels at 8 a.m. and sounding rather more like the squeaking of slate pencils or the filing of a tin can at 5 p.m. Conversations conducted in yells, and the incessant rustling of tissue paper. Everyone lays claim to a Dickensian appetite, but shows signs of latter-day squeamishness when faced with a third helping of plum pudding. In some cases, torpor and somnolence have their way; in others, excitement rises to the point of acute Anxiety Neurosis. But it is all very happy, with occasional surface irritations. . . . Christmas is best for children, and for those who are growing old; in middle life one's capacity for enjoyment is under the constraint of a thousand responsibilities.

• MONDAY AND POSTMORTEMAS •

✸ Boxing Day. There is a tradition that one will have a happy month in the coming year for every mince pie one eats on this day. In deference to tradition I did what I could, but choked on the first bite of October, and had to lie down with a cold cloth on my brow for some time afterward. ∮

• TUESDAY •

✸ Was reading the funnies today (just to keep in touch with what the common people are thinking) and was struck by the change in what may be called the dynamics of humour. When I first began to read the funnies this subject was simple; the greatest professor of humorous dynamics was Bud Fisher, the creator of *Mutt and Jeff*. When Mutt hit Jeff with a spittoon, the noise which came out of Jeff's head was "Pow," which was clearly printed at the appropriate spot; if Mutt threw Jeff out of a window, the trajectory of his flight was labelled "Zowie." Jiggs never made these noises; nothing ever came out of his head except stars and comets. But nowadays this dynamic field is vastly expanded. When a boxer is given a knockout blow his chin emits the word "BLAM" in big

∮ Pernickety readers may point out that earlier in this Diary—on Twelfth Night, to be exact—Marchbanks also made a beast of himself with mince pies in honouring this fine old custom. But if the good man chooses to lay down his digestion on the altar of tradition twice in a year, who is so mean-spirited as to find fault? Faultfinders—that's who. Narrow-gutted, thin-blooded, naysaying faultfinders, with whom Marchbanks will admit no kinship.

letters; when a man is kicked by a horse or a mule his afflicted part says "Zok!" Two of the dynamic sounds greatly used in *Barney Google*, have vanished from my ken; they were "Plop" (for falling on the floor) and "Wham" for being struck with a broom. There's no doubt about it, science is on the march in every sphere.

• WEDNESDAY •

This morning was compelled to listen to a long distance call. The telephone company was, as usual, quick and polite in getting my office, but then I became involved in a sparring match with the caller's secretary, who was determined not to let me speak to him until his full impressiveness and executive splendour had been paraded before me. This involved many repetitions of "Are you ready to speak to Mr. Squealy?" "Just a moment please," "Are you ready at your end, Mr. Marchbanks?" "Hold the line, please, Mr. Squealy isn't quite ready yet." This went on for quite a time and was punctuated with sounds like "Bzzzzt" which I think the secretary caused by blowing a raspberry into the phone. All this nonsense begot a somewhat morose attitude in my mind, and when at last Mr. Squealy burst upon me in all his glory, I was surly with him. Secretaries who seek to build up their bosses by such means merely make their Mr. Squealies detested by all honest men.

• THURSDAY •

A bus driver was telling me today about how he had been robbed of his underwear and a package of pork chops while driving his bus. Unfortunately a traffic snarl cut him off in the middle of the story, and I did not find out whether he was wearing the underwear at the time or whether it was in the parcel. I have seen a conjuror take off his shirt without removing his coat, and I suppose a clever thief might strip a man in the same way. I brooded on this problem for some time, and was reminded of my cousin Manfred Marchbanks, the organist, who once shocked the daylights out of a lady pupil by telling her that he was going to show her how to change her combinations without taking her feet off the pedals. . . .

• FRIDAY •

I see by the papers that Paramount is going to make a film called *Coming Through The Rye* in which the chief part of Robbie Burns will be played by Bing Crosby. It is to be "a semi-biographical story," I observe. I can just imagine it. Young Bing Burns is the child of poor but talkative parents who have Scotch accents. As Bing grows to manhood (or what passes for it in the movies) he discovers that he has The Gift Of Song. One day, when he is coming through the rye, he meets a body, and thinks that it is a sheep, and nonchalantly kicks it out of the way; it proves to be Highland Mary (Linda Darnell) who has a Brooklyn accent, and has disguised herself as a sheep in order to keep warm. Bing tells her that his Love is Like A Red, Red Rose. But there is an impediment; she is loved also by a birkie ca'd a lord, wha struts and stares, and a' that; though thousands tremble at his word he's but a coof for a' that. Bing rouses the tenantry against him, and personally brains him with an oat-cake. George Washington, who happens to be visiting Scotland, recognizes that Bing Burns is a true democrat and invites him to America. Bing and Linda marry, and get tight on Scotch whisky; they are na' fu', they're nay tha' fu', they've but a drappie in their ee'. They are last seen on a boat bound for America, and Bing is singing a special number composed by Eli Feitelbaum, called *The Star-Spangled Briar-Bush.*

• SATURDAY •

The last day of the year, and I passed part of the evening in melancholy reflection upon the waste of time which has always been my greatest sin. If only I could drive myself to do physical jerks for an hour a day, read improving books for an hour a day, practise on the piano for an hour a day, philosophize and ponder on life for an hour a day, eat less, drink less, sleep less, work harder, eat wholemeal bread, drink eight gallons of water a day, stop smoking, and overcome my ribald disdain for nice simple people who, whatever their shortcomings, Mean Well—if only I could do all these things, what a wonderful fellow I should be! Roused myself at last to make a final entry in this diary, which I leave with something of the feeling experienced by Gibbon when he completed the *Decline and Fall.* . . . To the reader who has read thus far, *Adieu.*

The Table Talk of Samuel Marchbanks

edited, and with Notes by
ROBERTSON DAVIES

• The Nature and Use of this Book •

*I*T IS A FREQUENT complaint of the sort of person with whom complaint is an ingrained habit that the art of conversation is dead. I do not believe this. I think that conversation is in a reasonably flourishing state and I assert furthermore that when I have the right company I am not a bad hand at it myself. I find that company most often seated around a dinner table. Encouraged, therefore, by the kindly reception which has been given to my *Diary*, which I published two years ago, I offer to the public these odds and ends from my Table Talk.

In the hope that such an arrangement may call up the atmosphere of the dinner table, I have set out my paragraphs (for a good talker should speak in paragraphs and not in disjointed utterance) under headings which trace the course of a good dinner. I do not mean a great dinner, for such things are almost impossible in private houses in our day; I mean a simple seven course dinner, consisting of a Soup (I like a choice of thick or clear), a Fish (I am very partial to lobster for this course), an Entrée (where the cook shows her utmost skill with a soufflé or some other complex and ingenious dish), a Remove (which is the proper name for a really good joint of meat or possibly a fine fowl if the meal is a simple one), a Sweet (and if anyone is thinking of asking me to dinner I may say that I am always well content with a Sherry Trifle), a Savoury (but no unnatural unions of prunes and bacon, if you please) and a simple Dessert of fruits, nuts and bonbons. In the matter of wines I do not insist, as some greedy diners do, on an array of fine vintages: a little Sherry, an honest Claret, a sound, wholesome Burgundy (or Vin de Champagne if you simply *must*) and a glass or two of Port, or better still, Madeira, to top off, will suffice me. If the Hostess insists, a Salad may be interpolated between the Entrée and the Remove, but I have provided no conversation for it; one does not talk while eating Salad; one crunches.

It should be understood by the reader that all the conversation recorded here was addressed to ladies, for at a well-regulated dinner the sexes are so disposed that every gentleman has a lady on his right and left. There are dreadful gatherings — dinner-parties I will not call them — where people are invited to sit higgledy-piggledy; at such affairs the hostess, with a vague wave of the hand, may even go so far as to say "Sit ye doon." This is base indeed and I never dine at such houses twice. I am, whatever my detractors say, a gallant man, and very fond of the fair sex and indeed even of the plain sex. So as you read, you must imagine me talking to right and left, to female hearers whose attention may be enthusiastic, or possibly lukewarm if the lady is anxious to snatch the talk to herself. But it is the mark of the Superior Woman that she plays fair in conversation and is able to disagree with her dinner partner without starting a hooley.

As to the use of this book, the reader may please himself, but I suggest that he may memorize pieces from it and cleverly pass them off as his own when next he dines out; in that way he will get a reputation as a talker. Those who wish to spare themselves the pains of getting passages by heart may take the book to dinner with them, and read aloud from it frankly. Those who, for one reason or another, are never asked to dine out, may create an agreeable illusion of society if they will read the book as they regale themselves with soda biscuits and weak tea, sitting at a corner of their own kitchen tables. To all, under every circumstance, I raise a glass (or, if total abstainers, a loaded fork) and cry "My dear Sir, (or Madam) — your very Good Health!"

The Junior Deipnosophists Club   SAMUEL MARCHBANKS
September 1, 1949.

Contents

Soup

• OF HIS GIFT FOR REMINISCENCE •

*B*EFORE DINNER, I observed, everybody seemed to want to talk about the Good Old Days. I am, generally speaking, better at this than anybody else, for I am not bothered by details of chronology, and tend to regard as my own, reminiscences which have been imparted to me by the Ancients of my tribe. Thus I frequently tell people about how I taught Disraeli to play croquet, because my Great Uncle Hengist did so, and I also have a good story about how I sent Sir John A. Macdonald his first brief, though I have a hazy notion that it was my second cousin, Bloodgood Marchbanks, who did it. Thus I embody in myself the whole Marchbanks Tradition, and possess what anthropologists call Racial Memory.

• OF HIS ECONOMICS •

A MAN WROTE to me today who says, "Why has Samuel Marchbanks no economic problem? To me no Canadian is real unless he is engaged in a death-grapple with his bank manager." This is easy to answer; I have no economic problem because I do not believe in economics. I am an atheist and an infidel in all matters relating to Mammon. I have never had a bank account; I keep all my money in a tin box under my bed, and I pay for it in cash. I am rarely tormented by the desire to own anything, and I would exchange the Towers for a tent tomorrow if tents were practical dwellings in Canada. I fight inflation by eating

---

Pernickety readers may complain that earlier Marchbanks referred to his bank account. When I used to point this out to him he would

cheaper food, and wearing my clothes past the bounds of hygiene. I have no insurance, and have made no provision for my old age, as I am resolved to become a whining beggar outside church and beverage-room doors when I am past work. All my life I have defied economics and I shall go on doing so. What is the result? I look at the world with the clear, bright eye of a man who has a tin box, and bank managers love me and sometimes give me blotters advertising their establishments. *⫽*

• REVENGE •

*B*EFORE I FELL ASLEEP last night a moth flew up my pyjama sleeve and tickled me excruciatingly. I overlaid the creature and slept on its corpse.

• OF CHARACTER REVEALED IN DEPORTMENT •

*O*N MY WAY to the dentist this afternoon, I was pursued by an elderly bum, who kept murmuring, "Hey Perfessor, wanna speakcha minute, Perfessor." Indigents almost always address me as Professor; I observe that men of very upright carriage are usually spoken to by beggars as "Captain," whereas fellows whose spines are noticeably out of plumb ("Bible-backed" is the phrase in some circles) are called "Professor." I suppose this is my fate, but I

---

wrap his overcoat about him in the manner of a toga, and declare (quoting Walt Whitman):

> *Do I contradict myself?*
> *Very well then I contradict myself.*
> *(I am large, I contain multitudes.)*

⫽ Readers will immediately divine that this was written before the advent of the credit card. After this invention grasped commerce in its clutch, Marchbanks found that unless he had one he was without Fiscal Credibility; if he had no debts he did not exist. Modern man is a debtor, or he is nothing, and money becomes more and more illusory. Marchbanks' ancestors dealt in gold; he finds it hard to accept plastic (nastily printed in tasteless typography) as a substitute.

wish that once in a while a beggar would call me "Sport," or something dashing of that kind, suggesting that he took me for a frequenter of race-courses, an habitual drinker of champagne, and altogether a knowing and dangerous character.

• OF ONE SEEMINGLY RETURNED FROM THE GRAVE •

I WAS IN TORONTO yesterday on business, and almost swooned at lunch when I saw a man at a table some distance away who had been killed, I thought, in the war. It was not possible to rush to him at once and say "Are you a ghost, or merely an Amazing Resemblance?" and so I was kept on pins and needles for an hour. But at last I buttonholed him, and it was indeed my friend. When I told him that I had thought him dead, mourned his loss, and filed him away in my memory, he laughed uproariously. Nothing amuses people under fifty so much as being told that you thought they were dead; after fifty the joke gradually loses its side-splitting character until, in the seventies, it is received with sour looks. Having established my friend's corporeality we exchanged news, but I could not shake off my doubt at once, and for half an hour or so I expected him to come out with some interesting revelation about the Life Beyond.

• HE CREATES A LEGEND •

T HE COMING OF summer has encouraged ants to invade my house, and this morning the bathtub was full of them. I drowned the lot, more in sorrow than in anger, and as they disappeared down the plug-hole, I reflected that I had probably started a Flood legend in the ant world, which in time will be recorded in ant Scripture.

• OF LOST CAUSES AND IMPOSSIBLE LOYALTIES •

I SAT DOWN today to rootle through a pile of mail which has accumulated during the week and which I have not opened, owing to its uninteresting appearance. I take my time about opening letters which look as though they contain unpleasant news, or information I do not want. I discovered in the heap a copy of a magazine called *The Celt*, published in Britain and devoted to what the publishers presume to be the interests of fanatical Scotsmen, Welshmen, Irishmen, Manxmen, Cornishmen and Bretons; large chunks of it are printed in Erse, Gaelic, Welsh and Breton by fellows called Dmurphaidh and Na Dhoaileach, who used to be plain Murphy and Dooley before the Celtic bug bit them. All of these Celts seemed to be uncommonly vexed with the English, and did not hesitate to say that if the English could be got out of the way everything would be dheaochd (jake) with the world. Being possessed of a considerable degree of traditional Celtic wisdom myself, I soon committed *The Celt* to the flames.

This seems to be my week to receive peculiar periodicals. Another paper called *The Jacobite* arrived from New Zealand, of all places; it was devoted entirely to that most lost of all lost causes. It boasted that a letter written by Mary, Queen of Scots, had recently sold for £1200, whereas one from Elizabeth had sold for a measly £500—an obvious victory for the Stuart cause. It spoke admiringly of Louis XVI as the man who had given the Americans their independence—an interpretation of history new to me.

· He Is Earthbound ·

I AM BEGINNING to be a little bit touchy about the fact that I have never been up in an airplane. Not so long ago I was among the majority in that respect; now I appear to be one of a timid minority, classed with people who think tomatoes poisonous, or who refuse to use the telephone during thunderstorms. Everybody seems to fly everywhere. The real reason why I do not fly is that I am a coward, and have not even been on a Ferris Wheel for twenty years. But I am getting sick of inventing lies about how I prefer train travel, or motoring, and some day I may be forced into a plane by my fear of losing face.

Totally false: Marchbanks did fly on several occasions until he was barred from the airways by all companies. He was rude to air hostesses, for he had been led by advertisements to believe that they were

• OF HIS TREATMENT •

AFTER A TRAIN journey at an ungodly hour I presented myself at the palatial offices of the eminent Dr. Aesculapius, and was told to seek him at the hospital. I went there, and asked for him. "Is it about a Growth?" asked the clerk, in a ghoulish whisper. "Heaven forfend!" I replied, and was pushed into a waiting-room, branded as an uninteresting fellow who had no Growth. But my companions in this sink of human misery all looked as though they had Growths, and for an hour and three-quarters I sat among them, wondering if I looked as ghastly to them as they did to me. At last I reached Dr. Aesculapius. "Tut tut," said he; "they should have kept you at the office, Mr. Marchbanks; you are to be

---

winners of beauty and talent contests, luscious morsels of dewy feminin-ity. But what was mistaken for insolence was simply pity. When he beheld the workworn, middle-aged slaves who toiled up and down the plane on aching feet—literally walking from Toronto to London—he was so moved that on one occasion he burst into song:

> *Och, I love the dear silver*
> *That twines in her hair,*
> *And the brow that's all furrowed*
> *And wrinkled with care:*
> *I love the dear fingers*
> *So toil-worn for me—*
> *Oh, God bless you, Air Hostess*
> *On B.O.A.C.!*

As if this were not enough, he applied a quotation from Anthony and Cleopatra—

> *". . .thou didst drink the stale of horses*
> *and the gilded puddle which beasts*
> *would cough at. . ."*

to his complimentary quarter bottle of white wine, offered with his rubber chicken, in a manner that was taken as injurious. If he does not fly, he has no one to blame but himself.

an ambulatory patient.". . . And so, later in the day, I engaged the attention of the great man once again, and he said Hum and Aha, and was so much more mysterious than any other doctor that I can readily understand his eminence in his profession. But at last he shoved me into an immense Atomic Frier which he kept in the back of his premises, and as I cringed under its blast I thought of the boys in the Fiery Furnace.

An ambulatory patient, I discover, is a fellow who would be in a hospital if there were room for him, but who is otherwise permitted to amble aimlessly about the streets when the doctor doesn't want him. The Atomic Frier made me feel thoroughly miserable; I was nauseated when I lay down and faint when I stood up, and so I crept about bent into a right angle, and moaned whenever anyone touched me or offered me food. This response to the treatment was apparently good, and Dr. Aesculapius was pleased with me.

• HE DESCRIBES AN ILLNESS •

YESTERDAY I finished the series of treatments. "You've been a good patient, Mr. Marchbanks," said the nurse as I climbed off the gridiron; "we've put 124,000,000 velocipedes through you and you haven't batted an eyelash." (She may have said something else, but I think it was velocipedes; these measurements of electricity are very confusing.) I said nothing. When one is praised by nurses it is best not to be too enthusiastic. They may like you so much that they insist on further treatments. I silently cursed the Atomic Frier, into which I have been slid like a roasting fowl for a month, and escaped to the cubby-hole where my clothes had been left. As always in doctors' dressing rooms, the mirror in this place was hung to suit the needs of women rather than men, and gave me a fine view of my navel. I was on my knees, tying my tie, when the nurse came in again. She thought I was praying, and bent her head reverently. While she was thus occupied I escaped into the blessed light of day, and bought a pound of candied peanuts and ate them all at once, to celebrate my liberty.

My experiences of the past week convince me that the world is full of Intuitive Diagnosticians and Vicarious Undertakers. Every third person I meet seems to know what ails me, and a good many of them have buried me so deep that they take it as a personal affront that I am still walking about. I have made up my mind to outlive all of these vultures, just for spite, and every year I shall defile their graves in some new and outrageous way on Father's Day. My family history is full of instances of Marchbankses who wouldn't lie down; they all outlived their physicians by several decades, and in one or two instances their cantankerousness was so powerful that they did not die at all, but were removed from this earth in heavenly chariots. I have every intention of following their example. ⫻

• OF TEMPTATION RESISTED •

ON MY WAY here this evening I saw a girl sitting on the stoop of a house, with a sign hanging over her head saying "Live Bait." They didn't catch me with that bait, though. Not pretty enough.

• OF HIS BASIC COSTUME •

I WENT TO a Fashion Show last evening to see what women would be wearing next season. I myself wore an outfit which I expect many men will favour during the coming year. It was a dark, three-piece ensemble with a plunging neckline which reveals, when I lean forward, the pencil-and-pen accessories with which the dainty waistcoat is embellished. Informality is

---

Marchbanks had been diagnosed, by several physicians of unimpeachable veracity, as having Something Very Dreadful, yet he outlived whatever it was, and even the horrors of the Atomic Frier. His doctors regard him now as a nasty, contradicting fellow, who doesn't know enough to let a good diagnosis alone. His lifelong disease, in the opinion of his present Editor, is Inveterate Hyperbole, for which there is no cure.

the keynote of the costume, accentuated by the extra fullness at the knees and the high gloss on the bosom of the trousers. With this I wore wool socks, with inserts of contrasting yarns, and conservative shoes of scuffed calf. For outdoor wear I put a topcoat over this ensemble, which presents a pleasing contrast of napped and napless cloth in the same colour, and complete the effect with a hat in the classic Canadian, or *pot de chambre* style. This is what is called a Basic Costume, suitable for office wear and, by the addition of a clean shirt and handkerchief, suitable also for dinners, dancing, and social engagements.

• OF UNKNOWN MARTYRS •

*O*FTEN, AS I have conned the pages of a newspaper, I have wondered who those people are who show such engaging frankness about their innermost secrets. There are their photographs, their names and addresses and all the lurid details of the years which they spent in martyrdom to gas, bloating, sour stomach, pains in the back and spots before the eyes, before they discovered the amazing patent medicine which cured them. But the question still remains: Who knows them? They must be real, but are they anybody's neighbours? . . . Yes, yes, I realize that it is not a nice thing to mention while eating Scotch broth.

• OF GARBAGE AND OUR CULTURE •

*W*HEN THE HISTORY of western civilization as evinced in Eastern Ontario is written, a long footnote will have to be devoted to the curious place which the garbage pail holds in our folk habits. A traveller from Mars, dropping suddenly upon this part of the Earth, might assume that we loved these vessels, and were proud of them. Every garbage-day the pails line the streets like sentinels — mute evidence of the amount of food we eat and the quantity of rubbish we throw away; every night, after the collection, they lie scattered in the snow, and at dusk they look like the bodies of soldiers, fallen in battle and frozen in death. Indeed, Napoleon's retreat from Moscow must have looked rather like one of these Ontario streets.

• OF WOMEN'S RIGHTS AND WOMEN'S LOOKS •

I RECEIVED A LETTER from the U.S. this morning, bearing a stamp with the heads of three women who had been prominent in the fight for Women's Rights engraved on it. As I lay in bed I reflected upon the uncompromising plainness of all three. Does an enthusiasm for Women's Rights kill beauty, or are none but plain women interested in the acquisition of Rights? Surely the engraver could have done something for these worthy but wooden-visaged females? An Italian coin which I had palmed off on me on Monday makes even poor Victor Emmanuel look regal — a staggering feat of artistic mendacity. But these crusaders in the cause of Women's Rights make the familiar picture of Laura Secord look like something spicy from *La Vie Parisienne.* ✍

• A MODISH NOTION •

I SEE BY THE PAPER that a Toronto burlesque house offers a striking novelty — a dance of chorus girls who are shackled together in pretty imitation of a chain-gang. If I am not mistaken the first appearance of this delicious new idea was in the *The Beggar's Opera* in 1728, which includes a Hornpipe of Prisoners in Chains. Inch by inch Toronto is creeping up on modernity.

• OF THE PURPOSE OF KISSING •

T HE FEDERAL DEPARTMENT of Health and Welfare is taking a strong stand against kissing, I see. They say it

---

✍ *The picture of Mrs. Secord referred to is no longer familiar, having been replaced on the famous chocolate box by a portrait of her in her girlhood, from the brush of the Canadian painter and fantasist, Mr. Clair Stewart. The earlier picture, from a daguerreotype, showed her in a bombazine gown and a starched widow's cap, and it appeared to have been taken after some serious personal bereavement. Mr. Stewart's portrait, which he declares appeared to him in a vision, shows her as looking as though a maple-cream soft centre would not melt in her rosebud mouth.*

spreads the Cold Germ. Very likely, though I must say I am less impressed by the germ theory than I used to be. But after all, who is so poor in spirit that he would not rather have his inamorata's head-cold than his perfect health?

• OF POETIC JUSTICE •

ACROSS THE STREET from my window this afternoon a handsome cat, smoke-grey with a rust spot on its back, sat in the sun. As I admired it a small boy of four or five approached, evil in his eye. With calculated malice he aimed a frightful kick at the cat, but overshot his mark and fell on his podex, whereupon he began to weep bitterly. I leaned out of my window and shouted "Sic semper tyrannis!" and then (as the Latinity of the child seemed doubtful) "Thus perish all tyrants!"

• OF NUPTIAL MERRIMENT •

I LIKE WEDDINGS. They are supposed to be a feminine taste, though I can't think why. Women often weep at weddings, whereas my own instinct is to laugh uproariously, and to encourage the bride and groom with merry whoops. The sight of people getting married exhilarates me; I think that they are doing a fine thing, and I admire them for it. If our society had any place for marriage-brokers I would certainly be one. A wedding breakfast is called so, of course, because people are supposed to go to their weddings fasting; a majority of brides, however, are chock full of nationally advertised breakfast food, bran muffins, bacon and eggs, citrus fruit, and coffee when they go to the altar; I have seen a few with crumbs still on their chins.

• OF A MINDER OF OTHERS' BUSINESS •

I WAS TALKING to a man today who complained that there were no towers on Marchbanks Towers, and that the name was therefore a cheat. I explained to him that although no towers of brick and mortar were to be seen, it possessed several spiritual and incorporeal towers — soaring pinnacles of aspiration and romance, vast fingers of fantasy reaching into the sky. He looked unconvinced, and asked me if the house were insulated? He also suggested that by crowding myself and my family into a space about as big as the Black Hole of Calcutta I could "duplex" the Towers and profit richly by the housing shortage. He even said that by not doing so I was Flying in the Face of Providence. In fact he worked himself up into such a state of mind over what was actually none of his business that I was afraid that he would make himself ill.

• OF WOMEN AND LADIES •

I LAUGHED MERRILY when I read in my morning paper that the Toronto City Council was in a fantod because a magazine writer said that Toronto women were "sleek, ravishing and sexy." Most of their complaint was incoherent but one councillor mastered his blood pressure for long enough to say that this constituted an attack on the good name of Toronto. . . . The root of this trouble lies in the belief of the Toronto Council that all female Torontonians are Ladies. A Lady, in Canada, is a dowdy and unappetizing mammal, who is much given to Culture and Good Works, but derives no sinful satisfaction from either; a Lady is without discernible sex, but can reproduce its kind by a system resembling radar; a Lady does not have to be attractive, because it is sufficient in this wicked world to be Good. There is nothing a Lady hates so much as a Woman, and women are occasionally sleek, ravishing and sexy. The idea that women have invaded Toronto would of course be repugnant to the City Council, which distinguishes itself every year or so by banning *The Decameron* or insisting that male and female authors be kept apart on the shelves of the public libraries, lest an unlicensed pamphlet make its appearance.

• MYOPIA A BOON? •

I LOOKED THROUGH my window into the window opposite this afternoon, and saw what I took to be a woman pouring water out of a jug on a hat; rubbed my purblind eyes, and wiped my spectacles, and found that she was refreshing the water in a vase of asters. Now here is a philosophical problem: Would I have been better off if I had not discovered the truth? Would not the wonder of my first impression have sustained me through a dull and unrewarding day?

• HE FEEDS THE BOOKS WHICH FEED HIM •

*T*HIS MORNING I put leather polish on the bindings of a number of nice old books which I am lucky enough to own. This is a regular yearly rite with me. There are people who would not dream of starving a child who will starve a fine old binding, and think nothing of it. But a child, be it never so stuffed with vitamins, may grow up to be a sorrow and a disgrace to you, whereas a good book will always be a credit and a friend. Let the admirers of the younger generation chew on that one!

• THE PLEASURES OF SILENCE •

I READ A LIST of the most popular songs of the year this morning. I have never heard any of them. Can it be that I live in an ivory tower? The last popular tune that I was able to recognize was *I Duwanna Walk Without You, Baby* which was played over and over again by the jukebox of a restaurant in which I sometimes ate. Now, when I think of it, the smell of stale fried potatoes comes back to me with disgusting clarity. I am probably one of the few men left on this continent who really likes silence. I am thinking of getting ear-plugs, like Herbert Spencer, and uncorking myself only when I am sure that I want to hear what is going on in the outside world.

• OF POLITICAL ORATORY •

*T*HE AVERAGE politician goes through a sentence like a man exploring a disused mine-shaft — blind, groping, timorous and in imminent danger of cracking his shins on a subordinate clause or a nasty bit of subjunctive. There is a popular

superstition that a politician who hangs himself in his own paren-
theses is likely to be an honest fellow, uncorrupted by schooling.
Personally I like my politicians to be literate.... No, madam, to
be quite frank, I did not know that your husband was an M.P....
Very well, if you wish it, I shall talk to someone else; I do not
believe in wasting good talk on people who are plainly unable to
appreciate it.

• OF CHILDREN'S PRETTY WAYS •

I DROPPED IN at a child's birthday party for a few minutes
on my way here, and a tot who had been eating chocolates sat on my lap and amused herself by blowing up a red balloon
and letting it disembarrass itself of its wind right in my face. The
mingled stench of chocolate and cheap rubber was too much for
me, and I fled.

• ABSTINENCE AND COLLYWOBBLES •

A FRIEND DROPPED IN to see me the other evening, and
I asked him to have a glass of beer. "No, thank you,"
said he; "I've got indigestion, and I don't think I ought to throw
any Alcohol down on top of it." Ignoring the coarseness with which
he had phrased his refusal, I said, politely: "Would you very much
mind not referring to honest drink as 'Alcohol'? The alcoholic content of beer is very small. You don't call bread Starch, do you?"
"It's all Alcohol to a man with indigestion," he replied. This I suppose is a great truth, and throws new light on total abstinence
movements.

• OF GETTING A JOB •

D URING THE PAST few weeks I have had chats with several young men and women who think that they would
like to get into the trade of which I am a humble practitioner. What
amazes me about them all is their frankness. "I'd like to get some
practice in a little joint like yours before trying for a job in the Big

City," they say, or words to that effect. As they all come to me without previous experience, this gives me somewhat the feeling of a professor in a kindergarten, whose job it is to set the feet of beginners upon the upward path, soon to be left behind and patronized by my former pupils. And yet they do not want to work for beginner's pay, nor do they seem to sense the painful fact that for six months or so they will be more of a hindrance than a help. I hope that I may be forgiven in Heaven for the bittersweet answers which I return to their demands. It seems odd to me that in our present educational system, in which virtually everything else is taught or half-taught, nobody teaches these young hopefuls how to behave when looking for a job. I do not ask for grovelling humility, but some hint of modesty, and some offer of honest service, would be welcome. Does any man like to be told that he is a given point which beginners in his trade soon hope to pass? *⸘*

• OF GREETING CARDS •

*I*T IS ST. VALENTINE'S DAY, and I received only one card, which was distinctly rude in its message. But even at that I was better off than a young lady I met who had not had even

---

⸘ Persons seeking to enter the profession of journalism are usually sodden with romantic notions about it, and particularly about the big rewards it brings. Marchbanks' Journalistic Training Course was simple: "(a) Read all of the Bible, or at least three-quarters of it, because it is a classical education, a history, and a compendium of ancient wisdom; (b) read the Book of Common Prayer, as a lesson in style, and also of good manners toward your superiors (a grave lack among journalists as a class); (c) read the Complete Works of Shakespeare, for knowledge of human nature and vocabulary; (d) read Defoe's Robinson Crusoe *until you have mastered his ability to make dubious, and even imaginary things seem true. Do not bleat about 'the public's right to know' when you really mean your own right to snoop. But snoop, all the same, and keep your trap shut about your sources or they will turn on you and destroy you."*

an insulting Valentine. The Valentine business has been driven just about as far as it can go by the greeting-card people, who neither slumber nor sleep. It seems to me that there is a card for every occasion that anyone could dream of which has any connotation of rejoicing. The obvious thing now is to devise cards for times of sorrow: "Sorry to Hear You've Lost Your Job"; "Hoping You'll Be Out of Jail Soon"; "Sympathy in Your Period of Receivership"; "Thinking of You During Your Disgrace"; "Bon Voyage, and Best Wishes for Your Deportation." It ought to be possible to work up a brisk trade in these.

• A NATIONAL DUTY •

*R*EADING AT MEALS is a vice to which I am a slave, and today at luncheon I was taking in the contents of the *New Yorker* along with a large plate of chopped cabbage, apples and nuts when I came upon an advertisement in brilliant colour, inserted by the Canadian Government Travel Bureau in order to lure tourists to our fair land. The attractions of Canada, according to this representation, comprise Mounties, totem poles, moose, Scotchmen (with bagpipes), Indians, rabbits, squirrels, deer, bears, sweet old ladies with spinning wheels, and goats with curly horns. This is the sort of thing which makes a Canadian like myself conscious of his lack of picturesque charm; I am useless as tourist bait, and to that extent I am a Bad Citizen. I suppose I could learn to work a spinning wheel, and in a heavy veil I might pose as an old lady if no tourists stopped to investigate me too searchingly. Lots of my friends could pass as totem poles of inferior workmanship. If thousands of Americans come up here expecting gaudy wonders, the least we can do is abet our Government in its pious fraud.

• OF AN IMPOSSIBLE TASK •

*S*OMEBODY WAS hounding me to talk to a women's club this afternoon. "Don't prepare anything; just tell them a few jokes," he said. Anybody who has tried to tell jokes to a horde of women, all wearing their best hats and expecting a cup of club tea, knows how stupid such advice is. "I can't," I replied: "my doctor says I'm dying by inches.". . . This is literally true. I die at the rate of about an inch a year, and the process began about a year ago. As there are only about seventy-two inches of me longitudinally and even fewer latitudinally it will be seen that I haven't long to last, and I must save myself as much as I can.

• OF THE COST OF FOOLS •

I PICKED UP a magazine this afternoon—one of those glossy eager magazines which give their impressionable readers the exciting illusion that they are really thinking—and read an article which said that it costs a family with an income of $5,000 a year the sum of $12,750 to raise a child to the age of eighteen. This seems an inflated price for most of the adults I know, many of whom would be extravagantly capitalized at $50. Still, it is a lamentable truth that a fathead or a mischiefmaker eats just as much, wears out as many clothes, and takes just as much room in a bus or a train as a Socrates or a Leonardo da Vinci. *✎*

• OF UNNATURAL AFFECTION •

T HE SCHOOLS reopened today and troops of children in unwontedly clean clothes rushed past my gate, all agog to resume their studies. I met one little girl who was crying because she had a cold and could not begin her kindergarten class for a few days. I eavesdropped as some of the groups rushed by, and found that they were assessing the relative crabbiness of their teachers. What has come over the children of today, I wonder? In my childhood nobody liked school, and with excellent reason. What

---

As the average income of a Canadian—not, of course, such favoured groups as doctors, dentists, plumbers and architects—is now about $25,000 it will be seen that the cost of the child in question has risen to $63,750. Roll on, birth control!

makes the modern school so attractive? Does the Minister of Education cause a powerful love philtre to be put in the drinking fountains? Stranger things have happened.

• OF ENCOURAGING THE GROWTH OF HAIR •

*A*S THE WEATHER grows warmer I see more and more men going without hats. For my part, I do not feel comfortable without a hat on, and much as I detest the felt chamberpots which are sold nowadays as suitable gentleman's headgear, I always wear one. The people for whom I really feel sorry are the bald men who go without hats in the hope that the sun will bring out a few spears of human hair on their naked noggins; it is my belief that the sun is an enemy of hair, and that if you have a tendency to be bald, the sun will encourage it. Consider this matter scientifically. Scotchmen have hairy knees, for although they wear no kneeclouts their climate is cold, damp and sunless. But African savages do not have hairy knees, because they get too much sun on their knees for the hair to flourish. If bald men really want hair, they should wear hats filled with damp and slimy moss; this would cause hair to grow as a form of protection.

• OF CHIVALRY SCORNED •

I TOOK A LADY'S ARM as she was stepping off a curb this afternoon, and she snatched it from me with a great show of offence. But I was raised in the Old School, and I automatically grab at any woman who is changing her level, to prevent her from tumbling down or wrenching her ankle. I cannot rid myself of a traditional belief that women are delicate creatures, though reason and observation assure me that most of them are as tough as old boots.

Fish

• OF ORTHODOXY IN BREAKING HIS FAST •

I AM STAYING in a hotel and suffer the inconvenience of being asked what I want for breakfast. I am not accustomed to answering such a question. For many years my breakfast has not varied by so much as a calorie, and I consider any breakfast but my usual one a heathen abomination. In the matter of breakfast, I am an out-and-out Tory. If my day is not to fall in ruins it must be founded upon a sliced orange, a dish of porridge, one slice of toast with marmalade, and three cups of weak tea. I know men of shifting and uneasy faith who change breakfast foods as easily as they change their minds; I know women of doubtful virtue who will jump from toast to hot rolls with a light laugh and a wanton glance from beneath their sweeping eyelashes. I know inordinate men who eat meat and eggs for breakfast, and deliquescent women who break their fast with a rusk and a glass of lemon juice. But mine is the one, true, apostolic breakfast, ordained at Creation, and enduring till the twilight of Time.

• OF SMUTTY JESTS •

A KIND FRIEND has sent me a Bay of Fundy lobster for Christmas, and I decided to eat it last night, as lobsters grow impatient if kept too long. I spent quite a time trying to undo its buttons and find its zipper, for a lobster is one of Nature's most baffling packages, though a noble sight. At last I had to call for skilled assistance. The Skilled Assistant laid the lobster bare in no time, reminding me of a jest much favoured by Gaffer Marchbanks, my great-great-grandfather: "What made the lobster blush?" "It saw the salad dressing." This was considered delightfully salacious when

Gaffer was a roystering blade, and he once had his face slapped for whispering it to a Nice Girl. The incident deepened his determination to marry a girl who was not Nice, and their descendants all suffer from a taste for ribaldry which I have never been able to root out of my heart. . . . You like smutty talk? My dear madam, why didn't you say so before?

• OF FLORICULTURAL FAILURE •

I RECEIVED a pamphlet this morning urging me to get to work on my lawn. "One can hardly do lawn work too early; grass seed loves cool weather, and so does the grass itself," I read. Looking out of the window I saw at least two feet of snow on the ground, and more was falling; even if grass seed does love cool weather, I am not going to dig through all that snow to oblige it. Nor am I going to make my sweet pea trench this week, as the pamphlet advises; I have planted sweet peas for three successive years, and I have not had a single bloom yet; therefore I cannot see that it makes much difference when I dig my trench; September would be early enough. Sam Sours Soil and Marchbanks Mars Mould. Just as women are forbidden to enter Italian vineyards for fear of blighting them, all sensible people keep me out of their gardens, and frankly, I am happy to admire them from the non-working side of the fence.

• OF WIND AND WATER •

A CHILD WHO received a plastic version of a tin whistle appealed to me today for a lesson in how to play it. This was a sop to my vanity which I could not resist, for I fancy myself as a performer on all tootling instruments. But when I took the thing to demonstrate, it slobbered half a pint of spittle on my waistcoat, and depressed me deeply. This is the trouble with all blown instruments; they drool. Brass instruments have special valves to collect this deposit, and one of the less pleasing sights in an orchestra is the frantic shakings of the trumpeters as they void their ptyalism upon the floor, and at almost any Wagner opera the conductor enters and leaves the orchestra pit in his rubbers. Nor is it nice to take over a wind instrument which someone else has been playing — particularly when one's pupil has been hitting the humbugs hard all afternoon.

• OF WORDS AND THEIR EFFECTS •

I WENT TO the movies last night and saw, among other things, a film about soil erosion called *The Rape of the Earth*. The word "rape" was so irresistibly humorous to two girls and their escorts in my neighbourhood that I thought they would burst; their sniggers were like the squirtings of a hose when it is first turned on. Some people are affected by some words as slot machines are affected by coins; feed in your word, and the result is invariable. Feed "Communist" into an old gent with a quarter of a million dollars, and out comes a huffy lecture; feed "Booze" into a prohibitionist, and out will come highly imaginative statistics about accidents and insanity; feed "Rape" into girls and boys and you get this bromo-seltzer fizzing.

• OF ADULT IGNORANCE •

A LITTLE GIRL asked me to read her a piece about clouds this evening, and I did so, although experience has taught me that reading things to children always ends up in an uncomfortable quiz, with me in the role of Marchbanks the Moron. Sure enough, she asked me where all the vapour comes from which forms the clouds. I took a leap into the dark and said that it was caused by the warm earth meeting cold air. Was the air wet, then, she asked. Yes, I said firmly. Then why weren't our clothes wet? They are wet, said I, feeling like a man stepping off a cliff. If the air is wet why don't we drown? Because our lungs are made to stand it. Like fish? Yes, like fish. Are people a kind of fish? Yes. . . . It just shows where a little child can lead you. . . . And yet it would be worse to say "I don't know." Children never forgive their elders for their ignorance. It is obviously a grown-up's business to know.

• OF THE CONSERVATISM OF YOUTH •

*C*HILDREN ARE the most confirmed Tories I have ever met. Today I heard a group of them boasting among themselves about how high they could count; such improbable figures as drillions and squillions were being lightly bandied about by the bragging tots. I remember that when I was in kindergarten the same sort of blowing to the teacher used to go on morning after morning. I never joined in it, for although I am almost illiterate mathematically, I grasped very early in life that anyone who can count to ten can count upward indefinitely if he is fool enough to do so. But apparently the kindergarten set of today are threshing the same old straw. Tories, that's what children are, perpetuating the same old nonsense from generation to generation.

• OF WASTED EFFORT •

I WAS AT A PARTY last night at which the refreshments consisted solely of cheese, biscuits and beer. This seems to me to be an admirable lesson in simplicity, and the party was a great success. Not, mind you, that I dislike elaborate parties; let the footmen cluster around me with the quail on toast, the caviar and the anchovies; let sherry trifle be heaped upon crêpes suzette and liqueur cherries swim in the zabaglione. I can take parties as elaborate as they come. But many times my heart has bled for the hostess who has slaved for hours to produce four kinds of sandwiches and two kinds of cake, and who is so exhausted by her labours that she casts a gloom over her own party. Far, far better to offer something simple and good, in a spirit of revelry, than to toil to produce pretentious mediocrity. It is the spirit that makes a party, and not dainty sandwiches, cut in the form of hearts and tasting like spades.

• OF HIS CONCERTINA BROW •

I CAME ACROSS a chart in *Life* magazine yesterday which was designed to help me decide whether I am a Highbrow, a Lowbrow, an Upper Middlebrow or a Lower Middlebrow. After some pondering I think I must be a Concertina Brow, for I like such Lowbrow things as beer and parlour sculpture, and I also like such apparently Highbrow things as red wine, art, ballet and pre-Bach music. But then I am a great fellow for the theatre, which is rated as only Upper Middlebrow. I even like front-yard sculpture, which is supposed to be Lower Middlebrow, though I also admire the fat naked female statues of Maillol, which are Upper Middlebrow. In short, my brow heaves up and down alarmingly, like a concertina, and I have a few tastes which do not fit into any of these categories, like my affection for corduroy trousers, and my fondness for bananas dipped in hot coffee. I am inclined to think that it must be very dull to have one's brow stuck at a particular point; I am glad my brow is able to expand and contract.

• OF BIRDS •

I MET AN ornithologist just before dinner and as the conversation lagged, I sought to beguile him by talking about his hobby. Dale Carnegie says that you should always talk to people about what interests them, whether it interests you or not, so I began thus: "I saw a funny-looking bird this morning; a blackish bird, or maybe it was a dirty brown; what would you say it was?" He pricked up his ears. "Had it a yellow spot about half a centimetre in diameter under each wing?" he asked. "I am not accustomed to peeping into the armpits of birds," I replied, haughtily, "but it had two feet, instead of the usual four, if that gives you a clue." "What size did you say?" he continued. "Roughly the size of a two-year-old child's shoe," I said after some thought, "but rather a different shape; it was shaped like an ocarina, or a sweet potato." "Was its mate nearby?" he persisted. "I couldn't say," I parried, "but it was on the lawn of a church, and I don't suppose it would go there with anybody else's mate, do you?" "I think you must have seen a squirrel," said he, in what I think was meant to be a satirical tone. And yet I am always nice to ornithologists when they talk about my subjects.

• OF HIS LACK OF SOCIAL GRACE •

OUR HOST asked me before dinner if I play bridge. No, I don't. An ancestor of mine was once a fair euchre player, but the talent for cards died out of the family when he passed. In my youth, when I still thought that by Herculean efforts I might turn myself into a social success, I tried to read a book about bridge, but it was worse than geometry. For the same reason I tried to learn to dance, and although I enjoyed it I found that I got on better without a partner than with one, and this was considered eccentric in the circle in which I moved. ∮ Still pursuing the fleeting goal of popularity, I attempted to become a raconteur, and memorized several funny stories and a number of witty rejoinders which I dragged painfully into any conversation in which I was engaged; this device failed me, also. It was quite a long time before I realized that I lacked the qualities which make a man the darling of a large and brilliant circle of friends, and resigned myself to being an outcast and a curmudgeon. Nowadays when I am asked to a party I sit in a corner and snarl at anyone who comes near me. This is called Being a Character, and although it is not very much fun for anyone, it is the best I can manage.

• OF DIVORCE •

A MAN BEWAILED the increase of divorce today until I could bear it no longer. "My dear creature," I cried, "you attack this problem from the wrong end. It is not the frequency of divorce which makes the times wicked; it is the wickedness of the

---

∮ As was so often the case, Marchbanks was ahead of his time. Nobody nowadays dances with a partner. Simply to step onto the floor and face a woman who is pretending to be spastic, while oneself feigning an epileptic fit, is enough for social success.

times which increases divorce. We live in an age when man is expected to waste and wear out as much as he can. Do we not call the ordinary citizen a 'consumer'? He buys 'lifetime' fabrics and soon wears them out. He buys a 'lifetime' pen and a 'lifetime' watch and in ten years he wants new ones. His books are not lifetime friends; they are the enthusiasm of a month. He is sneered at if he drives a perfectly good car which is ten years old. Is it any wonder, then, that he exhausts one 'lifetime' marriage and seeks another? Mind your economics, and your morals will take care of themselves." This bit of Marxian sophistry shocked him, and he fled. . . . No, madam, our hostess did not tell me that you were a divorcée. Tell me, are you a discard, or a discardee?

• OF DRABBERY AND SQUIRTDOM •

THE ENTERTAINMENT tycoons don't seem able to let musicians alone. I see that there is now a musical show in New York purporting to reveal "the romance of Tschaikovsky," though it has long been an open secret that Tschaikovsky had a neurotic dislike of women, and that much of the tragedy of his life arose from this cause. A new movie is based on the love of Robert Schumann for Clara Wieck, attributing his greatness as a composer to this inspiration. Bunk! Pure bunk! And yet I suppose it flatters a section of the public to think that the biological urges which they share with the great somehow reduce the great to their level. The points of resemblance between great people and paltry people are infinitely more numerous than the points of difference: they all eat, sleep, fall in love, catch cold, and use handkerchiefs. It is good business to pretend that no real difference exists, and Hollywood has long known how to exploit it. . . . But I am powerfully reminded of Théophile Gautier's division of men into two groups, The Flamboyant and The Drab; my sympathies and loyalties are always with The Flamboyant, of whom Churchill is one, though his followers are mostly Drabs. But this is very much the age of the Drab—the apotheosis of The Squirt. The Squirts and Drabs are not worth much singly, but when they organize into gangs and parties they can impose Drabbery and Squirtdom on quite a large part of mankind.

• OF TRAGIC FLAB •

*P*SYCHOLOGISTS, I read, now maintain that human fat is a sign of misery, and that fat people are immature, frustrated and anxious for protection. I have known this for years. Indeed I am known to the medical profession as the first man to identify Tragic Flab, a lardlike substance which is secreted under the skins of unhappy people, and which may be observed as a characteristic of many great figures in literature. Was not Hamlet described by his mother as "fat and scant of breath"? I have long maintained that Charles Laughton is the ideal Hamlet. I have also suggested that Romeo and Juliet should both be shown getting fatter and fatter as the play grows more and more tragic, until they are barely able to shift their carcasses about the stage in the final act. King Lear, too, should obviously be an immensely fat old man, weighed down with Tragic Flab. I wish psychologists would stop coming out with my old notions as if they were new discoveries.

• AVOIRDUPOIS A CROSS •

I LUNCHED EARLIER today with several men, one of whom was of generous proportions; a former athlete, the passing of years had softened his contours, while adding to his physical magnificence. I watched him with an eagle eye, and he ate consideringly, without haste or greed; calorie for calorie, he probably ate a little less than the others. Yet they tormented him unmercifully all through the meal about his weight, and about his entirely imaginary voracity. Gaunt, lank men who stoked themselves like furnaces paused only in their intensive fuelling to gird at him for his bulk. This is one of the great injustices of the world. A big man is always accused of gluttony, whereas a wizened or osseous man can eat like a refugee at every meal, and no one ever notices his greed. I have seen runts who never weighed more than ninety-six pounds when soaking wet outeat 200 pounders, and poke fun at the fat man even as they licked their plates and sucked the starch out of their napkins. No wonder fat men are philosophers; they are forced to it.

• OF CRUELTY TO VEGETABLES •

*T*HIS IS THE TIME of year when newspaper offices are embarrassed by gifts of deformed turnips, arthritic beets, spastic pumpkins and glandular potatoes. Whenever a farmer digs up something which should at once be returned to the merciful and all-covering earth, he rushes with it to his local paper, requesting that his shameful trophy be displayed in the window. I know what he wants; he wants people to laugh at that poor afflicted vegetable. Now it is several centuries since deformed people were regarded as objects of mirth. Even deformed animals are not the big attraction at the country fairs that they once were. Surely it is time that our pity was extended to include the Mongoloid, the moronic and the cretinous specimens of the root world? Has the Royal Society of Vegetarians and Nut Fooders nothing to say against this cruel practice?

• SCOTTISH SPORTS AND PASTIMES •

*T*HIS IS ST. ANDREW'S DAY, and although I do not belong to the Scottish Branch of the family (it spells its name Marjoribanks, which is wasteful, and therefore unScotch) I can never let the day pass unnoticed. My uncle Hamish Marjoribanks was an implacable Jacobite to his dying day, and at breakfast on St. Andrew's Day he would throw great gobs of porridge at the chromo of Queen Victoria which hung on his dining-room wall, crying "There's for ye, Hanover!" in a fierce voice. His wife, who was somewhat more reconciled to Culloden and the Act of Union, would spend the rest of the day swabbing the Royal Likeness with a dampened cloth. Uncle Hamish demanded a grand dinner at night, and when the capercailzie was brought in and carried round the table, he would insist that we all jump up on the seats of our chairs, put one foot on the table, and drink a largish glass of neat whisky, crying something which sounded like "Slachan!" at one another; then we all threw our glasses into the fireplace. After dinner Uncle Hamish would tell us how, if everyone had his rights, some obscure Bavarian prince would be King of England and he

(Uncle Hamish) would undoubtedly be a powerful figure at Court. It was all very exhausting, and cost a fortune in glass.

• OF MERRIMENT IN A MONASTERY •

*T*HE GENTLEMAN across the table was very much interested in my assertion before dinner that I hoped to spend the Christmas Season in a Trappist monastery in Quebec and asked me when I was going there. The fact is, I am not going at all. The Trappists won't have me. I spent a Christmas with them a few years ago and made a rather painful mistake. As everyone knows, Trappists live under a vow of silence, which I do not. I tried to keep as quiet as I could, and on Christmas Eve I consoled myself in my room in the guest-house with a bottle of rum. At midnight there was a tap on my door and the guest-master, Brother Eustachian, and his assistant, Brother Fallopian, stood outside; they showed me a typewritten notice which said "All guests are invited to join the brothers in the Oratory." I assumed (excusably, I still think) that an Oratory would be a place where one could talk, and when we got there I opened a discussion on the subject of Jehovah's Witnesses, and passed out a few pamphlets. In the ensuing hullabaloo, I only escaped with my life. When I wrote for a room this year, I got an immediate reply saying that they were completely booked up. After all, I was only trying to brighten their lives, and when I recited my limerick about the young maid of Madras, I was certain that some of them laughed—faint laughter like the unwrapping of tissue paper.

• A SYSTEM OF CALISTHENICS •

*F*ROM TIME TO TIME I am bothered by the thought that I ought to take some exercise. Usually I am successful in fighting down this ugly notion, but sometimes I toy with the idea of getting one of those machines which exercise a man against his will by rolling, hauling, squeezing and folding him. What I really want is a series of searching exercises which can be done while sitting in a chair. Years ago I read that caged lions and tigers keep themselves fit by stretching and for a while I used to stretch whenever I had a spare minute, straining my halliards and squirming my binnacle to the accompaniment of alarming cracks, creaks, and pops. But it is awfully easy to stop stretching. I think I shall re-examine this theory, and perhaps evolve Marchbanks Torso Tensions for the Sedentary. Advertisements will appear of me wrapped around my office chair, with the message: "Puny? Flabby? Torpid? In Thirty Days You can be like this Masked Marvel! No Costly Equipment! No Time Required! No Effort! Tear the Seat Off your Chair and send with Five Hundred Dollars for Trial Booklet! Be Muscular the Marchbanks Way!"

• OF SNOW REMOVAL •

I PERCEIVE THAT your city has no municipal arrangement for clearing the streets. As a result, when I went out for a walk this afternoon, I experienced a wide variety of footing. Before the houses of young and vigorous men, full of Civic Spirit and holiday food, the walk was clear to the cement; where less hearty citizens had their abode, there was a track about as wide as a snow shovel, and lumpy; the walks of the aged, the arthritic and the hung-over were pitiful muddles, with snow everywhere; in front of vacant lots it was necessary to break a track. Some citizens were shovelling as I passed. It is a pitiful sight, in a city renowned for learning, to see a graduate of the class of '07 with a prolapsed abdomen and eyes dimmed by much study trying to do a job which could be done much better by a horse or even, in these mad, rushing days, by a bulldozer.

• OF A DRAMA FESTIVAL •

I WENT TO THE Eastern Ontario Drama Festival last week, a function which, being of a cultural nature, was conducted with appropriate sedateness, as though a body were lying in the next room. Except for a few people of uncommon distinction, the gentlemen present forbore to dress; in histories of fashion, this will be known as The Century of The Sack Suit; I myself wore a dainty elephant-grey number, and a white shirt which I borrowed from my Uncle Fortunatus. . . .

On the Friday I went to see a group of accomplished Ottawa amateurs play Noel Coward's *Blithe Spirit*, which, as everybody knows, is about a man who has two wives — one alive and one a ghost — and enchants the audience with a spectacle of bigamy agreeably spiced with adultery. The final fit of the Festival was on Saturday night, and as some of the plays failed to grip my attention, I permitted myself to reflect on a few matters such as: (a) why amateurs in society plays never black the soles of their boots, which professionals are always careful to do; (b) why amateurs whose voices and deportment suggest a barn-raising at Pumpkin Centre choose to do plays about hoity-toity English people; (c) why plays about farm life (including the works of S. Marchbanks) invariably include a character who is crazy, or religious, or both. Perhaps the solution lies in a play by S. Marchbanks about the *bon ton* of Toronto or Ottawa — a play abounding in references to such hallmarks of high-toned society as butter knives, finger bowls, adultery and flush toilets.

• OF WEEDICULTURE •

*T*HIS HAS BEEN a great day for me! This morning the judges from the Horticultural Society arrived at the Towers, and made a tour of the grounds, murmuring with admiration. I was pleased by their approbation, but judge of my excitement when my name appeared in the Prize List. Let me show you my citations:

FINEST SHOW OF MIXED WEEDS (for garden tended solely by the owner): First Prize — S. Marchbanks.

FINEST SINGLE WEED IN NATIVE STATE: A magnificent *Amaranthus retroflexus* (Common Pigweed) — property of S. Marchbanks.

LARGEST FOLIAGE ON ANY WEED: A stupendous *Rumex obtusifolius* (Burdock) — reared with great care by S. Marchbanks.

FINEST RARE OR SPECIMEN WEED: *Cicuta Maculata* (Cowbane) — cherished under glass by S. Marchbanks.

At last I have found a branch of gardening in which I excel! From now on my course is clear, and the Marchbanks Weed Sanctuary begins tonight.

• OF RADIO •

I BOUGHT A NEW RADIO licence *f* today, although I don't suppose I use my radio more than twenty times a year, having full use of my vision, and being able to read advertisements for coffee, stomach medicine, and soap in the newspapers at my leisure. I grudged the $2.50, and I hope that the C.B.C. will not regard it as my personal endorsement of their artistic policy. Then I went to see a radio broadcast put on the air, and yearned mightily to get my hands on a Hammond organ which was being played. It has been a lifelong ambition of mine to lie at full length on the pedalboard of an organ, with the power full on, just to see what kind of apocalyptic roar the thing would emit.

• OF THE TRUE FUNCTION OF RADIO •

I LISTENED TO THE news on the radio last night — a thing I rarely do, as it is my experience that good news always seems better the following morning, whereas bad news at night disturbs my sleep. The news consisted of a list of people who died during the day in a variety of distressing circumstances. Such harping on death annoys and depresses me. What we want is a newscaster with second sight (they could probably import one from the Highlands of Scotland) who would give the names of children who had been born each day who would, in twenty-five or thirty years, be either great leaders and benefactors of mankind, or notable scoundrels. What we want is not news of who has left the earth,

---

f Radio licences were abolished in the Dominion Budget of 1953. Marchbanks, the Slave of Duty, always paid his, but many citizens took delight in cheating their country in this respect.

but something resembling the passenger list of an ocean liner, telling us who is joining the human race and what we may expect of them. There is no news about a death; one of the few certain things in life is that we shall all die. But if the radio could, now and again, announce the birth of a philosopher, or a great artist, or a nasty little baby who will grow up to be a Hitler, I would pay for my yearly licence in a somewhat more sprightly manner.

• OF EQUINE NONCHALANCE •

I WATCHED A MAN giving his trotting-horse a workout this afternoon. It was a noble animal with a great deal of what appeared to be adhesive tape on its legs, and when it moved it had the high-stepping, galvanized action of an usher at a society wedding. I was particularly entranced by the way it rolled its eyes. It has been my observation that the spirit of a man or an animal may be judged from this characteristic alone; a wildly rolling eye is invariably the accompaniment of a proud and daring spirit. Most of us, of course, have eyes like green grapes that have been partly squashed, floating in pools of mutton gravy, and we are incapable of moving them to right or left. . . . When the horse trotted its trainer allowed one of his feet to dangle nonchalantly from the side of the sulky; somehow this mannerism seemed to embody the whole devil-may-care attitude of the trotting fraternity. I watched until I was chilled, and then trotted home, trying to roll my eyes.

• OF UNCONTROLLED DESIRE •

*T*HE ONWARD MARCH of statistical research sometimes provokes me to incredulous protest. For instance, I see in the paper today a statement attributed to a "hair stylist" (which is what hairdressers now call themselves) that "Upswept hair-dos reduce woman's sex appeal 60 per cent." How does he know? Frankly, I think that he is wrong. Indeed, I once knew a fellow who found upswept hair-dos so provocative that he used to roam about at parties, nibbling the napes of the necks of any women whose hair was so arranged. It was the little curly wisps at the bottom of the hair-do, he explained, which drove him to this: they reminded him of hearts of celery. Sometimes the women were flattered; sometimes they screamed; sometimes their escorts offered to punch him on the nose. I gave up his acquaintance, considering his conduct embarrassingly eccentric, yet I suppose he did no more than yield to an impulse which afflicts all men at some time or other, but which they shove down into the reeking cesspit of the Unconscious.

· SOCIAL EMBARRASSMENT ·

*F*OR MANY YEARS I have used a cigarette holder to keep the smoke out of my eyes as I work. Last week I bought a new one, for which I have already conceived a hearty dislike. I have a supply of little bombs, filled with crystals which look like chips from a moth-ball factory, and I am expected to put a little bomb in the gizzard of the holder every now and then, and to remove it when it becomes discoloured and obviously drenched with poisons, tars and harsh irritants. But I find that two cigarettes are quite enough to turn one of these pretty, white little bombs into a stinking obscenity, and if I carry the holder, containing one of them, in my waistcoat pocket people whisper behind their hands and leave cakes of brick-coloured soap about the place in an obvious manner, wounding my self-esteem and causing me to lose face. I cannot possibly afford to change the little bombs every time I smoke a cigarette, nor do I want to become an object of loathing. And, being of a frugal disposition, I do not want to throw my new holder into the garbage, or give it to a tramp. Other people do not get into these embarrassing difficulties. Why am I thus cursed? *

Here Marchbanks reveals himself, without much shame, as a Smoker. Whether he would dare to do so if he were writing today is very much in question. But he has always insisted that every human creature has a right to one reprehensible habit, so as to avoid total perfection, and therefore social ostracism. What do the people do now who used to smoke? The mind recoils from speculation on the subject.

• OF HIS LEWD TONGUE •

I WAS TOLD TODAY by a friend that some of my more respectable acquaintances are deeply offended by the frequent references to privies and allied subjects which crop up in my conversation. There is an explanation for my grossness, madam, which I shall impart to you: when but an infant I was kidnapped by pirates and for the first twenty-one years of my life I shared their criminal pursuit, albeit unwillingly. During this time the vilest and most degraded circumstances of life—rapine, barratry, drunkenness, privies and cannibalism—were all that I knew; no childish innocence relieved the blackness of my character and no good woman's tears wore a channel through which delicacy of feeling might have penetrated my flinty bosom. But upon my twenty-first birthday I made my escape, and sought shelter in the hut of a snowy-haired old journalist who treated me with the first kindness that I had ever known, and instructed me in the rudiments of his lowly but necessary trade. In the employment of a journalist I have remained ever since, eking out a meagre but honest living and trying to forget those early horrors. But now and then, when swept along on the high tide of prose, some telltale evidence of my pirate days creeps into what I am saying, and the hateful word "privy" bursts upon the air. Now that you know my dreadful secret, can you find it in your heart to censure me? ✒

• OF HIS REMOTE BENEVOLENCE •

M ONTHS AGO I wrote to a class of school children in the U.S.A. on a subject in which they, and I, were interested. Today I received thirty-seven letters in return. One boy tells me that his appreciation of my letter is "greatly high"; another

---

✒ *This was written at a time when the understanding of the seamy side of life was much more restricted in Canada than it is now. But Delicacy is by no means dead. Even at the time of writing, Mrs. Margaret Laurence, a Canadian novelist of unimpeachable reputation, is under fire from the Forces of Refinement because she refuses to subscribe to the*

tells me that he was "greatly joyed" to hear from me, and wishes that we could meet because "to have a friend and not to see him is very uneasy"; a little girl ends her letter charmingly thus: "There are many other things I would like to say, but you know how it is in School"; my favourite, however, is the little girl who says: "I have often pictured a writer with a serious mind and a boredom for children." Several of them asked me for photographs of myself, which I shall not send, for fear of destroying the notion they have of me as a benevolent old gentleman who has no boredom for children. . . . The success of this venture leads me to wonder whether I do not get on better with children by letter than face to face? In a letter I am able to express all the easy-going affability which I feel when I am alone in a room; I find it hard to do this when I am in a room with thirty-seven children. Perhaps I shall go down in history as a Great Lover of Children By Correspondence.

• OF MONEY IN GALLSTONES •

I CHATTED WITH that man on our hostess' right before dinner, and he tells me that the Chinese value gallstones highly for their supposed medicinal properties, and that they will pay as high as $60 a pound for gallstones in good condition. The sale of extirpated gallstones should certainly be taken into consideration whenever it is necessary to finance the building of a new hospital.

• OF ANTISEPSIS •

I T WAS HOT LAST NIGHT, and as I brewed myself a refreshing pot of tea, I reflected that without tea and alcohol the human race would probably have perished of its own filthiness centuries ago. Our modern supplies of clean drinking

---

doctrine that babies are found in cabbage patches. Acceptance of the full gamut of human experience, from high to low, is greatly feared by a substantial number of Canadians.

water are a thing of the last sixty or seventy years; before that time water was so unspeakably polluted that nobody in his right senses drank the stuff, and used it for washing only with the greatest caution. ∯ The nations of the East preserved themselves by drinking beverages in which antiseptic herbs had been boiled; the nations of the West drank enough alcohol in one form or another to keep themselves reasonably pure, if a little pixillated. Even today alcohol is the great sterilizer, and water is used only if it has been boiled. I pondered on mankind's debt to booze for a while, and then pensively added a noggin of rum to my tea, just to make sure that I came to no harm.

· THE MIGHTY MINDS OF PHOTOGRAPHERS ·

I ATTENDED A lecture on photography this afternoon and was bemused by the complexity of it. It seems to resemble astrology closely, and also the mysterious tables by which the date of Easter is determined. If you want to take a picture of the baby, or your aunt gardening, and if your camera is anything more complicated than a pinhole affair which you have made yourself, you must base your calculations on the Golden Number, the Julian year, sidereal time, the helix of the parallax, and whether or not the Virgin has entered the house of the Ram. It brought back the sensations which overcame me years ago when I tried to read Chaucer's treatise on the use of the astrolabe. It gave me a new reverence for photographers, and convinced me forever that they are mightier fellows than mere painters. A painter, like Rubens or Velasquez, is just a chap with a knack; a photographer is a blood brother to the Astronomer Royal.

∯ Clean drinking water, indeed! Marchbanks must swallow those words —but not the water—now, when everybody except elected officials well knows that the filth of our water supplies is a greater threat to mankind than atomic fission.

• OF PROGRESSIVE COMMENDATION •

I WAS READING Dorothy Dix this afternoon; she says that it is permissible for a young man to tell a girl he knows fairly well that she has pretty ankles; from this I assume that the better he knows her the higher he may praise her.

• OF PAPER HANGING •

I UNDERTOOK a long-deferred job of paper-hanging this afternoon; there is a knack to this work which I have not fully mastered. It looks simple enough; the paper-hanger slops a lot of paste on a length of paper, throws it carelessly at the wall, gives it some swipes with a brush, and after a few repetitions of this child's play, the room is done. Unfortunately I was working on a ceiling, and no sooner had I fastened a bit of paper at one end than the other end descended with slow grace, like a ballet dancer, and stuck to my head. What I needed was a ladder on wheels, and somebody to push me rapidly back and forth, as I stroked the paper. Lacking this convenience, I got into some postures which reminded me of the famous statue of Laocoön struggling with the serpents. When the job was done, it lacked that rather character-less professional smoothness; at night the wrinkles catch the light in a manner which will undoubtedly soon be all the rage with professional decorators. "Marchbanks Log Cabin Style," it will be known as.

• DESIRING THIS MAN'S ART AND THAT MAN'S SCOPE •

I WENT TO THE country with some children to get pussy-willows the other day. They asked me how the pussy-willows became woolly? I did not know, but made up some quaint lies which pleased them. Psychologists frown on such conduct, I know, but I can't help it. Sometimes, however, I wish that my only ability did not lie in the direction of concocting untruths of one sort and another. I wish that I were a great woodcarver, or a wonderfully minute jeweller, or a bookbinder—somebody who can make something satisfying with his hands. In an earlier age I suppose I would have been a professional story-teller, sitting in the market place, spinning yarns and asking for alms — rightly despised by all the craftsmen who had tangible wares to sell. . . . But one must not quarrel with one's fate, and as it has pleased Providence to make me a sort of accredited prevaricator I must be content.

• OF DISCONTENT WITH ONE'S APPEARANCE •

*W*HY IS IT that people never like pictures of themselves? Earlier today I had a chance to observe a large group who were looking at a number of pictures in which they appeared in various guises, and while they agreed that admirable likenesses of everyone else had been caught they were deeply dismayed by their own faces and forms. Do we all cherish an ideal likeness of ourselves in our bosoms? Do we, when we peep into the mirror, refuse to see the wrinkled necks, the ant-eater noses, the cauliflower ears, the wens and bubukles which are indubitably our own? Or is it that we are all so discontented that we cannot bear the hideous forms with which nature, unwise eating and tight boots have endowed us? Or are we distressed that such horrible scarecrows should house such elegant souls as we know ours to be? I cannot answer these questions. I only know that I have never seen any-one look at a picture of himself with unalloyed pleasure. . . . No, madam, I did *not* mean anything personal by my remarks about wrinkled necks. . . . Oh, very well! If the cap fits, wear it.

• HE ENLARGES THE SCOPE OF MUSIC •

I INVENTED A new musical instrument today, by one of those happy accidents so often recorded in the lives of great men. I sat down to play my piano, which gave out a loud, wiry whine whenever I touched B natural in the middle octave. Raised the lid and investigated and found that some careless child had left a glass alley on the strings. In fishing the alley out I dropped it on the strings again, and it produced a succession of delicate, tinkling arpeggii, very pleasing to the ear. I repeated this a few times, and then got some more alleys and tried chucking them into the piano in handfuls; this was wonderful. Then I played a little piece on the keyboard, and threw alleys into the works at a musically appropriate moment. Superb! I shall patent this device of mine and market it as "Marchbanks' Fairy Harp." The soap operas will all snatch at it, I expect, and the electric organ will fall into disfavour.

• OF FEIGNED INDUSTRY •

I SPENT A BUSY DAY today, but got little done. This is because I am at last becoming perfect in the art of seeming busy, even when very little is going on in my head or under my hands. This is an art which every man learns, if he does not intend to work himself to death. By shifting papers about my desk, writing my initials on things, talking to my colleagues about things which they already know, fumbling in books of reference, making notes about things which are already decided, and staring out the window while tapping my teeth with a pencil, I can successfully counterfeit a man doing a heavy day's work. Nobody who watched me would ever be able to guess what I was doing, and the secret of this is that I am not doing anything, or creating anything, and my brain is having a nice rest. I am, in short, an executive.

• HYMEN HASTE! THY TORCH PREPARE •

I PASSED A CAR which had a crude sign on the back reading "Just Married and Away to the West to Build a Nest." The car was going east. I gaped at the occupants, a young couple who looked very serious, not to say worried. But as it can never be said that Marchbanks failed to encourage the noble institution of marriage, I waved at them, and shook hands with myself like a Chinaman or a boxing champion, and leered and wagged my head in what I believed to be a benevolent manner. They caught sight of me, and their jaws dropped, and they hastily looked away. It is very difficult to be a ray of sunshine in this self-conscious world.

• OF HIS BITE •

*M*Y DENTIST told me last week that modern man eats too much soft food, which weakens his bite and loosens his teeth. But this afternoon I bit my tongue with such vigour that I nearly bit it off. I do not understand how anyone could possibly have a stronger or more destructive bite than I have. Probably I am the only writer and critic in Canada of whom it can truthfully be said that his bite is worse than his bark.

• OF RATIONALIZING ANGER •

*T*HE LADY ON my right passed the afternoon at the hairdresser's. Such women are full of information, for they read old copies of digests and news magazines under the drier. She told me that a psychologist says that it is wrong to repress anger, as anger creates adrenalin and if this nasty stuff is not used up it poisons its owner, giving him indigestion, communism, rabies or ulcers. Anger, this fellow says, should be rationalized by violent physical action. It seems to me that the trouble with this idea is that the kind of violent physical action which follows anger is awfully hard to explain. If a man disagrees with me, and I become angry and pop him on the button and then say, "Nothing personal, you understand; I'm just rationalizing my anger and working off my excess adrenalin," he will probably secrete a lot of adrenalin himself and pop me back again. Then I shall fill up with adrenalin for a second time, and be compelled to re-pop him, and when the cops arrive it will look just like a low brawl, and not like a high-class adrenalin-rationalizing party. I wish psychologists wouldn't fill women up with such stuff; I am slopping over with adrenalin all the time and it doesn't seem to hurt me—very much.

• OF UNIVERSAL DEMOCRACY •

*I*WENT FOR A WALK this afternoon and pondered about democracy. Good as it is, no one can pretend that we have carried it out to its logical conclusion. The equality of man and man is now pretty well established, but what is being done to spread democracy among animals? Is the junk-wagon horse treated as the equal of the race-horse? Does the thoroughbred Boxer receive the same treatment as the mongrel? There is not even equality of opportunity within such fairly homogeneous groups as dogs and horses, much less among all beasts. Is a duck ever given a chance to run in the Grand National? And yet who is to say that a duck, given the proper education, and the right food and housing, might not some day win that famous race? And this question of equality among animals brings up the greater question: what is Man that he should consider himself the Lord of Creation? Will we not realize that all life is sacred and all animals — man included — equals (or "on all fours" if you prefer the expression)? There will be no real equality until our Parliament is filled with fowls, rodents, and horned cattle, as well as men. Then we will have earned the right to talk about Democracy.

• OF PROFESSIONALISM IN GRAMMAR •

I HAD A WRANGLE today with a man who said that there was no such thing as grammar, and that "the living speech" was good speech. He talked about "Everyman's grammar" — meaning anything anybody cares to say — as the only guide to usage. Humph! I wouldn't particularly like to trust myself to Everyman's medicine, or Everyman's ideas about the law. Why should I accept Everyman's grammar?

• OF FRENCH DRAMA •

Y ESTERDAY I SAW a play done in French by an excellent group of actors from Quebec. When this happens a synopsis of the play is printed for dullards like me, but these synopses are of very little assistance, being written, I suppose, by a Frenchman whose knowledge of English is about on a par with my knowledge of French. They generally run something like this: "Alphamet, the lover of Pheenaminte, is eager to break off his intrigue with Flanelette, ward of the miser Planchette, whose earlier affair with a woman of the town, Clitore, has been discovered by the wily notary Bidet. To achieve his end he disguises himself as a country cousin, Merde, and seeks the assistance of the maid, Vespasienne, who is in reality the disguised Comtesse de Blancmange. Meanwhile the miser has altered his will, leaving everything to the poet Tisane, whose love for the beautiful Parapluie is made known to her supposed father (but in reality her ward) Derriére, bringing the whole merry business to an end with a sextuple marriage and the birth of the triplets, Un, Deux and Trois."

• A BOON TO PUBLIC SPEAKERS •

*I*HAD TO MAKE a speech today, and was not in the mood for it. In consequence I lay in the bathtub and invented Marchbanks' Rhetorical Robot, a type of recording machine for the use of public speakers. You prepare your speech, and record it when you feel at your best. You then go to the meeting, and when the time for your address comes you turn on the Robot, which delivers the speech for you, while you loll at ease, picking your teeth, laughing uproariously at your own jokes, and leading the applause.

Entrée

• THE HORROR OF GRACIOUS LIVING •

I HEARD SOMEBODY use the expression "gracious living" today. Until now I have only seen it in print. It is a phrase I dislike. To my mind it suggests a horrible daintiness — salads made of cream cheese and pineapple, doilies scattered over everything and plaster book-ends supporting five books bound in imitation suede. People who go in for "gracious living" call beer "ale," when it isn't ale because they think "ale" sounds more refined than "beer"; they are the people who never want more food — they always "wish" it. "Do you wish further prunes?" they say, looking as though no one who was not a gormandizer could possibly want anything more to eat. "How warm I've grown," they say, when they are drenched in sweat. They never go to bed — they "retire." They spend their whole lives trying to be like characters in *The Ladies' Home Journal*. In my opinion, anyone who finds the expression "gracious living" creeping into his mind, is in mortal danger of becoming a pantywaist or a stuffed shirt. Good manners, decent hospitality and comfort are the reality; "gracious living" is a shoddy, sugar-coated substitute.

• OF UNSAVORY WHOLESOMENESS •

I SEE THAT Princess Elizabeth and Barbara Ann Scott *✒* have both been included among the "Six Most Whole- some Women of the Year" by the Women's Research Guild of New York. A dubious compliment, if ever I heard one. In my callow

---

✒ Princess Elizabeth (b.1926 and christened Elizabeth Alexandra Mary) is now H.M. Queen Elizabeth II. Barbara Ann Scott (b. 1928) was in the public eye when this was written, as a champion skater

youth, I was badly scratched several times before I learned that if there is one thing no girl wants to be called, it is wholesome. This word suggests that a girl eats a lot of turnips, laughs too loudly at clean jokes, wears too much underclothing of the wrong kind, and has not heard about depilatories. Wholesome is what one calls girls whom one cannot call beautiful, or witty, or charming without hurrying straight to the bathroom to wash one's mouth out with brown soap. Even a girl who takes a lot of outdoor exercise, like Miss Scott, need not be wholesome because of it: even a princess, with the eyes of the world upon her, can avoid the curse of wholesomeness. What girl would be a slice of bread, when she can be a piece of cake? I think that both these maligned young women are thoroughly unwholesome, so there!

· A Creature of Habit ·

*T*ODAY I SAW a baker wearing a pair of plastic pants over his ordinary trousers, and pondered idly on the purpose of this strange garment. A baby-sitter might advantageously wear plastic pants; I have known babies who themselves wore plastic pants; but why does a baker need plastic pants? Some modern mystery, beyond my comprehension, no doubt, for I am a poor creature, bound by chains of habit. The first butcher I saw as a child had a wooden leg, and to this day I have an unreasonable feeling that butchers with two genuine legs are impostors. Such is the strength of an early impression on a mind ill-suited to the giddy changes of modern life.

· Of Police Inefficiency ·

I READ WITH INTEREST that agents of the R.C.M.P. have been searching the offices of a Canadian magazine in search of a manuscript. "They searched the safe," says one report, "but found nothing in it except a stock of stationery." This shocks

---

who brought much renown to Canada, and also famous as the only girl known to have been kissed in public by Prime Minister William Lyon Mackenzie King.

me. The R.C.M.P. must really be very badly trained, or they would know that nobody keeps anything valuable in a safe any more, nor has anyone done so since 1910. The vault, or safe of most business offices contains all or some of the following:

(1) The accountant's rubbers
(2) Some disused ledgers
(3) The stick with a hook on it which is used for opening the windows.
(4) Two or three tarnished cups won by the firm's bowling team back in the days when it had a bowling team.
(5) A bottle of ink which has congealed but is too good to throw away.
(6) Vases in which the secretaries put flowers on the rare occasions when anybody gives them flowers. Valuables are kept in banks. Manuscripts are kept in confused heaps on desks.

• OF SEXUAL EXCLUSIVENESS •

I PONDERED AT LUNCH today on the fact that all waiters in good hotels are clean-shaven. Is this a reminiscence of the time—about a century ago—when all menservants wore powder in their hair on great occasions (although their masters had long given it up) and were forbidden to grow their whiskers as a mark of their servitude? At the turn of the century the only clean-shaven men to be seen in the streets were actors, clergymen, servants and a few lawyers.... A women's luncheon was going on near me. It looked deadly dull. Gatherings at which only one sex is represented are rarely enlivening. The only thing drearier than a pack of men eating together is a pack of women doing the same.... I quite agree with you, madam; the sexes are only tolerable when mingled.

• OF MALE COOKS •

I WAS AT A GATHERING last night where I ate cookies made by one man, discussed the chemistry of cooking with another, and examined a gingerbread house made by a third. The gingerbread house was particularly fancy and appeared to me to carry the pastrycook's art to considerable lengths. . . . More men can cook than is commonly thought, and I think that these male cooks are more concerned with the philosophy and mystery of cooking than are women. Women say, of course, that if men had all the cooking to do they would not like it so much. This is comparable to the frequent feminine comment that if men had to have babies there would soon be no babies in the world. Both remarks are equally untrue. . . . I have sometimes wished that some clever man would actually have a baby in a new, labour-saving way; then all men could take it up, and one of the oldest taunts in the world would be stilled forever. . . . I see that Shirley Temple has had a baby. Dear me, how time flies! Next thing we know that sweet little Mickey Rooney will be getting married.

• OF UNDESIRED INFORMATION •

I WAS EATING AN excellent slice of bread at lunch today, when I sensed a foreign substance in my mouth, and after some fishing and digging I found that it was a bit of paper. After I had cleaned it (by washing it in my tea, if you must know) I found that it was a union label, proclaiming that my bread had been made by organized bakers. I think, frankly, that I would rather have this information conveyed to me by other means than a label which I suspect had been licked by an organized tongue.

• OF SUPERFLUOUS HAIR •

I SEE A STRANGE gadget advertised—a special pair of circular scissors to remove hair from the nose and ears. Personally I regard hair in the ears as a sign of wisdom; the Chinese greatly esteem an elongated earlobe, and it seems to me that when such a lobe is allied with a splendidly hirsute ear, perfection has been reached, and should not be tampered with. As for hair in the nose, it is picturesque, and with a little practice it can be made to quiver, like the antennae of one of the more intelligent and sensitive insects. Anything which gives interest to the gloomy, immobile pan of the average Canadian citizen should be cherished and not extirpated with circular scissors.

• OF READING PLAYS •

*A*SMALL PLAY-READING group of which I am one met last night and had a very good time with Goldsmith's *She Stoops To Conquer*. Reading plays can be anything from the pleasantest to the most penitential of pastimes. I was reading in Thomas Davies' *Memoirs of the Life of David Garrick, Esq.* a few days ago about one of King George the Second's exploits in this direction. The King had reached the age of seventy-seven and had ceased to go to the theatre, but he was keen to hear Macklin's farce *Love à la Mode*, and Macklin had some hope that he might be asked to read his play to the King—presumably acting it out with great spirit. But, as Davies tells us, *Love à la Mode* was read to his Majesty by an old Hanoverian gentleman, who spent eleven weeks in the misrepresentation of the author's meaning; the German was totally void of humour and was, besides, not well acquainted with the English language; the King, however, expressed great satisfaction at the Irishman's getting the better of his rivals, and gaining the young lady. I have myself been present at play readings which were not much livelier than this.

• OF BONES •

*D*RIVING NEAR a railway siding this morning I beheld a sight of grim beauty—a gondola loaded with bones on their way to a glue factory. The load was heaped high and the rib-cages, spines and skulls of horses and cattle were seen in silhouette against a winter sky. Skeletons of all kinds have a beauty of their own; to me a house half-built, or a tall building which is still in the steel-structure stage, is a more pleasing object than the same building completed. Why skeletons are considered frightening objects I have no idea; most people would be far handsomer without their flesh than with it and I think this holds true of animals, as well.... And yet I will admit that there was an air of austerity about this load for the bone-yard. It was a gigantic reminder of our mortality, and if Sir Thomas Browne had been riding in the car with me he would no doubt have favoured me with a few rolling periods on the subject. And although the bones in themselves were beautiful there was something depressing about the thought that they would end, in all probability, as ten-cent bottles of mucilage, and that vile substance which bookbinders use so freely in their trade.

• THE LANGUORS OF TRAVEL •

AS I SAT ON A siding today I reflected upon the extraordinary slowness of our Canadian trains. There are, I know, fast trains in this country, but they never go anywhere that I want to go. The trains I am forced to take dawdle through the countryside, squatting every now and then to cool their bellies in the snow, while I yawn and try to read, a diversion which the lumpiness of the roadbed makes impossible. I was roused from a doze this afternoon by a fear that the train was on fire. There was no smoke, and I decided that someone must have left a pair of rubbers, or possibly a soiled baby, against the heating apparatus. But later I discovered that a man across the aisle had lit a pipe, at which he sucked with obvious enjoyment. There was a smoking section of the car, but he did not choose to go to it. Instead he blew his fetid exhalations everywhere, causing old ladies and expectant mothers to seek refuge between the cars, while men like myself, apparently in the best of health, turned grey in the face and wished for death to end our sufferings. I don't mind pipes; I smoke a pipe myself; but this was such a pipe as the damned must smoke in Hell.

• OF PRAYERS AND ENTREATIES •

A SCIENTIST WHOM I know was telling me this evening that ants and spiders sing quite loudly for their size, that flies scream and that weevils make noises like rivetters as they bore into wheat grains, yet none of these cries is audible to us, being far above the sound level of our ears. As he explained, the notion struck me that possibly our prayers and entreaties are not audible to God's ear. Perhaps as I walk in my garden ants and spiders send up the most terrific outcries to me for rain, or peace; maybe they think that I am being hard upon them when I do not answer their prayers, when the plain fact is that I do not hear them. Obviously they should lower their voices; and perhaps if we want to catch the ear of the Ancient of Days, we should moderate the eager shrillness with which we address Him.

• OF HIS FALLING-OUT WITH DOGS •

I WAS CORNERED before dinner by that solemn man over there who took me to task for my attitude toward dogs who are, he tells me, noble creatures. This grieves me, for the quarrel between me and the canine world was begun by the dogs themselves. I am the sort of man at whom dogs bark, rush wildly, and jump up. People who think that dogs are wonderful judges of character insist that this means that I have the soul of a burglar, or possibly a cat. If dogs think so poorly of me is it any wonder that I am distant in my attitude toward dogs? I get on well with horses, I mix freely with cows, cats are affable in my presence, and goats consider me one of themselves. Babies (also considered infallible judges of character) gurgle with fascination when I go near them. Old ladies ask me to help them across the street. But dogs dislike me. By a process of reasoning too complicated to go into here, this leads me to dislike dogs, and to regard them as idiotic and dangerous, or both. My household pet is the cat, which was man's friend while the dog was still unable to distinguish itself from a wolf.

• OF CHEWING GUM •

T HIS MORNING I had a brief chat with a gum-chewer, whose technique, I was interested to observe, was very poor. She chomped vigorously, with much wasteful jaw-movement and audible squelching. If I had had the time, I would have given her a lesson. The experienced chewer wastes no motion; he keeps his teeth together, merely nudging his quid from time to time with a single molar; he does not seek to produce the maximum of saliva, but is content with enough to keep his palate gently afloat; he does not work at his gum—rather let us say that he cherishes it; his technique is that of the cow, rather than the cement-mixer.

• OF THE FIEND CZERNY •

A LITTLE GIRL was showing me some of her piano exercises today. They were simple things with fanciful names, and she seemed to like them. When I was a child piano lessons involved an intimate acquaintance with the exercises of a fiend named Carl Czerny, *ƒ* all of which were intended to be performed at incredible speed. The pupil of those days began with a variety of Czerny, and soon passed on to thick books called *The School of Velocity, The School of Finger Dexterity* and so forth until he approached a work of blood-chilling difficulty called *The Virtuoso Pianist*. I never scaled this awful eminence (I broke down and was flung aside in *Finger Dexterity*) but I heard other students playing it, and such swoops, crashes and wrist-paralysing convulsions of sound were never heard. The object of learning all this, I was told, was so that if, in later life, one broke down in the performance of a concerto, one could always fill in with a few spasms of Czerny; the musically ignorant in the audience would never notice the difference, and the musically élite would understand that the pianist was perfectly capable of playing anything.

ƒ Czerny (1791-1857) came by his piano-bashing habits in the greatest style, for he was a pupil of Beethoven and his most celebrated pupil was Franz Liszt, of whom it was written—

> *The Abbé Liszt*
> *Hit the piano with his fist;*
> *That is the way*
> *He used to play.*

Music is identified by its composers in large hunks, called opuses. Many composers are content with a few hundred of these things, but Czerny wrote a full thousand of them.

• OF TRANSPLANTED TRADITION •

*T*HERE'LL ALWAYS BE an England while there is a U.S.A. I looked through a quantity of American magazines this afternoon and was amazed by the number of shaving creams, foods, leather goods and types of booze which are advertised with pictures of Windsor Castle, London clubs, Scotsmen in native dress and similar phenomena, suggestive of Ye Merrie Olde Englande. The more fiercely the socialists hack at Englysshe Tradition the more avidly do their American cousins embrace it, fake it, and attach it to their consumer goods. In Britain the stately homes are turned into hostels for Labour Youth Cycling Clubs, and the velvet lawns of noble lords are ripped up by miners pretending to search for coal; meanwhile in Akron, Ohio, Antonio Spigoni shaves himself with a soap which he thinks gives him an Old Etonian appearance, and in South Bend, Indiana, Mrs. Brunnhilde Klotz stuffs her friends with Olde Nell Gwynne Tea Biscuits (made in St. Louis, Mo.). A mad world, my masters, and one half of it doesn't know how the other half lives!

• OF THE MADNESS OF LOVE •

*T*HE PAPERS ARE full of news this morning about a gravedigger who killed a girl for love. Indeed, for several weeks I have been reading about murderers and suicides who are all described as "love-crazed." I wonder how many love-crazed people there really are? As I walk through the streets, what portion of the people I meet are in this distressing and dangerous condition? Quite a few, it appears. But from my newspaper reading I can make a few deductions about them. Most love-crazed people appear to live in boarding-houses, and a majority of them earn less than $2,000 a year. They are not extensively educated, as a usual thing, and none of them toil under the burden of a mighty intellect. But they are great lovers, and handy with knives, pistols and blunt instruments. Very few of them have steady jobs, and not many of them belong to the skilled trades. They do not eat regularly. (It is a curious fact that most of them have been grabbing a snack—a hamburger and a soft drink or something of that kind—within three hours before they commit murder.) Their physical health is good, but they tend to be puny above the eyebrows. They are under thirty-five. They need a good hobby and a larger circle of female acquaintance.

• OF BRITISH SOCIALISM •

I WAS TALKING TO a man before dinner who had recently returned from England, and was full of information about the harm which he thought the socialist government had done there. For one thing, he said, the dog-boxes have disappeared from English trains. This rattled me, I confess. Not long ago there used to be special holes between the carriages of English trains, in which dogs rode; they were happy in there, and they passed their journey in sleeping and trying to look out of a small window which other dogs had licked and blown their noses upon. But such dog-boxes are no more and dogs ride in the carriages with the people, whether Labour supporters or not. This man said that he had ridden fifty miles in a carriage with a dog as big as a calf, which stood on his feet, stuck its nose into his pockets, and beat noisily upon his newspaper with its tail. . . . This suggests to me that the Labour Government depends heavily upon the dog-lover vote, a very powerful political group in England where dogs are regarded as semi-sacred, along with such totems as crumpets, Brussels sprouts and umbrellas. "The voice of the people is the voice of Dog," say these zealots.

• WHY CANADIAN MEN ARE RESISTIBLE •

W ITH HEAVY HEART I went last evening to see a movie called *Bel Ami*, based on Maupassant's story. I had read several criticisms of it, all of which said it was bad. But I was in that mood which sometimes overtakes the true movie-enthusiast; I had to see a movie, however poor it might be. I was delighted to discover that the critics were wrong. It was an excellent picture, and also one of the dirtiest pictures (using the word "dirty" in its

Ontario sense, meaning "with sexual implication") that I have seen in many years. I can only believe that its suggestions and innuendoes were too recondite for the nice, simple souls who compose our censorship boards *f* . . . . It concerned a man who was irresistibly attractive to women. I believe that such fellows exist, but I have never met one, though I have met many who thought they belonged in that category. Women who are attractive to most men are common enough; men who are attractive to most women are rarities, in this country, at any rate. I think that it is because a man, to be attractive, must be free to give his whole time to it, and the Canadian male is so hounded by taxes and the rigours of our climate that he is lucky to be alive, without being irresistible as well.

• OF ONTARIO'S BACCHIC REFINEMENT •

I FOUND MYSELF yesterday by some mysterious chain of circumstances in the Cocktail Lounge of a large Toronto hotel. Although it was full of people, an awesome hush hung over the place, and there were three superior waiters at the door, to make sure that no undesirable guest (the kind of person, for instance, who shouts, "Well, here's looking up your address!" to his female companion whenever he takes a drink) gained admission. I saw three low fellows in their shirtsleeves come to the door and the waiters closed into a solid barrier of indignant flesh and

---

f This is unfair, but Marchbanks was often unfair. The film, starring George Sanders (1906-72) a notable player of cads, had as its most erotic moment a scene in which a woman, tormented by unrequited love, knelt at the feet of Bel Ami, and embraced his knees; he maliciously wound a tendril of her hair around one of the buttons of his coat, so that when she rose she was caught, hurt and humiliated; truly an erotic moment, if a nasty one, for the discerning. Canadian men seeking to reproduce any such effects as these must first of all reduce a woman to a beseeching posture, a virtually impossible feat in these liberated days. And of course they must wear coats, not windbreakers; there is nothing erotically stirring about hair caught in a zipper.

would not let them pass. After some palaver a sub-waiter was sent away, and soon he reappeared with three seersucker jackets; the lowlifers, now thoroughly cowed, put these on, and were shepherded to a table.... I approve of this sort of thing. It is very refined, and if there is one thing about which Ontario is particular, it is refinement. Fastidiousness was apparent everywhere in the Cocktail Lounge; all the men wore their coats, all the women wore gloves, and the only really loud sound was the silvery chinking of the waiters, as they ran to and fro with their pockets full of tips. My drink was not as good as I could have made at home, but it was worth the money to sip it in surroundings of such mortuary restraint.

• PHYSICIANS' PROGRESS •

I WENT TO SEE my doctor today, and while I lay upon his little table, waiting for him to finish off another patient, I passed the time by picking him out in the graduation photographs which hung about the walls. It is always instructive to survey the progress of one's doctor through the years in this manner. There he was as a young man — a lad, really — when he took his degree in Arts. Here we have him, a few years later, when he became an M.D. Smaller photographs show him with the eminent specialists with whom he did post-graduate work. And in each picture he looks older until the door flies open and the man himself, now gray-haired and with fingers a foot long and made of tempered steel, dashes upon one and begins to probe, pinch and squeeze. I think doctors must get their wonderful finger-development by tearing telephone directories apart.

• OF THE JOYS OF THE SMITH •

I SEE THAT A War Assets shop quite near my place of business is selling a lot of interesting things, including several forges. It occurs to me that a forge is just what I need, for I have long wanted a constructive hobby. I could set it up in my cellar, get a few bars of iron, and amuse myself during the long winter evenings by making beautiful and acceptable gifts for my friends. The upper chambers of Marchbanks Towers would resound with the merry ring of my hammer on the anvil, my loud Yo Hoes (is it blacksmiths who cry Yo Ho?), and the hiss as I plunged a white-hot book end or umbrella stand into the water to temper it. I would develop the biceps of a blacksmith, and the jolly great-hearted disposition of a blacksmith. The homes of my friends would be enriched with ornaments which I had beaten out at the forge with my own hands—wrought iron garden furniture, wrought iron cocktail sets, wrought iron spittoons—the possibilities are illimit-able. And any time anyone wanted a sword beaten into a plough-share, I would be just the man to do it (though I have often thought that a sword would make a pretty measly ploughshare). I shall phone tomorrow, and tell them to wrap up a forge for me.... Do you know that a smith is so called because he smites?... No, I am not sure that that is etymologically correct; I just made it up myself this minute.... Well, if you dislike guesswork, why don't you do some of the talking yourself.... Nonsense, madam, I am *not* "hog-ging" the conversation, as you so disagreeably put it.

• OF RECLAIMED INEBRIATES •

A MAN WHOM I had never seen before turned up in my office today and seated himself in the uncomfortable chair which I keep for guests with the air of one who bears a great mes-sage. Indeed, he wore the dedicated look which I have learned to associate with magazine salesmen and agents for worthless ency-clopaedias. "Mr. Marchbanks," said he, "I saw by a recent article of yours that you have been absent from your work, undergoing treat-ment for an illness; you assured your readers that you were not taking the Gold Cure, but that may have been an attempt to pull the bull over their eyes. Now, Mr. Marchbanks, I represent an organization of which you have doubtless heard—the Nameless Drunks, we call ourselves—and if we can help you, we certainly will. You too can overcome your habit, Marchbanks! You too may become a Nameless Drunk if you so choose!" I allowed him to talk for an hour or so, during which time he imparted to me the secret sign of the Nameless Drunks: you raise an imaginary glass, but instead of putting it to your lips, you pretend to pour it into your eye; you then make motions as though shaking a drink out of your right ear. By means of this simple, hardly observable sign, Nameless Drunks can recognize each other anywhere.

• OF THE DEPRAVITY OF BEES •

*T*HIS IS THE SEASON of flowers, and everybody I meet is either boasting about his garden, or groaning because it has not come up to his expectations. I can be philosophical about flowers, and I conduct my own garden on strict philosophic principles; if flowers grow, I am pleased but if they do not grow I will not permit my life to be darkened by their absence. I do not blind myself, as many gardeners do, to the fact that flower gardens are cultivated principally for the pleasure of bees. A bee gets more fun out of a single iris than a human being can get out of a vast herbaceous border. The bee drags its feet in the flower, rolls in it, takes a bath in it, swigs the nectar out of it, and revels in the sound of its own voice while doing so, just as we sing in our resonant bathrooms. Sometimes as many as three or four bees enjoy mixed bathing in the heart of a rose, and The Dear knows what goes on in there when they are all plastered with nectar, and think that they are out of sight. Flowers are just bagnios for bees, and while I take a broad view of these things, I feel no impulsion to wear myself out providing for insects who would not do a thing for me if they could possibly help it.

• OF FEMININE ALLUREMENTS •

I SEE THAT QUEBEC is getting worked up over two-piece bathing suits again, and an ardent do-gooder has declared that they threaten all that is best in French Canadian life. I remember that after the First World War it was rolled stockings which were nibbling at the foundations of the universe. What fascinated me at the time was that the evil power lay in the female patella itself, and not in any beauty which it might exhibit. Men's knees were not harmful, and Scotchmen were, as always, encouraged to show off their gnarled joints. But any female knee, however like a cabbage or the skull of a goat it might be in appearance, was charged with vice, and the male who beheld it was in danger of being turned to stone, as if he had beheld the face of the Gorgon. Since those days knees have become an old song — indeed a weariness of the flesh — and it is that comparatively undistinguished portion of the female anatomy comprising the lower ribs and the diaphragm which is now the focus of holy horror. If women showed their navels with texts from the *Song of Solomon* tattooed around them, I might see some sense in all this fuss, but they don't, and I don't.

• A CURIOUS CHARITY •

*L*OOKING THROUGH a catalogue of rare books last evening, I found one written in 1806 by a William Turnbull called *Manual Containing General Rules & Instructions to Those of Both Sexes Who Are Afflicted With Ruptures and Prolapsus Ani*. This work was published under the auspices of The Society for The Relief of The Ruptured Poor, of which the Archbishop of Canterbury at that time (the Rev. Dr. Charles Manners-Sutton) was honorary patron. I yearned for this fascinating volume, but I am much too poor to buy all the books I want. But a flame of curiosity devours me; does this benevolent body still exist, and does the present Archbishop still visit among the poor, his little basket of trusses upon his arm?

• PREDICAMENT •

*S*OME WORK THAT I was doing kept me in a room today which adjoined one in which a service club was meeting. I was thus made privy to their mysteries, and very odd they were, too. For instance, one member was congratulated on a wedding anniversary, and immediately afterward they all sang *The Old Gray Mare, She Ain't What She Used To Be*, which I thought was somewhat pointed, under the circumstances. Perhaps nothing was intended except a general reflection upon the flight of time, however. I also suffered the puzzlement which always comes upon a man who is alone in a room when *God Save The King* is being sung next door: should I stand up and feel foolish, or sit down and feel unpatriotic? ⫯ The same problem arises when I hear somebody praying on the radio: should I stop flogging my dog, or forging cheques, or whatever I am about, or should I pretend not to notice?

• OF TIMEPIECES •

THE DAY OF THE ornamental clock seems to be done. This morning I poked about in an antique shop and saw two: the first had a large brass woman on it, holding a harp with four uncommonly thick strings; the other had a man in the dress of the early 19th century sitting on its top, holding a pen in one hand and a scroll in the other, and surrounded by globes, papers and mathematical instruments. I cannot guess who he was; some great figure in the horological world, no doubt. Such clocks are rarities now. Even marble clocks with brass lions' heads poking out of the ends of them are rarely seen. Modern interest centres upon watches, and watches which tell time, date, year, phase of moon, and forecast the weather are not uncommon. But I like strange clocks, and particularly those which have moving figures on them. Most of these are of ancient workmanship, but I think the idea might well be brought up to date. A clock upon which,

---

⫯ *Written at a time when standing for the National Anthem was a custom with mythic sinew. Nowadays Marchbanks comments that at the movies, when the new national anthem is played—O, Canada!— many people remain seated. He does not despise them, though he always rises himself. They may be protesting against the Income Tax. Anyhow it is easier to revere a living monarch than a land-mass of 3,845,774 square miles with less than twenty-five million people on it, while listening to a tune which, to a sensitive ear, is commonplace when it is not downright plagiaristic.*

every hour, a figure identifiable as a taxpayer was pursued by a figure with a pitchfork and a sheaf of Income Tax forms would command a good price at Marchbanks Towers.

• OF PHOTOGRAPHS •

I HAD SOME photographs taken today, an experience which always leaves me limp, with my ego quivering and bounding like an uncoiled spring. "Take a natural, easy pose," says the photographer, and when I do so he winces and says, "Oh, no, not all slumped, like the leavings of a torso-murder." So then I strike a pose which seems to me to suggest dignity and vast stores of reserve power, and the photographer laughs merrily and says that I'm not to make faces. The fact of the matter is that I cannot be at ease when a man is pointing a machine at me, and jumping and ducking about the room, pulling curtains, flashing lights and looking at my face as though it was something on a butcher's bargain counter. "I am trying for a characteristic likeness," says he. But that is just what I do not want. I want a picture which looks the way I should like to be, not the way I am. I can face facts in the mirror whenever I choose. I do not see why I should pay good money to have my nose rubbed in the bitter realities. "You don't mean to say you want to be flattered?" he asks, and as I nod my head wildly he clicks the shutter. In the picture I shall probably appear to have a broken neck, like the body just before the police cut it down.

• OF PIGEONS •

I WAS TALKING TO a young person who attends the kindergarten, and she gave me some interesting details about the teaching of music, as it is done at her school. All the children must sing, and are divided by the teacher into canaries (the best singers), robins (fairly good singers), bluebirds (definitely not choral material) and pigeons (creatures who croak moodily upon one note). The young canary with whom I spoke expressed deep scorn for pigeons. It seems to me that this name has been well chosen. I once lived in a house which was very popular with pigeons, and their croaking was a great nuisance, and caused me to look up a recipe for pigeon pie. Poets have affected to find a pleasing melancholy in the note of the pigeon, but poets are notoriously heavy sleepers, and are not wakened by these pompous, detestable, strutting birds in the early hours of the morning. I never made the pigeon pie, for the labour of skinning and cleaning enough birds daunted me. But to this day I never see a pigeon waddling in the street, eating something disgusting, without wanting to let it have the toe of my boot. Have you ever kicked a pigeon?

• OF MEAT BALLS •

I HAD MEAT BALLS for lunch today. This is a delicacy of which I am very fond. But I insist upon the True Meat Ball—prepared in an open pan and tasting of meat—rather than the False Meat Ball—prepared in a pressure cooker and loathsomely studded with raisins. The pressure cooker is all very well in its way, but there are some dishes with which it cannot cope, and the meat ball is one of them. A meat ball made in a pressure cooker has a mild, acquiescent taste—the sort of taste which I imagine that a particularly forgiving Anglican missionary would have in the mouth of a cannibal. Your True Meat Ball is made of sterner stuff, and if he tastes of missionary at all he tastes like some stern Jesuit, who died dogmatizing.

• HE IS OF A PIECE WITH ROYALTY •

I TOOK AN OPPORTUNITY which presented itself today to see a film about Princess Elizabeth, which showed her from earliest babyhood to the present day. I found this impressive and moving, for I admire royalty, and am sorry for nations which have none. Scores of my obscure and unmeritable ancestors have shared with the Royal House the task of building Great Britain and its Empire and Commonwealth, though I am the first to admit that the Marchbanks tribe were more active in the South Sea Bubble, the Rebecca Riots and the War of Jenkins' Ear than in the more spectacular events of history. There were a few bad kings, and many a dubious Marchbanks, but they all wove the tapestry of history together, and will do so, I trust, for many centuries to come. ✒

• OF A POSSIBLE CRUSADE •

I THINK SERIOUSLY of launching a crusade against the custom of removing the hat in an elevator. I wear my hat in the lobby of my hotel, and I wear it in the corridors. Nobody expects me to take it off in a streetcar or in an automobile when I ride with a woman. But as soon as a woman comes aboard an elevator all the men in it sweep off their hats as though she were the American Mother of the Year; some extremists even hold the hats over their hearts and assume that colicky look which indicates nobility of feeling in the Canadian male. The elevator operator is a woman, but nobody bothers about her. The whole thing seems to me to be false and foolish.... Frankly, I should like to see a corresponding custom decreeing that women should keep their heads covered in the presence of men, as a gesture of respect toward the Defender, Bread-Winner, Prophet, Sage, Seer and Begetter of the Race. Why should I show respect for any strange woman who flouts my manhood by running about with a bare head? A fig and a resolutely pulled-down fedora for all such hussies!... No, no, madam,

---

Marchbanks has lived to see the Motherland brought low; remembering the glories of Empire he is sad, but as a Celt he is not surprised. It is not that the pound has become an object of derision; it is not that the French regard the whole Common Market scheme as their revenge for Waterloo. It is that the English have taken to making movies and TV shows in which they depict their stupidity and snobbery in India. When the English admit that they have ever been wrong, Marchbanks, Welshman and Scot that he is, knows that Chaos Has Come Again.

it is quite unnecessary for you to cover your head with your fruit-plate. Desist, I beg!

• OF CURATIVE GROANING •

I TOOK TO MY BED last week-end, for my bones ached and my tripes felt as though I had swallowed a porcupine. I treated this malady by drinking countless glasses of luke-warm water. I wish it were the fashion to groan when one is ill. I like groaning, and I believe it helps me to bear suffering; what is more, groaning helps to pass the time. But modern sickroom practice is all against groaning. In Victorian times it was different; everybody groaned when they were ill; it was considered the right thing to do. Their roars were an inspiration to their doctors and nurses, urging them on to greater flights of bleeding, purging, leeching and poulticing. Furthermore, groaning has curative powers. A Hindu, when he is ill, repeats the mystic syllable "Om" as loudly and as resonantly as he can until he is well; it is his belief that the resonance provides a gentle and beneficial massage for his suffering insides. And what is "Om," I ask you, but a stylized groan? There is more to groaning than Western medical science has yet recognized.

• OF AN UNFORTUNATE PERSONALITY •

I SEE A LETTER to the press complaining that Toronto is terribly abused, and that the jokes about Toronto are the fosterlings of cankered minds. Personally I always think of Toronto as a big fat rich girl who has lots of money, but no idea of how to make herself attractive. She has not learned to drink like a lady, and she has not learned to laugh easily; when she does laugh, she shows the roof of her mouth; she is dowdy and mistakes dowdiness for a guarantee of virtue. She is neither a jolly country girl with hay in her hair, like so many other Ontario cities, nor is she a delicious wanton, like Montreal; she is irritatingly conscious of her own worthiness.... Toronto ought to read the advertisements which explain why girls are unpopular and get themselves whispered about. Maybe she needs more bulk in her diet. ✒

• OF THE DIVINE WILL •

I HAD A LETTER this morning from some association which is agitating for the repeal of the Sales Tax which is, its pamphlet assures me, "a straight violation of the laws of God." This is fascinating. Not long ago one of the larger Canadian churches notified me of its intention to "prepare a statement of God's Will concerning marriage." How lucky we are to live in a country where God's Will and His Laws are so thoroughly understood, and so zealously publicized!

• OF JUVENILE LITERATURE •

I WAS LOOKING through a pile of books this afternoon, which I had not read since I was a boy. To my astonishment I found that I remembered the stories in some detail. But in those days my mind was young and impressionable, and had not been subjected to the horrible wear and tear of book reviewing; nowadays my poor brain is a sort of incinerator, which seizes upon huge amounts of literary garbage, quickly reduces it to ashes, and spits them out, retaining only a disgusting slime upon its walls. . . . As I leafed over the pages of these boys' books, I was delighted by the unambiguous style in which they were written, and particularly the way in which the characters were named. When in a boy's story, you find a character called "Sir Judas Snake" you can be pretty sure that he is up to no good, and will probably get seriously in the way of the hero, who is quite likely to be called "Justyn Bloodygood" or "Samkin Steelheart." Indeed, it is amazing how closely these villains resemble one another; they are all fancy dressers, they are

---

✒ Times have changed. Toronto is now the soignée enchantress of Canadian cities, wearing her necklace of murders and crimes of violence with an air of international chic. Montreal still holds her head high, but has bags under her eyes and wears mended stockings.

all thin, they all talk in a nastily grammatical manner, and they are all cowards at heart. My life has not brought me into close association with many important criminals, but I have known a few very unpleasant types who were fat, sloppy, illiterate and braver than the average Good Citizen. But then, art is always superior to truth.

• OF HIS LINK WITH THE QUEEN MOTHER •

*T*HE PAPERS tell me that Queen Mary will be eighty next Monday. There is an interesting link between myself and the Queen Mother which I do not think Her Majesty would see any reason to suppress, and of which I am very proud. In the days when I earned my living in the disreputable but amusing profession of an actor I once played the role of Snout the Tinker in a production of *A Midsummer Night's Dream* at the Old Vic in London; Her Majesty brought her granddaughters to a matinee, and in one of the intervals summoned the stars of the play (I was not one of them) to her box. "You know, I once played in *The Dream* when I was a girl," she said; "I played Snout." When this news was told to me, I immediately prepared myself for a summons to the Royal Box, being sure that the Queen would wish to discuss the fine points of the role with me; after all it is not every day that a couple of veteran Snouts get together. But, alas, the summons never came. An oversight, no doubt, or some jealousy of me in Court circles. *✍*

• OF PERFORMING ANIMALS •

I WENT TO A CIRCUS last night and the first thing on the program was a girl who exhibited some trained goats. My mind immediately flew to Hugo's *Notre Dame de Paris*, in which

---

✍ Astonishment! Who would ever have supposed that Marchbanks, the Recluse of Skunk's Misery, had ever appeared upon the boards! But there he was, on the stage which had once known Edmund Kean, not to speak of Gielgud, Olivier and Richardson, appearing before royalty! Queen Mary (Princess Victoria Mary Augusta Louise Olga Pauline Clau-

the heroine, Esmeralda, had a trained goat which could spell out the name of her lover, Phoebus de Chateaupers, which is no small feat, when you think about it. There are plenty of stenographers who couldn't do as well. But the circus goats were not nearly so accomplished, and the act retired in disgrace after the star goat fell off a bar on which it was walking, and almost hanged itself in its halter.... There are people who object strongly to performances given by animals. Indeed, I believe that there is an organization called The Jack London Society, the members of which are pledged to rise and leave any place in which a performing animal appears— even if it be only on a movie screen. I think that is carrying humanitarianism to extremes. When I see a dog like Lassie or Rin-Tin-Tin in the films, I realize that it is the pampered darling of the studio, and has more money in the bank than I have, and probably rides to its job in a Dusenberg with special body work.

• Of Ennobled Mummers •

*T*HE KING HAS MADE Laurence Olivier a knight "in spite of the fact," says one paper, "that Mr. Olivier was divorced in 1939." I wonder if this is the first time that a divorced actor has been given such an honour? Usually theatrical knighthoods are distributed for good conduct more than for ability, and I have even heard wicked actors refer to such a knighthood, sneeringly, as The Order of Chastity. The first actor to be knighted was Henry Irving, about whom Queen Victoria had never heard anything bad, and who had in the highest degree the Victorian ability to look noble and spotless; his runner-up in the contest for the title of Most Respectable-Looking Victorian was, of course, Mr. Gladstone, and

---

dine Agnes of Teck, 1867–1953) was a keen playgoer and frequently brought her grandchildren to the Old Vic at the time when Marchbanks was falling from great heights, turning somersaults, and throwing and receiving custard pies in the lively versions of Shakespeare devised by the late Tyrone Guthrie (1900–70).

it is a well-known fact that the heads of the Landseer lions in Trafalgar Square are a composite portrait of Gladstone and Irving. ✒

• OF CURIOUS MEDICAMENTS •

*T*HE LADY ON MY LEFT was telling me a few minutes ago two "cures" which were highly esteemed in the time of her grandmother (who was born in 1800). The first was a cure for "gathered face" (what we now call an abscessed tooth) and it consisted of digging up the skull of a dead horse and carrying it under the arm for a few days, or until the gathered face ungathered itself. The second was a sure cure for goitre, which was brought about by stroking the goitre six times with the hand of a dead Negro. In spite of occasional evidence to the contrary it seems to me that medicine has advanced a good deal in Ontario during the past 150 years. Hand a horse's skull to a modern doctor, and he probably wouldn't recognize it as a valuable medicament at all; very likely he would make an ash-tray out of it. . . . You wish I wouldn't speak of such things? Very well, eat your sautéed brains in silence, madam.

• OF SPLENDID ACTING •

*I*WENT TO SEE John Gielgud's production of *Love For Love* last evening, and was carried away by the brilliance and artistic completeness with which it was presented. The drama, in its finest flights, gives me a satisfaction, an elation and a recreation which makes the pleasures of the greatest music seem thin and chilly in comparison. Music is an intellectual extract of life; drama is life itself, raised to the highest pitch. I reflected also that great acting (and there were some rare examples of it in this play) makes

---

✒ It may be thought that Sir Laurence's career took a backward step in 1970, when he was raised to a baronetcy; to be a knight may be a guarantee of respectability, but lords have always been a dubious lot, just as were all actors before 1895 when Henry Irving was knighted and made them respectable. Who ever says "Drunk as a knight"?

heavy physical demands on the actor. To move with grace and vigour, to speak complex prose so as to be heard and understood everywhere in a large theatre, and to look exactly right at every moment of a long part requires no mean athletic equipment and physical stamina. *⫯* How hard these actors worked, and yet how easy and inevitable seemed everything that they did! How strong an actor has to be, in every muscle, in order to be graceful without seeming affected! It is in this physical aspect of acting, as well as in imaginative grasp that our amateurs are disappointing. . . . It is not often that we see a play perfectly done in Canada, but when we do we chew the cud on it for months and sometimes for years.

• OF AMATEUR WRITERS •

*H*OW OFTEN and how bitterly I regret the fact that my work makes me read so many books. Reading is one of my great delights, but I like to read books by men of letters; I loathe reading books by soldiers, sailors, airmen, engineers, explorers, politicians, economists and other imperfectly literate persons who write like amateurs. The world was better off when there was a recognized clerkly caste, by whom all reading and writing was done.

• OF MAGIC OPPOSED TO REVELATION •

I READ AN UNUSUALLY good novel this afternoon, called *Herself Surprised*, by Joyce Cary; I was particularly struck by the skill with which the principal character was given life; I shall remember her for years. When I laid the book down I reflected for a time on the rarity of such novels; how few of the books which

---

⫯ This was in the days when actors thought it part of their job to be audible and comprehensible. Many modern mummers, working on the principle that much conversation is inaudible, have altered stage speech to a point where only some of a play is heard, and varying amounts of the remainder are overheard.

are pushed at us by modern authors contain any really interesting or memorable people. Yet there are books, not of the first quality, which give us such experiences. Consider *Lorna Doone*, the darling of our grandfathers; how real Lorna seems, and how potent her charm is, compared with the heroines of most modern novels, about whom we are told so much more! We do not know how Lorna looked in bed, or the state of her digestion, or what parts of her tingled when John Ridd kissed her, but we love her still. Magic, not psychology, is the stuff of which great stories are made.

• OF THE UNSIGHTLINESS OF AUTHORS •

I RARELY play cards, but I was taken to the cleaners this evening by a couple of young women in a spirited game of "Authors." I reflected as I played upon the appearance of authors, as a class. They are a mangy lot. Shakespeare appears to have been a dapper fellow, but look at James Fenimore Cooper, who kept turning up again and again in the hands I was dealt. And look at Ralph Connor and Sir Gilbert Parker, the two Canadians included in the game. Scarecrows, all of them. Authors should be read, but not seen. Their work unfits them for human society.

• OF A DRAMATISTS' QUARREL •

B EFORE DINNER that gentleman over there with the cubical head was expressing disappointment that so little attention was paid to the centenary of the birth of August Strindberg, the Swedish dramatist, which occurred on January 22. I have the centenary habit rather badly, but this one escaped my attention. The fact is, I have never been able to admire Strindberg since I made the acquaintance some years ago of a Swedish girl whose grandfather had been his near neighbour. She said that the neighbourhood was made intolerable by the noise of his quarrels with his three wives, and that his hatred of Ibsen bordered on the demoniacal. He invariably referred to Ibsen as "Gammal Snorlje," meaning "Old Grouchy," whereas Ibsen spoke of Strindberg, even in his public speeches, as "Gammal Nutsje," meaning "Old Nutsy," which was a sly reference to Strindberg's frequent spells of violent insanity. Coldness between dramatists is not unknown, even in our day, but it seems to me that the affair between Strindberg and Ibsen had got out of hand, and as the younger man, it was Strindberg's job to patch it up. The girl also told me that Strindberg's genius defied translation, and I can well believe this.

The Remove

• OF SCIENTIFIC REVELATIONS •

I SEE THAT Professor Kinsey has published the first volume of his study of sexual behaviour in the human male. ⫔ This emboldens me to publish a study of a somewhat similar subject on which I have long been engaged, to wit: how many men wear only the tops or bottoms of their pyjamas? Of course, speaking to you on a social occasion like this I cannot be completely frank; children, or young girls tottering upon the threshold of womanhood might accidentally overhear me and be brutally awakened to an aspect of life hitherto undreamed of by them. Therefore I shall only say that my investigations reveal that 47.3 per cent of adult males wear only the t-ps of their p-j-m-s, and 32.9 per cent (usually thin, muscular men) wear only the b-tt-ms thereof. And in summer 83 per cent of adult males (excluding only university professors, clergymen, chartered accountants and people who habitually sleep in their underwear) wear no p-j-m-s at all; they describe this custom by a revolting expression, to wit, "Sl--ping r-w." I hesitate to tell you this, but science knows no bounds, and the spotlessness of my own private life is well attested.

The lady on my left, to whom I whispered my comment on the Kinsey Report, and on my own researches regarding the wearing of the t-ps and b-tt-ms of p-j-m-s replied to me thus: "A curious use of the p-j-m- is illustrated by a married couple of my acquaintance;

⫔ *Though in large international centres of population it had long been an open secret that the human male had some form of sexual expression, the publication of Kinsey's study in 1953 put the matter on a scientific basis, and doubters were forced to accept the brutal fact.*

Mrs. A. wears the p-j-m- t-p and Mr. A. wears the b-tt-m and thus they make one pair do. Do you think that this sort of thing is widely prevalent in Ontario?" Frankly, my investigations lead me to believe that anything can happen behind the pressed brick, lace curtains, and phoney leaded glass of an Ontario home.

• OF TWANGLING INSTRUMENTS •

*E*VERY NOW AND THEN I am seized with the notion that my life would be transformed if I had a new hobby, and I passed an hour this morning considering the possible consequences of my learning to play the guitar. Nobody plays it much nowadays except the radio cowboys, and they use it only to accompany themselves while they sing miserable songs about their mothers' graves or their own imminent (but too long deferred) deaths. The guitar has slipped sadly in the social scale. During the nineteenth century it was a favourite instrument of the nobility and gentry, and no picnic was complete without at least one girl who could play the thing. Of course, that was the Spanish guitar, an instrument of some artistic respectability. The present guitar is likely to be the Hawaiian model. The Spanish plunks, the Hawaiian yowls. Tunes can be played on the Spanish guitar if you have long, strong fingers and immense concentration; the Hawaiian guitar will yield nothing but shuddering wails. The mandolin (which did not so much plunk as plink) has also fallen into disrepute, though Mozart and Schubert thought well of it.

• OF THE MOCKERY OF ANIMALS •

I WENT TO THE movies last night and saw a short about wild life which made me angry, for it made fools of a lot of handsome wild creatures. A moose appeared, whom the commentator felt impelled to call "Elmer the Moose"; the moose's mate was called "his mooing momma." A fawn was referred to throughout this tiresome piece as "Junior," and when the fawn was being suckled by its dam there was a lot of facetiousness about cafeterias. A fine owl was seen blinking in the sun, and the commentator shouted wittily: "Hey, I gotta get my sleep!" The whole thing was on the lowest level of taste and vulgarity, and the commentator had a voice which would have seemed needlessly uncultivated in a baseball umpire. God knows I have little interest in animals, but I do not like to see them insulted. I used to feel the same thing in the days when I was a frequent visitor at the London Zoo; in the lion house there were always ninnies who mocked the captive lions. I often wished that the bars would turn to butter, and that the great, noble beasts would practise their particular form of wit upon the little, ignoble men.

• OF THE LONELINESS OF WISDOM •

I TALKED THIS AFTERNOON to a university professor who told me that he recently had the job of overseeing a large group of students who were writing an examination in psychology; at least half of these young sophisticates, he said, had lucky pennies, or rabbits' feet, or ju-ju dolls, or other good luck charms on their desks as they wrote. This strengthens my belief that education does not really alter character, but merely intensifies it, making foolish people more foolish, superstitious people more superstitious, and of course wise people wiser. But the wise are few and lonely.

• OF INORDINATE SMOKERS •

I T IS A CURIOUS fact that some people can create a great deal more stench, fog, dirt and annoyance with a single cigarette than most people can make with a bonfire. The common cigarette smoker is not much of a nuisance; he keeps most of his smoke to himself, and what he spreads about is not too offensive. But there are fellows who blow out cubic feet of rank gas after a single inhalation, infecting the air around them for several yards. They also cough, rackingly and nauseatingly, until you wonder if they are getting ready to throw up. They blow ashes over everything, and when they have done with a cigarette they allow the butt to smoulder. What is more, their smoke has not the ordinary smoky smell; it is sour and bitter, and their clothes smell like ash-heaps. I had to do some work today in a room with one of these people, and for a time I watched him fascinated: he sucked in a third of his fag at one gasp, gulped, looked sick, and then blew out a great greenish cloud; when this had dispersed he was racked with coughing; then the whole dirty, noisy business was repeated. What could such a man not do with a big pipe? He would be a secret weapon in himself.

• OF A TAXING POSITION •

I MET A MAN TODAY who exhibited such unusual social grace and savoir faire that I was immediately curious about him; I learned that he was the chief Inspector of Income Tax for a large district. This explained everything. Such a man would be forced to develop a winning manner in order to overcome the social handicap imposed by his position. In the same way an habitual strangler of children, or a man who was known to have his pockets full of rattlesnakes, would have to develop remarkable ease and brilliance if he hoped to have any social life whatever. In his office, too, he would constantly have to meet trying situations, such as enraged taxpayers armed with fire-axes, hysterical taxpayers who wanted to tear off their clothes in the Doukhobor manner, or ice-cold taxpayers with soft voices and a mad light in the eyes, who obviously had revolvers in their overcoat pockets. To charm and soothe such visitors, while at the same time dipping deep into their jeans, would demand an unusually polished address.

• OF SONG •

I MET A FELLOW TODAY who is very fussy about the spoken word, and he was groaning that the radio provides little for persons of his kidney, although it serves those of musical taste very well. He was particularly critical of the people who speak on the Metropolitan Opera broadcasts, and became quite wild because Milton Cross *�𝆑* pronounces "Mignon" as though it were "minion" and pronounces "Wilhelm" with an English instead of a German "W." He moaned also about the poor speech of the Opera singers who speak in the intervals, and who call a tune a "toon" and in other ways assault the sensitive ear. As a matter of fact I myself have often marvelled at the ability of many singers to divorce speech from song, though it seems plain enough that song is a kind of glorified speech. But then, my views on singing are unusual and unpopular, for I am always amazed by people who announce that they cannot sing at all; it seems to me that anybody who can speak can sing, though he may not sing very well. There are even children who say that they cannot sing, though for a child it should be as easy to sing as to spit. How did this cleavage between speech and song arise, I wonder? . . . You are going to sing after dinner? And what sort of singer are you, madam? A real singer, or a musical gargler?

• CHILDREN AND POLITICIANS EQUATED •

I WATCHED A LARGE GROUP of children skating this afternoon, and was impressed once again by the shameless boastfulness of the young. One little girl kept falling down on her behind, and each time she did so she would shout, "I did that on purpose!" to the spectators; I reflected that if her thinking becomes fixed in this channel the only career open to her will be politics, for her technique is precisely that of some of our most eminent statesmen, who never execute a pratfall without declaring that they had some subtle design in doing so.

✒ Milton Cross (1897–1975) was famous as the commentator on the Saturday afternoon broadcasts from the Metropolitan Opera. The rich fruitiness of his voice struck awe into the breasts of the uncultivated, and his pronunciation of Italian words was Ultra-Italianate. His swooping, lyrical style of utterance was in itself an adaptation of the German Singspiel, but juicier.

• THE MISERY OF KINGSHIP •

SOME OF THE MEN here were discussing the late Victor Emmanuel of Italy before dinner, and they all agreed that he was a weakling and a peewee, and should have "stood up" to Mussolini and told him "where he got off." I would not dream of contradicting these experts, deeply versed in statecraft and familiar with court procedure, but I wondered what would happen to H.M. George VI if he were to say: "No, I refuse to appoint Sir Stafford Cripps ∮ as one of my ministers; he has repeatedly advocated the abolition of the Throne upon which I sit, and I detect seeds of tyranny and oppressiveness in him which I refuse to encourage." The King would, I am sure, be invited to abdicate, just as his brother was when he revealed a mind of his own. Not kings, but politicians, are the rulers in our day, and no king dares thwart a politician. Indeed, I can imagine no worse fate today than to be a king, and also a man of independent, humane and agile intellect. When he encouraged Mussolini poor Victor Emmanuel was encouraging The People's Choice, and the voice of the people, as we all know, is the voice of God. The Aristocratic Principle is a puny babe; the Demagogic Principle rages unchecked.

• OUT OF THE MOUTHS… •

A LITTLE GIRL OFFERED to read to me out of a book of Bible stories this afternoon, and announced the title of the one she had chosen as "Ruth, the Frightful Daughter-in-Law"; I was somewhat drowsy, and this sounded so normal — so in accord with everyday experience — that it did not occur to me until she

---

∮ *Sir Stafford Cripps (1889–1952), British politician and one-time Chancellor of the Exchequer, was even more famous as exemplifying the cast of countenance known as Reformer's Face, compared with which the mugs of the most determined Puritan divines seemed as jolly as Santa Claus.*

was well launched on the tale of Ruth and Naomi that she had misread the word "faithful."

• OF MELANCHOLY REFLECTIONS •

A GROUP OF professional floor waxers invaded The Towers today. They brought with them a great deal of equipment including several large wheels which appeared to be covered with the skins of whole cows. Their first move was to pile all the furniture in every room in a heap in the middle of it, and I was saddened to see how quickly the old home could be made to look like a junk shop. If I were to choke on a crumb, or collapse while shovelling snow, or be struck by a falling icicle, or fall backward down the cellar stairs while struggling upward with an armful of wood, or perish through any of the hazards of daily life, it would only be a matter of a few days before the auctioneers would invade the scene of my sloughed-off existence, and pile up my furniture in exactly this way; and when people came to the sale they would despise my furniture, and conclude that I was a sordid fellow, who had lived shabbily. These reflections depressed me so much that I itched all afternoon to get the waxers out of the house, so that I could set it right, and reassure myself.

• PERSONAL AND REMINISCENT •

A DISTANT RELATIVE of mine sent me a genealogy of part of my family today. I passed the evening reckoning the ages at which my ancestors died; save for a few who pegged out miserably in infancy the average age is eighty-seven years and a few months. Now this seems to me to be thoroughly praiseworthy. These primeval Marchbanks without the aid of vitamins, central heat, balanced diets, or any medical care save bleeding, purging and mustard plasters, managed to survive to an average age of eighty-seven, and usually died by falling off roofs, being gored by bulls, or otherwise violently. They ate till they were full, drank till they were drunk, hated fresh air, and thought tomatoes were poisonous, yet they lived valiantly, God rest them.

• OF TAILORS AND THEIR MYSTERY •

*A*S IT MUST to all men, the realization came to me today that I must order a new suit. I am sorry for men whose work demands that they present an appearance of neatness and prosperity; I rejoice that I belong to a traditionally frowsy trade. But even the vilest rags must be refreshed from time to time, and I went to the tailor's with a heavy heart. Soon I was fingering little squares of cloth and trying to imagine what they would look like if swollen into suits and hung upon my frame; this is the sort of job at which my imagination boggles, and when my imagination is boggling, my mouth drops open, my tongue lolls out foolishly, and a film creeps over my eyeballs. "This is a nice thing," I say, trying to curry favour with the tailor, "but I think I like this even better"—as I pick up my own pocket handkerchief or perhaps a penwiper from the desk. At last the tailor puts me out of my agony, and measuring begins. Here I exhibit devilish cunning, sucking myself in where I am too big, and blowing myself out where I am deficient, in a Protean manner, so that the record gives a completely false impression of my figure. "You sit a good deal at your work, Mr. Marchbanks?" says the tailor. "When I'm not lying down," I reply. "We'll allow a little extra for that," says he, and makes marks on his chart which he will not allow me to see. In time I escape into the street, shaking like a leaf.

• OF ANIMAL DEFENDANTS •

*I*SEE IN THE PAPER that a dog has been destroyed because it knocked down and frightened an old woman. In the Middle Ages such a dog might have received a full-dress trial; animals were often tried for serious offences. The court records before the Reformation are full of cases in which a dog was tried for preventing someone from going to church, or for biting somebody important, or for barking during a political speech. The animal was provided with a defence lawyer, and if he lost his case his client was likely to be hanged, or even tortured. Many a young barrister in those days got his start defending animals, and a court would as soon subpoena a herd of sheep or a couple of oxen as anybody else. This was because animals were thought to be easy hideouts for evil spirits — an opinion which I think modern jurisprudence has abandoned without sufficient thought.

• OF GUEST-ROOM BEDS •

I WAS TALKING to a lady before dinner who was shaken by an experience she had had with a bed in her guestroom. One night recently her spouse was sick of a salt rheum, and in order to escape infection and the sound of his coughs and moans she betook herself to the guest chamber, and tried to sleep upon one of the beds which her guests had been using for years. But to her horror the bed was too short, and too narrow, and was inclined to buck and throw the sleeper, so that she landed on the floor twice in the night. She was up at dawn, writing letters of apology to all her guests, and as soon as the shops opened she rushed forth to buy a new bed. Personally I think that everybody should sleep in their guest-bed once a year, to test it, and I am seriously thinking of giving the wretched palliasse at Marchbanks Towers a try-out one of these nights. Perhaps that bagginess of eye which I have observed in my guests at breakfast is in some way related to its deficiencies. Perhaps I should shove more hay into the tick.

• OF SOLEMN TIDES AND FESTIVALS •

I TRIED TO EXPLAIN the significance of Lent to some children this morning, but found it hard to make the principle of self-denial comprehensible to them. That one should refrain from doing something one wants to do as a spiritual exercise seems peculiar to a child, and as I agree with them with the heretical half of my mind, I cannot put my full weight into any theological dispute which may ensue.... I was asked what I myself was giving up for Lent. "Showy displays of personal prowess such as running upstairs, lifting heavy weights and walking great distances," I replied, without batting an eye.... I have also been looking over the year's

Valentine displays, which are more degraded in verse, and more vilely spotted with doggies, pussies, and bunnies than usual. Modern love, as reflected in Valentines, is on a depressingly infantile level.

• OF BONHOMIE IN TRAINS •

I HAD TO MAKE a train journey yesterday. In an advertisement for a mystery story I read a testimonial from Miss Hedy Lamarr, in these strange words: "It made my blood curl.". . . On the train were four happy extroverts who drank copiously from flasks, and were bosom friends in less than an hour; in ringing voices they discussed their investments, private fortunes, the Palestine situation and the difficulty of getting any wearable underpants. When any woman under seventy passed down the car they whistled after her, to show that they were full of hormones. They rushed to and from the lavatory, shouting as they went. As train lavatories have direct access to the roadbed, I hoped that they might fall through, but none of them did so.

• OF BIBLIOPHILY •

O NCE AGAIN, after a pause of many years, catalogues are beginning to reach me from sellers of old books in England. If I had any strength of character I should throw these into the garbage pail as soon as they arrive but I am a weak creature, and I always risk a peek. This is fatal, for in no time at all the concupiscence of the book-collector burns hotly within me. I send off an order, and in the course of time a new treasure is added to the cupboard at Marchbanks Towers. . . . Real bibliophiles do not put their books on shelves for people to look at or handle. They have no desire to show off their darlings, or to amaze people with their possessions. They keep their prized books hidden away in a secret spot to which they resort stealthily, like a Caliph visiting his harem, or a church elder sneaking into a bar. To be a book-collector is to combine the worst characteristics of a dope-fiend with those of a miser.

• OF DAY AND NIGHT •

OUR HOST REMARKED to me before dinner that the days are already drawing out. It is true, and I disapprove of it heartily. If I had the ordering of such things, it would be dark every winter day at five o'clock and every summer day at seven. Day should be day, and night night, and the present careless mingling of the two is distracting and annoying. As a matter of fact I think that time was much more sensibly dealt with in the Middle Ages when everybody got up at about 4 a.m., worked during the hours of daylight, and was in bed by 7 p.m. Midnight in those days was really the middle of the night, and not the hour when most people begin to think about bed. But for some inexplicable reason we now compound our normal day out of half the light and half the dark hours. And I stoutly maintain that when a man has done his day's work it should be dark. This is sheer cantankerousness, and I glory in it.

• OF UNCOUTH SPEECH •

THE AUSTRALIAN LADY on my right has been telling me of her labours to rid herself of her native accent under the tuition of an elocution master. She had to say "How now, brown cow?" over and over again, as apparently this greeting is a very hard one for an Australian to utter with complete purity. This amused her greatly, for it appears that in the Antipodes the word "cow" is applied to any unfortunate person, male or female, and a set of disagreeable circumstances or a distressing personality may also be called "a fair cow." Only in Australia, so far as I know, could a man be a black sheep and a fair cow at the same time.

• OF DAME NATURE •

I WENT TO SEE an exhibition of modern Canadian paintings this afternoon, and liked them very much. But there were a few people present who appeared to consider the pictures an insult to themselves — a kind of aesthetic hot-foot. They muttered and mumbled, but none of them seemed able to explain just what it was that bothered them. My own guess is that the pictures disturbed their ideas about nature, and made them reconsider certain notions which they have cherished, but not examined, for years. Music and pictures are able to churn the soul without using the medium of words, and as most people are quite at sea when they have to transform feelings into words they were affronted and gagged at the same time.... Most people, too, appear to think of Nature as a dear old lady with steel spectacles and a bonnet, mouthing platitudes. To have Nature presented to them as a wanton, decked in gayest colours and obviously not wearing a foundation garment, hit them smack under the Moral Sense, which is to a Canadian as its shell is to a tortoise.

• OF KINGS GREAT AND KINGS GOOD •

*T*HE LADY ON MY LEFT was complaining to me about the foolish caricature of King Charles II which appeared in the film *Forever Amber*; the Merry Monarch was shown as a man surrounded by silly little dogs, to whom he cried "Come children!" from time to time.... I replied that I had been annoyed by the same thing, and also by repeated film caricatures of Henry VIII as a gross monster, gorging, swilling, burping and pinching the bottoms of court ladies. Charles and Henry were two of the ablest kings ever to occupy the British throne, and it is not wise to forget it. They would never have become Sunday School superintendents, of course, but they had many excellent, and indeed admirable qualities as statesmen. For some reason the British rulers who have been chosen by common consent for adulation are Alfred the Great (about whom we know nothing save what is told us by his personal chaplain, who was on his payroll), Charles I, who was pious, but had no tact and owes much to the fact that Van Dyck was his court painter, and Victoria, who carried goodness to a point where it became indistinguishable from self-indulgence.

• OF MODERN HOUSES •

I PASSED LAST EVENING in the company of some people who have bought a lovely old house, and are having great fun fixing it up. Of course the furnace is not in very good condition and shoots most of its heat up the chimney, and none of the sashes fit, and there are cracks in the foundation, but it is a dear old place all the same. Admittedly they have to burn their own garbage in the furnace (which makes a smell) and they have to bury their tin cans privily at dead of night, and the water supply is capricious, but it has lovely high ceilings (some of which need replastering). Yet, in spite of their woes, I see what they are after. They are in rebellion against the modern vogue for houses which our ancestors would not have accepted as almshouses, and which are undoubtedly the nastiest human habitations ever to be built since man emerged from the Mud Hut Period of architecture. An old house is a nuisance, but it is obviously intended for men and women to live in. Much modern housing would be better called kennelling.

• OF A LOST ART •

A SCHOOLTEACHER confided to me today that there is nothing so useful for sticking things to a blackboard as shaving cream. It holds as well as glue, and yet it does not harden, and it imparts a delicious scent to the schoolroom, slightly ameliorating the customary effluvium of chalk, Vapex and wet sweaters. This lady told me that she used approximately a tube a term for this purpose.... What she said reminded me of my childhood, when I used to get my hair cut in the tonsorial parlour of an elderly barber called Murphy; in front of his two chairs were mirrors elegantly framed in walnut, and on these mirrors it was his custom to write improving sentiments in lather, such as "Treat Your Wife and Your Hair Right and They'll Never Leave You" or "God's Finest Gift—A Mother; A Man's Best Asset—A Fine Head of Hair." Murphy's spelling was not always equal to the demands of his philosophy, but he wrote a flourishing hand with the lather brush, and surrounded these profound reflections with curlicues and even flowers delicately executed in lather. The art of lather work has died out, I fear.

• OF A DISCOVERY •

I BOUGHT SOME ROPE today, for the first time in my life, I think, and was amazed to find that it is sold by the pound, like cheese. Who would think of going into a shop and asking for two pounds of nice fresh rope, suitable for a suicide? Yet the request would be a perfectly sensible one. I bought twelve feet, or about an eighth of a pound, and it cost me seven cents.

• OF YOUNG FOGIES •

*A*N ACTOR FRIEND of mine left a copy of *Variety* in my office today, and as I looked through it I was amazed to find a full-page advertisement which said, "Gabriel Pascal and Bernard Shaw wish all their friends a Successful New Year." I wonder if Mr. Shaw really paid for half of that insertion? It doesn't seem like him to deliver good wishes in that wholesale manner. . . . The magazine also contained an article headed, "Is Radio Burdened with Young Fogies?" It seems to me that the probable answer is "Yes." The whole world is burdened with young fogies. Old men with ossified minds are easily dealt with. But men who look young, act young, and everlastingly harp on the fact they are young, but who nevertheless think and act with a degree of caution which would be excessive in their grandfathers, are the curses of the world. We have a good many young fogies in Canada—fellows who, at thirty, are well content with beaten paths and reach-me-down opinions. Their very conservatism is second-hand, and they don't know what they are conserving.

• OF THE SIESTA •

I COMPOSED MYSELF after lunch for my noonday snooze, but was called three times on the telephone; in consequence my afternoon was ruined. It has long been my contention that the siesta is needed far more in our cold climate than in the languorous South. Southerners snooze at midday because they are lazy; Canadians should snooze at midday because they still have several hours of hard work ahead of them, including a certain amount of battling with the wintry blasts, and slipping and slithering on the ice. They need to prepare themselves for what lies ahead.

But it happens far too often that when I compose myself for fifteen minutes of delicious torpor some fellow who either has high blood pressure or is in a hurry to develop it calls me. He never wants to tell me that I have inherited a fortune, or that a beautiful dark woman is anxious to make my acquaintance; he invariably wants me to do something right away, usually of a vexatious nature. By the time I have lied my way out of doing whatever it is he wants, the shy nymph Snooze has fled, and there is nothing for me to do but begin the afternoon's toil.

· OF AN OPPORTUNITY MISSED ·

I HAVE RECEIVED a great many letters relating to a radio broadcast in which I took part a fortnight ago. They all make the same complaint and if I may I will give you the substance of a representative letter, sent to me by an elderly clergyman in Sault Ste. Marie: "There you were, with a national hook-up, and what did you do? Talked in a smarmy, Nice Nellie way that nearly made me throw up! Why did you not do what any man of spirit would do if he had a chance to address the whole of Canada — shove your face as near the microphone as possible and shout a dirty word? Such as '— —,' or '— —,' or better still '— —'? It is such a chance as I have long dreamed of. You had it, and you missed it. — —you!" The others are in much the same vein. . . . But what was I to do? Naturally the idea occurred to me, as it would to any man worthy of the name. But there were a lot of big C.B.C. bullies watching me, and I knew that if I yielded to my impulse I should be dragged from the microphone, beaten with rubber truncheons, and shipped to Ottawa under guard, where I would be forced to wash out my mouth with soap in the office of the Minister of National Revenue. I know that I was weak, but try to understand my position. I am not of the stuff from which martyrs are made.

• OF A USEFUL DOG •

I SAW A DALMATIAN dog today — one of those curious spotted animals which used to be called "blotting-paper dogs" when I was a boy. They used also to be called Coach Dogs, presumably because it was the smart thing to have one bounding along the road after one's coach, getting even more spotted from the spatter of the wheels. But of the three names I like "blotting-paper dog" best. It suggests that a Dalmatian has literary qualities not given to other dogs — that it lends itself to use as an auxiliary penwiper, or to rolling gently on large manuscripts. The average dog is a nuisance to a writer, as it lies on his feet, snuffling, coughing and having bad dreams, while he tries to collect his thoughts. No dog has ever whispered poems into its master's ear, as was the case with Victor Hugo's cat, but at least the Dalmatian has tried to make itself useful in the study.

• OF A MEDICAL CONSPIRACY •

I WAS TALKING this evening to an nineteenth-century Liberal who accused me of being an eighteenth-century Tory. This was because I had been holding forth at some length about the conspiracy against the home life of our nation on the part of the medical profession and the nurses. There was a day when a man took pride in the fact that he was born in the house in which he lived, and looked forward with confidence to dying in the same house, and perhaps even in the same bed. This gave a richness of association to a dwelling which has entirely been destroyed by modern medical usage. Babies are now born in hospitals, and there is a powerful and subtle move on foot to persuade everybody to die in hospitals. My desire is to die in my own bed, leaning back on a heap of pillows, wearing a becoming dressing-gown and a skull-cap, blessing those of whom I approve, gently rebuking my enemies, giving legacies to faithful servants, and passing out clean handkerchiefs to the weepers; I should also like a small choir to do some really fine unaccompanied singing within earshot. But will I be able to stage such a production in a hospital? Never! I'll be lucky if the nurse answers the bell in time to jot down my last words.

• OF AN UNACKNOWLEDGED AILMENT •

I READ IN A magazine this morning that gout is just as prevalent today as it was in the eighteenth century, although some doctors do not recognize it when they see it, believing the disease to be extinct. *℘* It seems to me that several other diseases are in the same ambiguous position. For instance, in *The Anatomy of Melancholy* Robert Burton makes frequent reference to a disease he calls "crudity," the symptoms of which were distress in the stomach, wind, and a sensation of having swallowed hot pennies. Lots of people that I know have these symptoms; if they are poor they consume patent medicines; if they are rich they permit surgeons to do fancy whittling and knot-tying in their entrails. They give the ailment many names, but it is just plain crudity, and I should think that doctors would recognize it. A sure sign of crudity, says Burton, is what he calls "hard, sour and sharp belching." Everybody knows how common this is; at service club luncheons you can hardly hear the speaker because of it. I have even heard it mentioned on the radio. Crudity numbers its victims by the millions, yet doctors refuse to acknowledge its existence.

℘ Gout is far from extinct and has had a remarkable upsurge in recent years. It affects men only, but the Women's Lib forces are agitating to have it made available to their sex. It is notorious that gout affects only men of superior intellect, and Marchbanks is humiliated that he has no faintest twinge of it, and feels at a disadvantage among his many gouty friends. It is a vulgar error to suppose that it is a consequence of high living; it is a deposition of sodium ureate and even the humblest and most poorly fed, such as university professors, may have it if they are sufficiently bright in the head.

· OF MOTHERHOOD ·

I SEE BY THE PAPERS that the champion milch cow of Great Britain drinks twelve quarts of stout a day, and is habitually soused. Also there is a cat in California which never drinks anything but Scotch, is seventeen years old and has produced 111 kittens. These are fascinating bits of information, but I fear that brooding on them will only lead to the formation of socially unacceptable theories concerning Motherhood.

· OF THE PYTHAGOREAN NOTION ·

E VERY DAY I SEE a dog which lies in wait for passing cars, and rushes at them, snarling. It is my theory that this dog is a reincarnation of a traffic cop. The belief of Pythagoras that the souls of men may return to earth in the bodies of animals, and vice versa, seems to me to be no more unreasonable than a lot of things we are expected to believe nowadays, and there is a good deal of circumstantial evidence to support it.

· OF HOT WEATHER ·

Y ES, I THINK the heat wave reached a new level this week. I do not greatly mind the heat; I simply drink water by the pailful, and go about my business. But some of my friends are in a sad state. This leads me to wonder whether the use of the fan by men might not be revived in Canada. Men carried fans in the eighteenth century; Orientals carry fans to this day. Of course the modern craze for utility would make it impossible to revive the fan as a thing of beauty, but a fan which was also a notebook, or which had actuarial tables printed on it, or which bore a large advertisement of one's own business would surely be permissible. Golfers could keep their scores on special fans, and preachers would write their sermons on them.

294

• OF EDITORS •

I SEE THAT THE U.S.A. is going to issue a stamp with the head of William Allen White of Emporia on it. ✐ I think that Canada is wise never to have created a stamp with the head of an editor on it; editors at best are disagreeable fellows, professional contradicters and sassers back. An editor of any degree of experience becomes incapable of complete agreement with anyone, and he reads the dictionary so much that he always knows more nasty names for any particular offence than the man who has committed it. Whatever an editor may be in his private life, he is professionally ferocious, and he can turn on his tap of belligerence at a moment's notice. There was a time when the horsewhipping of editors was a common sport, and shooting their hats off in the street was regarded as mere pleasantry. Now the law forbids both these manly pastimes. . . . But glorifying an editor by putting him on a stamp is as inexplicable to other nations as is our Canadian custom of worshipping the beaver, that other unattractive, gnawing, surly mammal. To be obliged to lick even the back of an editor's picture would be intolerable to a free man, though, an instant later, he could punch the picture in the face with his thumb.

• OF SCHOOLTEACHERS •

T HIS IS SUMMER, unmistakably. One can always tell when one sees schoolteachers hanging about the streets idly, looking like cannibals during a shortage of missionaries. Of course, schoolteachers are not idle all summer long; no, no. Very soon the well-paid ones will be travelling, the poorly-paid ones will be sweat-

---

✐ *White, who edited the* Emporia Gazette *from 1895, was recognized in journalistic circles as a fearless innovator. His most fearless innovation was his custom of writing his own editorials, instead of pinching them from other papers and then publishing them without attribution or else with "We agree with the Bingville* Bugle *which says . . ." tacked on top. This innovation was long in reaching Canada and there are still remote areas where it has not penetrated.*

ing in summer jobs, and great numbers of others will be in summer schools, stoking themselves with knowledge which they will disgorge next autumn. Here and there a few mad eccentrics will be found reading and thinking, having somewhere received the impression that this indulgence is somehow connected with their work. But for a few days at the end of every school year teachers of whatever degree may be seen roaming the streets, slightly dazed and a trifle irresponsible, like the slaves immediately after Lincoln signed the decree of emancipation.... You are a school teacher? Then what are you doing in that attractive gown, you little skeezix!

• THE RITES OF PICKLEMAS •

I ATTENDED A PLAY which I myself had written and at the end of Act One two women hurried past me, making for the door. "I don't care what happens, those pickles have got to be done tonight," said the larger and more determined one. It is incidents such as this that keep authors from getting swelled heads. And indeed at this time of year pickles are the prime concern of every really womanly woman. The subtle alchemy which transmutes a mess of tomatoes and celery (which looks like something the police have swept up after a disastrous bus collision) into chili sauce cannot be understood by men; nor can the coarse male hand compound mustard pickles which do not scorch the epigastrium of the eater, and give him a breath like the monsoon of the spicy East. There are indisputably some jobs which women do better than men, and making pickles is one of them. Women cannot make wine — Sir James Fraser tells why in *The Golden Bough* — but they are priestesses of the pungent mystery of the pickle, and the 25th of September is their Picklemas.

• OF SALVATION BY WORKS •

O F LATE I HAVE been much in the company of some professional Canadian actors, who were engaged in the production of a play. Most Canadians still think of actors as gay, carefree souls and not quite respectable by our grisly national standard. (In Canada anyone is respectable who does no obvious harm to his fellow man, and who takes care to be very solemn, and disapproving toward those who are not solemn.) But my experience of Canadian actors is that they are intense and earnest folk who work very hard and spend the time when they should be asleep chewing the rag about a national theatre for Canada. For this reason I think that it is wrong to call pieces which are written for the theatre in Canada "plays," for that word suggests lightness, fantasy and ease of accomplishment. Canada will only respect her theatre when plays are called "works." Canada has a high regard for anything that involves toil. Therefore I think that in future I shall describe all my plays as "works," and if they ever reach the apotheosis of print I shall take care to call them *The Complete Works of Marchbanks*. Let triflers talk of plays; Canada wants to be given the works. . . . Yes, madam, I entirely agree: all works and too few plays makes Canada a dull nation.

• NEW LIGHT ON HISTORY •

O N TWELFTH NIGHT my host offered me a drink of Drambuie; plainly marked on the bottle was a statement that this was the drink favoured above all others by Prince Charles Edward. It seems to me that this throws a light on the history of the 1745 rebellion which historians have unaccountably neglected. If Bonnie Prince Charlie was in the habit of drinking Drambuie freely he was in no state to lead armies, though it is obvious why he so grossly overestimated the size of his forces. That look of being delightfully fried which he wears in all his portraits is explained, too.

• OF DOG HAMS •

I SAW AN AMATEUR production of *The Barretts of Wimpole Street* last week; the audience had come to admire the actors (who were high school boys and girls) but were much taken by the goings-on of the spaniel who played the role of Flush. Dogs and babies are impossible creatures on the stage; they have only to gurgle or scratch a flea and the careful art of the human actors is set at naught. Somebody should write a play in which a dog has to do something difficult, and meet stern criticism. In Victorian England there was a popular version of *Hamlet* in which the Prince was accompanied at all times by a huge dog (a Great Dane, of course); in the Play Scene it was the dog's duty to leap at the throat of King Claudius. Often the dog-actor missed his cue, or wagged his tail at the gallery, or licked Claudius affectionately; such dog-hams were given short shrift by the critics of the day and many a dog-actor disgraced himself by snarling over the footlights at the critic's row, with bared teeth. This is only just; if a dog appears on the stage, it should be expected to do something difficult, and not loll about, stealing scenes from hard-working humans.

• OF DEATH BY GREED •

CONSIDERING THE AMOUNT of time and ingenuity which is devoted to making it hard for a man to get a drink in this country, I think it strange that nothing is done to keep people from digging their graves with their teeth. I have just finished two volumes of historical studies by Dr. C.H. MacLaurin, the celebrated diagnostician, in which he shows that a surprising number of the most eminent people in history have died of diseases which began in their habit of overeating. Drink is a spectacular vice, but comparatively few people have any inclination to drink to excess. But the quiet, day-to-day cramming, guzzling, stuffing, bolting and gormandizing which goes on is thoroughly alarming, when we consider its effect on the nation's health. And everywhere we permit signs and advertising positively encouraging people to eat; little children are plied with cake and pie; the old are urged to eat "to keep their strength up" when in reality food will only sclerose their poor old arteries and blow the fuses in their shaky nervous systems. Frankly, I think that a move should be set on foot to limit the retail outlets for food, or perhaps bring it under government monopoly, making it too expensive for people to get much of it.

· He Faces an Ugly Fact ·

*B*Y A COMPLEX SYSTEM of my own I cushion myself against the shocks of daily life, but today I was forced to face the fact that I must have a new winter overcoat, and a few discreet enquiries made it clear to me that prices have been going up, and that clothes cost more now than they did. I grudge money spent on clothes. But from time to time it is absolutely necessary for me to replenish my wardrobe, and then there is always a disquieting struggle between my need and my ingrained penuriousness. I cannot bear to spend money on anything except pleasure, and I do not consider the buying of new clothes as a pleasure. If I could have a red overcoat with a fur collar, that might be fun, but to face the dreary choice between grey and blue again at my time of life, and to have to fork out several months' income in payment is more than I can bear. Still, I suppose that by a painful process of screwing up my resolution, I shall come to it.

· Of a Quaint Simile ·

*T*HIS AFTERNOON I had a long conversation with a man who comes from Lincolnshire; he says that the peasants in his native shire have a pretty simile to describe a baby which has just awakened; they say it looks "like a louse peerin' out o' an ash heap." It is such flights of untutored poesy as this which inspired Wordsworth.

· Of Audience Participation ·

*I*WENT TO THE movies last night. I always buy a stall, or loge, as I am by nature a snobbish fellow, and also because those seats give me more room for my legs. But the people who get to the loges before me all seem to bring provisions for a week, and attach themselves to their seats with cobbler's wax and glue, so that I usually spend the first half of any film sitting in a cheaper seat, poised to pounce if any loge-squatter should be called out by the demands of nature or the death of a near relative. Tonight I sat next to a couple of spirited girls who were not content to follow the story on the screen; they acted it, as well. When the heroine bridled, they bridled; when the hero hit the villain on the jaw, they cut the air with desperate haymakers. When there was kissing on the screen, they squeaked with their lips and wriggled in their seats. It was fascinating but unnerving, this audience participation; I was never sure that they might not involve me in the game in some embarrassing way. But at last a slide was flashed on the screen: "Whole West End of the City Wiped Out by Tornado — Hundreds Killed." One man rose and departed reluctantly from the loges, and I vaulted into his seat, beating an old lady by a nose. ✍

• OF A MALE DELUSION •

*B*EFORE DINNER I joined in a great discussion about the forthcoming rise in the price of bread, and I heard several men planning to have their wives make bread at home. I know this will not last long, for home bread-making, though not difficult, is a nuisance. Home bread is greatly superior to the purchased article, but it has to be made two or three times a week, and the average housewife would rather pay more for the customary ration of half-cooked dough than be bothered with it. Many men are speaking nostalgically of breads which their mothers used to bake — fancy confections with odd names, like Old Hoe Handle Bread, Barnyard Pandowdy, Corncob Bumblepuppy, and the like. They tell me that they always ate these luscious breads with baked beans. It is odd how all men develop the notion, as they grow older, that their mothers were wonderful cooks. I have yet to meet the man who will admit that his mother was a kitchen assassin, and nearly poisoned him. Yet there must be some bad cooks who are also mothers.

✍ It may be asked why the sale of loge tickets was not governed by the number of loges available, but such a question reveals a pitiable naiveté. The proprietors of cinemas are rarely persons of iron principle.

• OF CHILDREN AT PLAY •

I WENT TO CALL on some people today and stumbled into a children's party—a type of entertainment which I usually study to avoid. No sooner was I in the door than a young woman of about six pushed an apple core into my hand, saying "Here!" in a peremptory tone. I immediately assumed the guise of Marchbanks the Child-Lover and grinned at her forgivingly; I tossed the apple behind a sofa. Not long afterward I was called upon to umpire a game of Pin the Donkey's Tail, and barely escaped with my life, but not before a small girl showed me her doll. It was one of those dolls which can be fed water from a feeding-bottle at one end, and shortly afterwards rejects the water through a sort of brass drain in its bottom. I am not easily embarrassed, but this doll made me blush; its lack of reticence was appalling. Live babies have drenched me, and I have borne it with good humour, but this awful effigy of a baby with its hideous painted smile!... "Don't you think your dolly would like a rest?" I asked hopefully. "NO!" said the moppet, with iron decision, and began to ply it with water again. Whatever served the office of kidneys in the doll gave a gurgle, and I hurried away. Why not a doll which burps? Babies burp, and a doll with a bellows and a squeaker in it, which could belch like a sailor or an Indian chief, would sell like hotcakes. After refreshments the party grew rough; one lad kept jumping off the top of the piano, landing in a sitting posture on the keyboard; he did this a number of times—leaving no tone unsterned, in fact. As soon as was decently possible, I left; children were beginning to go upstairs to be sick, and I was willing to leave them in abler hands.

• OF YULETIDE DECORATION •

I WAS FACED TODAY with the necessity to decorate Marchbanks Towers against the coming Christmas, and passed many hours perched on a shaky ladder twisting paper streamers (which immediately untwisted), getting sharp pieces of tinsel under my nails, and arranging elaborate festoons which, as soon as I looked at them from the floor, proved to be miserable in conception and lopsided in execution. I also knocked down a good deal of plaster and made dirty marks on the wallpaper. The effect, when I was finished, was that of a cheap dancehall decorated by a drunken sailor. However, I had a great artistic success with the younger members of my family, who think my efforts greatly superior to Michelangelo's decorations of the Sistine Chapel. This disposed me to be friendly toward them, and we ate a great deal of candy, which caused them no inconvenience, but makes me feel pensive even at this moment. . . . No, no more chocolate mousse, thank you.

• THE PLEASURES OF OFFICIALDOM •

I WAS A JUDGE at a county fair today: I was invited to give my opinion on the turnips and the cats. There were only three turnips exhibited and as all of them came from the farm of the son of the man who was my colleague in judging, we awarded him the prize with beautiful unanimity. There was only one entry in the cat show; it belonged to the other judge's daughter, so we gave her the First, Second and Third Prizes, as well as the silver cup. I then strolled around the fair, with a large purple ribbon with "Judge" printed on it in gold adorning my bosom. It was an "Open Sesame" to all the treasures of the fair. I rode free on the merry-go-round, and the Dodge 'Em. I then judged the whole of the midway, poking the Fat Lady with a stick to see if she was genuinely fat or merely padded, patting the midgets, and accepting the gift of a cigar from the Turkey-Faced Man. Oh, it is a beautiful thing to be a Judge, to be honoured wherever one goes, to get things for nothing! If all life could be passed as a Judge at a fair, what a glad, sweet song it would be!

• HE CEASES TO BE A TENDERHORN •

I WENT ON MY first hunt last week with a group of friends; they were Old Hands, and I was what they call a Greenfoot or a Tenderhorn, so I kept quiet and tried to learn woodlore. We motored fifty miles, then crowded our eight selves, 400 pounds of equipment, four dogs and two Indians into a rather small boat, bringing the gunwales down almost to the water-line. We journeyed by water for a considerable distance and then debarked after sundown. Then we carried the junk a further five miles in the dark — at least, it was supposed to be five miles, but as none of the Old Hands knew the way and there was no road or path, it was more like eight. At last we found the camp and the guide, who had prepared a supper of salt pork and fried potatoes two hours earlier; it had congealed curiously, but we ate it. Then the Old Hands "turned in." Being a mere Tenderhorn, I simply went to bed.

Next day it was raining cats and dogs, and the Old Hands complained that their feet hurt; my feet hurt too but being a mere Greenfoot I was ashamed to say so. We breakfasted on salt pork and fried potatoes. We decided that it was useless to try to hunt in the rain; it kills the scent, or depresses the dogs or gives the Old Hands colds, or something. The Old Hands did not seem to be feeling very woodsy, and talked about the merits of different kinds of cars all day. Dinner and supper were of salt pork and fried potatoes. One Old Hand produced a package of bicarbonate of soda, and we all had a snort. We went to bed early. The bunks were boards with marsh-grass strewn lightly over them, and I dreamed of Hell.

The next day was better, so we stoked ourselves with salt pork and fried potatoes and went out. I was put by a rock and told not to budge or fire at anything unless I was sure it was a deer. I gave my word.... Hours passed. At midday I cunningly buried my package of salt pork and fried potatoes, and ate some of the biscuits and things I had secreted in my pockets; I wouldn't dare admit to the Old Hands that I have such babyish tastes. Nothing happened except that I grew to hate my rock and wished I were sitting in my swivel chair in my nice stuffy office. At last ennui became so great that I sneakingly smoked a cigarette — a hideous crime. *∫* When we reassembled at camp for salt pork and fried potatoes, I noticed

---

∫ Because it arouses an insatiable lust for tobacco among the deer, who slink up to the hunters, imploring a cigarette or two with their great, beautiful eyes, thus spoiling the sport, which consists of killing them treacherously, when they haven't got their horns crossed.

that all the Old Hands had biscuit crumbs on their fronts, and smelled of tobacco. Two of the dogs were lost.

I was put in another place the next day, with a better view. I found a dead bear in the woods and performed an autopsy; it had been eating salt pork and fried potatoes. After some hours I saw an Old Hand approaching with a strange light in his eyes; he jerked his head at me, and I followed; he had picked up a trail. At last we crouched behind some scrub. He put his lips to my ear, and in a moist, tickly whisper said, "See his antlers?" "Her horns?" I enquired. "Tenderhorn," he whispered; "a magnificent spread of antlers; a buck." I peeped over the scrub. "A Holstein," I whispered back, but already he had aimed. He trembled. His eyes bulged. Bubbles came out of his mouth. He fired. The cow squalled and fled. The milk was sour at supper, which did not help the tea with which we washed down our salt pork and fried potatoes. Being a Greenfoot, I said nothing. There seemed to be an air of depression in the camp; the Old Hands massaged their stomachs and brooded.

By the next day I had decided that I shall never understand this hunting business. I hadn't even fired off my gun, and I had stood still for seventeen hours, and I had stomach ulcers from the food, saddle-galls from the bed, and to top it all we were going home! Nobody explained anything but the chief Old Hand was in a terrible temper, and had a bullet hole in his hat, and wouldn't speak to one of the other Old Hands, who looked defiant and pouty, like a little boy who has broken a vase. The rest of us talked a lot and agreed that there were too many hunters in the woods, some of whom didn't know how to handle a gun (the chief Old Hand and the pouty Old Hand both snarled at that) and that it was not our fault that we hadn't killed eight or ten deer. We retraced our steps, but as we were short a pair of dogs the boat wasn't quite so full this time. Motoring home we passed car after car with its engine smothered in deer. They trapped them, probably.

I was glad to be back at work. "My foot is on my native heath; my name's MacGregor!" I kept exclaiming, while my colleagues stared. "Have a good hunt?" people asked me. "Capital sport! Capital!" I replied, knowing that the Old Hands would expect this of me. People pestered me for cuts of venison; I explained that I had sent all mine to the Hospital for the Deaf and Dumb.

But I received a brusque note from the chief Old Hand today, asking me for twenty-five dollars—my share in the price of the lost dogs. Those dogs must have had hearts of gold; their carcasses were not worth fifty cents apiece. But never mind; I have been on a hunt, and I shall never be a Tenderhorn again. From henceforth I am an Old Hand, and I shall boast and lie about my prowess in the woods, avowing that I am every bit the equal of Natty Bummpo, Robin Hood, and Frank Buck. I have even burned a hole in my hunting hat with a poker, so that I can pass as a genuine Old Hand. That is the sign by which they are known, I am told.

• A System of Marking •

*I*N A WEAK-MINDED moment last autumn I agreed to serve as a judge of some undergraduate writing; today my Fate overtook me and I had to spend two or three hours reading ambitious pieces of all kinds—poetry, criticism, short stories and whatnot. I am a wretched judge of such things, for I am capricious, irresponsible, unmethodical, utterly without conscience and what my grandmother used to call "notionate." Anyway, I wasn't interested in any of the stuff I read. The right people to judge such contests are sober, keen-minded fellows who are ready to take all sorts of trouble to arrive at the right decision—not whirligigs like me. At last I put all the manuscripts on the floor, whirled round three times, and shook my fountain pen over the heap; the manuscripts with the biggest blots on them received prizes, the rest got nothing. I do not defend this method of judging; I merely explain it. I also recommend it to university professors and teachers who have a lot of troublesome papers to mark.

• Of Energetic Histrionism •

*I*T WAS FOGGY yesterday; I met several people who referred to it as "English weather." It is a popular idea in Canada that England is under a blanket of fog about 300 days in the year. As one who has lived quite a while in both places, I can assure them that fog is about as common in Ontario as it is in England, though English fog tastes worse. I went to a play through the fog, the plot of which was the ancient one of the husband, presumed dead, who turns up again after his wife has remarried. This palsied wheeze was beaten to a pulp by the playwright and the cast, and the evening was somewhat exhausting. I was not sure whether the actors were trying to divert the audience, or just working up a good sweat; they rushed on and off the stage, they shrieked, waved their arms, and tumbled into chairs; they were diverting, but it wore me out to watch them.... Frankly, I don't think many women would mind having two husbands, if they could get away with it, and therefore the play was founded on an unsound argument, so far as I was concerned.

• OF AMOROUS SELF-SUFFICIENCY •

A FRIEND OF MINE was showing me his aquarium this afternoon; he had some pretty tropical fish, and I looked at them with an intelligent expression and pretended to understand what he told me of their species and habits. But I woke up when he pointed out his Japanese snail, and informed me that this creature is its own mate, and produces young without entangling alliances. At first it seemed to me that this was carrying egotism too far, but then I began to reflect on the advantages of such a plan. It is cosy, to begin with, and love, which is for mere human beings an emotion involving painful dependence upon another person, is for the Japanese snail merely a period of delicious introspection. Moralists should make this snail their emblem, for it knows no divorce, no marital disagreement, and no triangle murders. And the Japanese snail, instead of keeping his wife's picture on his desk, as so many men do, merely tickles himself when he feels uxorious and says "Ah, you slyboots!"

• THE ADVANTAGES OF MORALITY •

A JUICY BIT of gossip reached my ears today to the effect that a puritanical fellow of my acquaintance has been paying court to a lady who is not his wife. My informant expressed surprise that so straight-laced a man should err, but it does not surprise me in the least. Puritans are always thinking about sin, and consequently they are quick to see a sinful opportunity when one presents itself. A Poor Lost Lamb like myself, who never bothers his head about sin, is far less subject to temptation than a convinced Puritan. Furthermore, Puritans enjoy sin more than ordinary people; not only do they have the fun of doing whatever it may be that is wrong, but they have the fun of self-accusation, repentance, penitence, and similar emotional binges. A Puritan gets more of an emotional jag out of a miserable little sin like stealing a postage-stamp or kissing an hotel chambermaid than I would out of robbing the Bank of England, or, more profitably, the U.S. Mint. Consequently, Puritans lead gaudy lives, while mine is a life of bland respectability.

• RELIGION WITHOUT TEARS •

NEWS REACHES ME that in the kindergarten which my nephew Belial attends they recently gave point to the Easter lesson by acting out Our Lord's Passion, and Belial was chosen for the coveted role of the Saviour. This was an egregious piece of miscasting, as Belial is much better suited to the part of a torturer, demon or tormentor. However, he was tied to a cross (made from a couple of yardsticks) with tape, and in due time he was taken down and laid in the tomb of Joseph of Arimathaea which was represented by the schoolroom cupboard. "And did you rise again on the Third Day, Belial?" his parents asked him. "Yes, I came out of the cupboard," he replied. "And what did you do then?" they enquired. "I went to my seat," said Belial, apparently without any sense of anticlimax.... The new system of religious education is working wonders in the land, and I hardly meet a child these days who has not been an angel, or the Virgin Mary, or the Paraclete, or Original Sin, or some other notable character from Holy Writ in one of these classroom epiphanies.

• OF COMPULSORY AFFECTION •

A MAN IN THE States proposes that a date be chosen for International Grandmother's Day; I suspect that he is being egged on by the greeting-card cartel. The average grandmother is, I suppose, a worthy old party, and it has been my observation that grandmothers are kept pretty well stocked with sweetmeats, flowers, cocaine and bottles of gin by their loving relatives, without any social compulsion being exercised. But once grandmother-worship becomes official and obligatory a great many untrammelled spirits will rebel against it. Look what happened to Mother's Day. From the dawn of civilization mothers, as a class, were held in reasonably high regard until Mother's Day was established, with the purpose of compelling every man, under pain of social ostracism, to declare that his mother was the greatest woman who ever lived, and to give proof, in consumer goods, of his tremendous adoration of her. In consequence a lot of men—just to show that their souls are their own and without any ill-will toward the authors of their being—kick and buffet their mothers all over the house on Mother's Day, although during the other 364 days of the year they take them to the movies, buy them bags of nut fudge, and provide them with lacy shawls and crime-story magazines. Men can be led but they won't be driven; mice, of course, do what they are told.

• OF HYGIENE RESISTED •

CIRCUMSTANCES MADE it necessary for me to take a walk through town at half-past five this morning; I had the streets to myself and was able to look about freely. I was astonished by the fact that a great number of my fellow citizens appear to sleep in sealed rooms; if they get any fresh air, it is certainly not through their windows. I dread to think what my old school nurse, Miss Toxaemia Dogsbody, Reg. N., would have said about this; retrospective fear of that old harridan has compelled me to open my window on nights of bitterest cold, and because of her admonitions I still brush my teeth up and down, instead of crosswise which is much more fun. . . . Indeed, I must confess that fear of Miss Dogsbody (although she is now in Abraham's bosom and is probably scrubbing it with carbolic soap) is the moving principle in my struggle for health. Like most people I have a natural tendency toward unhealthy practices which are pleasant, such as drinking with my mouth full, eating heavily before going to bed, and sleeping in an atmosphere of warm frowst.

• OF THE MISERIES OF ELEPHANTS •

I WAS LUNCHING with a person today who has travelled a good deal, and has had contacts with elephants, both wild and in captivity. I was astounded to learn that most elephants suffer to some extent with indigestion, as they eat a lot of damp grass and vegetable matter which gives them gas and bloating (like the people in the patent medicine advertisements). I didn't like to be too curious on this subject, which had a slight tinge of indelicacy and was not entirely suitable for lunch-table conversation, but it explained a few things about elephants which I have pondered from time to time. That look of patient resignation, for instance, is familiar to all victims of indigestion. And the saggy skin of the elephant is probably Dame Nature's way of providing the poor beast with plenty of stretch during periods of bloating. A full-blown elephant must be an astonishing sight. What hiccups an elephant must suffer! What apocalyptic belchings, what rumblings of that vast paunch, how sonorous those pachydermatous borborygmies!

• ANOTHER DRAMA ORGY •

I SPENT A GOOD DEAL of time last week making arrange-ments to go away. This is one of the curses of our over-organized modern life — nothing can be done simply. I cannot wrap a crust of bread and a rind of cheese in a bandana handkerchief and set out when the spirit moves me: I must buy several tickets, make reservations at hotels, redeem my collars from the Oriental who washes them, grapple with the confusion between Daylight Saving and Daylight Wasting, issue instructions in all directions and work myself into a frame of mind in which all travel seems hateful, and a six-by-eight prison cell, with no possibility of escape, the highest reach of human bliss. Oh to be a gypsy, with one shirt and no necessity to be anywhere on time!

Then at last, I reached Toronto, and went to the Big Pub, where I had reserved a room: but of course it was not ready, so I went to the home of some friends, and when I had eaten and drunk them poor I returned to the B.P. at 1 a.m.

Then on the next day I went to London, where the Dominion Drama Festival *ƒ* was in the throes of its final competition. This city has the windiest station in Ontario, and my hat blew under a train, acquiring an oily patina. At the hotel and the Grand Theatre hundreds of amateur actors and producers were milling around, addressing one another in the merry shrieks which theatrical people consider obligatory in conversation. I had not been in the hotel a minute before I was greeted by the front legs of a horse of which I had been the back legs in a pantomine in 1933. The years sat lightly upon these front legs, and we tried out our act then and there: nobody noticed, for everyone else was horsing around, too.... During the afternoon I engaged in several invigorating fights about a Canadian National Theatre — a sort of Loch Ness monster which rears its ugly head at every Drama Festival.

I was surprised and delighted by the number of pretty and smartly dressed women attending the Drama Festival. Though really there is no occasion for amazement: pretty women like to act and show themselves off, and acting and showing off tends to make women pretty. I am no admirer of the retiring violet, who forgets to powder her nose and straighten her stocking-seams, and who prides herself on being natural and unspoiled; if the human race had persisted in being natural and unspoiled we should all still be swinging from tree to tree by our tails. Women are the flowers of human-

---

ƒ *The Dominion Drama Festival was a highly praiseworthy association of amateur theatrical companies that met every year for regional
and Dominion-wide contests, which were judged and criticized by adju-
dicators brought in from Great Britain and the U.S.A. Its avowed desire
was to render itself superfluous by bringing about a professional theatre
in Canada and in this philanthropic aim it was wholly successful. Let us
remember it, therefore, with gratitude. And let us remember also the
spirit of pow-wow, palaver and corroboree which marked its meetings
and made them immensely pleasurable.*

ity, and I find it hard to be patient with poor bloomers, and worse still tiresome thorny shrubs that never bloom at all.

At a matinee performance I sat between two parties of elderly people who enjoyed the comedies in a somewhat moribund way. Their praise was all negative. "Glad this isn't one of those gloomy ones," said an elderly man, with a despairing face: "Yes, I don't like those plays about death," agreed his female companion, who wore false teeth made apparently out of bone buttons and red sealing wax, and whose gayest smile was a ghastly *memento mori*. The elderly usually crave comedies, even though they have no touch of the Comic Spirit: it is the young, the dewy, the not-quite-dry-behind-the-ears who applaud the grim plays.... A performance of *Jane Eyre* one evening suffered from the fact that theatrical wigs are virtually unobtainable in Canada; consequently Mr. Rochester wore a thing on his head which had apparently been made from a dust-less mop, and gave him an unfortunate resemblance to King Kong.

• OF FESTIVAL AWARDS •

*T*HE LAST DAY OF the Festival was the best and there was wild excitement everywhere. After the adjudicator had announced the usual awards, I was called to the stage to make the Marchbanks Special Awards. These were:

THE MARCHBANKS SHIELD FOR THE BEST COUGH IN FRENCH OR ENGLISH TO BE HEARD DURING THE FESTI-VAL: In spite of strong competition from some sharp Western coughs, this went to a fruity old Eastern cough, like coal sliding down a chute, from the Eastern Ontario region.

THE MARCHBANKS TROPHY FOR THE MOST SUCCESSFUL LATE COMER: Won by a lady from Quebec whose gown was caught in the doors just as they closed on Friday night, and who sat out the performance in her chemise, to the envy of the remain-der of the spectators, who were overheated.

THE MARCHBANKS SCOLD'S BRIDLE FOR THE MOST TACT-LESS REMARK: Awarded to a lady from the West who approached the only Canadian playwright to have a long play in the Festival immediately after its performance with the query: "Well, and when are you going to write a novel?"

• OF DISCIPLINARY MAYHEM •

A FRIEND PLAYED ME a gramophone record of a song called *"Little Sir William"* yesterday, which is about a small boy who was murdered by his school-teacher. When his mother calls piteously for him outside the school he replies:

> How can I pity your weep, Mother
> And I so sore in pain?
> For the little pen-knife
> It sticks in my heart
> And the school-wife hath me slain.

This song is obviously a relic of the good old days when teachers were not forbidden to inflict corporal punishment on troublesome pupils. If we had the school-wife's side of the story we should no doubt find that little Sir William had been throwing spit-balls, or pinning signs saying "kick me" on the seat of the school-wife's gown. Many a teacher has fingered her knife reflectively under such circumstances.

• OF A NICE POINT IN LAW •

T HE CROSSROADS at which I live has recently treated itself to a few score parking meters; the hitching post having gone out of fashion, the parking post has become the mode, and rude fellows have been referring to them as pay-toilets for dogs. A more seemly attitude was shown today by two Wolf Cubs whom I observed from my window. "Let me show you how these things work," said one of the lads, pulling a cent from his pocket and putting it in the slot of a meter. When the indicator swung into view his small friend was suitably impressed. Now, I should be interested to know the legal position of that boy, who had bought twelve minutes worth of parking time, but who had no car. Would he be within his rights if he stretched himself prone beside his meter, and took a twelve minute nap? And if so, would it be legally possible for me to unfold a deckchair by one of these gadgets, buy an hour's time, and sun myself in the street, in the Mexican fashion? What would happen to a man who parked his trailer by one of the things, and kept his rent paid by stuffing the meter with money? There are some pretty problems of jurisprudence inherent in this question of parking meters.

· OF DANTE ·

A NEW TRANSLATION of Dante's *Divine Comedy* came to hand today, and I took a quick look at it before putting it on the review shelf. Reading Dante is a valuable corrective to too much reading of American political philosophy, for Dante had no use for the Common Man, although he was one of the great democrats of the ages. People who had done nothing in life were of no interest to him, and he states plainly that such people are of no interest to either God or the Devil, and are condemned to spend eternity in a nasty, cold place (like the recent Spring) outside the gates of Hell. . . . What fun, what deep, marrow-warming satisfaction Dante must have had in the composition of this mighty poem! Putting all his enemies (including the reigning Pope, Boniface VIII) into Hell, and attributing various unsuitable and undignified sins to them, doling out praise and blame, and vicariously spitting in the eye of anyone who disagreed with him! Nowadays of course the law of libel (that cloak of scoundrels and ruffians) would restrain his hand.

· OF THE HORSE SENSE OF CHILDREN ·

A CHILD ASKED me today to explain a picture it had found in a magazine, which showed some mailed warriors walking toward a castle carrying branches of trees in front of them. It was an advertisement for Scotch whisky, and the picture was Malcolm's forces advancing upon Macbeth's castle — Birnam Wood moving toward Dunsinane, in fact. I explained this to the child, and gave a rough and expurgated version of the Shakespeare play, in which I happened to mention that the Witches had told Macbeth that this very thing was likely to happen. "If a witch had told me that, I'd have cut down the forest right away," said the child. I agreed that this would have been a wise precaution, but that if Macbeth had done so there would have been no tragedy, and the whole course of Scots history would have been altered. She looked up at me searchingly and said: "That's silly." Sometimes I think that the reins of government should be put in the hands of children. They have remarkably direct minds, and when a witch tells them something, they pay attention.

• THE BYRONIC ENDING •

I SAW IN A PAPER today that Hollywood is going to make a film based on Byron's poem *The Corsair*. My guess is that the movie boys will take their cue from the lines:

> His heart was form'd for softness — warped to wrong;
> Betray'd too early and beguiled too long;

and will turn the whole thing into an exposure of juvenile delinquency, altering those lively scenes in the Pasha's harem to a sequence in which some rough boys with pea-shooters have fun in the ladies' section of a Turkish bath.... It is a matter of surprise to me that Hollywood has not yet attempted a film on the life of Byron. True, the facts are too lurid for the censors, but the moviemakers could always use one of their tried-and-true stories about poet meets girl, poet loses girl, poet gets girl. The truly Byronic conclusion — i.e., poet, having got girl, kicks her into the street — would not suit Hollywood's customers.

• OF SHORT SKIRTS •

I READ IN THE fashion news that the Handkerchief Skirt is coming back; this garment, fashionable in the twenties, is short and hangs in rags, as though the wearer had been fighting a particularly sharp-nailed wolf. I hope that this is not true, and that the Handkerchief Skirt will remain in Oblivion, where it belongs. I do not like short skirts; I like long skirts which swish and whirl. A short, tight skirt on a girl is ugly enough, but on an older woman to whom life and her metabolism have been unkind it is a cruel joke. Some men whose notion of Fashion is to bring women as near to utter nakedness as possible like short skirts because they reveal a lot of leg; but to my mind a really graceful woman is shown to greatest advantage in a skirt which compliments the poetry of her walk, instead of revealing the muscular action of her *gluteus maximus*. And though I yield to no man in my admiration of the female leg, I do not want to see all the legs in the world: there are thousands which I am ready to take for granted as useful, sturdy servants. Let us be spared Nature's rougher handiwork.

• OF HIS POLL •

I WENT TO THE movies last night and on the newsreel saw the Hon. George Drew ✒ welcoming some immigrants. I started a clap for him, in which only one other person joined. I do this whenever I see a politician on the screen, to test his popularity; I am President, Statistician and only field-worker of an organization called the Marchbanks Poll of Worthless Public Opinion. If I raise a big clap for a politician I know at once that (a) it is payday, and the audience is in a generous mood; (b) the audience consists chiefly of married couples, who are not holding hands. If the

---

✒ *George Drew (1894–1973) was a Canadian statesman of considerable celebrity in his time, who might have been Prime Minister if he had not tactlessly referred to our French-descended brethren in Quebec as "a conquered race." This, of course, was unforgivable, just like suggesting that the English won the Battle of Waterloo. That was, long before our Bill of Rights, which guarantees that no minority, under any circumstances, can be wrong.*

response is small I know (a) that the hands of most people in the audience are otherwise engaged; (b) that the audience does not expect the feature picture to be any good and only came to the movies to get away from home; (c) that the audience consists chiefly of people who have never heard of George Drew and think the figure on the screen is Eva Peron, or the Pope, or some other distant dignitary. I am compiling a large volume of my findings, and will shortly sell it to industrialists who will be impressed by the price and the word "Poll" in the title.

• OF THE GREATNESS OF THE HUMAN SPIRIT •

*A*HEALTH NUT assailed me today. "Are you getting plenty of water?" said he. "You know, surely, that you are about 70 per cent water?" "You astonish me," said I, determined not to encourage him. "Your brain alone is 79 per cent water," he continued, "and 90 per cent of your blood is water. Obviously you must take care to get lots of water." "If you didn't get enough water, is there any chance that you would dry up?" I asked, but he was too full of facts to be affected by sarcasm. "Really you are just a big lump of carbon, with a few salts and minerals thrown in," he continued. "I could buy all your ingredients in a drug store for about sixty cents, and get enough free water out of a tap to mix them up." "Vain man," I cried, "in the hereafter we shall see what I am — a dollar's worth of slops and condiments, or one of the Sons of the Morning. Go, pinhead, lock yourself in a room, and stay there until some inkling of the greatness of the human spirit dawns upon you, then see if you can buy THAT in a drug store." He fled, hustling his sixty cents' worth of chemicals and his water down the street at about fifteen m.p.h.

• OF THE VIRTUES OF ARTIFICE •

*I*SAW A MOVIE of Oscar Wilde's play *An Ideal Husband* last week, and enjoyed it greatly. The movie reviewers had assured me that the piece was slow and dull, but I did not find it so. The plot and the dialogue were artificial, of course, but so are the plot and dialogue of all other movies; more artificiality on the Wilde level would improve the movies immensely. I have never understood why people object to artificiality; almost everything that has raised man above the beasts is artificial in some respect. I am an exceedingly artificial creature myself; my teeth are preserved artificially, and I have artificial aids for my eyes; I wear artificial coverings of cloth and leather upon my body; I eat no food which has not been artificially treated. And, unlike a great many of my hypocritical fellow creatures, I like frankly artificial entertainment.

Last night I went to a private showing of a Russian film, *Ivan the Terrible*, which was one of the best films I have ever seen. True, I have never looked up the nostrils of so many Russians before, and I hope that it will be some time before I do so again, but it was a film after my own heart — full of poisoned wine, spies peeping around pillars, and people wearing trains approximately twenty feet long. This was artificiality on a grand scale. Ivan in the film bore no resemblance to the Ivan of history, who was as mimsy as a borogrove and spent his time alternately in doing unpleasant things and repenting, but it was a fine bit of propaganda and not more distorted than the films we see about Lincoln and George Washington. . . . I was much impressed by the scene in which Ivan was cured of a severe illness by having a prayer book placed over his face. I shall try this on myself when next my ulcers go back on me.

• A Scheme to Improve Bureaucracy •

I PREPARED MY Income Tax form today, and reflected that it costs me just about as much to be a Canadian as it would to be an Englishman, and twice as much as it would cost me to be an American. This is a time of year when I think sourly of Government expenditures. I reckon that my Income Tax pays the salary of one minor official, such as the censor of books. What does this minor official do for me that I should support him? Can I march into a government office, seek him out, and say, "You're my man. I pay you. What are you doing, and are you making a decent job of it?" No, I cannot. Frankly I think it would be a good idea if every taxpayer were told what government stooge he maintained.

Small taxpayers would then feel that they owned an eighth of a charwoman; modest taxpayers like myself would own petty officials; wealthy men, who pay a lot of taxes, would be allotted ten or twenty clerks, or a brace of deputy ministers. With this knowledge we could go to Ottawa from time to time and chivvy and nag our hirelings. Such a scheme would give a taxpayer some pride in his taxpaying and would greatly increase bureaucratic efficiency.

• OF WINES RUDELY MINGLED •

I ATTENDED A BANQUET last night at which an appropriate quantity of wine was consumed. But there were a number of people present who were plainly devotees of hard spirits, for they drank little or no wine, leaving it in their glasses. Now when the affair was over I noticed one of the cleaners collecting these remains in a large jug. Sherry, claret, and port were poured without discrimination into the mixture, which had the murky, threatening colour of cough medicine. What did he intend to do with it? I am convinced that later, in some secret bower of his own — some sequestered broom closet or coenobitical lumber room — he drank the contents of that jug in which the conviviality of sherry, the sturdy manliness of claret and the episcopal blessing of port mingled in vinous kaleidoscope. I hope he had a good time, but I would not have his head on my shoulders this morning for a mine of gold.

• OF ANCIENT PROFANITY •

I WAS READING Ben Jonson's play *The Poetaster* this afternoon, and found this passage:

OVID: Troth, if I live, I will new dress the law
        In sprightly Poesy's habiliments.

TIBULLUS: The Hell thou wilt!
        What, turn law into verse?

I had not thought that this special use of "the hell you will" was so old, for *The Poetaster* was written in 1601.

• OF THE BIG HINGE •

I SHOVELLED A LOT of snow today, and rather enjoyed it, though I had had enough at least half an hour before the job was finished. But a friend of mine who sets up as a great authority on health tells me that snow shovelling is wonderful for sedentary workers, because it makes them use their Big Hinge. Apparently "Big Hinge" is what health maniacs call the waist, because it bends. If you use your Big Hinge a lot it squeezes your tripes, causes your juices to squish and slither about inside you, wrings out your liver and spleen, and puts accordion pleats in your vermiform appendix; it scrapes your epigastrium on your backbone and increases the traffic on your alimentary canal. No doubt this is all very fine, but I find that any prolonged use of my Big Hinge makes me extremely hungry, and by the time I have satisfied my hunger I have short-circuited all my inner workings, and my Big Hinge is incapable of moving more than a degree or two in any direction. My juices are solidified, my liver and spleen are like rocks; my appendix is throbbing like a Congo drum and my alimentary canal is closed to navigation. You can't win in the fight for health.

Sweet

• OF PURITY TOO LONG SUSTAINED •

I WAS INVITED to a private showing of a sex education film this morning, along with prominent members of the clergy, judiciary, police chiefery and fire departmentery. This is because I am a Great Moral Force in my community. My sex education is now complete, and I have given my word of honour that, whatever temptations life throws in my way, I shall never have an illegitimate baby. I was fascinated by a distinction which the film insisted upon between "sentimental love" and "sensual love." The former is what nice people feel, and the latter is what low scoundrels feel. But my dictionary says that the word "sensual" means "connected with the gratification of the senses," and it has been my observation that when a young man monopolizes a girl's time without making at least a half-hearted attempt to gratify a few of her senses (her passion for nut-fudge sundaes with chocolate and marshmallow sauce, for instance) she soon passes him up for a more adventurous fellow. The plain fact is that however hard a young man may try to live up to his Scout Oath, and to keep his love on a purely sentimental plane, girls don't encourage him to do so. And just as well, too. There is a point beyond which purity should not be allowed to go.

• OF DOWDINESS •

N OT ENOUGH attention is paid to the negative side of fashion. Great effort is exerted to make people look smart, but somebody should face the fact that a lot of people will never be smart, and that they should be given some assistance in maintaining their fascinating dowdiness. Lists of the favourite colours of the dowdy ought to be published in *Vogue*: Fever Pink, Outcast Brown, Bile Yellow, Lustkiller Red, Linty Black, Housedust Grey, Skim Milk White, Pondweed Green—these colours are the favourites of thousands, and they ought to be identified and kept handy on the shelves of drygoods merchants. Some assistance should be given too to men who wear those ties that look as though they had been made out of a worn piece of carpeting; as such things are never seen in shops it must be that their wives make them; it would be a boon if some haberdashery were to take over this useful and profitable work. Shops now attract a certain trade by advertising that "Smart people shop here": think of the untapped source of trade which would be set flowing by an ad which declared that "Within these walls the invincibly dowdy will find everything they need"! . . . Oh, I assure you, madam, I think your gown most becoming. What made you think otherwise? . . . I have observed that women have no knack for impersonal speculation.

• OF THE PERILS OF SELF-CONTROL •

*A*S MY ALARM CLOCK beat feverishly with its tiny fist upon its bell this morning, I stretched slothfully beneath the covers and mused on the flight of time. The people of the Balkans, I read somewhere yesterday, live to great ages. Their average life expectancy is eighty-seven. Some doctors think that this is because they eat a mysterious goo called Yoghurt, which resembles sour milk, and is said to keep senility at bay. I do not believe a word of it. My own theory is that the Balkans live to great ages because they never trouble to keep their tempers, because they never take baths, and because they never repress a nasty remark when they think of one. Our civilization is one which demands an unconscionable amount of holding-in; in the Balkans you never hold in anything. Holding-in creates horrid poisons which wear us out before our time. There are more deaths caused by ingrowing, suppurating self-control than the medical profession wots of.

• OF ILL-SUPPORTED CLAIMS TO BEAUTY •

I SEE BY A Toronto paper that "a pretty co-ed" has distinguished herself by eating a grasshopper. The thirst for beauty in Toronto press circles is astonishing. They will describe anyone who gets into jail, or lost, or murdered, or who eats something inedible, as "pretty." What they will say when a really pretty girl gets into the news, I cannot imagine. Their standards are so low that even I—! But I can imagine the report: "Lovely Samuel Marchbanks, glamorous Eastern Ontario redhead, appeared in court today charged with kicking the stuffing our of a dog which he alleged had been rummaging in his garbage can. Testimony was given by Dr. Flop, well-known psychiatrist, that the winsome defendant had developed an idea that he was persecuted by dogs owing to the fact that he really was persecuted by dogs." I am forced to conclude that Toronto reporters think any female who is not a certified gorilla is a beauty, or that Toronto news photographers are bunglers.

• OF BASEBALL •

O UR QUAINT NEIGHBOURS, the Americans, have concluded the local baseball tournament which they boastfully call the World's Series. What would happen, I wonder, if some Norwegian or Siamese baseball team were to insist upon entering this cosy little contest, and beat them? They would drown the stage with tears, and split the general ear with horrid speech. I have always thought that the international nature of cricket served as a useful check on English pride. Just when the Motherland was beginning to think well of herself a pack of gangling Australians or Dutch-speaking South Africans would land on her shores, and knock the spots off the Old Girl at her national game. The Americans are very careful that nothing of the sort should happen to them. . . . I read today that the man who invented the curve pitch had died. I am sceptical about the curve pitch, and I should like to have a scientific showdown on the matter. Once when I was a boy a friend showed me a metal cup which he concealed in his hand, and which he had bought on the understanding that it would enable him to pitch a curve. As a matter of fact, he couldn't hit the side of a barn.

• OF FEMALE BEAUTY •

I WATCHED A Santa Claus parade this morning, and was greatly struck by the fact that all the figures on the floats were made of plaster, and the giants and gnomes and princesses were fixed eternally in one position. The parade seemed to give great satisfaction to the children round about, but children are not searching critics and will take anything that is palmed off on them. It seems to me that in a parade which symbolizes goodwill toward men it is wrong to use plaster people instead of real people, simply because plaster people are cheaper. Also I like Santa to appear surrounded by movement, and particularly by lots of pretty girls. I mentioned all this to a man who immediately wanted to know what pretty girls had to do with Santa Claus? I decided to give him the Theological Treatment. "Sir," said I, "female beauty is an important Minor Sacrament which cannot be received too often; I am not at all sure that neglect of it does not constitute a sin of some kind." That fixed him. . . . Yes indeed, madam, I am a great admirer of female beauty, particularly when, as in your case, it is partnered by a gossamer wit.

• OF DUMBOTAL •

M Y HAY FEVER is getting out of bounds. I attended a meeting last week which was up three flights of stairs and when I reached the top, I was wheezing like a cab-horse. The day before yesterday, therefore, I sought a Learned Physician, who brought out his stethoscope and listened to my chest, for so long, and with so much enjoyment, that I wondered if he had accidentally tuned in on some favourite radio program. But at last he put his instrument aside, and surveyed me through narrowed eyes. "I can't do anything until these symptoms are disposed of," said he; "I'll give you an antispasmodic to quiet them." This filled me with fear, for I am very credulous and timid where doctors are concerned. "What's that?" I quavered. "Oh just a few grains of Dumbotal," he said. "If you find yourself dropping off to sleep at odd times, or falling down in traffic, decrease the dose." He is going to survey me for allergies next week. What shall I do if he discovers that I am allergic to paper, ink or any of the tools of my trade? Nothing then but the life of a hobo will remain for poor Marchbanks.

I began my course of Dumbotal yesterday morning. The first tablet had excellent effect, and my wheezing abated. After lunch I had another tablet of Dumbotal, and during the afternoon I felt like a bloodhound. I loped when I walked, my eyelids drooped, and every now and then I tumbled down and had a nice rest; but I was breathing beautifully. At dusk another Dumbotal. I read a book for an hour and discovered that I had no idea what I had read, so I took a two-hour nap. I woke up and crawled to bed without unnecessary effort, rather like a snake. But I was sucking in the good air in mighty draughts all the time. If the price of easy breathing is semi-coma, I shall pay it without a whimper.

Thanks to Dumbotal, I breathe freely once again, and I spent quite a lot of this afternoon sitting in the open air, thinking how good it smelled. A human being is an extraordinarily delicate creature, capable of tremendous physical and mental feats; but push his bodily temperature up a few points, or tinker with his blood pressure, or shoot a few bubbles into his bloodstream, or drop a little camphor into his eye, or reduce his breathing capacity slightly, and he is miserable. He can bear the martyr's fire or the torturer's rack with fortitude, but a comparatively trivial inconvenience floors him.... Next week several professional sooth-sayers are going to find out what gives me hay fever; I anticipate their investigations with no special delight.

• OF IMPROVED FALSE TEETH •

I INVENTED THE Marchbanks Dental Wurlitzer today. It is a set of dentures in which each tooth has been hollowed out and fitted with a miniature organ pipe. It has been my observation that most false teeth whistle, but mournfully and unmusically. The Dental Wurlitzer will ensure that if the teeth whistle at all they will whistle in a pleasing and tuneful manner. Clever wearers will learn to play tunes upon their dentures, thus giving amusement to their grandchildren, and perhaps acquiring a talent which will make them favourites in fashionable drawing rooms. My invention should add something new to choral singing, as well. At present choir singers who have grown elderly, and whose whistling is thought offensive, are asked to resign, or to devote themselves to arranging the chairs in the concert hall. But a small body of elderly singers (say five in a choir of thirty) equipped with my Dental Wurlitzer would be able to provide a rich supplementary tone to the whole, and would be especially effective in the rendering of bird-calls, echo effects and the distant carolling of angelic choirs.

• OF CANADIANISM •

I WAS CALLED BY THE Mayor today. "The Governor General is coming to town," said His Worship, "and the only way we can get him up to my place is past Marchbanks Towers; what about getting some of that junk out of your front yard? If you like, I can send a gang up from the Works Department, and bill you for it." "Have no fear," I replied; "Marchbanks is no man to affront His Majesty's representative, and the Towers will be a bower as you sweep by with your fine friends.". . . But as I laid down the telephone I reflected that His Excellency will be honouring my street on a Garbage Day, when my neighbours and I conspire to turn the whole avenue into a replica of Hogan's Alley, and the jolly doggies strew our kitchen rubbish in a thick carpet all over the pavement. When Catherine the Great of Russia passed through a village, false fronts, like Hollywood scenery, were put on all the huts, and sleek, well-dressed peasants stood in front of the fakes while the real owners cowered hungrily behind the dunghills. Could not something like this be done here?

For the visit of the Governor General and his Lady I attired myself suitably in Canadian National Costume, consisting of a cowboy hat, a Red River flannel shirt, a Quebec doeskin wamus, Bay Street trousers (made of imported cloth and beautifully creased) and St. Catharines street shoes (patent leathers with buttoned cloth tops); under this I wore a hair shirt (to represent the Canadian Puritan Conscience) and a pair of underpants which have been sitting for thirty years and are due for retirement (to represent the Civil Service); in addition I wore a tartan cummerbund (to represent the Maritimes, sometimes referred to as "the soft underbelly of Canada") and a string of ice-cubes around the brim of my hat (to represent the immense promise of our Northland). At some little distance from myself I chained a Newfoundland dog, to personify our tenth province. In this picturesque garb I stood at my gate and as the Vice-Regal party drove by on its way to refreshment with the Mayor I cheered lustily in English and French, and cheered again as the party drove back to the teetotal Meat Tea which had been prepared downtown.... The costume was quite a strain and gave me a new realization of what a difficult country Canada is to unify.

• OF X-RAYS •

ONCE I PUT MYSELF in the hands of the medical profession, I am a gone goose for several weeks. I endured more injections and X-rays today. My inside has always fascinated photographers, though none of them has ever shown the least enthusiasm about my outside. "Lock your hands behind your head, tie your legs in a knot, cross your eyes, touch the end of your nose with the tip of your tongue; now hold still, Mr. Marchbanks," says the X-ray technician, and there I am, a spectacle of discomfort to the eye, but a thing of beauty to the X-ray camera. After the film is developed they all say, "That's lovely," though I don't think these pictures show me at my best. I have never worn my heart on my sleeve, and I certainly have no intention of turning myself inside out, even if I do look more fascinating that way.... Yes, madam, I have a few duplicates of my X-rays, and I would be happy to inscribe one for you, if you like.... Not at all; I find your request most touching.

• OF THE SYSTEM •

THE APPLE SEASON is now at hand, and I shall partake hugely; it was not for nothing that I gained the name "Cider-Press Marchbanks" in my youth. Fondness for apples is with me partly sheer greed and partly therapeutic. I have inherited from my pioneer ancestors a belief that no real harm can befall a man who eats plenty of apples. In my grandmother's time it was widely held that apples were good for The System, just as tomatoes were thought to be deleterious, and perhaps fatal, to The System. This System implied the whole of the bodily plumbing, wiring and ventilation. Apples "toned up" The System; tomatoes poisoned The System. It was as simple as that. I toned my system with a couple of prime McIntoshes this evening before coming here to dinner.

• HE DECLINES TO WINTERIZE •

I SAW A PIECE IN the paper this morning advising readers to "winterize" themselves. "We all winterize our automobiles; do the same thing for your bodily mechanism," it said. This is not true: I don't "winterize" my automobile; I prepare it for winter. I would scorn to use such a word as "winterize." Nor would I dream of winterizing myself. Of course, I change my lubricant from a light lager to a thick Jamaica, but otherwise I do nothing. There was a time in my youth when I was prepared for winter by the consumption of a special thick grease, made of the bodies of decayed cod and halibut, which I ate on a biscuit three times a day. It made me reek like a trawler's raincoat, and no germs could get near me. Sometimes I heard people whispering about it behind my back (as happens in advertisements) but most of my contemporaries stank of the same, or similar, "winterizers" and so no social ostracism resulted.

• OF A NEW USE FOR HOLLY •

T HE POST-CHRISTMAS dullness persists. There is a curious hush in the air, which puzzles me until I realize that it is caused by the cessation of the carol-singing which, until Christmas Eve, was launched upon the ether by loudspeakers in shops, offices and municipal buildings. From time to time Scotsmen hail me, and want me to join them in celebrating the New Year which is, they explain, the great festival of their homeland. But although

I appreciate their kindness, I am a Welshman by descent and in spirit, and for me Christmas is the great day, and when it is gone I cannot work up much enthusiasm for what is, after all, a purely chronological event. . . . I dined yesterday with some friends, who had a large bowl of holly in the middle of the table. This gives me an idea; could holly, toasted, be launched upon the world as a new breakfast food? Its effect upon the intestines might be quite miraculous. Eat Marchbanks' Holly for breakfast: You Pick It and It Picks You!

• OF HIS ETERNAL SALIVATION •

I BEGAN MY HALF-YEARLY seance with my dentist this afternoon, and as usual, cost him a fortune in cotton wads. It is my good fortune to have splendidly robust salivary glands, and at the mere sight of a dentist my mouth waters as though he were a steak or Hedy Lamarr. Before he can begin his work he has to make a kind of Holland of my mouth, draining elaborately and erecting dikes of cotton wads to stem the sea which threatens to engulf him. He must then work quickly before my levels rise to the point where all his work is washed away, his tools rusted beyond reclaim, and his arms drenched to the elbow. Most of my dentists have been very nice about this peculiarity of mine. They understand that I do not do it to vex them, but because I cannot help it. Nevertheless, there are times when I can see a shadow crossing the dentist's face and I know that he is wishing—without malice —that I would drown in my own spit. Little does he know how near, sometimes, his wish is to being granted.

• PREPARATIONS FOR A FEAST •

T HERE WAS A great deal of sense in the medieval custom of fasting before a feast. Today I ate lightly and drank a lot of water, in order to give my insides every possible advantage, in the approaching conflict with turkey, plum pudding, mince pies, hard and hot sauces, chocolates, nuts, candied fruits, cheeses, lemon custards, butter tarts and similar seasonable indigestibles.

Nobody expects a boxer to do a day's sewer-digging before an important match; why expect our gizzards to meet such an onslaught in a condition of fatigue? I just put this question to the lady on my right who said, "La, Mr. Marchbanks, you are always considering your stomach." "Madam," I rejoined, "that is true, and I expect my stomach to return the compliment."

• OF MUSCLE AND CHARM •

I WENT TO THE movies last night. The newsreel contained some pictures of a female weight-lifter, a girl who tossed 250-pound barbells around with great ease. For some reason I found the sight of her depressing; I cannot decide why this was so. Obviously it is a good thing for a girl to be strong, but it is not becoming for her to look strong. The Ideal Woman, I suppose, would have the deliciously languishing, aristocratic appearance of a du Maurier beauty, and the physical constitution of Mammy Yokum. She would then be able to do a full day's work at home or in the office, dance until midnight, and refuse or accept proposals of marriage (and whatnot) until 3 a.m. every night in the year. But she would never permit her muscles to show; really beautiful women should look as though their skins were stuffed with nice firm blancmange.

• OF HOUSEHOLD MARTYRDOM •

T HIS AFTERNOON I listened to an act or so of the most laughable of all operas, Gounod's *Romeo et Juliette*. A great deal has been written about the power of music to ennoble words; I think it is high time something was said about the undoubted power of music to render fine words trivial. . . . Then I went out to struggle with the week's accumulation of snow. In no time at all three children appeared to help me, and as fast as I threw snow aside they tumbled it back into the path. There are men who endure this sort of thing philosophically, but I am not one of them; I made a short but passionate appeal to my helpers to go elsewhere and help my worst enemies, and they went. Then I settled down to the back-breaking job of heaving snow which had achieved the texture and weight of plaster. My spectacles fogged, my hat fell off at every fifth heave, and my overcoat twisted around until I seemed to be wearing it back to front. But by dint of Herculean effort, Job-like patience, and Franciscan spiritual abasement I shifted enough of the nasty stuff to make it possible to get from my house to the street, and at every heave of the shovel my heart yearned for flower-crowned Spring.

• OF POVERTY IN PROFANITY •

I WENT TO SEE A play last evening—a play which contained a measure of profanity. Not the rich, refreshing, imaginative profanity of Shakespeare, but just ordinary swearing. I noticed several members of the audience swallowing their Adam's apples and distending their nostrils at this, but as the play was a highly moral work, directed against divorce, they made no serious complaint. . . . This caused me to ponder on the crying modern need for new and more ferocious oaths. The few tattered old rags of blasphemy and obscenity which we have inherited from our church-going ancestors are insufficient to deck out the tremendous angers of the Atomic Age. An era of new terrors, amplified treachery, vastly extended political cynicism, and starvation on an undreamed-of scale surely demands an extended gamut of objurgation to cope with it. But our age is uncongenial to poetry, and swearing, at its best, is a kind of diabolic poetry.

• OF MEALINESS OF MOUTH •

I WENT TO SEE AN English movie last night, called *The Notorious Gentleman* which was very good indeed. In Britain it was called *The Rake's Progress*, and when I asked why the name had been changed I was told that it was done to prevent unsophisticated audiences from imagining that the film depicted the evolution of the popular garden tool. But I don't believe any such thing. I think it was to spare our movie theatre employees the distasteful task of spelling out a dubious word like "rake" in electric lights. In movie circles on this continent they have a rooted objection to calling things by their right names. In the newsreels, for instance, Eva Braun is referred to as Hitler's "good friend," although everybody knows that she was his mistress, and later (for a few nasty moments) Mrs. H. But "mistress" is a Dirty Word, and may not sully the chaste lips of a newsreel commentator, or befoul the antiseptic ears of a movie audience. What will be the result of this nonsense? In a few years the words "good friend" will have achieved a lewd secondary significance, and will be unusable by those who do not wish to be misunderstood. "Do you love John?" the Canadian Mama will enquire of her Innocent Daughter. "No, Mumsie, I am merely his Good Friend," the I.D. will reply, and will then be surprised when Mama locks her in her room with bread and water, shrieking the house down as she does it. Nothing but evil comes from mealiness of mouth.

• OF VILE PHRASES •

*F*ROM TIME TO TIME I hear a word or an expression which I mentally resolve never to use myself — not if entreated to do so by wild horses on their bended knees. Today, for instance, I heard a man refer to a motor car as a "transportation unit." A vile phrase! It might mean anything. A horse is also a transportation unit, and so is my wheelbarrow. Even my degraded old carpet slippers are transportation units. . . . Could a romance between Civil Servants blossom in an immobilized transportation unit, possibly resulting in a little vital statistic?

• OF HOLIDAY PREPARATIONS •

*P*RE-HOLIDAY PROSTRATION has overtaken me. Today I tidied my desk, mowed the lawn, hid the hose, collected my shirts, packed my bags, shot the iceman, poisoned the bread-man, drowned the milkman, ripped out the telephone, pushed chewing gum in the keyholes, broke the electricity meter open with an axe, and hid the silver in a hollow tree. To frighten away robbers I have prepared two cunning wax images of myself, and have laid one of them in a deck chair on the verandah, and posed the other one over the garbage box at the rear door. Having thereby complied with all the newspaper advice to people about to go on vacation, I am waiting for the dawn to break, and my yearly respite from slavery to begin. *

• OF THE FOUR DOLDRUMS •

*E*VERYBODY I MEET these days seems to be suffering from one or more of the Four Doldrums which are guaranteed by our Canadian Way of Life *—Doldrum from Want, Doldrum from Fear, Doldrum of Religion and Doldrum of Speech. A great many of them are still victims of post-vacation coma; they have been out in the sun too much and their brains have dried up. I am no better myself; I have been dull at many periods of my life, but never so dull as now. My dullness is so complete and all-embracing that it constitutes a kind of mystical experience—the merging of the Null with the Void. Shall I found a new religion? A Cult of

---

His hatred of such holiday preparations gave rise to one of March-banks' most brilliant Thwarted Inventions. Visiting a friend in the U.S.—a gentleman famous for growing rare specimen trees—he learned that one of the arboriculturist's great problems was to keep the deer who were numerous in the district from devouring his tender seedlings. This he overcame by bringing in tiger's dung from a nearby zoo and sprinkling it in the plantation; the deer, sensing the presence of a fierce predator and enemy, kept their distance. In a flash Marchbanks conceived the ultimate protection for his household and its treasures; he would secure and sprinkle R.C.M.P. dung (human, not equine) around the Towers, thereby scaring off thieves. But the whole plan was negated by the R.C.M.P. who, though sympathetic in principle, proved to be inexplicably prudish, and utterly refused to co-operate, blushing as red as their famous tunics. Thus, once again, Science was defeated.

During the 1939-45 war we were assured by our Leaders that the struggle was to ensure the Four Freedoms which were also, strangely enough, the Four Doldrums in cheerful guise.

Blaa? So much of modern religion is imbued with a busy dullness that the world might welcome a nice, passively dull faith, specifically designed for the poor in spirit.

• OF THE TRIVIALITY OF APPENDICES •

A MAN MENTIONED casually to me this afternoon that his brother was in a hospital, having his appendix removed. This operation is now undertaken without qualm; surgeons regard it as a pastime, something to keep the hands busy, like knitting or eating salted nuts. But I can remember the day when a man whose brother was undergoing such an ordeal would have been at the hospital himself, probably accompanied by a robed choir and two or three powerful evangelists. When my brother Fairchild had his appendix out, in the early days of anaesthesia and antisepsis, it was customary to refuse water to those recently relieved of their appendices, and the poor fellow was reduced to drinking from the flower vases near his bed. When he left the hospital, he was given his appendix in a jar of alcohol, and after a few months as a mantel ornament this relic was thrown out. Dogs drank the alcohol and cats ate the appendix, and so for a night Fairchild brought joy to the animal world.

Savoury

• OF HIERARCHY AMONG MAGAZINE READERS •

DESPERATE FOR Christmas gifts I have been driven to giving subscriptions to magazines this year to many of my friends who deserve something better. The tragedy of magazines is that nobody has any time to read them; only those who are condemned to lonely vigils in doctors' waiting-rooms are able to wade through those pungent comments on world affairs, those brilliant disquisitions on married happiness, those tales of adventure, for which magazine publishers pay so much. But most of us like to have a few magazines coming to the house, if only to proclaim our intellectual status. Thus readers of the *New Yorker* and the *Atlantic* curl the lip at those whose living-room tables boast only *Life*, *Time* and the *Reader's Digest*; and these too are given the sneer of contumely by readers of *Horizon* and *Partisan Review*; and all of the foregoing suffer embarrassment in those homes where *Country Life*, *The Tatler* and *Punch* lie beside the chairs, though I cannot quite explain why. So all week I have been tearing those hard little cards out of magazines, and accepting the Special Offer whereby I can give subscriptions at bargain rates. It is a coward's way out, but what am I to do?

• OF DENTISTS FAR AND NEAR •

I HAD A TOOTH filled today. My dentist wears a tasteful white smock with a high collar; I can remember the first dentist whom I visited in my childhood, who wore a morning coat, and worked his drill with a foot pedal. His operating room was as dark as a church, and he had not been trained to stand any nonsense from children; my recollection is that he knelt on my prone form while drilling, and that every now and then he drilled a piece out of my tongue, just to learn me.... In odd corners of the world strange dentists still lurk; an Irish friend of mine told me recently of visiting a dentist on the West Coast of Ireland who had no running water, and bade his patients to spit into a potted fern which was conveniently placed by the chair.... The fanciest job of dentistry I ever saw was done on a Welsh farmer; a travelling dentist pulled all his teeth in the kitchen one afternoon, and sold him a false set to be inserted at once. The total service cost just under five dollars. The man was wearing the teeth when I met him, and there was a rugged grandeur about the lower part of his face which suggested the Sabre Tooth Tiger in the Royal Ontario Museum.

• OF PLEASURE TOO DETERMINEDLY SOUGHT •

*E*VERY YEAR, about this time, I take a vacation, as a result of social pressure. I do not really like vacations; I much prefer an occasional day off when I do not feel like working. When I am confronted with a whole week in which I have nothing to do but enjoy myself I do not know where to begin. To me, enjoyment comes fleetingly and unheralded; I cannot determinedly enjoy myself for a whole week at a time. A day's work when everything goes smoothly, or an evening when I am thoroughly happy and at ease, or an unexpected stroke of luck — these are the things which I enjoy. But when I go after the coy nymph Pleasure with a blunderbuss, determined to make her my mistress for a whole week, she vanishes into her fastnesses, and hurls ordure and makes rude noises at me whenever I approach.

• OF THE CAPRICE OF SYMPATHY •

*M*Y HAY FEVER continues unabated. Several people have told me that I should go to the seaside — useless advice for I have no money for gallivanting. I am toying, however, with a new invention, Marchbanks' Maritime Mask. It will be a respirator, filled with sea water, and worn over the face and mouth like a dog muzzle; every breath the wearer takes will be filtered through the sea water, and thus he will have all the benefits of the seaside, while living inland.

As I wept, sneezed and coughed my way through my day's work, I reflected that the world judges disease by unjust standards. Anyone who has a migraine headache, for instance, receives the keenest sympathy, for his ailment is heroic and—this is important—silent. But a man who has hives is a joke, though hives are desperately painful. Similarly it is heroic to suffer with one's sinus, but a man who has catarrh, and who, in consequence, hawks, hoots, snorts, roars, gags and spits is thought to be making a great and disgusting fuss about nothing. The healthy can endure invalids only when the latter are quiet and motionless. Let them but cough or scratch, and sympathy flies out of the window.

• OF SELF-TORTURE •

*W*HEN I AWOKE this morning there was a smell of burning in the air, and for a moment I wondered if the northern bush fires had crept up during the night, in the hope of engulfing me and my neighbours. While dressing I wondered what I would do in such an emergency: would I form a firebreak by chopping down the puny hedge of Marchbanks Towers, order my dependants to go and stand waist-deep in the nearest lake, and take up a menacing position on the lawn with a soda syphon; or would I phone the fire department, shrieking, "Save me! Save me!"? Like all men whose work consists of dreaming, word-spinning and prophesying, I like to torture myself with these problems; nothing so entrances a man of words as to imagine himself in a situation in which words are powerless. It is this which keeps him humble. Men of action, I notice, are rarely humble, even in situations where action of any kind is a great mistake, and masterly inaction is called for.

• THE INNER VOICE •

I SAT ON MY verandah last evening, reading Winston Churchill's new book, which I do very slowly, because I seem to hear that wonderful phlegmy voice declaiming every word.

How many people, I wonder, hear voices as they read? I always do. I read American books with an American accent, and English books with an English accent, and Canadian books in the voice of a friend of mine who speaks the best Canadian I have heard. People have told me that I would be able to read much faster if I gave up this indulgence, and clutched groups of words and whole paragraphs with my greedy eyes, but I pay no attention to them. My method is the one I like, and it is an infallible touchstone for judging a writer's style. The man who writes only for the eye generally writes badly; the man who writes to be heard will write with some eloquence, some regard for the music of words, and will reach nearer to his reader's heart and mind. Of course, fools and clods will write like fools and clods, whatever means they use. . . . No, madam, I do not read the works of foreign writers in broken English.

• OF A WITTY POLITICIAN •

I REFRESHED MYSELF today by reading a few chapters of *Peck's Bad Boy,* a book which delighted my childhood. I wonder if children read it now. Rereading with the eye of bawdy eld supplanting that of dewy innocence, I was astonished to discover what a suggestive work it is. George W. Peck, who wrote it, was a Milwaukee journalist, and he became so popular as a funnyman that he was elected mayor of that city, the first and last time in history that any city ever elected a consciously funny man to be its chief magistrate. He scaled even dizzier heights, however, and was Governor of Wisconsin before he died. Let this be a lesson to our Canadian politicians; wit and politics are not mutually exclusive.

Published in 1883 and popular at least until the twenties of this century. The Bad Boy spent his time in such merry tricks as putting ants in his Pa's liver-pad, getting him falsely arrested for murder, and in other ways making the old man's life a burden. It was written, of course, in the days before it became the fashion to believe that boys had souls, and write books about them like The Catcher in the Rye.

• OF AN INJUSTICE •

*T*HE MEDICAL profession had some fun with me this afternoon. They extracted blood from me at various strategic points, and did strange things with such of my by-products as they could obtain. They took pictures of my insides, and put me in a machine which rendered me transparent. They gouged and banged me to see if I would scream, but I remembered that I had once been a Wolf Cub, and kept a stiff upper lip (though why I should have done this when my underlip was trembling like a blancmange in an earthquake I cannot say). But the final injustice came when they decided to weigh me. I craftily left off my coat, hoping thereby to gain a slight advantge, but the doctor who had just used the fluoroscope to see through me saw through me again and ordered me sternly to put it on. This I did, and consequently the weight of two books which I had in my pocket, as well as $2.35 in silver, was entered on the charge-sheet against me. This is the kind of unfairness which drives men to rash acts. However, it will be easy for me to make a good impression next time I visit my doctor, for I shall simply leave my books and money at home, and he will think that I am losing weight.

• OF THE STRANGE POWER OF WOMEN •

*Y*ES, THANK YOU, my cold is improving. I went to the movies last night; they always cheer me when I have a cold although I expect that I spread germs in a thoroughly antisocial manner. The film was *Anna Karenina*, and I liked it greatly. Some girls sitting near me appeared to find it funny. Will any of them, I wonder, ever discover themselves in a situation comparable to that of the heroine? Often I look at women on the streets, or in restaurants, and wonder if anybody has ever loved them to distraction, or if they have ever wrecked a man's life. Most of them have not done so, of course, but a few must have lived out some passionate story, or will do so before they die. The curious thing, of course, is that it is by no means always the beautiful or attractive ones who have caused these upheavals. Little mousy women, or fat, cow-like women have often inspired ill-fated romances, driving men to suicide or murder, or simply to that living death which is worse than either. Statistical records show that women commit suicide rarely, as compared with men; are they more philosophic, or merely more stupid and unfeeling?

• OF HIS RHEUM •

*A*LL THIS WEEK I have had a cold. At least, I hope it is a cold. My head feels like a pumpkin, and when I breathe my left lung makes a noise as though a kitten were playing in a basketful of crumpled paper. I dare not go to my doctor, for he will send me to bed, and I want to save my usual Autumn holiday-in-bed for later on, when the weather is not so fine. But the man who occasionally sells me a little benzine with which to clean my clothes diagnosed my case today. "You've got muck in your bronikkles," he said, as I gave an agonizing cough. "There's only one thing that'll do you any good and that's mustard tea. Just get a pint of stout, heat it nearly to the boil, and put a couple of good tablespoons of mustard in it and drink it off quick. That'll fix you!" I thanked him and went away, thinking that it would fix me indeed, and probably for good. I suppose in the dear dead days beyond recall, when doctors were scarce, thousands of people were killed every year by wholesome home remedies given to them by sadistic old creatures with a taste for experiment.

I have suffered from extreme stupidity all day, which I attribute to my cold. I would begin a piece of work, and twenty minutes later would recover consciousness to discover that I was staring into space with my mouth open, making a noise like a sleeping bulldog — snuffle, snuffle, glrrk, woof, snuffle. Is this sort of Hypnosis by the Common Cold well known to medical science, or will I get my name into the medical books under some such heading as "Marchbanks Symptom (Hypnogogia Marchbankensis)"? . . . Very well, madam, if you are not interested, let us talk of something else. Is that all your own hair?

• OF FAIRY-TALE FATHERS •

A YOUNG WOMAN whom I know, who is just learning to read, kindly undertook to read me a story from her schoolbook today. It was one of those pieces about a king who promises his daughter's hand to any man who can make her laugh. It is this sort of promise which makes me wonder about the psychological make-up of fairy-tale characters; they seem to be ready to marry their daughters to anyone at all, for the most extraordinary reasons. I have never known a Canadian father who would permit a young man to marry his daughter, merely because he could make her laugh. (And I may say in passing that to make a really well brought up Canadian girl laugh is no easy task.) Canadian fathers don't care whether their sons-in-law are funny or not; all they want to know about is their prospects and how much money they have in the bank, and whether they drink. In fact, I have received the impression that Canadian fathers prefer sons-in-law who do not laugh. No doubt this attitude explains why Canada has no body of native fairy-tales. Many a Canadian father might justly say: "If you can get a laugh out of this sourpuss, you can have her." But he doesn't.

• OF THE SUBTLETY OF CATS •

N EXT WEEK, I see, will be observed as National Cat Week. It is a good thing to do honour to this noble, dignified and beautiful animal, but I don't imagine for a moment that the cats will co-operate. Cats don't mind being worshipped, but they refuse to be organized. They have always insisted that their lives are their own, to be lived as they see fit, and their attitude toward everything which is symbolized by the American passion for "weeks" of one sort and another is contemptuous, contumacious, and insulting. Can anyone imagine cats walking in a parade? Does anyone seriously think that cats are interested in civic betterment? When have cats ever shown a united front on any subject whatever? The great charm of cats is their rampant egotism, their devil-may-care attitude toward responsibility, their disinclination to earn an honest dollar. In a continent which screams neurotically about co-operation and the Golden Rule, cats are disdainful of everything but their own immediate interests and they contrive to be so suave and delightful about it that they even receive the apotheosis of a National Week. Smart work, cats!

• OF PRECOCIOUS CHILDREN •

I MET A MAN today who boasted intolerably about his child. It is eighteen months old, I think he said, and he asserts without a blush that it has a vocabulary of three hundred words. I believe that I was expected to show awestricken admiration, but as I have no idea what vocabulary may be expected in a child of that age I held my peace and nodded as though prodigies were an old story to me. Frankly, I do not care how large a vocabulary any child has; I am only interested in what it says, and not always in that. What is the use of a large vocabulary of words, if the child has only a small range of ideas?

• OF COMPLACENCE •

O F LATE PEOPLE have been picking on me because I am what they call "complacent." By this they mean that I refuse to share their hysterical fears about another war, about Russia, about the atom, about the commercialization of Sunday, about divorce, about juvenile delinquency and whatnot. Because I do not leap about and flap my arms and throw up all my meals when these things are mentioned, they assume that I am at ease in Zion. As a matter of fact I have my own well-defined field of worry, which I exploit to the full. But it seems to me that a little complacency would do nobody any harm at present and I am thinking of incorporating complacency into the platform of the Marchbanks Humanist Party—a retrograde movement of which I am leader and sole support. "Tired of Clamour? Try Torpor!" How's that for a campaign cry?

· OF REALISTIC SPORTSMANSHIP ·

*M*Y MORNING PAPER expects me to sympathize with a man who shot a bear cub, and then was charged by the mother bear; he and his companion fired eleven shots at her before they finally killed her. But before I congratulate him on his escape, I would like to know why he shot at the cub in the first place? Had he never heard that bears are strange, unpredictable beasts, likely to chase people who shoot their young? And what is the fun of shooting a bear, large or small? Is it the pleasure of seeing it fall down? Or does a shot bear leap comically into the air, shouting, "O my goodness!" thus providing the hunter with a hearty laugh? It seems to me that I once read in an old musty book (very much out of date, probably) that it was unsportsmanlike to shoot the young of any animal, or to shoot a female who was running with her young. But it is plain from the reports which appear in the papers every season that ideals of sportsmanship have changed, and that the tactics which, in political circles, are called "realistic" are now in fashion.

· OF SILOS AND SILAGE ·

I WENT TO THE country to see the autumn colours yesterday, and reflected for the thousandth time on the difficulty of finding any place in Ontario where a man can walk without being warned off as a trespasser. In England the walker's rights are protected by Footpath Societies and local use: here the landowner is as tyrannous as he pleases, and particularly so in the neighbourhood of lakes. I saw a good deal of wild aster and hawthorn berry, but not much leaf-colour yet. I collected a little more material for my book *Silo Architecture in Canada and Its Relationship to the Campaniles of Southern Europe*. So far as I know there has been no extended treatment of the aesthetic side of silo-building.

The word "silo" comes, I find, from the Greek "siros," meaning a storage pit, and the use of silage as fodder was known to the Greeks and Romans, and to the Spaniards, from very early times. The first silo I ever saw was a very grand concrete one which reeked of sour corn so powerfully that it seemed to tear at the lungs as one peeped into it. Cows fed on its silage never drew a sober breath all winter, but leaned against the sides of their stalls, hiccuping; their udders ran pure eggnog. Every Spring they were driven reluctantly to the meadows to take a kind of agricultural Gold Cure, and everyone remarked on the change in the milk. What Alcoholics Anonymous might have done for those cows I cannot now say.

• HE ANIMADVERTS UPON DOGS •

A DOG ATTEMPTED to end it all under the wheels of a car in which I was riding this afternoon. The suicidal instinct seems to be strong in all dogs, but amounts to an overmastering passion in collies and Airedales. My theory is that dogs go mad from the boredom of being dogs and seek to take their lives in consequence. The much advertised intelligence of dogs is mythical. A recent article in *Saturday Night*, written by a scientist, asserts that dogs have even less intelligence than chickens, which is a strong statement. A dog can't begin to compete with a monkey, the writer says, and horses simply laugh at the pretensions of dogs to be sagacious. A pig can learn more tricks than a dog, but has too much sense to want to do it. All this supports my lifelong contention that Man's Dumb Chum is a fraud, and has only wormed his way into the hearts of dog-lovers by undignified self-abasement. The dog is a Yes-animal, very popular with people who can't afford to keep a Yes-man.

• A HINT FOR THE WEALTHY •

I WAS DELIGHTED to read of the great good luck of Dr. Williamson, the Canadian who has discovered the biggest diamond mine in the world, and is now one of the world's richest men. I am afraid that Dr. W. is in for some annoyance, though. The South African government will want its slice, quite rightly, but I am betting that the Canadian Ministry of Finance will want a bit, as well. The idea of a Canadian having all that money will drive Ottawa crazy unless they can devise some way of getting at it. If I were Dr. W. I should pay my Income Tax in cash—copper cash—and go to the tax office every year with a procession of Negro porters, each one carrying a big bag of pennies. I should then stand by and make insulting remarks while the clerks counted the boodle, and demand a receipt in full. When leaving I should toss a huge diamond (with a huge flaw in it) among the herdsmen of the Golden Calf, and watch them scramble, claw, kick and bite for possession of it. What's the good of money unless it gives you some real fun—preferably of a vindictive nature?

• OF HIS ALLERGIES •

I DELIVERED MY body into the hands of Learned Physicians this morning confiding that they may discover why I have hay fever. As soon as they got me out of my clothes I ceased to be a man to them, and they began to talk about me as though I did not understand English. "My guess is that his heart is too small," said the 1st L.P. "I've read some of his stuff, and I'll bet his heart is a little, shrivelled black thing, like a prune," said the 2nd L.P. Whereupon they whisked me into a dark room, and made me stand in a machine that revealed my heart, which they observed with unflattering interest. Then they handed me over to a young woman who removed blood from me and sent me on errands which modesty forbids me to specify in detail. Then the Learned Physicians got me again, and poked tickly things up my nose and peeped down my throat, and wrote cryptic notes on pads. At last I was released, completely demoralized, and sent to a technician whose job it was to test me for allergies.

I was fastened in a chair with thongs, and various substances were brought to me. First of all, a vacuum cleaner was emptied right under my nose, and I sneezed. "Allergic to House Dust," wrote the clinician. Next a flock of geese waddled by, under the care of a pretty Goose Girl. "Kerchoo!" cried I. "Allergic to Goose Feathers," was the comment. Then a farmer rushed in, carrying a truss of weeds ("truss" in the sense of "bundle," of course, and not one of those light-weight, comfortable affairs you see advertised in magazines) which he brandished in my face. "Allergic to English

Cockleburr, Golden Rod, and Old Man's Nuisance," wrote the clinician, as I nearly burst my bonds asunder with sneezing. The next thing to parade past me was a beautiful girl in a lowcut evening gown, which I blew off with my sneezes. "Allergic to Musk and Orris Root," was the notation. And so it went until I was completely exhausted, and I didn't miss a single allergy. I am allergic to everything, it seems. Why, when I looked in the mirror this evening, I sneezed violently. ✒

• OF UNKNOWN PERILS •

*L*OOKING THROUGH my pocket notebook today I discovered that it contained much valuable information which I had overlooked, including a list of antidotes for common poisons. I jumped slightly when I discovered "hartshorn" listed as a poison, with an antidote of vinegar in water. My amazement was caused by the circumstance that as a child I could never distinguish between "hartshorn" and "horehound" and until this day I imagined them to be the same thing. But hartshorn is a nasty ammonia extracted from the horns of deer, whereas horehound is a nasty flavouring extracted from a harmless herb. As an infant I was wont to trot into drugstores with five cents in my chubby palm to ask for hartshorn candy; what would my amazement have been if the chemist had taken me at my word! I would soon have been writh-

---

✒ The reader will by this time have observed that Marchbanks suffers ill-health, even if it is no more than the hypochondria characteristic of so many literary men. One of his worst trials in his visits to the medical profession was the Basal Metabolism Test, which was required of him often. It involved arriving at the physician's office without breakfast, and lying on a cold table while a rubber bag was strapped over his mouth and nose; the bag was never cleansed, and God knows who had puffed and blown into it; breathing in and out while it was in place was like giving the Kiss of Life to somebody on Skid Row. Under such circumstances Marchbanks was unable to obey the doctor's command to breathe quietly and easily, and in consequence the record of his Basal Metabolism is a medical marvel of inaccuracy.

ing upon the floor pleading—perhaps in vain—for vinegar and water. What unsuspected perils beset us, all the days of our lives!

• Of The Flabbered Gaster •

"*Y*OU FLABBERGAST ME!" said the man sitting beside our hostess to whom I had imparted a slightly surprising piece of information. His word caught my fancy; I am a bit of an etymologist myself, and I well recall the Greek word "gaster," which the Elizabethans used to mean the stomach and digestive organs. Now when a man is amazed his stomach and digestive organs bear the brunt of it; sometimes they tremble violently; the word "jellybelly" has been coined to describe this condition of tremulousness. Therefore, when a man is flabbergasted, it means that someone has flabbered his gaster. And what is "to flabber"? Does not the word explain itself? To flabber means to flap or violently agitate something which because of its saponaceous or oleaginous nature does not flap readily—the middle section of a human being, for instance. Therefore when my friend said that I flabbergasted him he meant that I wobbled his tripes, which was interesting if true, and I know many people upon whom I would be happy to produce this effect.

• Of Suffering •

*T*HE COLD which has been hovering around me for the past month found a chink in my armour last week, and began its horrible invasion of my person. I passed the next day in bed—confined to my rheum, so to speak. The mail brought its usual yield of junk, including a catalogue of what were described as "Rare, Exciting, Unusual, Entertaining Books!" Among them were *Famous Hussies of History*, *The Book of Torture*, and *Thrilling Tales of Pep and Spice*. The one which interested me most, however, was one called *The Seven Keys to Power* which promises to teach me many useful things such as "How to gain the mastery of all things," "How to banish all misery," "How to cast a spell on anyone, no matter where they are," and "How to gain the love of the opposite sex." As it retails at the modest price of one dollar, I do not see how I can go wrong on that one. If I could cast a spell on anyone I would not really need another book in the catalogue, on Lightning Ju Jitsu, which has a special chapter called "The Answer to Pawing Hands." Nor, if I could compel love at will, would I need the book called *How To Write Love Letters*. I might risk fifty cents on the book which teaches Ventriloquism, and thus, for a mere $1.50 become one of the choice and master spirits of my age. I might even discover how to cure a cold.

• A FOOLISH QUESTION PARRIED •

I TYPED A LETTER today, and was annoyed to find that I had put the carbon under it in such a way that it printed on the back of my original instead of making a copy. But a boob who saw me do this said, "Why did you do that? Is it for some special kind of filing system?" I replied, "No; the man to whom this letter is going is the most cross-eyed man I have ever known, and if he happens not to have his glasses on when he gets this letter he won't be able to read it. But if he turns it over and reflects this backward copy in a mirror, he will be able to read it perfectly." "Oh," said the boob, looking mystified, "I never knew that before.". . . As the Good Book says, "Answer a fool according to his folly and when he is old he will not depart from it."

• NO TRUCK WITH ANGELS •

I LISTENED TO THE opera broadcast this afternoon for the first time in a long spell. It was *Hansel and Gretel*, to my immense delight, but I cannot help feeling that children who had fourteen angels to guard them all through the night should not have got themselves into such dreadful trouble as soon as they woke up. Probably that is the moral of the opera: if you depend on guardian angels, your moral fibre and common sense will rot, and you won't be able to look after yourself.

• LEAR'S FOLLY NOT IMPROBABLE •

*I*WENT TO SEE Donald Wolfit *⸙* in *King Lear* last week. He is advertised as the greatest actor since Henry Irving; unless everything I have ever read or heard about Irving is wrong, this is a somewhat over-confident statement. He had fine moments, but the shabbiest scenery and costumes I have seen since the days of the Marks Brothers (not to be confused with Groucho, Harpo and Chico) did nothing to help him. Charles Lamb said that *Lear* could not be acted, and all sorts of people have parroted that foolish remark ever since; it is as sensible as saying that Beethoven's Ninth Symphony cannot be played. Wolfit acted Lear admirably; if he had had more nobility and more pathos he would have been wonderful. Somebody said to me in the interval that it was unbelievable that any man would be so stupid as to do what Lear did — put himself at the mercy of his children. I don't know about that: I have seen at least three cases in which parents did the same thing, and with not dissimilar results.

• TRAVEL AMONG STATESMEN •

*O*N THE TRAIN again yesterday I was travelling with a number of men who were obviously Senators and members of the Commons on their way to Ottawa for the opening of Parliament. They wore that dedicated, holy look which is only to be

---

⸙ Donald Wolfit (1902–68) was an actor of extraordinary courage and determination, uninhibited by self-doubt, who in his professional life presented a large number of the plays of Shakespeare, and some of Ibsen, acting with intelligence and clarity of focus. Without any advantages of person, and with a somewhat harsh voice, he was at his best in the roles of tragic heroes, but had no turn for scenes of tenderness. Marchbanks saw him often, and thought him best in the title role in Ben Jonson's Volpone, *the brilliance, ferocity and abrasiveness of the character being perfectly suited to Wolfit's gifts. He was also greatly admired in the larger-than-life role of the protagonist in Marlowe's* Tamburlaine. *In the age of Gielgud, Olivier and Richardson, Wolfit exemplified the earlier tradition of the great roaring actors.*

seen on the faces of men who are travelling on passes and expect to be wearing their best suits within twenty-four hours. The members of the older parties gravitated naturally toward the chair-car; the socialists rode in the coach, ate box-lunches, and occasionally exclaimed, "God pity the poor engineer on a day like this!" whenever there seemed to be a member of the Brotherhood of Railway Men within earshot. I did a good deal of spying and eavesdropping in all parts of the train, but learned nothing.

• OF SABBATH OBSERVANCE •

I SHOVELLED SNOW yesterday aftenoon. As I laboured, a passer-by said, "Considering the dispute that has been going on about Sabbath observance I'd think you would be afraid to be seen doing that." Leaning on my shovel, and holding my poor bent back, I replied, "Sir, if Providence sees fit to send snow on Saturday night, Providence will have more sense than to condemn me for clearing it away on Sunday. If I am not greatly mistaken, it is pleasure-seeking on the Sabbath which gives pain to the godly; shovelling snow is not a pleasure to me, but a penance, a mortification of the flesh, and a Lenten misery. I offer this labour — which I heartily detest — as an expiation for all my sins of pride, lust, covetousness, greed, sloth, anger and envy during the past six days. And now will you please go away before I sin further by washing your face in this snow bank?" He hurried away, tut-tutting.

• OF UNWONTED EXERTION •

S EVERAL LARGE and dangerous icicles hang from the roof of my house, and I decided that I had better get them down before they fell on the milkman and clove him to the brisket. So I spent quite a long time heaving snowballs at them, this afternoon, trying to knock them off the eavestrough. Throwing things is not one of my accomplishments; I can hit a dog with a baseball bat at ten feet, but picking off icicles with snowballs is quite another thing. However, I threw and threw, until my right shoulder became numb and my appendix gave notice that it was going to burst, but very few of the stalactites (or are they stalagmites?) came down, and those that did smashed uncomfortably near me. . . . The result of all this stretching is that my right side is now several inches longer than my left side, and I walk with a hippety-hopping gait, like a dwarf and a giant tied together for a three-legged race.

• EDISON THE CALLIGRAPHER •

*T*HE PAPERS ARE full of hullabaloo about Edison, 𝄢 who appears to have been not merely an ingenious fellow, but also a major philosopher and saint (as well as the only man who could write the Lord's Prayer on a piece of paper the size of a dime). Edison's chief impact was made upon me by means of his phonograph. My great-aunt Lettice had an early model, and as soon as I was strong enough to lift the records (which were as thick as manhole covers and about the same weight) I played it frequently. As a result of this early training, I am still able to recite large portions of a monologue called *Cohen On The Telephone*, and sing all the hits from a forgotten musical comedy called *The Yokohama Girl*. Edison's admirable autograph appeared on each record, and I am surprised that in all the praise of him there has been no word of his genuine skill as a calligrapher.

• GEOGRAPHY AN IMPERTINENCE •

I HAD AN OPPORTUNITY to examine a rather fine stamp collection today. As a usual thing stamps leave me cold; I regard them simply as dirty bits of paper which foreigners have

---

𝄢 Thomas Alva Edison (1847-1931) was the inventor of hundreds of remarkable devices, and seems to have been the Yankee Handy-Man raised to the nth *power. His lifelong deafness was caused when he was a newsboy on the Grand Trunk Railway. Running to catch a train, he was seized by the ears by a brakeman and dragged aboard, with irreparable damage to his hearing. Children and dogs should never be lifted by the ears, as U.S. President Lyndon B. Johnson once discovered, to his cost.*

licked. But I had to admit as I turned the pages, that some of the stamps were pretty; the pre-revolutionary Russian ones, for instance, had great charm and the Japanese stamps were delicately beautiful. The possessor of the collection assured me that it was a great aid in learning history and geography, which is probably true, but the kind of history which can be learned from stamps is of no particular interest to me, and I have no desire to learn any geography under any circumstances. The fact that I am never sure where any place is gives a special charm to my consideration of the daily news and if I shattered my ignorance another of my retreats from reality would have been ruined. I think that all this dabbling in geography is rather bad-mannered and nosy, like peeping through people's windows.

· THE NAÏVETÉ OF OPERA ·

*T*HE LAST OF THE opera broadcasts was on the air this afternoon, so I settled down in my armchair with a bag of peppermints to enjoy it. But luck was not with me; things kept cropping up which had to be done, and people kept calling me to the phone who wanted taxis and other things which I couldn't give them, and altogether the union of Mozart and Marchbanks was incomplete and unsatisfactory. By the time the broadcast was over I had a headache and a peppermint hangover. Nevertheless, opera broadcasts exercise a powerful fascination over me, and every winter I try to hear as many as I can. There is a childlike, unsophisticated quality about opera which commands respect in this wicked world. All that hooting and hollering because somebody has pinched somebody else's girl, or killed the wrong man, or sold his soul to the devil! These are commonplaces in daily life (particularly the latter) and it is astonishing to hear them treated with so much noisy consideration.

· HE YEARS FOR THE REVOLUTION ·

I MADE A TRAIN journey yesterday. As always I was impressed by the amount of rude staring that goes on when a train is standing in a station. The stay-at-homes on the platform gawp rustically at the people in the cars, while the urbane and world-weary travellers stare back, down their noses. As in an aquarium, it is impossible to say who is staring and who is being stared at.... When the train reached my stop I wrestled my own suitcases to the door, for the porter thought I was going to Toronto, and had fallen asleep. Yet, I gave this neglectful blackamoor a quarter — an act of sheer cowardice; I should have stared into his chocolate eyes like a lion-tamer, and kept my money. But in such matters I am contemptibly lacking in resolution. My face is perpetually ground by those who are, in a purely technical sense, the poor. I shall welcome the Revolution, after which I shall not be expected to tip anybody.

· OF WITCHES ·

A LITTLE GIRL was telling me about a dream that she had last night: "A witch was chasing me, and she had germs all over her fingers," the child said. This is a good example of the way in which superstition keeps abreast of science, instead of being displaced by it, as foolish people believe. In my childhood I sometimes dreamed that witches were chasing me to tear out my liver and lights, or to bake me in a pie, but never to infect me with germs. The next generation, I suppose, will dream that witches are after them to make them radioactive. The fashion in scientific horrors may change, but the witches will go on, and on, chasing generations of horror-stricken children down the shadowy labyrinths of sleep.

· HOW TO DISCOURAGE EVIL SPIRITS ·

I SAW A CHILD whizz across the road on her tricycle today, directly in front of a car; when she grows up she will be the kind of woman who darts across the streets against the red light, holding back traffic by sheer power of the human eye. In India it is regarded as a good idea to dart in front of an oncoming car, for the car is sure to kill the evil spirits who are pursuing you, and all the rest of your life you will have good luck. There are a lot of Canadians who seem to be trying to get the best of their evil spirits by this dubious method. Of course, if you are a little out in your calculations, and the car reduces you to a large splash of tomato sauce, your evil spirits may be said to have won the final trick.

• GROWTH OF INCREDULITY •

I SAW A LARGE shell in a friend's house the other day, and for old times' sake I held it up to my ear and heard the familiar roaring which is supposed to be the sound of the sea. When I was a child I listened to this sea-noise eagerly, and believed in it. But now I am of a less easily satisfied disposition; the Scientific Spirit has got hold of me and it gives me little peace. If I hold an empty beer bottle up to my ear I hear a noise, too; am I to believe that is the sound of a brewery? And when I hold an old marmalade jar to my ear, must I believe that the suspiration which I hear is the whisper of the zephyrs through orange-groves? No. As a modern poet has put it:

> The noise
> Which is so easy to explain to girls and boys,
> Serves only to insult
> The keener intelligence of the adult.

• OF CENSORSHIP •

I HAVE A PARTICULAR affection for the city of Toronto; the mere contemplation of its moral sublimity puts me in good humour for days at a time. The latest outbreak of virtue in the Queen City takes the form of a declaration on the part of one of the city controllers that the Public Libraries of Toronto have been circulating dirty books, including *The Decameron*. At first I was a good deal startled by the thought that a Toronto alderman had been reading *The Decameron*; I had not imagined that they read anything more taxing than the portions of the *Reader's Digest* which are printed in large type. But I now discover that the alderman had not read the book; he had simply been told by somebody else that it was not a proper book for anyone to read. . . . The first indecent book I ever read was *Quo Vadis*, which I got out of a Sunday School library; I found the descriptions of Roman highlife deeply stirring. Later I became very partial to *The Song of Songs* (which is Solomon's) which was sold to me by an agent of the British and Foreign Bible Society in a plain wrapper.

• OF DOGS •

A BEAUTIFUL NEW dogproof garbage box was installed on the back stoop at Marchbanks Towers today. For several years all the jolly doggies of the neighbourhood have looked upon my back stoop as a rendezvous where they can drop in for a snack, a chat, a fight or to enquire after some bitch of easy virtue with whom they can pitch a bit of woo; dogs create their own form of bebop, and discuss big deals involving dozens of bones on my back porch, and I make no secret of the fact that I am sick of it. Therefore I have caused to be constructed a large and durable chest, heavily ribbed and studded with brass screws, in which I shall keep my garbage pails in future, and the dogs can find some new Kasbah in which to carry on their raffish social life.... For a time I used to lie in wait in my kitchen until the dogs gathered for the evening, and then (choosing my time very precisely) I would rush out among them, striking to right and left with a broom, and uttering loud and terrifying cries, like a Japanese warrior going into battle. Then I would pick up the garbage and go inside, congratulating myself on a good job well done. But I found that the dogs looked upon me merely as the floorshow, or comedy act, of their evening's entertainment.... Well, they'll laugh on the other side of their muzzles when they see my new box.

• OF HAPPY PRIVACY •

A LL YESTERDAY'S papers informed me that this would be International Shut-Ins Day, and when I awoke I found that rain was descending in large greasy blobs about the size of marbles. This meant that I was a shut-in myself until this evening, for though I enjoy a walk in the rain a recent misadventure with my umbrella put such an amusement out of the question. Personally I do not greatly mind being a shut-in. I have often longed to have my sphere of activity sharply limited. Whenever I see an advertisement telling me that it is now possible for me to get to Britain in eight hours, or that the wonders of South America are within my easy reach, I recoil; when a speaker begins his remarks by saying that the world is shrinking, I shrink too. I shall end my days, beyond a doubt, as a happily cantankerous old shut-in, reading, eating and sleeping in one small room, with doors and windows sealed, and a hole in the ceiling for the entry and removal of necessities. At last my corpse will be dragged up through the hole, and only my memories will be left.

• OF NATURE'S MALICE •

*I*T LOOKED LIKE rain this afternoon, and I gave it every chance to do so. But nothing happened, so I girded up my loins and cut my grass, after which the heavens opened and the rains fell. The malignancy of Nature in these matters is past belief. If I am not to enjoy the beauty of my lawn when I have cut it, why should I bother with it? I often think that I should abandon the futile struggle and allow Nature to reclaim the pleasure grounds of Marchbanks Towers. Let the velvet lawns grow rank; let briars and thistles choke the Lovers' Walk; let scum accumulate on the lily pond; let the grape arbour and the Temple of Diana fall into ruin. Let the place assume the aspect of Tobacco Road, and I shall sit happily on the decaying verandah, spitting tobacco juice at the passers-by.

• OF HIS UNCLE BRIAN •

*T*HERE SEEM to be a good many advertisements for Irish goods about these days, and most of them give the impression that everything in Ireland is made by peculiar fellows in bobtailed coats, who wear bog beards and smoke clay pipes. If memory serves me aright the word "shantycraft" was used in one such billboard that I saw. It is a lucky thing that my great-uncle

Brian Boru Marchbanks never lived to see those things. He was a proud man, and any suggestion that Irishmen kept pigs under their beds or habitually went about with holes in the seats of their pants (for the airiness of it) used to put him into a state of passionate resentment. It was his opinion that Irishmen were just the same as other people, and frequently in the street he would call loudly upon anyone who was with him to point out just one respect — only one — in which he could be singled out from the crowd as an Irishman. Often his protestations of ordinariness would draw quite a crowd, which he would offer to fight, man by man, until he was dragged away by his wellwishers.

• OF THE MANX SHAKESPEARE •

*T*HE LADY on my right has just asked me if I remember the novels of Sir Hall Caine. ⁋ I replied that with Hall Caine, as with Sir Walter Scott, I had never been able to read one of his books through. All of Caine's characters lived in an atmosphere of agony and molasses, which was intolerable to my ribald mind. The lady then confessed to me that she, too, had no admiration for Caine, but thought that I might recall in which of his novels it was that the heroine dried her baby's diapers by wrapping them around her own body, next to the skin. I could not recall the source of this astounding instance of mother love but said that any heroine of Hall Caine's was quite welcome to get rheumatism, so far as I am concerned. It was a little surprising, however, to hear that Caine ever acknowledged the existence of anything so closely related to the baser functions as a diaper. . . . You've never heard of Hall Caine! *Sancta simplicitas*!

Sir Thomas Henry Hall Caine (1853-1931) was in his heyday a best-selling author and enjoyed some reputation as a prophet and seer. He was known as the Manx Shakespeare because he had a strong affection for the Isle of Man (though born in Cheshire), wrote plays, and cultivated a resemblance to the Bard, firmly based on partial baldness. Like many writers of the highest popularity, he had little humour. When his drama The Eternal City *was being rehearsed by Herbert Beerbohm*

• A WOMAN OF PARTS •

THE LADY ON MY left tells me that she wants a job in my Institute for the Re-Gruntlement of Disgruntled Persons. As qualifications she tells me that she is a bad cook and a terrible dancer; the latter circumstance she attributes to a Methodist upbringing, which still causes her to drag one leg. She says that she gets devilish ideas easily, and advances some very original notions for treating disgruntled persons with Epsom Salts. She seems to be the ideal appointee for the post of Matron. I have already put the Business Management of the institution into the hands of a man who was unfrocked by the Income Tax division of the Department of National Revenue for extortion above and beyond the call of duty. ✒

• OF CALENDAR REFORM •

I CHATTED THIS evening to a man who is in the calendar business and who tells me that one mighty industry recently distributed several hundreds of thousands of calendars in which April was credited with thirty-one days. This is probably the result of a secret coup by the calendar reformers. I do not personally favour calendar reform as I am a friend to inconvenience and inconsistency, believing that the illogicality of our present calendar serves as a useful reminder of the capriciousness of fate and

---

Tree in 1902, Caine wanted Tree, who played the villain, Count Bonelli, to drag the heroine, Roma, played by Constance Collier, around the stage by her hair and conclude by bashing her head on the boards. "Yes, yes," said Tree, "but my dear Caine, I seem to remember that incident being worked into another very famous tragedy." "Good gracious, Tree," said Caine, "whatever play was that?" "It was," said Tree, thinking deeply, "yes, it was called Punch and Judy." Caine was not amused.

✒ This was, of course, written at a time when the tax-gatherers admitted that there was such a thing as Going Too Far. They have long since overcome any such inhibiting scruple.

the mutability of all things. The calendar reformers just want to be cosy. A pox on cosiness!

• OF LUMPISM •

*I*BECAME INVOLVED in an argument about modern painting, a subject upon which I am spectacularly ill-informed; however, many of my friends can become heated, and even violent on the subject and I enjoy their wrangles. In a modest way, I am an artist myself, and I have some sympathy with the Abstractionists, although I have gone beyond them in my own approach to art. I am a Lumpist. Two or three decades ago it was quite fashionable to be a Cubist, and to draw everything in cubes; then there was a revolt by the Vorticists who drew everything in whirls; we now have the Abstractionists who paint everything in a very abstracted manner. But my own small works (done on my telephone pad) are composed of carefully shaded, strangely shaped lumps, with traces of Cubism, Vorticism and Abstraction in them for those who possess the seeing eye. As a Lumpist, I stand alone.

• OF UNIVERSITY VERSE •

*I*RECEIVED AN undergraduate magazine this morning, containing the kind of poetry which boys and girls write between eighteen and twenty-one, full of words like "harlot," "stench," "whore" and the like. The young have a passion for strong meaty words, and like to write disillusioned verses with jagged edges about the deceit and bitterness of life. I idly turned my hand to versifying, and produced this nice bit of undergraduate poetry, which I offer free to any university magazine:

> DISILLUSION
> Ugh!
> Take it away!
> Life — the thirty-cent breakfast
> Offered to vomiting Man
> In this vast Hangover —
> The World.

> Onward I reel
> Till Fate — the old whore —
> Loose or costive
> Drops me in the latrine of Oblivion —
> Plop!

I have not lost the youthful, zestful university touch with a bit of verse.

• OF AN AGREEABLE PASTIME •

ON MY WAY HERE tonight I found that an icy crust had formed on all the snow, about an eighth of an inch in thickness, and as I trod it broke into large flat chunks, like dinner plates. I smashed a few of these, experimentally, and found it an admirable release from tension. I began to pretend that the chunks of ice were valuable pieces of china, and this was even more fun. "Here goes a Spode dinner plate!" I cried, and smashed it to smithereens. Then — "Bang goes a half dozen Crown Derby demitasses!" — and bang they went. Next — "Here's for those ruddy soup cups I've always hated!" — and an armful of them dispersed into atoms. It was glorious. I was a bull in a china shop — an embittered, vindictive bull, revenging itself for a thousand annoyances and injuries. I suppose that, by the time I had finished, I had destroyed about an acre of ice or $50,000 worth of china, and I felt fine. If people had more cheap releases of this kind, there would be fewer deaths from heart failure.

• OF BEETHOVEN'S WIT •

THE PAPERS TELL me that an admirer of Deanna Durbin's ∮ has paid $60 for a lock of Beethoven's hair to give her, to be added to her collection of musical relics. I hope he

---

∮ Deanna Durbin (b. 1921) was a Canadian girl singer of great charm who enjoyed ten years of success on the screen, when an increasing plumpness brought about her retirement. Would a lock of Beethoven's

sniffed it before paying. It is well-known that Beethoven, who was a nasty man in many ways and possessed of a thoroughly Germanic sense of humour, was pestered all his life by women who wanted his hair, and on more than one occasion he cut a swatch off a goat and sent it to a fan, who presumably wore it in a locket, or sewed it into her corsets next to her heart. I doubt if the smell of goat would wear off, even after 150 years.

• OF HIS PROTEAN PERSONALITY •

I TRAVELLED BY train yesterday, and observed a remarkable change in my character, which would undoubtedly be of the deepest interest to psychologists, if I chose to make it public. There was a queue for the dining car, and as I stood in the narrow corridor, beside the axe, hammer, saw and crowbar which railways display in a little glass showcase (doubtless for sale to tourists) I imagined, and mentally ate, several meals, wondering meanwhile how the gluttons in the diner could take so long. It was sheer malignance, I decided. But when at last I was shown to a table I forgot all this, chose my meal with a gourmet's care, and then ate it as much like a gourmet as its decidedly poor quality permitted, forgetting all about the needy wretches in the corridor. But when I passed them on my way out their fiery and indignant eyes burned through my waistcoat, giving me heartburn.

---

hair have added anything to her gift of song? Marchbanks once bid up to $15 at an auction sale in Port Hope, for a disgusting object under a belljar which was described as a cigar butt thrown away by the great Franz Liszt. Marchbanks believed that if he set it on the lid of his own piano it might improve his playing, but stinginess proved his undoing, and another amateur pianist got the cigar butt for $17.

Dessert

· OF HEBRAISM AND HELLENISM ·

*T*HE DIFFERENCES between Montreal and Toronto are basic and significant. In Montreal I see dozens of men wearing wigs, and almost as many who obviously wear corsets. In the Queen City of the Trillium Province wigs are a great rarity, and prolapsed abdomens are commonplace. The shiny dome, the swaying paunch—these are marks of respectability in Toronto, and are carefully cultivated; a special wax is used by Toronto barbers for polishing those heads, and the tailors cut the trousers in such a way as to throw the bay window into prominence. They seem to say, "I am a plain, blunt fellow and I scorn subterfuge; the flesh may be weak, but the spirit is of brass." In Montreal, on the contrary, fanciful wigs are worn by old men, and cruel stays are endured by them, as a tribute to the charm of youth and beauty. Your Montreal man, at thirty or so, cries to the Fleeting Moment in the words of Faust. "Ah, stay, thou art so fair!" and then he buys anything he can get which will keep up a pretence—however scarecrow-like—of youth. It is the old conflict of Hebraism and Hellenism, and upon the whole I plump for Hellenism, even when it means wigs and circingles.

· OF MEAD, OR METHEGLIN ·

*S*OMEBODY HAS sent me a clipping which attempts to prove that the drinking of mead was given its death-blow by the Reformation. The implication is that the Reformation was therefore a Bad Thing. It may be so. I can never decide the matter to my own satisfaction. On Mondays, Wednesdays and Fridays I am a rollicking Chestertonian medievalist, shrieking against the Reformation, exulting in any manifestation of unreason, and shoving wads of my shirttail into delicate machines to harm them and show their inferiority; on Tuesdays, Thursdays, and Saturdays I am a fiery-eyed Puritan, attempting to reconcile modern progress with the blackest Old Testament morality, and yelling for a church which is both completely secular and all-powerful. On Sundays I rest from these theological exercises and read Voltaire. . . . As for mead, I have been told that it is a delectable drink, and I suppose that my Welsh ancestors drank it out of the horns of rams, in true Celtic style. But they were hearty, outdoors types, innocent of the complications which beset a man today, and I suppose that if one of them had a horrible mead hangover nobody noticed it, or mistook his mutterings for poetry.

· OF SCIENCE ·

I SEE IN THE paper that a celebrated Canadian educator said today that no one should consider himself educated unless he has some knowledge of science. I wonder if I am educated, by this standard? As a schoolboy I failed with monotonous regularity in chemistry, but I was rather good at physics, which seemed to me to make more sense. Chemistry appeared to consist of efforts to make crystals in a test-tube — efforts which were doomed to failure because the tube was wet, or the chemicals old, or simply because I put too much of something in the mixture. But physics was good fun, permitting me to blow bugles in the classroom (to learn about sound) and to slop happily with acids (to produce electricity) and to grind the cranks of old rusty machinery in order to study the centrifugal principle. My present knowledge of science is not profound; when a car will not go I know enough to say, "Dirt in the gas-line" in a weighty manner, and I can replace a fuse, if goaded to it. I also know that the pressure of the atmosphere on my body is fourteen pounds to the square inch (or is it an ounce to every fourteen pounds of body?). All I know about atoms is that they are teeny-weeny. Does this make me educated? Don't answer.

· OF INTERESTING PHONIES ·

C ANADA IS growing up. Why? Because we are beginning to have interesting phonies upon our national horizon. Of late I have seen two or three good examples of the Phoney

Westerner. This type is interesting, for although he comes from the West, he is a business man, in no way different from his Eastern counterpart. But he wears a big hat, and a horse-head pin in his tie, and he is very, very breezy. He walks with the gait of a man who is carrying a keg between his thighs, and this is meant to suggest a familiarity with horses. He is full of tangy, open-air oaths and he treats women as though they were idiots, this being his way of showing respect for their purity. He corresponds to that American type, the Phoney Southerner. We shall see more of him, as time passes, and the West becomes more and more sophisticated. ⁊

• A BAS LES ANIMAUX! •

I ATE MY FIRST Canadian margarine today and found it disappointing. It was neither the nauseous concoction of train-oil and soap which the dairymen had led to me to expect, nor did it taste of glorious liberty and the Triumph of the People over Vested Interests. It just tasted like butter. And yet this might have been expected. Surely man can produce, by scientific means, something as good, or better than the goo which a cow exudes without using her mind at all? Having beaten the cow at her own game, Triumphant Man will march onward to the synthetic egg and then to laboratory-made beef-steak. At the moment a whole large class of society is doomed to coddle and valet a lot of idle, ungrateful animals. Get rid of the animals, say I! Kick them back into the forests whence they came! They have leeched and battened upon man for aeons, but their day is done. In the world to come there will be no farmers — only scientists, leaning on the

⁊ *Since Marchbanks wrote this the Phoney Westerner has added two new items to his costume — the shoelace necktie and cowboy boots (made in Switzerland) of richly worked leather. Because these boots have uncomfortably high heels the PW not only walks as if straddling a barrel, but hobbles as if afflicted with terminal bunions. . . . Every politician now has a large white Stetson that he wears when travelling in the West, beseeching the prairie-dwellers for their votes.*

gates of their laboratories, yammering about the low prices they get for their stuff, and whining if it is suggested that they pay income tax.

• OF BABY TALK •

A MAN WAS HOLDING forth to me before dinner about how much he disliked baby-talk; anyone who used baby-talk to a dog, or a woman, or even a baby, was in his opinion a contemptible creature, capable of any inanity. But I am not so sure. I don't care for men who have no silliness in them, and I have known some men of remarkable character who were not above a spell of baby-talk, upon a proper occasion. And indeed that wonderful man Dean Swift used a lot of very babyish baby talk in his letters to Esther Johnson, whom he called "Stella." One winces a little as one reads it, but one winces far more sharply when one thinks what Swift might have become if he had not been able to let himself go in that manner. There is a certain spiritual indecency in overhearing any man talking baby talk or making love, but that does not mean that it is wrong or indecent of him to do so.

• A RETURN TO THE GOLDEN AGE •

A FRIEND WAS telling me today about a little girl he knows who was sent some handkerchiefs for her birthday. "Look, Mummy," cried the moppet in amaze; "cloth Kleenex!" This child will be an ideal citizen of the Age of Substitutes, into which we are fast moving. For a time we shall use nothing except foods, fabrics and substances which have been made in imitation of the age-old gifts of nature. Then as time passes, distinguished scientists will discover that a cloth of superior properties can be made from the wool of sheep, that amusing drinking cups can be made from the horns of beasts, and that a piquant beverage can be produced by allowing honey to ferment. And thus, by the roundabout methods which appeal to scientists and worshippers of Progress, we shall return to the Golden Age. I hope that I live long enough to see it.

• OF THE LANGUAGE OF STAMPS •

*Y*EARS AGO I possessed a dictionary in the back of which was some information about the language of flowers; it appeared that the most complex messages could be expressed by a properly composed bouquet. Mind you, those speaking floral tributes might not always be pleasing to the eye: to say, "I shall love you till death; meet me at the hollow oak tomorrow evening; my laundry has come back and I shall wear a clean shirt," one might have to combine a pansy, a gladiolus and a truss of Baby's Breath — a difficult bunch to make presentable. Later I learned that there is also a language of stamps; if the stamp is stuck on the envelope cockeyed it means, "I despise you" or "I adore you," according to the way the King's head is pointing. There are other variations, some of which I invented myself. To omit the stamp from the letter altogether means "You are richer than I am and can well afford to pay double postage." To glue a cancelled stamp on a letter means "I am in revolt against our Country's fiscal system." To draw spectacles on the King's head means "I harbour subversive opinions."

• OF TATTOOING •

I SEE THAT THE art of tattooing is said to be in decline. When I lived in England I passed No. 72 Waterloo Road every day on my way to work, where a great artist in this field, G. Burchett, had his atelier. I never ventured inside, but I admired the rich display of designs in the window, and sometimes I would see a man going in or coming out, wearing a special defiant look. I am too timid to do anything so irrevocable as to have my hide ornamented but I understand and sympathize with those who do so. The ordinary designs — fouled anchors, flags, ships, naked women and the like — obviously would appeal to many men; but who, I wondered, took up G. Burchett's offer to tattoo the Apostle's Creed on his chest, or his thigh? Did divinity students creep through the door at night, for this service? Or did atheists cause themselves to be so tattooed that whenever they sat down they affronted, so to speak, the whole of Christendom? Perhaps I shall never know.... No, madam, I did not know that your husband is a clergyman.... Yes, as a child I often sat upon the whole of Holy Writ, in large print and fully illustrated, in order that I might reach the level of the dinner table.... Very well, if you choose to take that attitude.

· A GIFT TO HOLLYWOOD ·

I SEE THAT A family has died of carbon monoxide poisoning at a place called Ingomar, in Pennsylvania. Was the town named after the old play of *Ingomar* adapted by Maria Lovell from the German drama by Eligius Franz Joseph Munch-Bellinghausen, called *Der Sohn der Wildnis* which was popular from 1842 until the beginning of this century? *Ingomar* is such tripe that I wonder why the movies do not do a version of it. Ingomar is a wild man of the woods, who laughs a great deal until he meets a very civilized girl who quickly has him twining rose wreaths, working sixteen hours a day as a farm hand, and eating cooked food. Then he stops laughing, and realizes that in Civilization Woman has the Upper Hand (a philosophy widely popular on this continent at the moment). A movie of this piece, with Bing Crosby as Ingomar (singing Boo-boo-boo instead of laughing) and Joan Fontaine as the Civilized Maiden should prove one of Hollywood's most successful boobsqueezers and I give them the idea free. *

The Women's Lib groups should investigate Ingomar; *it has much to recommend itself to them, though they might find it sentimental. The reiterated couplet—*

> *Two minds with but a single thought,*
> *Two hearts that beat as one—*

might get on their nerves, as it does on mine. But some rewriting, and the setting of the play changed to some fashionable theatrical milieu of our day, such as a prison or a madhouse, would work wonders.

• OF HISTORICAL NOVELS •

*T*HE LADY ON my right who has had quite a bit of experience of lending libraries tells me that a great many people demand a historical novel, "but not too far back," for weekend reading. Now why "not too far back"? Perhaps because of the widespread belief that people who lived long ago were not as smart as we are, and did not do very interesting things. Modern historical novels have spread the delusion that in the seventeenth and eighteenth centuries people gave all their time to sex, and in the nineteenth century devoted themselves wholly to sex and adventures, such as building railroads. But previous to the seventeenth century people had neither sex nor railroads, and were consequently of no interest to anyone, even themselves.

• OF TALKING DOLLS •

I WATCHED A very small child playing with a Mama-doll this afternoon; when the doll emitted its painful, catlike cry (as much like the squeal of an overloaded stomach as the voice of a child) the face of the tot would be filled with concern, and it would stare deeply into the eyes of its toy, obviously wondering what ailed it. I take a mild interest in dolls and I am always a little irked when I hear the Mama-doll referred to as a triumph of American ingenuity. As a matter of fact it was invented by Johann Nepomuk Maelzel, who died in 1838 and was a German; he is best known for his invention of the Maelzel Metronome, to the

---

Why not an epic on the evolution of the Male? We begin with Glug, the Cave Person who slew the sabre-toothed tiger. When Mrs. Glug said "Oh, Glug, you are wonderful!" Glug would blush and drag her around the cave a few times to show that Romance was not dead (though he was all of seventeen and thus, for a Cave Person, over the hill). Onward, by difficult stages to modern man, or the Apartment Person, who proves himself to his mate by opening packages that have been sealed in plastic—a severe test for the over-forties. This would be an historical novel on the grand scale.

nagging tick-tock of which millions of music students have practised their pieces. He was an inventor and handyman of unusual ability, and among other things he invented an ear-trumpet which his friend Beethoven wore for many years; it was an awesome crumpled horn which was affixed to the head with a clamp. Maelzel's Mama-doll may have had a better voice than the modern product, for it contained a more elaborate works, and it could also say "Papa."

• OF DISTRESSED FURNITURE •

I WAS TALKING to a man whose job it is to reproduce antique furniture, which he does remarkably well. When he has made a perfect piece, he then knocks a few bits out of it, scratches it and digs a hole or two in it. This process is called "distressing" the piece, he told me, and it is not to be confused with faking. There is no intention on his part of selling the distressed piece as a genuine antique, but he finds that people do not want antique reproductions that look too new. There is some moral obliquity in this matter, but I cannot discover exactly where it lies. The thing which interests me is that mankind does not yet appear to have improved upon the designs for chairs which were perfected in the eighteenth century. What is wrong? Has human inventiveness reached a dead end?

• OF A LAUGHABLE DELUSION •

N O MAN'S NEWSPAPER writings should be saved and produced in evidence against him. Take the case of G.B. Shaw, who served a term as a drama critic about 1895; today I was reading what he said about the first appearance of *The Importance of Being Earnest*; he did not think much of it; this play, which is now pretty generally acknowledged to be one of the great farces of our literature, appeared to Shaw to be old-fashioned — as if that made any difference, so long as it was good. But the funniest thing in the review is Shaw's assertion that the comedy was not of a high order because he was not "touched" by it. It is a popular delusion (and therefore the last thing one would expect G.B.S. to embrace)

that really funny things are also "touching." Sentimental twaddle!
And, by the way, was anybody ever touched by any of the comedies of Old Barney Shaw, the Swan of the Liffey?

• OF TELEPHONIST'S NECK •

*A*T THE RISK of giving offence to any living descendants
of Dr. Alexander Graham Bell, I must confess that I hate
and fear the telephone. There is something superstitious in my
attitude toward it; I credit the thing with the ability to see, as well
as hear. When I speak on the phone I wear a false smile; while I
am listening I grin and nod my head and flash my eyes, to show it
that I am paying attention. Real men of business, who are not
afraid of phones, do not do these things. They grab the phone and
spit in its face; I have even seen them grip the thing by pressing it
into the flesh of their necks, and then use their hands to write,
strike matches, and push buzzers. I have tried this neck trick once
or twice myself, in a spirit of bravado, but I merely drop the phone,
giving the impression on the other end of the wire that I have
fainted, or been shot. My neck isn't strong enough, or adhesive
enough, I suppose. A deeply creased neck, with hundreds of tiny
suckers in it, like the tentacles of an octopus, is what's wanted.

• OF KEROSENE •

*A*S THE ONTARIO Hydro is suffering from what certain
advertisements (not theirs) call "waning powers and general debility" I have to install a kerosene heater in one room of my
house which I used to heat with electricity. This has brought to
my notice the appalling rise in the price of kerosene since my boy-
hood. In those days everybody had a large can of the stuff in the
woodshed, with a potato stuck on the spout, and if a stove was not
burning satisfactorily you poured a gallon or two of kerosene on
the flames. Women were burned bald, doing this, and children
were consumed like little phoenixes (although they never rose again
from their ashes) and even fathers of households were Called to
Their Reward blazing like heretics in the fires of the Inquisition,

and shrieking to be extinguished. But with the cost of kerosene nowadays only the very rich would be able to afford this form of spectacular demise.

• OF THE PLEASURES OF SELF-PITY •

I LISTENED TO some people discussing an absent friend this afternoon, and as always on such occasions, they were much franker than if the friend had been within earshot. He was, they agreed, sadly given to self-pity; they seemed to regard this as a grave defect. I wonder why people are so down on self-pity? It is a cheap, agreeable amusement, requiring no elaborate equipment, like golf or polo. It imparts a pleasing melancholy to the countenance and a note of gentle charm to the voice. Most people despise self-pity in others because it makes them slightly uncomfortable, which is a selfish reason for disapproving of anything. But I have always found that there is nothing like a good wallow in self-pity when my spirits are low, and I do not grudge to others an indulgence which has given me so much harmless pleasure.

• OF NUT INTEMPERANCE •

I WAS INVEIGLED yesterday to help a friend stretch some new canvas over the frame of a chair. I should have more sense than to get myself involved in tasks which lie beyond the limits which Nature has set upon my capabilities, but I never learn wisdom. We fastened the canvas on, and of course there was a bubble in it, so we chased the bubble up and down for an hour, pulling out nails and knocking them in again and getting them crooked and smashing our thumbs and growing very ill-tempered. To soothe our nerves we ate most of a heart-shaped box of salted nuts which he had given his wife as a Valentine; prohibitionists talk about the devilish hold which Demon Rum takes on its devotees, but it is a trifle compared with thralldom to the salted nut. We both tied on a sizable nut bun, and the whites of our eyes were turning yellow before midnight.

· OF THE CHARMS OF PRISON ·

*E*ARLIER THIS EVENING I joined in a discussion as to whether hanging is not to be preferred to life imprisonment; they all thought it was, particularly the ladies. But I am not so sure. Life is sweet, even when it is confined, and I am sure that if I were imprisoned for life I could, by various winning ways, get myself a soft job in the penitentiary library, or as the Warden's chef, and contrive quite a pleasant existence. I would tell the warders funny stories, and suck up to the Chaplain so that he would let me play the organ on Sundays, and become the Prison Pet. In time I would be a "trusty," perhaps even a stool-pigeon, and in the kingdom of the mind I should roam freely. So much for prison. But what of hanging? The trap drops, down I go, and then—? No, no; not for Marchbanks. Social security and a nice cell for him, every time.

· OF AN IMPROVING BOOK ·

I WAS READING that great Canadian classic, *Beautiful Joe* by Marshall Saunders, ∮ to some children today. I had forgotten what a grisly book it is. Cruelty, drunkenness and meanness abound in it, which accounts for its popularity with the young, who love cheap sensationalism. But, oh how good the good people in it are! In one chapter a poor sailor boy, who owns a parrot, confesses to a clergyman that he calls his pet "Beelzebub." This

---

∮ Marshall Saunders (1861—1947) was a Canadian author who wrote something like thirty books, of which the most successful was Beautiful Joe, *an autobiography (1894), a stirring revelation of the beauty of the canine soul. Marchbanks, whose affection for the canine species was always under iron control, had reservations about the book but read it to children because it made them cry, which children love. He never failed, however, to point out that the book is also a vile racist attack on the Welsh people, for the cruel milkman who crops Joe's ears and makes him hideous (his beauty was wholly of the spirit) was gloatingly described as a Welshman. The Welsh have enough to put up with without being set upon by the wealthy and influential Dog Lobby.*

flummoxes the parson, and one of the parson's little boys "turned away with his face a deep scarlet, and walked to the window murmuring 'Beelzebub, Prince of Devils.' " How the child got this notion I do not know; an adherent of some church with a very loose theology, no doubt, for when I went to Sunday School "Beelzebub" meant "Prince of Flies," and was considered a very third-rate sort of devil. . . . In modern children's books no boy ever flushes a deep scarlet; they are too dumb. The heroes and heroines of modern children's books are all feeble-minded. . . . But the good clergyman persuaded the sailor boy to rename his parrot "Bella," thus whitewashing it. I never knew but one parrot, which was called "Stinker," for the best of reasons. It lived in a pub.

• OF IRREGULAR MENSURATION •

*T*HAT GENTLEMEN over there, whom I met just before dinner, remonstrated with me about my careless statement, hastily thrown into the conversation, that Thackeray drank 1,500 bottles of wine a year; the correct figure, he said, was 500. This seems very likely, and I attribute my use of the larger figure to the rich generosity of my nature. I have never been good at remembering figures and statistics depress me. When I was a schoolboy I was the despair of the teachers of mathematics, and since my escape from the education-mills I have had as little as possible to do with their dismal mystery. When I have to estimate a yard of anything I do it by stretching whatever it is from the tip of my nose to the end of my outflung arm; when I have to estimate heights, I mentally judge how many times I could lie at full length in the distance to be measured. These are not the methods of an Isaac Newton, but they suffice for my humble needs. I live a non-mathematical life, full of uncertainty, unreason and delicious surmise. /

Marchbanks made wretched the lives of countless good men and women who sought to teach him mathematics. He suffered from what Catholic theologians call Invincible Ignorance. But he has lived to see the coming of the Computer Age, when nobody has to know mathematics, because the computer knows it all, and if you press the right button will

• OF PASSION IN TORONTO •

I VISITED A famous Toronto confectioner's this afternoon and found all the salesgirls wearing their coats and shivering with cold. One large window was out and was being replaced with a new sheet of plate glass. It appears that last night two men had an argument in front of the shop and one of them was thrown through the window, wrecking the pane and bringing about the ruin of two dozen Maids of Honour. Outside a young man walked by with his arm in a sling. "That's the fellow who was hurt the other day by the young girl," said one of the coated waitresses, but did not say how, or why. What violent creatures these Torontonians are! What passions smoulder beneath those flat bosoms, what rage lurks behind those lack-lustre eyes! There is a Sicilian strain in the people of Toronto, ready at any moment to shatter their exterior of blancmange-like calm.

• OF STAGE IRISHMEN (A WEARINESS OF THE FLESH) •

L AST WEEKEND I went to Kingston, to attend the Eastern Ontario Drama Festival. All these festivals have many factors in common. The small people are always seated behind the big people, and even the biggest people are apt to find themselves behind middle-sized people who have fuzzy hair or are wearing huge hats; the proportion of coughers in every festival is constant, and they whoop up the rags of their lungs with the same revolting relish year after year; the pictures of theological professors on the wall are as disapproving as ever, though as their paint fades they become more remote from the scene; the actors, whether they are playing earls or garbage men, are all linked in the same conspiracy never, under any circumstances, to polish their shoes; doors which opened inward at dress rehearsals show a baffling tendency to open outward at performances; and, among the audience, blood lust against the adjudicator rises hour by hour, as he

---

give a plausible but not necessarily a correct answer. Nowadays March-banks could take a job as a teller in a bank, or even as its President if he would get his clothes pressed.

probes the sore spots, the malformations and the tuberculous lumps of each festival offering with a pitiless finger. It is all fascinating but painful, and in Spain where the bullfight is enjoyed, drama festivals are strictly forbidden as inhumane.

I found time in the midst of the festival to make a hospital visit, and had a chance to observe several interns, while cooling my heels in the halls. In the movies, whenever Gregory Gable or Clark Peck pretends to be an intern, he wears a beautifully fitted white suit which shows his hairy forearms (and if a nurse had wool like that on her arms she would be thrown out of the profession as unsanitary, but never mind that) and swathes his neck in a round-about collar which gives him a fetchingly clerical look. But in real life interns tend to be fellows with no chests, and their pants have been so shrunk by the laundry that they walk as though they were being sawn in two, which is probably the case.

A play about Irishmen, written by a man with a German name, engaged the attention of the festival-goers at a matinee. It made a liberal — not to say prodigal — use of a peculiar type of speech never heard in Ireland, or anywhere but in such plays as this. In this play, if one character said "Good morning" to another, he was likely to get some such answer as this: "Houly St. Pathrick, Barney O'Lunacy, sure and bedad 'tis yerself is just afther kissin' the Blarney Stone, at all, at all!" I rather like plays in which pretty girls confess their readiness to be loved by anybody at all, and in which old Irishmen cry into red handkerchiefs without any apparent reason, and in which policemen are much wittier than they ever are in real life — but I cannot bear these things when expressed in phoney Irish dialect. If I have to listen to more than one act of such stuff, sure an' 'tis meself is the boyo that's after throwin' up in the aisle. So I crept from the scene, and refreshed myself by listening to a couple of real Irishmen who were digging a hole in the street nearby, and who conversed solely in grunts.

• OF ALL WEEKS' WEEK •

I AM ALARMED by the increase of special "weeks." "Eat an Apple Week," "Immunization Week," "Education Week," "Sterilization Week," "Swat the Fly Week," "False Teeth for Pensioners Week"—there is no end to them. Every seven-day stretch is two or three "weeks." There was a time when the Holy Church suffered from so many saints' days that nobody was able to observe them all and do any work as well, and a calendar had to be arranged with a very few important saints who got a whole day to themselves, while the remainder were taken care of on All Saints' Day, November 1. I recommend that an All Weeks' Week be decided upon, and that every form of enthusiasm be given free rein while it is in progress. But once it is over there must be no "weeks" at all.

• OF IMPUDENT TRACTS •

*A*N ENVELOPE full of tracts came for me in the mail this morning. Tracts always ask foolish questions. "Are you on the way to Heaven?" said one of these. "Are you prepared to meet God?" said another. "Are you prepared for Eternity?" asked a third. "Are you going to a Christless grave?" enquired the last of the bunch. Really, I do not know the answers to these questions, and I doubt the ability of whoever writes the shaky English grammar of these tracts to answer them for me. I am not even prepared to meet Professor Einstein or Bertrand Russell; why should I vaingloriously assume that God would find me interesting? And I really cannot claim to be prepared for Eternity when I have so many doubts about today. I wish that whatever God-intoxicated pinhead directs these inquiries to me would cease and desist. In the struggle of the Alone toward the Alone, I do not like to be jostled.

• WHAT KILLED THE PARLOUR ORGAN •

*A*N OPPORTUNITY presented itself to play a reed organ, or "parlour" organ this afternoon, and I seized it eagerly, for it is many years since I had a whack at such an instrument. Really it is not more than a gigantic mouth-organ, blown by foot power. And what foot power! It is popularly believed that our grandmothers were unathletic, but no girl who operated a parlour organ lacked exercise, pumping with her feet, clawing at the *Vox Humana* and *Celeste* stops with her hands and wagging her head to keep time. But the parlour organ went out when short skirts came in. Many a young fellow of the nineties, charmed by his girl's command of her organ, married her, only to discover on his wedding night that she had legs like an eight-day bicycle racer — the result of furious pedalling. When skirts were raised, the jig was up.

• OF SPORTS AND PASTIMES •

I HEARD LAST evening about a physical fitness test which was used in the Air Force, called the Harvard Step Test. Here it is: step on and off an ordinary kitchen chair once every second for three minutes. If, by the end of that time you have not dropped dead, your physical condition is satisfactory, and you probably will not drop dead until tomorrow. As soon as I heard of this I was agog to try it, and lasted splendidly for about twenty seconds; then I heard a sound in my ears like the boiling of a cauldron of maple sap, and I decided to sit down and accept a cool drink. The only physical exercise at which I really excel is walking downstairs.

Many people complain to me that the world has become degenerate, and that we now rely on mechanical entertainments, instead of making our own fun. This is not true in one aspect of life, at least; nowadays we all make our own wrong numbers. There was a time, before the dial phone, when we relied on the operators at "Central" to get wrong numbers for us, and very good at it they were, too. But now we do it all by ourselves; somebody hoiked me out of bed at 7:10 this morning absolutely unaided. . . . Those "Central" girls developed wonderful voices and stupefying accents. One lifted the receiver from the hook. "Nubbaw?" said a voice. "9999," one said. "Nyun, nyun, nyun, nyun," said the voice, and after a few clicks one was talking to 9989, who had got out of his deathbed to answer the ring. Effete, dependent old days!

• A TREND? •

I AM DEEPLY interested in a news dispatch from South Africa which tells of twin girls who suddenly became boys. I want to know more about this. Was the change the result of deep emotion generated by the Royal visit? What are the feelings of the girls with whom, until now, they mixed on terms of girlish intimacy? Is there any sign of a trend toward this sort of thing in the Sister Dominion? Have bearded Boer farmers begun to look speculatively at their reflections in the glass, wondering how they would look in one of those saucy Voortrekker bonnets? Canada is outclassed now. All we can show is a set of Quintuplets when our King visits us, but in South Africa they are ambisextrous.

Personally I like being a man, and I can face with stoicism the possibility of becoming a woman, but I dread the intermediate period, during which I should be an It, tossed hither and thither on the turbulent seas of irreconcilable ambitions.

• Pitfalls of Cleanliness •

I TALKED TO a man this morning who is financially interested in Ontario wines. I asked him why they were no better than they are, and he replied by telling me of the extreme care and cleanliness shown in manufacturing them. "But that's just the trouble," I said; "you make wine as though it were a disinfectant. In the wineries of France they concentrate on flavour, and not on cleanliness, and as a result they produce great wines; wine must be made by vintners, not by analytical chemists. Wine and cheese are two things which cannot be made under laboratory conditions if they are to be good. It is better for the connoisseur not to poke his nose into the cheese factory or the winery. Cleanliness is the bugbear of this continent, and too much is sacrificed to it." He goggled a bit, and then said that he didn't know anything about it; he was a rye drinker himself. Oh, for a glass of real wine from grapes pressed by the feet of joyous, pleasure-loving Ontario farmers.

• Of Illogical Persons •

I ARGUED TODAY with the most illogical opponent I have met in a long time. For my part, I can argue quite logically when it suits me, having been trained to it at my school, where there were a number of clever young English masters who supervised our boyish wrangles. "That's an *argumentum ad hominem*, Marchbanks," they would cry, when I was buttering up my opponent before giving him a verbal K.O. Or they would shriek, "*Tu quoque!*" when I sought to unnerve my rival by shouting "The same to you, with knobs on!" at him, hoping to make him lose his temper. They were also very critical of something called "an undistributed middle" which I apparently made use of when I was being particularly foxy. Under their tutelage I learned the useful art of logic, which permits me to hold my opponent very closely to the rules, while pulling a dialectical fast one on him whenever I can. But when I argue with someone who scorns logic, and even reason, I have to depend on my talent for abuse if I hope to win.

• SIN, GLUTTONY AND SLOTH •

*A*T CHRISTMAS someone gave me some Russian cigarettes, wrapped in black paper and with elegant gold tips. From time to time I smoke one, enjoying a deep sense of sin as I do so. Thus it is to have been brought up in a household of Continuing Presbyterians; when others wallow happily in the fleshpots I gather up the skirts of my immortal soul and dabble my feet timidly over the brink.... I shovelled a lot of heavy snow this afternoon, which caused a great lethargy to come upon me. But I revived myself with a glass of sherry, which made me so hungry that I ate a huge tea, after which I could do nothing but loll by the fire and yawn until it was time to come here. Physical activity of any kind is my downfall; in order to keep my brain working and my productiveness at its height, I should be carried everywhere in a chair, like a Chinese mandarin.

• OF CALLIGRAPHY AND TURPITUDE •

*T*HERE WAS A time when I took a modest pride in my handwriting; of late years it has degenerated into a scrawl. This probably means that my moral stature is increasing, for I have observed that beautiful writers are usually uncommonly wicked men. One of the most exquisite writers who ever lived was Casanova, and everybody knows that he was a fellow you wouldn't trust even with your old Aunt Bessie; another impeccable master of the cursive hand was Poggio, who used it chiefly to write down dirty stories about the clergy. Of late years I have grown so moral that I am becoming dull company for myself, and it is my invariable habit to remove my hat to all wearers of back-to-front collars. Result: I can hardly read my own notes. ✒

• MARCHBANKS NO COMMITTEEMAN •

I ATTENDED A committee meeting this afternoon to decide certain matters bearing upon the public weal, and tried to look serious for three hours and a half. As I am incapable of concentrating on any single theme for more than an hour at a time, this was a strain on my histrionic powers. My imagination wandered; I thought about what I would do if I had a lot of money, what I would do if I were wrecked on a desert island with Joan Fontaine, and what I would do if I were a woodcarver of the genius of Grinling Gibbons. I drew funny faces on the paper which had been given to me for the purpose of making serious notes. I wondered what would happen if an evil fairy were to sneak into the room through the keyhole and strike us all stark naked. I wondered if I would be able to eat a woolly old Life Saver which I found in my pocket with my keys, without being rebuked by the Chair. It is useless to put me on committees: I have an incorrigibly frivolous and vacillating mind.

✒ *Not true. Marchbanks was vice-president of the Canadian Society for Italic Handwriting during its brief life. Like so many movements to elevate mankind it perished quietly after a few years, but he can still produce a few lines of passable script.*

• JONSON'S MESSAGE FOR OTTAWA •

I WENT TO SEE Donald Wolfit in Ben Jonson's *Volpone* last evening, and liked it much better than I liked *Lear* last week; the company seemed more suited to the satirical work. This play is all about avarice, and was a delightful change from most modern plays which are all about love. But avarice, as a vice, seems to have gone out of fashion. Nobody is miserly in the grand manner nowadays. Of course, following the trend of the times, the State has taken over avarice, and for genuine grasping, grinding, scrunching, scraping meanness and extortion it surpasses immeasurably all miserliness based on individual whim. In fact, I think it would pay the Income Tax Payers' Association to engage Mr. Wolfit and his company to stage a special performance of *Volpone* and give free seats to the Government, the deputy ministers, and the heads of all bureaux and boards at Ottawa as a lesson in avarice punished. . . . The genius of Jonson never fails to astonish and refresh me. What a torrent of golden words! And what a magnificent detestation of cant and folly.

• OF AN IMPERFECT WIG •

W HILE ON THE train today I sat near a man who was wearing a particularly fine example of a $5 wig. Like many other things, the excellence of wigs increases directly with their cost, and $5 procures the absolute minimum of deception and aesthetic satisfaction. This fellow had bought a somewhat larger wig than he really needed, perhaps in the hope that his head would grow, and in consequence it shifted a little every time the train lurched. Sometimes it dropped down over his eyes, and I was treated to the spectacle of a growing gap between art and nature at the back: at other times the thing jerked backward, giving him a high forehead, like pictures of Shakespeare; when it tilted over one eye he had quite a rakish appearance. His hair alone entitled him to challenge Lon Chaney's right to the name of "The Man With A Thousand Faces." I should judge that he had owned this wig for many years, for it had grown a trifle mangy, and he had tried to rejuvenate it by smearing it with brilliantine. The result was rather as though he had decorated his pate with a piece of cotton waste which someone had used for cleaning an engine.

• CANADIANS AT THE PLAYHOUSE •

I WENT TO SEE John Gielgud's production of *The Importance of Being Earnest*. I have never understood why some people call this an "artificial comedy"; true, it does not sprawl, and it wastes no words in foolishly reproducing the emptiness of everyday speech, but it is no more "artificial" than the music of Mozart is "artificial.". . . It has been a long time since Canada saw comedy acting as perfect as this. . . . It is a wonderful thing to watch the audience at a performance of this quality; every time they laugh they seem to roll forward a little in their seats, and the cumulative effect of this movement is as though the whole theatre had given a tiny hop toward the stage. And what a wonderful thing it is to see an Ontario audience laugh! Those stony, disapproving, thin-lipped faces, eloquent of our bitter winters, our bitter politics, and our bitter religion, melt into unaccustomed merriment, and a sense of relief is felt all through the theatre, as though the straps and laces of a tight corset had been momentarily loosened.

• OF BEING POORLY •

I ATTENDED A meeting of a Strength Through Joy committee of which I am a member this afternoon, and we talked about the encouragement of hobbies. There was no mention, however, of Ill Health, which is the hobby of a lot of people I know, and a very satisfactory hobby, too. You can pursue it anywhere, with simple materials which are to be found in every home, such as a bed, a rug, an easy-chair, or even a box of bicarbonate of soda. If you want to go in for it in a big way it is well to spend a dollar on a clinical thermometer, which you can carry in your pocket, and a watch, so that you can take your own pulse. The object of a hobby is to broaden your outlook and develop your personality, and mild invalidism will do both. Once you establish the fact that you are Poorly, you will be able to impose on your friends in a variety of delightful ways, and as a means of dominating your married partner, and subduing your children, it has no equal. It is a mistake to omit Ill Health from any list of hobbies, for it has its devotees in every class; I think it would be a good scheme to get all the Ill Health hobbyists together, and let them be Poorly at one another, and select a Champion. And instead of an annual Festival they could hold a Depresstival.

• OF A FAVOURITE SWEETMEAT •

I BOUGHT MYSELF a small bag of dragées yesterday; life has been using me rather shabbily, and I thought I deserved a little treat. They are delicious sweetmeats, my favourites. The modern dragée is an almond coated with hard sugar, delicately flavoured with (I suspect) talcum powder; eating one always reminds me of my childhood when I was occasionally commanded to kiss ladies who tasted just like that; old ladies tasted like mauve dragées and young ladies tasted like the delicious pink and white dragées; I always gave them a little unobtrusive lick as I kissed, to test their flavour. Modern face powder affords no such delights. . . . The dragée has not always been an innocent indulgence. A century ago physicians concealed their most detestable purges in those sugar shells, and poisoners have also made use of them. . . . Dragées are the sugar-plums about which one reads in old children's books, and they are still more wholesome than chocolates. I sat before my fire sucking, champing and wallowing in the nostalgia which the sweets evoked.

• OF LAGLES •

W HILE DRIVING this morning near a lake I saw a large group of seagulls swooping and wheeling over its surface. Among the most graceful of birds, they have the ugliest faces; in the countenance of a seagull we observe all the bitter hatred and malignance which we usually associate with the faces of money-lenders or book censors. To my mind the inland seagull is misnamed; it ought to be called a lake gull, and as seagull is commonly pronounced seagle, I suggest that lake gulls be known as lagles. I have several ornithologist friends to whom I shall mention this, but I do not expect that they will pay any attention. Ornithologists like to give birds a Latin name, with a Latin version of their own names stuck on the end. But it is rude, untutored nature-lovers like myself who give birds their common, deeply poetic names, like the Marsh Grommet, the Wheat Teazle, and the Double-breasted Ninnyhammer, or Film-Star Bird.

• OF ROMANTIC POVERTY •

A CHILD WHO IS interested in music was telling me about her favourite composers today; according to her they were all desperately poor, and never had a square meal. "Where did you pick up that notion?" I enquired; "you are wasting your pity on Chopin, who was really very well off; Beethoven had a pretty bank book, Haydn was well-heeled, Mendelssohn was born in the lap of luxury, and made a small fortune on his own account, Handel made and lost a couple of fortunes, and even Bach was in easy circumstances, according to the standards of his day. The only poor composer of the first rank that I can think of was Mozart. Dry your tears, my poppet." But she did not want to be comforted and was annoyed by my array of facts. Why people like to think of composers as poor I cannot say, but they do. My observation has been that most musicians were as sharp as a tack in their attitude toward money, long before the days of Petrillo.

• OF HIS CHOICE OF BOOKS •

T HE WEEKEND approaches, and I want to collapse with a book during the whole of it, seeking surcease from the cares of the world. But what book? Ah, there is the question! For when I am in this spiritually depleted condition I lack the strength to tackle a book with any substance to it, but I am too cranky to endure a foolish book. Today in a bookshop I picked up a new novel and, as is my custom, looked for a picture of the author on the back of the jacket. I judge most books by the pictures of the author. If he looks a congenial fellow, I read his book; if not, not. Upon the back of this book was a picture of a fellow with large intense eyes and his hair combed forward in a fringe. Obviously, I thought, this fellow has a grievance of some sort, and his novel will fall into the great category of Gripe Novels. So I looked at some others, but found none with pictures of authors who pleased me. They all looked like Gripers, or people with a Social Conscience, or Oh-God-The-Pain-Of-It writers. I like authors to look sassy and bright, like Evelyn Waugh.

· OF FREEDOM IN TEACHING ·

I WATCHED A CHILD attracting a bit of steel with a magnet this afternoon, and realized with a sudden shock that the bit of steel was a five-cent piece; I can remember when those coins were made of silver, and were much in vogue for Sunday School collection. As a child I was a regular Sabbath Day scholar, graduating from the Infant school to the Intermediate, but never rising to the Bible Class, which was taught by a lawyer whose scriptural teaching was inextricably mingled with his deeper knowledge of baseball; sometimes he would devote most of a lesson which was supposed to be about the Prodigal Son to an analysis of the Babe's batting form. This led to a widespread belief in his class that the Prodigal passed his years of riotous living as a professional ballplayer. Sunday School teaching is one field into which the modern pedagogical approach has never penetrated. And I still think that children learn more about life and conduct when an interesting man is given the run of his tongue, and is not chained to a syllabus which dictates everything, including the opening and closing of the classroom windows.

· OF DISTINCTION ·

"*D*ON'T YOU THINK Mr. X looks very distinguished?" the lady on my right asked me just now. As a matter of fact I think that X looks as though he had a clinker stuck in his grates, so I gave her an indirect reply. I never know what people mean by "distinguished" when they apply it to a man's appearance. Often the person so described looks as though he smelt a bad drain, or had a nail in his shoe, or had been to the barber and got his hair down his neck; the alliance between distinction and an appearance of suffering appears to be unbreakable. Nobody who looks as though he enjoyed life is ever called distinguished, though he is a man in a million. For some reason the world has decided that an expression suggestive of pain and disgust is a mark of superior mental power, for the world assumes, quite wrongly, that to be happy is a simple thing, within the reach of any idiot.

• OF FAUST EXAMINED •

I WAS THINKING about the Faust legend today, and began to wonder what I would ask for if I had sold my soul to the devil, on condition that the devil grant my wishes on earth. Faust was a painfully unimaginative fellow; he asked for youth — I would prefer a hearty middle age. He asked for a fortune; I would prefer a purse which at all times contained an exact $1,000 in five dollar bills. He asked for that tiresome simpleton Gretchen, and what a sanctimonious mess she turned out to be! And in Marlowe's play Faust asked for Helen of Troy, a notorious trouble-maker. In fact, as a philosopher, Faust appears to have been in the dunce class; money, women and the torments of youth — what a choice! I cannot think what the devil wanted with the soul of such a numbskull. With his opportunities I think that I should devote myself to politics, and for recreation I would demand the power to transform myself into a beautiful woman, and in that guise I would overthrow governments. And after a few years I would command the devil to explode himself forever. How would he meet that situation, I wonder?

Marchbanks' Garland

A Nosegay plucked from
the Musings, Pensées, Obiter Dicta,
and Apophthegms as well as
the Letters of Samuel Marchbanks
and Some of his Friends
(to say nothing of Enemies)
provided with Notes
and Explanatory Matter
by Robertson Davies

AS WELL AS being a keen guest at the banquet of life, as is shown in his *Diary* and *Table Talk*, Marchbanks has always been a voluminous correspondent, and as well as his published writings has accumulated many notebooks filled with his occasional thoughts and reflections. Printed in full, this matter would fill several volumes, and would doubtless deserve some such title as *The Marchbanks Archive*. But as both he and I have observed that the full correspondence of any man is a mind-numbing bore, and that most fleeting thoughts would do well to go right on fleeting, we have decided to offer a selection only, and to include letters received by him which throw light on his many-sided nature.

The Editor

· To Samuel Marchbanks, Esquire · ✒

Dear Mr. Marchbanks:

I hear that you are going on a trip abroad, and that you are going by plane. Of course I wish you the best of luck but I suppose you have been reading the papers lately? These plane accidents are the limit, aren't they? Every day a plane or two seems to crash somewhere. This being so, will you be wanting your garden hose if anything should happen? I mean you won't, of course, but what I mean is can I have it? We have never been very close friends, but I would like something to remember you by, and mine is going all to pieces.

Bon voyage and happy landings,
Dick Dandiprat.

The Editor will attempt to identify, so far as possible, Marchbanks' principal correspondents, where their relation to him is not immediately obvious. RICHARD DANDIPRAT, born in 1927 of obscure parentage and minimally educated, was at the time of his legal dispute with Marchbanks engaged in a paramedical capacity at the local hospital; he was, in fact, Chief Teller in the Sperm Bank. His job was always in hazard because of his objectionable habit of winking knowingly at any depositors at the Bank when he met them at parties and—far worse —nudging women who had appeared at the Withdrawals wicket, murmuring lewdly, "Anything doin' yet, kid?" He was an incorrigible practical joker even in his domestic life and his wife was known to go home to her mother at least twice a month.

• TO RICHARD DANDIPRAT, ESQUIRE •

My good Dandiprat:

No, you may not have my garden hose under any circumstances. If evil should befall me while in flight, it will become the property of my heirs. They will, I presume, have to water the grass just as if I were alive. Your attitude suggests that of the vulture.

Indignantly,
Samuel Marchbanks.

• TO SAMUEL MARCHBANKS, ESQUIRE •

Dear Mr. Marchbanks:

Although it is some years since we met I am sure that you will remember me perfectly. I hear that you are going to Edinburgh by air, and I write at once to ask a small favour. Will you take my sewing-machine with you, and send it on to my sister in Aberdeen? For some years I have been looking for an opportunity to send it to her, but I would not trust it to unfriendly hands. The machine will reach you tomorrow. I know that you will not mind doing this, as I have read all your books in our Public Library.

Yours sincerely,
Minerva Hawser.

• TO MISS MINERVA HAWSER • ✒

Dear Miss Hawser:

I am returning your machine, which weighs seventy-five pounds collect. I am only permitted sixty-six pounds of baggage.

Yours without regret,
S. Marchbanks.

MINERVA HAWSER, born 1887 (so far as anybody knows) was a maiden lady of Scottish antecedents, who entered Marchbanks' life as a supply teacher for a few days when his regular teacher was ill; he

· To Amyas Pilgarlic, Esquire · ✒

Dear Pil:

You have often complained that the art of correspondence is in decline, and I suppose you are right. Everything seems to be in decline, one way or another. The long eighteenth-century letter is a thing of the past. I seem to spend quite a large part of each day writing notes of all sorts, though I rarely get a chance to write long budgets of news to my friends — among whom I am proud to number you, you frowsy old pedant. I shall send you a postcard from abroad.

With warm good wishes,
Sam.

· To Samuel Marchbanks, Esquire ·

Dear Mr. Marchbanks:

As you are in Edinburgh I know you will not mind doing a favour for an old friend and well-wisher. I have long wanted to honour the land of my forebears in some striking fashion. Will you buy, therefore, sixteen or eighteen yards of material in the Hawser tartan — the Dress Hawser, not the Hunting Hawser — and bring it back to me when you come. You might as well see it through the Customs, to avoid any trouble. I shall cause an evening dress to be made from it, which I shall wear on any occasion that seems to

---

was eight years old at the time. On this slight acquaintance she behaved as though she had taken out a lease on his time and energies for the remainder of one of their lives — probably his.

✒ *It was as AMYAS PILGARLIC that Marchbanks concealed the identity of the Editor of these Works when first he published his Correspondence. If Pilgarlic appears as a dull pedant it was thus Marchbanks saw me, and if I wanted to make him appear as an overbearing mountebank in these pages it would be easy to do so, but I am too fine for such petty revenges.*

warrant such a display. I hope you enjoy your stay in "the land o' cakes."

Lang may your lum reek!
Minerva Hawser.

• TO MISS MINERVA HAWSER •

Dear Miss Hawser:

When I made enquiries here concerning the Hawser tartan I was greeted with oblique glances in several shops, and all knowledge of your family was hastily denied. Are you sure that you know all the circumstances which led to the migration of the Clan Hawser? ✍

Long may your blood boil,
Samuel Marchbanks.

• TO SAMUEL MARCHBANKS, ESQUIRE •

Dear Mr. Marchbanks:

As you are in Edinburgh I write to you for information on a matter which arouses me to anger. I read that the British, subverted by foreign *restaurateurs*, are now eating horseflesh. If this is true it must stop at once. Cruelty or indignity to dumb creatures is a thing I will not tolerate, even when it is posthumous. I demand that you get to the bottom of this story at once. And if you yourself have been eating any of our dumb friends, I command you, in the name of Canadian Womanhood, to desist immediately. Cows, yes; pigs, yes; fowl (so long as they are not singing birds) yes. Of cats I forbear to speak. But horses and dear, dear doggies—NO! Please reply immediately this reaches you. The eye of Canada is upon you.

Yours,
(Mrs.) Kedijah Scissorbill.

✍ *If Marchbanks appears in a harsh light in this letter it was certain that he knew the motto of the Hawser Clan—acted upon remorselessly by Miss Hawser herself—was* Vexo *(I pester).*

• To Mrs. Kedijah Scissorbill • 🖋

Dear Mrs. Scissorbill:

Pray compose yourself. I have not seen any horseflesh consumed as yet. If I have eaten it, I knew it not. Canada may therefore take its eye off me. I may perhaps quiet your suspicions regarding British Dogdom by telling you that there is a statue to a dog in Edinburgh; it is Greyfriars Bobbie, a dear doggie who used to go regularly with his master to a restaurant in Greyfriars; when his master died the doggie kept on going to the restaurant for twenty years, begging for food. Everyone was touched by this act of fidelity, including the restaurant-keeper, who reckoned that in that time Bobbie had sponged 7,300 meals from him which, at six pence a time, amounted to a little over £180. He felt he had been extraordinarily touched. The statue of Bobbie was erected by American admirers of the dog. No other dog in history is known to have been faithful to one restaurant for so long. I am, Madam,
Your servant,
Samuel Marchbanks.

🖋 *Mrs. KEDIJAH SCISSORBILL was another lady who, like Miss Hawser, had entered Marchbanks' life when he was too young and innocent to defend himself. An ardent feminist, she was a zealous detector and denouncer of Harassment in the Workplace. (She always pronounced the word with a heavy emphasis on the second syllable, as HarASSment, giving it a sinister connotation, as though hinting at sodomy behind the filing cabinets.) Her unusual given name was chosen by her father Elihu Crossbite, when he was a prominent figure in the imported Arabian date trade; the name is that of the wife of the Prophet Mohammed. Kedijah married the prophet when she was forty, and fifteen years his senior. Despite a late start she bore him five children. Mrs. Scissorbill was founder and for many years Perpetual Chairperson of WAHIW (Women Against Harassment in the Workplace); a woman of unspotted virtue, she was never personally harassed. It was Marchbanks who pointed out to her that the word "person" in "Chairperson" was open to objection, as it implied someone slightly declassé; he proposed "Chaircreature," the word "creature" being entirely neutral, and it was as a Chaircreature that Mrs. Scissorbill rose to a limited fame.*

• To Samuel Marchbanks, Esquire •

Dear Mr. Marchbanks:

What a disappointment about the tartan! Please try again. And another thing; I am anxious to possess some personal relic of Mary, Queen of Scots. Could you possibly get me something—one of her sweet little shoes, for instance. You must remember, Mr. Marchbanks, that I have been an orphan for the last forty-five years. Surely I deserve some consideration from one who, whatever his faults, is a man, and should be glad to assist the weak and helpless.

Yours confidingly,
Minerva Hawser.

• To Miss Minerva Hawser •

Dear Miss Hawser:

Really I cannot get the eighteen yards of the Hawser tartan you ask for. Could you manage with an equal length of something else? I was talking two days ago with Mr. Telfer Dunbar, who is said to know more about tartans than anybody else in Edinburgh, and he says there is no earthly reason why anybody should not wear any tartan that pleases them. From my recollection of your person, a few yards of a hound's-tooth tweed suggests itself for an appropriate evening gown. As for Mary Queen of Scots' shoes, I have not seen any for sale. What makes you think, by the way, that it would be sweet and little? Are you aware that Mary was six feet tall? With such a physique she may well have had feet like a policeman. I fear that you are a romantic.

Yours unromantically,
Samuel Marchbanks.

• To Samuel Marchbanks, Esquire •

Dear Marchbanks:

While you are in Scotland will you collect and send me a dozen new Scotch stories? I have just been appointed to head the Speaker's

Committee of the Rowanis Club for the next year, and good funny stories are scarce. I find that stories about Scotchmen are always popular. Oh, yes, and will you send me a few tips about the Scotch accent? Everybody thinks I tell stories very well, but I have only one funny accent and it has to do for Scotch, Irish, Jewish, Negro, etc. I would like to specialize in Scotch stories. Please hurry about this, as I haven't any time to waste.

Yours eagerly,
Dick Dandiprat.

• TO RICHARD DANDIPRAT, ESQUIRE •

My presumptuous Dandiprat:

I have no time to send you Scotch stories, even if I knew any. Nor can I help you with your assault upon Scottish vernacular. Everyone speaks it here, but it defies analysis. Yesterday a lady of my acquaintance said to me, "Hoo lang is it sin' ye pit meat in yer wame?" She was enquiring when I had last eaten. Having some acquaintance with Scottish vernacular speech I was able to reply, "Lang syne, and I hae na' suppit cockieleekie sin' Hogmanay." The acquisition of the right accent for such a remark is far beyond your feeble powers so no more from

Yours regretfully,
S. Marchbanks.

• TO AMYAS PILGARLIC, ESQUIRE •

Dear Pil:

At last the flood of letters subsides, and I have a moment to write to you.

Dandiprat was a singularly obtuse creature, or he would have realized that ethnic jokes, founded on the supposed comical characteristics of people other than Canadians, were falling into disfavour. The decline of the Ethnic Joke left funnymen with nothing to be funny about

The Edinburgh-London journey took from 10:40 a.m. until
8:15 p.m. Meals in English trains are perhaps a little worse than
they used to be. That brown soup is somewhat browner, the coffee
is somewhat weaker, and the cheese hints more strongly than ever
at an origin in a soap factory. The English are not really a puritanical people, but railway meals suggest a dreadful mortification of
the flesh—an urge to take the joy out of travel.

As I wander about my fancy is greatly caught by the unusual
names which I see on signs and advertisements. Just as I left Edinburgh I saw a beauty over a clothing store—Clinkscales. Now if I
wrote a book in which anyone was called Clinkscales the critics
would accuse me of being fanciful. Yet it appears that people of
that name really exist. Wonderful! Travel is so broadening.

Yours broadly,
Sam.

• TO SAMUEL MOCKBANKS, ESQUIRE •

Dear Mr. Mackbonks:

In your correspondence with the Passport Agency and Fiscal Control Board recently, your "Form Z" was returned to this office
unstamped. It is therefore invalid, and the sterling currency now
in your possession has no legal existence. In order that your position may be regularized as soon as possible, you must secure Forms
H and Q from the British Currency Legitimization Authority, and
obtain permission to export one cent (1¢) in Canadian currency to
us. We shall purchase a one-cent stamp for your "Form Z" with
this sum. A further charge for service in purchasing, moistening
and affixing the stamp, amounting to five dollars, will also be

---

except Sex, with depressing result. Marchbanks, who was born in an era
when sex was regarded as a private pleasure, like reading or drinking,
has lived to see it become a public, vainglorious display, like jogging or
dieting—even more discussed than practised.

charged. Please attend to this matter immediately, as until you do so your money is a fiction.

Yours,
Haubergeon Hydra.
(Sub-deputy Fiscal Repressor).

• TO HAUBERGEON HYDRA, ESQUIRE • ✒

Dear Mr. Hydra:

Far be it from me to dispute the word of a government official, but my sterling currency seems to be quite real. The people of Edinburgh were willing, and even eager to accept it. However, if you want a one-cent stamp I happen, by a lucky chance, to have one in my pocket, which I enclose. You overestimate the difficulty of getting it on to the document; it is not five dollars worth of work even for a Civil Servant. Just a quick lick and a slap, and it's done.

Yours, with dripping tongue,
Samuel Marchbanks.

• TO MISS MINERVA HAWSER •

Dear Miss Hawser:

Yes, I quite understand your passion for relics of eminent persons. You have asked me for Sir Walter Scott's walking-stick and for Robert Burns' snuffbox; I regret that both of these interesting objects are in museums, and I am too timid to steal them, even in order that you may exhibit them to the Canadian Authors' Association, who doubtless need them.

The meteoric career of HAUBERGEON HYDRA in the Canadian Civil Service is one of the wonders of the twentieth century. He might make an appearance in any Government Department. His stern application of all rules and regulations was the delight of his superiors, and the terror of such oppressed citizens as Marchbanks.

The only relic I can get you is associated with Haigh, the Vampire; ℱ no doubt you read that he was hanged on August 10, 1949, for murdering no less than eight persons of about your own age and general character; after each murder he drank a glass of his victim's blood, mingled with a liquid which he supplied from his own person. How's that for connoisseurship? A friend of mine has a tumbler which he is practically certain was used by Haigh in one of these curious toasts, and he will let me have it for only £10. If you want it please cable this sum immediately. I am sure your branch of the Authors' Association would be thrilled. All friends around the punchbowl!

Yours amiably,
Samuel Marchbanks.

• TO HAUBERGEON HYDRA, ESQUIRE •

Dear Mr. Hydra:

As I understand that you are permanent secretary of the Government Alcoholic Discouragement Board, I write to ask you why

---

ℱ Marchbanks has always been interested in murder and murderers, strictly as an amateur. John George Haigh, referred to here, was born in 1910 and in 1949 became notorious as the Acid Bath Murderer, and was dispatched by the hangman on August 10. He admitted to eight murders, the last being that of a sixty-nine year old widow, Olive Durand-Deacon. He had shot her through the neck and dissolved her body in a forty-gallon drum of sulphuric acid, except for an acrylic plastic denture by which what remained of her—described by the police as "sludge"—was identified. Haigh confessed blithely, saying, "Mrs. Durand-Deacon no longer exists. I've destroyed her with acid. You can't prove murder without a body." Haigh based his belief on a misunderstanding of the Latin phrase corpus delicti *without which a criminal charge cannot be laid; he thought it meant the body of a dead person. But in Law Latin it means "evidence of the crime," and the soup in the vat was damning evidence. Evidence, surely, of the stupidity of neglecting Latin studies in modern education.*

there is no cider for sale in my part of Canada. Since coming to Britain I have renewed my acquaintance with this wonderful drink (or beverage, as I suppose you call it) and I want to know why I cannot get it at home. Canada is a great apple country: then why no cider? Cider rejoiceth the heart of man (and of woman) Hydra, old boy, and the Canadian heart could do with a good rejoicing.

Yours merrily,
Samuel Marchbanks.

• TO SAMUEL MARBLINKS, ESQUIRE •

Dear Mrs. Matbanks:

Your letter re cider to hand and contents noted. In reply would beg to state that (a) the Civil Service cannot entertain suggestions from unofficial sources and (b) cider is objectionable to the Medical Association, as being a notorious Physician Repellent, and a prominent feature in the coat-of-arms of the Royal College of Chiropractic Healers.

Yours semi-officially,
Haubergeon Hydra,
for Government Alcoholic Discouragement Board.

• TO SAMUEL MARCHBANKS, ESQUIRE •

Dear Marchbanks:

I am offering you $50, cash down, for your car. It is a good make, only two years old, has first-class tires and has plainly been well cared for. That is why I am offering you $50, instead of the $25 which is what a dealer would give you.

The fact is that Chanel, that skunk that has been hanging around Marchbanks Towers for years, has been living in the garage since you went away. It looks as though she had made a nest in the back seat, and last night she was badly frightened by my dog, Bowser, who happened to be snooping around.

Take it or leave it; $50. I say nothing of the shock to Bowser's nerves, as you are a neighbour and I want to treat you decently.

Yours decently,
Dick Dandiprat.

• To Amyas Pilgarlic, Esquire •

Dear Pil:

It is high time I came home. Dandiprat and his dog have sabotaged my car and that accursed old crone, Min Hawser, is hounding me to run down relatives of hers who have titles. I cannot write to them now, as I am on a train bound for Wales, and you are the only one who can read my train-writing.

Railway travel in this country has one great advantage over train journeys in Canada; I can get unlimited reading matter in every station. There is a book-and-paper stand on every platform, offering the most delightful train literature. At present I have *The Matrimonial Post*, and *The Girl's Own Paper* with me. Have you read either? They are very rich feeding, let me tell you. Consider this, from the *Post*: "Attractive, witty, physically opulent lady of modest means seeks correspondence with gentleman of refined but not inhibited mentality. Object, a mutual exploration of intellect, with a view to intimacy and possibly matrimony. Photograph offered and expected." Or how does this appeal to you: "Lady, twenty-eight, who has lost left leg seeks congenial gentleman friend lacking right ditto. Friendship and possible matrimony." Or what do you say to this choice offer: "Gentleman, mature but well-preserved, amusing, presentable, experienced, seeks ditto lady with private means. Offers unlimited comradeship and fun." I can dream over the *Post* for hours, calling up the opulent ladies and comradely gentlemen before my mind's eye. ⸙

⸙ *Of course this was before the present frankness which permits otherwise respectable newspapers to publish advertisements from people who want partners of all sorts — not invariably human — for amorous sport.*

The Girl's Own Paper I read for its style. Here is a sample paragraph: " 'Crumbs, girls,' cried Crackles Crompton, bursting into Dormitory Thirteen where her special chums Bubbles, Giggles and Foibles were washing their hair, preparatory to the great lacrosse match against their hated rival, St. Rawbones, the coming Saturday, 'have you heard the news?' 'Oh go and eat coke,' cried Giggles, lifting her ruddy head, thick with foam, from the basin, and cramming another fig-bar into her mouth, 'your news is always about boys since Foibles' brother Derek took you to the Natural Science Museum last hols.' 'Oh boys are rot,' cried Crackles, a flush mounting from the top of her navy blue serge blouse toward her chestnut hair, 'boys are utter, piffling, footling rot, and you know it. There isn't a boy on earth I wouldn't give for a really spiffing hockey stick — except Daddy, of course,' she said and her liquid brown eyes grew even more liquid as she thought of Major Crompton, who was in Africa subduing native tribes. 'Miss Checkrein's stop-watch has been stolen, and until it is found the whole school is confined to the grounds.' " — This sort of writing still flourishes in spite of all the books and films about St. Trinian's; the really deep things of life are impervious to satire. *ƒ*

You know, I really think that I shall have to have the law on Dandiprat.

Yours determinedly,
Sam.

ƒ As proof observe the spectacular success of the schoolgirl drama Daisy Pulls It Off *by Denise Deegan, presented at the Globe Theatre, London on April 18, 1983 and still playing to full houses at the time of writing. In it the heroine, Daisy, wins a scholarship from her State school to a posh girls' school where she meets with snobbish contempt until she exposes the Chief Snob as a rotten cheat, scores the goal that wins the Big Game for her school, solves the mystery of the Hidden Treasure (thereby saving the school from ruin) and discovers her long-lost father who is of aristocratic birth — so* sucks *to the girls who thought Daisy wasn't of their class.*

• To Mouseman, Mouseman & Forcemeat •

Dear Sirs:

Will you, as my legal advisers, give your attention to the following matter: A neighbour of mine, one Richard Dandiprat, has caused his mangy old dog Bowser to chase a skunk into my car, which I have left in my garage during my absence. The skunk has, I gather, done its worst. I know that Dandiprat did this on purpose, and now he wants to buy the car at a ridiculous price. I want to put Dandiprat in court, and take his shirt. He is a low scoundrel, and I want to show him that I am privy to his base design. If you will begin legal proceedings I shall be home in a week or so, and then we will get after him.

I hope that the rheumatism of the senior Mr. Mouseman is much improved.

Yours faithfully,
Samuel Marchbanks.

• To Haubergeon Hydra, Esquire •

Dear Mr. Hydra:

I have now reached Wales, from which country some of my fore-bears emigrated to Canada. I became conscious that I was on un-English ground at Gobowen, a Welsh junctional point where the ticket-taker thanked me in the Welsh form—"ddiolch yn fawr." How pleasant, I thought, and how characteristic. And this made me wonder whether some distinctive form of thanks could not be devised and adopted in Canada. "Thank you" is excellent, but for-mal and English in effect. "Thanks a million" is excellent, but it has an American extravagance which is unbecoming in Canadian mouths. What would you think of "Thanks a hundred thousand"? It seems to me to strike the right Canadian note. 𝄞

At the time of writing Marchbanks is attempting to equate Cana-dian gratitude to the value of the Canadian dollar against its Ameri-can equivalent. Thus "Thanks 74.3" or some similar wording hitched to the latest quotation would serve.

I direct this suggestion to you because, as Permanent Secretary to the Royal Commission on the Arts in Canada, you might be able to popularize it. If you can do so, you may take all the praise which such a happy thought will surely evoke.

Yours self-effacingly,
Samuel Marchbanks.

• TO SAMUEL MARCHBANKS, ESQUIRE •

Esteemed Sir:

I am in receipt of your letter in which you instruct this firm, as your legal advisers, to bring action against Richard Dandiprat for having wilfully and with malice aforethought induced, instructed or compelled a skunk to commit a nuisance in your motor car.

Immediately upon receiving your communication I dispatched my efficient and discreet secretary, or confidential clerk, Miss Prudence Bunn, to Marchbanks Towers to examine the scene of the alleged misdemeanour. Miss Bunn's report was as follows:

Confidential to Mr. Mouseman: "At a distance of a quarter of a mile from Marchbanks Towers the atmosphere became noticeably heavy. Asked to describe this odour in court I should use the phrase 'burning old gym shoes.' At one hundred yards from the Towers it was clear that a skunk, or some animal indistinguishable therefrom, had committed a nuisance. In order to carry out my instructions I was compelled to soak my handkerchief in eau de Cologne and hold it over my mouth and nose. Thus protected I examined the garage, but found no evidence of violence or felony. Determined not to fail in any requirement of duty, I opened the door of the car, and at once lost consciousness, collapsing head foremost into the rear seat. I regained consciousness to find that I was being sniffed in what can only be described as a searching manner by a large white dog with pink eyes — a bull terrier, I should judge. Whether this was Mr. Dandiprat's dog Bowser I cannot say, though I have my opinion (which is not evidence). However, I can state without fear of successful contradiction, and if necessary upon oath, that a skunk or some animal indistinguishable from a skunk has been living with the utmost freedom in Mr. Marchbanks' car and has sustained an emotional shock therein."

Yours faithfully,
Prudence Bunn.

Now, Mr. Marchbanks, we cannot advise you, as your lawyers, to prefer a charge against Richard Dandiprat without further evidence to show that it was he who put the skunk in the car. My father, Mr. Jabez Mouseman, is at present unable to attend to business, as rheumatism and great age render him incapable. However, I have consulted our other partner, Mr. Cicero Forcemeat, who does all our court business and his report is as follows:

"Tell Mr. Marchbanks that unless we have something to pin the skunk to Dandiprat, we wouldn't have a Chinaman's chance in court."

"Chinaman's chance," Mr. Marchbanks, is Law Latin signifying "slight likelihood of success."

Yours faithfully,
Mordecai Mouseman,
(for Mouseman, Mouseman and Forcemeat).

• TO AMYAS PILGARLIC, ESQUIRE •

Dear Pil:

I am making a short stay in Wales with my Uncle Fortunatus before coming back to Canada, and to work. You have never been to Wales, I believe? A great country, and the people have immense charm. For some reason the English seem to think of the Welsh as rascals and cheats, and this unjust notion has taken hold in Canada. Of course some Welshmen are curmudgeons, but on the whole I think they are wonderfully high-spirited. As a matter of fact, the only man in medical history who died of joy was a native of the very district where I am now staying. His name was Edward Burton, and in 1558, when Queen Elizabeth came to the throne, his own patriotism and the celebrations drove him into such a frenzy of delight that it killed him. He died while roaring with laughter, and uttering loyal yells.

He was refused burial in the churchyard of St. Chad's, in Shrewsbury. Presumably the authorities took the view that no real Christian can be as joyful as that, and didn't want him making trouble among the glum ghosts. So he was buried at home. I would like to meet Burton in the hereafter, and ask whether the strange manner of his death caused him any trouble with St. Peter.

From my bedroom window I can see the hill upon which Thomas Parr lived his uncommonly long life, from 1483 to 1635 — 152 years. This remarkable old party married for the first time when he was eighty, and was made to do penance for adultery when he was over 100. Rubens painted his portrait when he was 140.

I am not surprised that Parr refused to die: life here is too good to be given up — though I must leave soon.

Yours,
Sam.

• To Samuel Marchbanks, Esquire •

Dear Mr. Marchbanks:

May I call upon you on Monday in order to borrow some books of reference of which I know you to be the possessor? I am about to begin work upon an historical study which I have long pondered, to be called *The Rise, Decline and Fall of the Toothpick, with an Appendix on the Toothpick in Canadian Lumbering*. Also, have you any old toothpicks which I might have photographed for illustrations? My own forebears always used gold or silver toothpicks which they carried upon their watch chains. It occurs to me that someone of humbler birth, such as yourself, might have the wooden toothpicks I need.

Yours in hope,
Minerva Hawser.

404

• To Mouseman, Mouseman and Forcemeat •

Dear Sirs:

Are you men or mice? Of course we must take legal action against Dandiprat. I know he put the skunk in my car because I know Dandiprat, and it is just the sort of thing he would think of. ∥ I am amazed by Mr. Cicero Forcemeat's suggestion that the case would not hold water in court. If Forcemeat wants water-tight cases, he will not get them from me. A lawyer who cannot bridge a few unavoidable gaps in evidence is a disgrace to his profession. Now, think again, gentlemen!

Yours in expectation of fireworks,
S. Marchbanks.

• To Amyas Pilgarlic, Esquire •

Dear Pil:

At last I am back in Canada. I flew home from Scotland. I made my way thither from Wales by two trains—the Flying Scot and the Creeping Scot. What a country Scotland is, and how wonderfully the characteristics of the countryside are repeated in the people! The British Isles is rich in eccentrics, and those of Scotland are among the most flavoursome. Consider those two wonderful eighteenth century Lords of Session—Lord Gardenstone, who always slept with his pet pig for warmth, and Lord Monboddo, who thought that all children were born with tails! What has Canada to show to equal them?

I may tell you that as I made my way to Prestwick, I passed the Johnny Walker distillery, and the works of Shanks of Barrhead, the great makers of sanitary pottery. "The Alpha and

∥ Attempts had been made by friends of Dandiprat to soften Marchbanks' heart by saying that Dandiprat came from a Broken Home. This was a tactical mistake, for Marchbanks gave a surly reply to the effect that he wasn't at all surprised and supposed Dandiprat had broken it himself, having demonstrably been a malefactor from his mother's womb. Cain similarly gave a nasty twist to the Primal Family.

Omega of many a good party," said my companion, bowing her head respectfully.

Yours as always,
Sam.

• HOME REMEDIES •

*A*N ALMANAC FROM a patent medicine company arrived in the mail this morning—a gaudy reminder of the immense tonnage of pills, the vast ocean of jalap, the heaped-up mountains of salts which are consumed by the Canadian public every year. Not that I have any prejudice against patent medicines. They are a relatively harmless indulgence and may even contribute to human well-being. It does a man good to take a few pills every day. It gives him a feeling that he is taking care of himself, and this persuades him that he is in good health—but only just. It is not advisable to feel too well. People who boast about their good health are apt to overtax it. They want to lift things which should be left on the ground; they insist upon walking when it would be much simpler to ride. Everybody should have some slight, not too obtrusive ailment, which he coddles. Nobody should be without some harmless medicine which he takes. These things enable him to husband his strength, harbour his resources, and live to a ripe old age.

• LAUGHABLE NUDITY •

*T*HIS EVENING some worldly acquaintance took me to a nightclub, where I watched the floorshow with simple-minded wonder. One of the chief attractions was a blonde young woman, said to be Finnish, who danced in an Eastern costume that afforded her strategic but not complete protection. She was less graceful than supple, and when she had got her feet very dirty she showed us how she could waggle them over her shoulders. Then she turned herself into a wheel of irregular contour and rolled lumpily about the floor. Her abdomen was rubbery and less taut than many I have seen, and every time she fell on it there was an audible and rather comical "Splat!" which amused me greatly. However, I was frowned on for laughing. In Toronto, it appears, one may leer desirously at underdressed girls, or gape at them with the costive expression of one who considers Nudity and Art to be synonymous terms, but one must not laugh. Which is unreasonable, considering that many people are even funnier stripped than clothed.

· ILLUSION OF PROGRESS ·

A CHILD SHOWED me a comic book that sought to show how much better life is today than it was in the eighteenth century. It pointed out rather smugly that in those days there was no electricity, that many people could not read, and that life was somewhat inconvenient. So far as I am concerned life is still far from convenient, but pleasant for all that, and many people who can read do not seem to do so. Further, some things achieved a perfection in the eighteenth century which has never since been surpassed: we have never bettered their window-sashes, for instance; nor have we designed any chairs which combine beauty and comfort as theirs did; our glass and chinaware are not, on the whole, as good as theirs, nor are our textiles. In fact, in virtually every phase of architecture and industrial design, they beat the heads off us and we still copy them because we cannot do better. It is dishonest to give children the notion that we are cleverer than our ancestors in every respect. We make many things more easily than they, but not necessarily better.

· AGREEMENT WITH SATAN ·

A LADY WRITES to me, unreasonably angry because I have let it be known that I dwelt within myself and peeped out at the world. "I know the kind of man you are," she writes; "you are the kind who would agree with the lines —

> The mind is its own place, and in itself
> Can make a heaven of hell, a hell of heaven.

And do you know who said that?" Yes, my dear madam, I know who said that: it was Satan, in *Paradise Lost*. And a remarkably intelligent and able fellow he was, too, and quite the best character Milton ever created. . . . But I make no such vast claims for myself; I can make a hell of heaven but the other trick is too much for me.

• VICTIM OF SCIENTIFIC COMFORT •

*W*OKE FEELING like a piece of pemmican; my electric blanket had dried me out during the night. Two years ago a kind friend gave me this luxury, and I owe many a snug night to it, but from time to time I curse its remorseless efficiency. If it is cold when I go to bed I push the controller on the blanket up as high as it will go, and compose myself for slumber with a smile, knowing that nothing short of a new Ice Age can harm me. But sometimes the temperature changes sharply in the night, and after dreams I am lost in the desert, where my dromedary has dropped dead from thirst, I awaken to find that it is thawing outside, and I am in danger of bursting into flames. I then drag myself to the bathroom, fill the tub with water, and leap into it. There is a sizzle and a suck, and all the water has disappeared, but I am back to my normal size and wetness, and feel much better. But one of these times I shall not wake, and the cinder which will comprise my mortal remains will be buried in a pillbox.

• DR. SHAKESPEARE •

*R*ECEIVED A CURIOUS pamphlet from a doctor in West Virginia; it was a reprint of a speech he made before the Section on Diseases of the Chest at the Ninety-ninth Session of the American Medical Association in 1950, and is called "Shakespeare's Knowledge of Chest Diseases." In this strange work the good physician proves that Shakespeare knew that people had lungs, because he mentions them nineteen times. He also knew that there was such a thing as consumption and asthma, and one of his heroines (Beatrice in *Much Ado About Nothing*) suffers from a cold in the head, so we must assume that Shakespeare knew that there was such a disease as a cold. All this seems to amaze the West Virginian doctor, and suggests to him that Shakespeare was a pretty smart fellow. But I can take this information calmly. Though I am no Shakespeare, I have long been acquainted with all these facts myself. People who are not poets are often astonished to find that poets know anything at all; they seem to think that poets are born stupid, and get worse as they grow older. But I have long recognized the fact that true poets are among the very few sane people in a mad world.

• A FORGOTTEN COMPOSER •

LOOKING THROUGH a song-book in a friend's house today I came upon a ballad which was a great favourite with contraltos in my childhood; it was *Three Fishers* by John Pyke Hullah, with words by the Rev. Charles Kingsley. The moaning of the harbour bar in the song was trifling compared with the moaning of the large, hollow-voiced women who sang it at church concerts and "musical evenings." Hullah was an odd man, who thought that he could devise an easier way of putting music on paper than the usual system of notes. He also composed an opera for which Charles Dickens wrote the libretto, a work which seems to have disappeared completely. That would be a curiosity, indeed, if it could be found. *Hullah was the composer of *O That We Two Were Maying*,

Marchbanks is careless again. This operetta, The Village Coquettes, is to be found in the British Museum, from which an offprint was obtained and the work performed at the Christmas Gaudy at Massey College, in the University of Toronto, on December 13, 1970. If Marchbanks were not such a curmudgeon he would probably have received an invitation to be present. The operetta has some charming passages, owing to Hullah's pleasing music, but Dickens' libretto is wooden and his verse the work of a man determined to write verse rather than the effluxions of a true poet. Dickens, who longed for stage success, did not achieve it until after his death, with the production of Nicholas Nickleby by the Royal Shakespeare Company in London in 1980 and later in New York to great acclaim.

another favourite of my childhood, usually sung as a duet by a slate-pencil soprano and a fog-horn contralto; the audience always concurred heartily in their wish to be elsewhere.

• VICTIM OF THE WEED •

I WAS IN CONVERSATION with a merry fellow who knew many odd scraps of history and told me that William McKinley, twenty-fifth president of the U.S.A., died of a tobacco heart. "Surely he was assassinated by the anarchist, Leon Czolgosz?" said I. "Czolgosz shot him," said he, "but McKinley lingered for some time, and when he died several papers of strong moral tendency said that if his heart had not been weakened by tobacco smoking, he would have pulled through. I was alive then, and I recall it well; you can't imagine how powerful the anti-tobacco faction was in 1901." *∮* He also told me that the name of the killer was pronounced Cholguss, and many wits at the time said he had been driven to madness, and his rash act, by a lifetime of hearing it mispronounced.

• NAÏVETÉ OF CANADIAN FOXES •

W AS TALKING TO one of the few people in Canada who hunts foxes on a horse, and with hounds, in the English fashion. It is not generally known that there is a small but persistent survival of the fox-hunt in this country. But this man told me

---

∮ O yes, we can; it was nothing to what it is today, when smoking has been accorded the character-destroying, health-diminishing powers which were, in the nineteenth century, reserved for masturbation. But, Marchbanks has frequently demanded, what of the horrible effects wrought upon mind and body by cheap thinking and shallow reading, which poison the mind and bring about a foolish life, after which mere physical demise is barely discernible? But as Marchbanks has learned, if you attack Stupidity you attack an entrenched interest with friends in government and every walk of public life, and you will make small progress against it.

that Canadian foxes are either stupider than English foxes, or do not realize what is expected of them; the last fox he hunted, he said, ran in a circle of about a hundred yards, rushing directly at the hounds, who ate it as best they could while rolling around on the ground, holding their sides and laughing in their rich, doggy voices. Because of this lack of gumption among foxes, it is usual to drag a sack of some strong-smelling stuff over a good long course, and let the hounds follow that. The question which occurs to me is: would there be any money in training foxes for this highly specialized work? It would be wearing for a man of my temperament to drag a fox on a rope through streams, in and out of holes, and over ploughed fields, but I am willing to try it if I can thereafter rent the fox to hunters at a stiff fee. If they kill my trained fox, of course, I shall expect to be pensioned for life.

• NATIONAL CHARACTERISTIC •

*A*TTENDED A theatrical performance and was impressed once again by the amount of coughing which a Canadian assembly can manage, and by the freedom with which this national habit is indulged. Not merely the aged and the infirm, but the young and the hearty, the valiant and the fair, cut loose with coughs like the roarings of lions. Mentally ran off a new verse for our national song, thus:

> O Canada, our home, our native land,
> Chronic catarrh makes all our tubes expand;
>> With raucous cough we greet the dawn,
>> With snorts we hail the noon,
>> The emblems of our nation are
>> The kerchief and spittoon;
>>> Post-nasal drip!
>>> Woooof! Let her rip!
>> We face the future trusting in our grippe—

(Exultantly and accompanied with loud coughs, hawkings, gaggings and retchings).
  DE-FY The World with Freedom in OUR GRIPPE!

· THE CAMERA CAN LIE ·

*A*SSISTED THIS afternoon at one of those meetings where a concert committee decides what musicians it will engage for its series next season. Having decided how much money we had to spend, we passed two happy hours figuring out whom we could get for it—Monsieur Strummo, who plays the piano with his hands and feet, and who wants five thousand dollars to do it for an hour and a half, or Signor Thumbo, who plays the musical saw all night for twenty-five dollars; Madame Y, who had a wonderful voice twenty-five years ago, or Mademoiselle Z, who is expected to have a wonderful voice in a few years? As we pondered, I looked at the pictures of the artists in the catalogue which we used; what liars photographers are! There was a picture of a soprano, looking like a virgin of seventeen, whom I saw recently, with a neck like the bellows of an accordion, and bags under her eyes like golf balls. There was a tenor, showing his magnificent chest and leonine head, but omitting his legs, which are about ten inches long. Another tenor was shown with his eyes closed in ecstasy; when they are opened, I happen to know that one of them is a bad glass job which he made himself, from the bottom of a beer bottle. Ah, human vanity! Ah, photographic artifice!

· PERILS OF MUSEOLOGY ·

*V*ISITED THE Royal Ontario Museum, and was concerned to notice that a lot of the stuffed animals are fading badly. The laborious researches of the Royal Society of Taxidermists, continued for over a century, has not yet discovered a way of perventing this deterioration, which can turn a beautifully striped tiger into something like a polar bear in ten or twelve years. Museums are by definition temples of probity, or the curators might touch up the animals with some of the preparations so lavishly advertised for fading hair. But if a Museum Director were to countenance such deceit he might be drummed out of the profession at the very next International Conference of Museologists. This is a dreadful ceremony, in which the offender, having been stripped naked, is locked into an Egyptian sarcophagus, upon the cover of which his former colleagues drop rare coins in an irregular rhythm, until at last he is released, raving mad, and good for nothing but light work as a Museum guard.

• TO HAUBERGEON HYDRA, ESQUIRE •

Dear Mr. Hydra:

I am in bed with flu just now and my pyjamas are a dreadful nuisance; they creep up. A lady visited me yesterday, and when I mentioned this to her she said that she had the same trouble with her nightdresses.

Then — in a flash! — inspiration came to me and I forthwith invented Marchbanks' Nightwear Stirrup. This consists of two metal stirrups, to which stout elastic cords, with clamps, are attached. The wearer puts his feet in the stirrups, clamps the cords to the bottoms of his pyjamas (or the hem of her nightdress) and the device keeps the garment in place all night long.

How does this appeal to you? As Preliminary Examiner for the Board of Patents and Copyrights, do you — as the current phrase is — go for it?

Yours in breathless anticipation,
Samuel Marchbanks.

• TO SOLOMON MUCKBANKS, ESQUIRE •

Dear Mr. Mackbonks:

I was alarmed and displeased to receive a note saying that you are in bed with Flo, and as a servant of this Dominion I have no desire to enter into a correspondence with you so long as you occupy any irregular situation.

The device which you describe — a Nightwear Stirrup — does not interest me, for in common with many Civil Servants of the better sort, I have slept at my desk for many years.

Yours very conditionally,
Haubergeon Hydra.

• TO SAMUEL MARCHBANKS, ESQUIRE •

Honoured Sir:

The tone of your last letter was very strong — very strong indeed. As your legal advisers, we must caution you against such layman's phrases as "take the shirt off his back" and "make him eat crow," when referring to a possible legal action. We lawyers do not like such expressions: they savour of violence.

In our opinion, your case against Richard Dandiprat is uncommonly weak. You have only circumstantial evidence that he introduced a skunk into your car. Your suggestion that we should in some way bridge the gap between guesswork and certainty alarms us by its sinister implication.

Lawyers do not like to go to court. Anything may happen in court. The magistrate may be a skunk-lover, or a card-companion of Dandiprat's, or anything. Besides, courts are invariably draughty, and our court partner, Mr. Cicero Forcemeat, is trying to postpone catching his winter cold for as long as possible. We suggest that you empower us to seek a settlement with Dandiprat out of court. This is the proper legal way of doing business.

Yours for caution,
Mordecai Mouseman,
(for Mouseman, Mouseman and Forcemeat).

• TO MOUSEMAN, MOUSEMAN AND FORCEMEAT •

Dear Sirs:

Your mealy-mouthed letter disgusts me! Settle out of court, indeed! What are you lawyers for, if not to go to court? Eh? Answer me, Mouseman! Don't sit cringing there, in your stuffy office! Get on the job, man!

What do I care for Cicero Forcemeat's cold? If he catches cold in court I will personally send him a mustard plaster.

Now, keep your temper, Mouseman, while I explain: you say that evidence is lacking that Dandiprat put the skunk in the car. I know that he did it; I can tell by the ugly leer he gives me whenever I see him, and by the way he pretends to sniff the air when he passes my house. If you want evidence, why don't you send that sensible secretary of yours, Miss Prudence Bunn, to Dandiprat's house, disguised as a government inspector, or a Hydro snoop, or something. Then when nobody is looking, she can nip upstairs, pinch one of Dandiprat's handkerchiefs—an initialled one—and then we can say we found it at the scene of the crime.

What you lawyers need is enterprise. I shouldn't have to do all your thinking for you.

Yours for brighter law,
Samuel Marchbanks.

• To Samuel Marchbanks, Esquire •

Dear Sir:

It has been brought to our attention that you have several times and in divers places alleged that our client, Richard Dandiprat, Esquire, introduced a skunk into your motor vehicle and there induced, coerced or suborned the animal to misconduct itself in a characteristic manner. Should you persist in this allegation we shall take action against you for defamation.

Yours,
Craven and Raven,
Attorneys.

• To Mouseman, Mouseman And Forcemeat •

Dear Mouseman:

Now look what you have done! I am sending you a letter from Craven and Raven, a firm of cheap shysters who are Dandiprat's lawyers, in which they threaten me with a libel action if I tell the truth about Dandiprat. Why don't you get on the job and put Dandiprat in court for what he has done to me? I don't want to be bothered with law: I just want Dandiprat thrown in the jug, where he belongs. Why don't you do something?

Yours passionately,
S. Marchbanks.

• TO SAMUEL MARCHBANKS, ESQUIRE •

Wretch!

Ignoring your rudeness in your last letter, I write to inform you that Outraged Womanhood is once more upon the march. You have heard (as who has not?) that a quarter-pint of rum has been added to the birthday cake of H.R.H. The Prince Edward Antony Richard Louis. Now I ask you, what will happen when that infant has eaten his piece of cake? Staggering, bleary-eyed, he will drive his kiddy-car recklessly around his nursery, his co-ordination reduced perhaps 30 per cent, until he maims his nurse. And what sort of example is that, I ask you, for the infants of the Empire? Rum in cake will lead to demands for rum-and-butter toffee, and then his little bootees will be firmly set upon the Road to Ruin.

I enclose a protest for you to sign. If you do not sign it, never hope again to hear from

Yours,
(Mrs.) Kedijah Scissorbill.

• TO AMYAS PILGARLIC, ESQUIRE •

Dear Pil:

I don't suppose you have seen the movie of *Madame Bovary*? I beguiled an idle hour with it last night when some fragments appeared on TV, and was moved to reflect that there is something deeply phoney about American actors pretending to be Frenchmen. And when a French classic is translated into American all illusion of French atmosphere is lost. In this piece, for instance, Mme. Bovary goes to her aristocratic lover and says:

MME. BOVARY: I must have 150,000 francs.
ARISTOCRATIC LOVER: Uh don't have ut.
MME. BOVARY: Yuh don't have ut?
ARISTOCRATIC LOVER: Naw, uh don't have ut.
MME. BOVARY: (collapsing) Aw, yuh, don't have ut!

Frankly this seems as un-French to me as if they had spoken with Scottish or Lancashire accents. There was a time when actors had a good clear speech of their own, which was not related to any special place and so was suitable for everything, but this excellent tradition was never incorporated in the movies. Ah, well—

Yours,
Sam.

• TO SAMUEL MARCHBANKS, ESQUIRE •

Honoured Sir:

You have been most indiscreet, Mr. Marchbanks, indeed you have! Now that Mr. Dandiprat's lawyers have been brought into the matter, I confess that I scarcely know which way to turn. Craven and Raven, whatever you may say to the contrary, are very astute. Indeed, they took a case to court and won it, so recently as 1924. I have consulted with the elder Mr. Mouseman, and also with Mr. Cicero Forcemeat, and we are agreed that we are pitted against some of the keenest legal talent in the country.

Oh, Mr. Marchbanks, why, oh why did you utter libel against Mr. Dandiprat? Before we know where we are this matter will come to court and, as I have told you before, anything can happen in court.

Your grieving attorney,
Mordecai Mouseman,
(for Mouseman, Mouseman and Forcemeat).

• TO SAMUEL MARCHBANKS, ESQUIRE •

Dear Sam:

I have been curious lately to discover what notable or merely notorious persons in history have at some time been actors. The list is surprisingly long and contains some strange fish. Did you know, for instance, that Oliver Cromwell once appeared, when a young man, in a play called *Lingua, or the Combat of The Tongue and the Five Senses for Superiority*? It sounds rather a dull piece. Cromwell played Tactus, which, as you are rather an ignorant creature, I hasten to explain means "Touch." Appropriate, is it not, that a man with Cromwell's views on taxation should have played such a part? It is said that his experience as an actor inspired him with ambition to rule.

Possibly so. Many a man who has had a taste of acting takes to politics. / The critics are less severe toward politicians than toward those who pursue the player's art in its more demanding form.

Yours,
A. Pilgarlic.

• A FANCIFUL NOTION •

*B*RUCE HUTCHISON, whose love-affair with the Canadian nation takes many a strange turn, writes this of Sir John A. Macdonald who gave us, he says, "our first portrait of a Canadian." Here, it appears, is the portrait: "In that strange old man with the wine-red face and fantastic nose, in all the queer clutter, contradiction, comedy and tragedy of his life, we can see ourselves as in a mirror.". . . Can we, indeed? I look eagerly at my fellow-Canadians, and not a wine-red face do I behold, except in early spring, when the sun-bathing mania claims its first victims. Fantastic noses, likewise, are all too few. Clutter, contradiction, comedy and tragedy are, I confess, to be met with on every hand, but they are not exclusive to Canadians. . . . No, I cannot think that Sir John A. was much like a Canadian, or like anything else, except his excellent self. As well say that Laurier was a mirror of Canadians. If any statesman really epitomized the Canadian char-

---

/ *May I modestly call attention to the prophetic nature of my comment? What about Ronald Reagan (b. 1911), hero of the ominously named film* Accidents Will Happen *(1938) and the even more ominously named* Nine Lives Are Not Enough *(1941), to say nothing of* The Killers *(1964)? Not since the Empress Theodora, who was the daughter of an animal trainer in a circus and had quite a career on the boards as a dancing girl and actress before her marriage to the Emperor Justinian in the year 523 and her elevation to joint authority with him in 527, has a member of the theatrical profession attained to such gaudy public honours.*

acter and appearance, it was probably Sir Oliver Mowat. ∮ I do not hold with pretending that our exceptional and great men are made in our image. We honour and follow them for the very reason that they are not.

• COMMUNIQUÉ •
(thrust under my door)

To Big Chief Marchbanks:
How, Marchbanks!

Maybe you not know me, Marchbanks. How, anyhow.

You got money? I got no money. Get out of jail two day ago. Want money. Beg. Cops chase me. So I ask fat woman in house for money. You clean up yard I give you two dollar, she say. Awful mean face, Marchbanks. So I clean up dirt in nice pile behind garage. Then she say I got no cash but I give you cheque. She give me piece of blue paper. This no money, I say. Ha ha you poor ignorant savage, she say. You take cheque to bank, she say. I tear up cheque and steal three dollars worth her tools. She squawk. Cops chase me and take tools. Then I got no money and no tools. So I work one hour to dirty her yard again. Put back all her dirt and some new and stale dead cat I find under snowbank. Lots of work for nothing. Women awful hard to manage and fat ones worst. You got money? I need money.

How again,
Osceola Thunderbelly,
Chief of the Crokinoles. ∮

∮ *Anyone desiring to test the accuracy of this observation will find an effigy of Sir Oliver Mowat (1820–1903) in front of the Ontario Legislature's main building. Neither an Apollo nor yet a fascinating grotesque, he stands there in all weathers, a typical Canadian statesman. The rendering of his spectacles, in bronze, has been much admired.*

∮ *The fascination of the character of OSCEOLA THUNDERBELLY is equalled only by that of another great Canadian Indian, known to fame as Grey Owl, who was in cold fact an Englishman named Archibald*

• GARDENER'S PROBLEM •

I AM ALWAYS A little later than other people getting my garden in, but it is the autumn flowers, and asters in particular, which appeal to me. While I made my careful map of my garden on ruled paper, as the garden book said to do, I reflected how hard it is to get a satisfying bed of annuals which sounds good when you describe it. Spiderflower and feverfew look well together, but they sound as though the garden had been planted by Frankenstein's monster. And though Mourning Bride and Bouncing Bet make a nice combination, it seems to be tactless to put them together. As for bugbane, gasplant, tickseed and sneeze-weed, nothing would induce me to plant them, pretty as they are. I would not know how to mention them to people who wanted to see my garden.

Stansfeld Belaney (1888–1938); despite this accident of birth Belaney became the most famous Indian of his day, widely admired as an author and lecturer and exemplar of all that is finest in the Canadian native peoples. Thunderbelly, self-styled Chief of the Crokinoles, was also an Englishman, Algernon Moncrieff-Worthing, scion of a noble English house: he came to Canada suddenly after the breaking of the Oscar Wilde scandal in 1895. His family made him a very small remittance, and he eked out a leisured existence by assuming the guise of an Ignoble Red Man. Those who treated him with derision must not therefore be accused of racism or prejudice, because of course Thunderbelly was really a WASP, and thus a member of the only Canadian ethnic group which it is perfectly all right to abuse. Whereas Grey Owl said to his audiences, "You are tired with years of civilization. I come to offer you what. . .? A single green leaf," Thunderbelly often said to Marchbanks, "What the hell do you mean, civilization? I come to ask for what. . .? A measly greenback." Marchbanks, whose compassion for impostors was as boundless as his tongue was rough, never refused.

Most embarrassing of all is that pretty plant sansevieria trifasciata, *for if you identify it that way for your lady guests they will think you are a chauvinist pig, attempting to flatten them with Latin, but if you call it by its common name, which is Mother-in-Law's Tongue (because of its extremely abrasive leaf) you will be lucky not to be snatched bald.*

· YOUR PET BETRAYS YOU ·

*A*MAN I KNOW who is very fond of dogs called my attention to a newspaper article today, which said that a dog
grows to be like its owner. Nervous people have nervous dogs;
savage people have savage dogs; stupid people have stupid dogs.
Well, it may be so, though I have never seen any dog-owners among
my acquaintances nosing their pets away from a garbage can, or
chasing each other amorously over a newly-seeded garden. But it
is a fact that married people grow alike from living together, and
no true dog-owner would admit that his dumb chum was less sensitive to atmosphere than his married partner. It may be that this
theory about dogs throws new light on some of my friends: Professor
A, the celebrated economist, has a dog which always forgets where it
has buried its bones; Madame B, the fortune-teller, has a dog which
cannot foresee what will happen when it goes to sleep with its tail
under the rockers of Madame's chair; modest little Miss C owns a
pooch of notorious wantonness and infidelity. Can it be that these
beasts reveal the truth about their owners? Beware of the Dog!

· THE SEX WAR ·

*W*ALKING HOME from my work this evening I passed a
group of children who were busy, as children so often
are, in taunting and torturing one of their number. "Teddy's got a
gurr-ul! Teddy's got a gurr-ul!" they screamed, while Teddy, who
appeared to be about six, denied the charge with a remarkable
command of blasphemy and obscenity. I pondered upon this scene
for some time. Why is it considered disgraceful for little boys to
play with little girls, though a little girl who can get herself accepted
in a gang of little boys gains prestige by doing so? The equality of
the sexes, about which there is so much futile blather in the adult
world, is unheard of among the young. Women's suffrage, and equal-
pay-for-equal-work would never have come into being if children
had had any say in the matter. I toyed with the idea of going back
to the children and saying: "My pretty dears, the fact that Teddy

has a girl shows that he is more mature than the rest of you; do you not know that girls will grow up to be the equals, in all respects, of men? Don't you know that girls will sit on the juries which will condemn you to hang, which, if I may judge by your language, is the fate to which you will all come?" But I was rather busy, and went home instead. ∮

• TO MOUSEMAN, MOUSEMAN AND FORCEMEAT •

Dear Mouseman:

Get busy at once and apply for a patent on the greatest of my inventions—the Marchbanks Alert Mask for the Weary Face.

Thumbing through a magazine yesterday, I came upon an advertisement for a rubber mask which, pulled over the face, makes the wearer look like Boris Karloff in his role as Frankenstein's Monster. A toy, Mouseman: a trifle meant to enliven an evening party. But it touched off an explosion in my mind. Why not a rubber mask which makes the wearer look like himself—yet not himself as he usually appears, but himself at his best—alert, kindly, intelligent and yet also noncommittal and reserved?

Think what a boon this would be to judges on the bench, newspaper editors, psychiatrists, university tutors, and others who have to spend hours every day listening to tales of woe, boring accounts of boring events, and threshing of old straw in general. Under the mask the wearer could relax, allowing his jaw to slacken, his lips

---

∮ The bitter fact is that harassment related to sex is a two-way street. The girl who is tormented by her boss (who is old enough to remember, and whistle, "Gimme a little kiss, Will ya, huh?" when he passes her desk) is partnered by her brother, who dreads the moments when the Vice-President, a woman, beckons him to accompany her into the stockroom. The results of this sort of thing are incalculable; a few days after the incident recorded above Marchbanks saw Teddy in the same ring of tormentors, who were chanting "Teddy's got a boy-ee! Teddy's got a boy-ee!" which made it clear that sexual harassment (or as Ms. Scissorbill prefers it, harASSment) had driven Teddy to adopt an Alternative Lifestyle.

to curl, his cheeks to slump and his dewlap to throb like a frog's, while to the observer he would seem a model of solicitous goodwill.

This will crown my career as an inventor and philanthropist. You may have stock in it to cover the amount of your bill, thus getting in on the ground floor.

Yours triumphantly,
Samuel Marchbanks.

• To Amyas Pilgarlic, Esquire •

Dear Pil:

You know where I stand on dogs: I am not a person in whose life Man's Dumb Chum has played a leading role. But a day or so ago I had to attend a dog show, and as I watched the eager crowd I was visited, for perhaps the fiftieth time in my life, by the reflection that if people had to meet the rigorous standards of physical appearance which are set for dogs and other show animals it would go hardly with most of us.

The judges at the show, for instance, would have cut poor figures if the dogs had been judging them. The most important of them had a really shocking head—coarse muzzle, apple-domed skull and, so far as could be seen, a poor coat. The other judge had a narrow, splayed front, a snipey muzzle, and ears set far too high. The third judge was a woman and, though I hate to say it, a poor mover, being cow-hocked and badly spaced between her shoulders, hips and stifles. None of the judges had a bright eye nor, I should say, an affectionate nature. They did not answer readily to words of command, and showed a strong tendency to turn right when it was necessary for them to turn left. Poor creatures, useless for breeding; it would have been better to drown them as puppies.

Have you observed that a miserable-looking dog is regarded, quite rightly, as a poor-spirited creature, probably in need of worming, whereas a miserable-looking man is usually taken to be a philosopher, or at the very least, an economist? There is food for profound reflection in this.

Yours,
Sam.

• TO HAUBERGEON HYDRA, ESQUIRE •

Dear Mr. Hydra:

It will hardly come as a surprise when I inform you that the pace of modern life is increasing. A statistician of international repute (myself, if you want to know) has reckoned that every adult now gets through three times as much in a day as his grandfather; we are not measuring achievement, naturally — only activity. But when it comes to running about, meeting one another, hurrying from town to town, and taking papers in and out of brief-cases, our generation is vastly superior to any of which we have record.

This remarkable increase in activity could not have been achieved without a great deal of hard work, and I think that we owe much to the organizers, heads of speakers' committees, pep and ginger groups, and others who have made it possible. And in order that they may meet frequently and exchange ideas on how to goad the rest of the population into even greater activity I am organizing an international association for them alone, to be called "The Friends of Thrombosis." The emblem of the association will be a small wire wheel, with a demented squirrel in it.

I am sure that there are many potential members of this association in the ranks of the Civil Service, and you, as Expediter of Needless Activities, will know best who they are. Will you get them together, therefore — I beg your pardon, I should say "alert them" — and lash them into frenzied activity in preparation for our inaugural meeting. ∥

∥ *Hydra stole this idea and secured $25,000 for himself from his Minister in order to conduct a "feasibility study" which was in due course "laid before a committee" and like so many things that get laid, brought forth no fruit, which is sometimes just as well.*

I intend to be Perpetual Past President of this as yet unorganized society. It is said that at the exact centre of a vortex there is utter calm. If you should want me, you'll find me at the centre of the vortex.

Yours for earlier thrombosis,
Samuel Marchbanks.

• To Samuel Marchbanks, Esquire •

Dear Wee Sammie:

The other day, while pursuing my peaceful rounds as a junk man, I was in the house of a lady who had a good many odd bits of rock and a wheen auld jugs in a glass-fronted cupboard. "And what would ye call those, madam?" said I. "That is my collection of Chinoiserie," said she; "those pebbles are pieces of jade, and the jugs are fine old porcelain." "And why Chinoiserie?" said I. "That is the proper word for Chinese curios," said she.

As you well know, I have a cupboard of my own, in which I keep a scrap of Marchbanks tartan found in a thorn bush after the Massacre of Glencoe; our ancestor Auld Nosy Marchbanks was there as a war correspondent. And I have the sporran of our Great-great-grandfather, Close Jamie Marchbanks, which is believed to contain a bawbee, but as it is rusted shut I have never been able to get it out. And I have an empty bottle, thrown at our forebear, Fu' Charlie Marchbanks, by Robbie Burns. And as well I have a stomacher belonging to our ancestress, Sonsie Meg Marchbanks, given to her by Bonnie Prince Charlie; it is heavily encrusted with cairngorms. I am going to refer to these in future as the Marchbanks Collection of Scotchoiserie.

Your affct. uncle,
Gomeril Marchbanks.

• Of Life Beyond the Grave •

M Y VISION OF the afterlife is Celtic and undemocratic. The Lordly Ones, with their male and female followers and their bards shall dwell among the Delectable Mountains, passing

their days in hunting and their nights in feasting, song and poetry
—and of course love. The Mediocrities shall enjoy the Lesser Hell,
travelling by air from Nowhere to Nowhere without ever landing,
eating tasteless food out of plastic trays and watching movies of a
piercing badness: from time to time a voice will halloo over the
Tannoy—"Lays and Jemmun, thiz yer Captain speaking—" and
then dissolve into incomprehensible crepitations and squawks. The
Truly Evil shall descend to the Greater Hell and there the base of
heart shall dwell in damp caves among serpents who reject them,
and their food shall be the droppings of vultures. I hope to end up
as a bard, providing marvels of song and improvisation by night,
and passing the day sitting happily under a tree, quaffing and laughing at the new jokes I am concocting for the evening's after-dinner
performance.

• A LASTING CHARM •

I LISTENED RECENTLY to some gramophone records of
a woman called Yma Sumac, a Peruvian who has an astonishing voice with a range of a little more than four octaves. She
can tweet like a bird, sing like an ordinary woman (an ordinary
woman with a very good voice, that is) and roar and rumble like
the voice of Fate itself. It is a fascinating and uncanny performance.
One of her songs is about the Xtabay—supposedly a poisonously
alluring and beautiful woman who attracts men with her voice;
once that voice has been heard, a man is her slave until he dies. I
reflected that such women are uncommon in our great Dominion.
Our women are not lacking in their share of good looks, but they
will never attract international attention by the beauty of their
voices. And yet what a potent charm a lovely woman's voice is! I
would rather hear an Irish girl say something nasty to me, than
hear most Canadian girls say, "Take me, Mr. Marchbanks, I am
yours." A man likes his eye to be refreshed, but beauty perishes. A
beautiful voice, however, goes on until death, and it can call up
the ghost of vanished physical beauty more readily than any other
spell. Let the Canadian Female ponder this in her heart, and remedy her customary dispirited croak, caw or screech.

• THOUGHTS ON LEONARDO •

*H*AD TO TAKE a bag of potatoes into the cellar of the Towers, and as I heaved and struggled with the formless monster I reflected that it is now a little over 500 years since the birth of Leonardo da Vinci who, if he had been asked to take a sack of potatoes downstairs, would undoubtedly have rigged up some ingenious machine to do so for him. Although we know him chiefly as a painter, Leonardo was one of the great engineers of all time, and never lifted anything personally, because he knew all about hoists and levers. No doubt (I reflected as my arms were dragged from their sockets and my heart was moved four inches to the left) this was why he lived to be sixty-seven in an age when most people thought they had done well if they hung on till forty. I think it is shameful that boys are not taught a little elementary engineering at school — enough to teach them how to get a bag of potatoes into a cellar, for instance. When at last the task was done I prepared a restorative cordial and drank it, and remembered that Leonardo was a teetotaller. But then, he never lifted anything; we toiling peasants have some justification for our vices.

• WILLS AND THEIR WAYS •

I HAVE BEEN pondering about my will. As a literary document it lacks interest and surprise. Recently the wills of a number of notable Canadians have been printed in full in the metropolitan press and I have read them with interest and a degree of envy. Not that I thought much of their style; I am sure I could write a fancier will; but I was impressed by their length and complication. How can I complicate my few miserable bequests? Shall I make them conditional upon the prolonged bad conduct of my heirs? Shall I leave my library — which, at the usual second-hand dealer's price of ten cents a volume, would bring close to $20 — to a university, conditional upon their erecting a million-dollar building, with a big statue of me in the rotunda, to house it? Shall I give the Towers, with all its bills for back-taxes, to the community, to be preserved in perpetuity as a memorial to myself? Who is to get my wheelbarrow, which I coated afresh with aluminum paint last week? Shall I leave my silver tray (a splendid piece of electro-plate, nine inches in diameter in all directions) to the Ontario woman to have the greatest number of triplets within ten years of my demise? My present will simply won't do.

• TO AMYAS PILGARLIC, ESQUIRE •

Dear Pil:

I am impressed by the huge new banks which have either been built, or are now in the process of building, in the fair city of Toronto. As the towers of cathedrals in the Middle Ages were thought to point the way to heaven, these vast temples of commerce obviously stretch themselves toward the clouds as symbols of unimaginable wealth. And how typically Canadian these huge bank buildings are! They have a kind of stony austerity about them, and a frowning, tight-lipped expression around their doors, which strongly suggests our national attitude toward the really important things of life, such as money.

But their modern sculpture displeases me. The older bank facades were guarded by thick-waisted girls who contrived, though naked, to look unapproachable and No Fun, and by excessively muscular young men, who were tensed like young executives trying to Get Ahead. These creatures were all gods and goddesses in Banker's Mythology, and the more important ones were easily identified:

FRIGIDIUS

a god usually represented with a beard and washboard muscles on his stomach; he is the deity of branch bank managers, and is always represented with a frown, like a manager refusing to lend $50 to a small business man.

AVARICIA

the goddess of thrift, and she is usually represented naked but unamusing, with a look in her stony eye as though she could buy a fur coat, if she wanted to be silly, like other girls.

USURIUS

the god of compound interest, and he is always represented with a thoughtful look, like a banker doing a sum in his head, and wondering whether he should check it on the calculating machine.

TRANSPIRIA

the goddess of professional secrecy. She usually has one hand over her open mouth, and looks as though she were hinting to a Government Loan salesman that there is a farmer out in the county with $5,000 in cash in a coffee can under the pigsty floor, and that his wife has $800 of egg money in a Savings Account.

BAROMETRUS

the god of Future Security, and he is represented seated, gazing into the future, like a bank president trying to guess whether the credit companies will cut into his business much more during the coming year. Now and again one sees a representation of a young man chasing a young woman: this is not what you would expect, but Good Money driving out Bad.

So far as I know, this school of sculpture, done with a sandblasting machine, was peculiar to Canada. Let us cherish the examples that remain.

Yours,
Sam.

• TO MRS. MORRIGAN • ∅

My dear Mrs. Morrigan:

I was at a concert last night where a pianist played Handel's variations called *The Harmonious Blacksmith*. Of course Handel never called it anything of the kind and the name was not attached to the piece until long after Handel was dead. But the program note

---

∅ The precise identity of Mrs. MORRIGAN cannot be determined. The name is that of the Great Queen of Celtic mythology, a woman of extraordinary sympathy and wisdom. Readers may consult mythologi-

repeated the old story of how he received his inspiration for the piece while sheltering from a thunderstorm in a smithy. How good old George Frederick would have snorted! He loathed flapdoodle.

But this reminded me of that other legend, preserved in the old Ontario Third Reader, of how Beethoven, walking through the streets of Vienna with a friend one night, heard a piano being played in a basement; peeping through the window, he saw that a blind girl was playing to her aged father. "Alas, papa," said she, "if only I could go to the concert tomorrow night, to hear the great Beethoven play, how happy I should be! But (sob) we have no money." Without a word the great composer rushed into the cellar, sat down at the piano, and played a magnificent program, improvising the *Moonlight Sonata* at the conclusion, and wowing the simple music-lover. As a child I was much touched by this story.

What disillusion awaited me when I began to look through the private papers of my Viennese ancestor, Wolfgang Amadeus Marchbanks, who was a close friend of Beethoven. Indeed, he was the very friend who accompanied Beethoven on that memorable walk. And my great-great-great uncle Wolfgang says that in reality Beethoven pushed his head through the window, and said, "Stop that row, woman; if you must play my stuff, stop vamping the bass." Beethoven was not an easy man to please.

Truth, alas, is sometimes even uglier than fiction.

Your humble servant,
Samuel Marchbanks.

• To Miss Nancy Frisgig • ⨍

Charming Nancy:

Last night a friend of mine showed me a book which he has, illustrative of photography during the nineteenth century. It was a

---

cal dictionaries or The White Goddess *(1948) by Robert Graves for details. Who was Marchbanks' Morrigan? A pretty problem for Ph.D. students in years to come, but beyond the present editor.*

⨍ *Miss NANCY FRISGIG was Marchbanks' god-daughter, with whom he maintained a happy relationship, sending her a birthday gift*

wonderful book, and a revelation to me, because it contained photographs of virtually every celebrated beauty of that era. And how plain they were! Empress Eugenie, for instance, looked as though she needed a dose of liver salts, and the glamorous Lola Montez looked like the back of a hack. The Princess Alexandra was by no means what tradition avouches, and indeed the only one of the lot who really lived up to expectation was the ill-fated Empress of Mexico. Is the beauty of women, then, an illusion which cannot safely be transferred from one era to another? Would Cleopatra, if we could see her today, be merely a scruffy gypsy, and Helen of Troy a greasy girl with a garlic breath? I shrink from such conclusions, but as a philosopher I must face them.

One of the most interesting photographs in the book to me was that of Rigolboche, the dancer who made the can-can famous. Nobody thought Rigolboche beautiful, or even wholesome-looking, but she waggled a wicked shank and was full of high spirits, and Paris loved her. And when she retired wise little Rigolboche bought a high class boarding-house with her savings, and was the perfect landlady until she died at a great old age.

For years thoughts of Rigolboche have made me look at my landladies with a speculative eye. Could they, I pondered, once have been glamorous courtesans and can-can dancers? Did noblemen drink champagne from their slippers in the days before they abandoned slippers in favour of lark-heeled house shoes with scuffed toes? I have come to the conclusion that boarding-house landladies of the Rigolboche type are uncommon in Canada. Most of them

---

whenever he remembered. A revealing incident happened at Nancy's christening, a very High Church affair where Marchbanks at a solemn moment was handed a candle by the clergyman, who said "Receive the light of truth." "Ah, that it were so," said Marchbanks, "but you must allow me my reservations as a determined Gnostic." The parson, who was not accustomed to back-talk from the minor characters in the drama was further disconcerted by the infant Nancy, who was heard to laugh for the first time in her life. It was this and a thousand later laughs that made her very dear to Marchbanks.

are profoundly melancholy women, and if they were ever in the public eye it was certainly as hired weepers at undertaking parlours.

Yours regretfully,
Sam.

• TO CHANDOS FRIBBLE, ESQUIRE • ✒

Dear Fribble:

I do not get to the movies as often as I could wish, but I saw one a few days ago which you really must study before you write your book on The Screen Epic. This particular Epic was presented to the audience as a wonderful evocation of the spirit of the Renaissance. It contained fine examples of three of the elements which are inseparable from celluloid epics. (1) The Virgin Heroine: in this piece she was married to an old man, and in a very pointed speech he made it clear that he had brought her up strictly as his daughter; this meant that when she was at last free to marry the hero she was, so to speak, leaping from the refrigerator into the frying-pan, which is what audiences expect. (2) The Good Villain: movie audiences like a villain to have large streaks of good in him, like the streaks of fat in a slab of restaurant ham; this gives them a comfortable feeling that although villainy is obviously fun, it is also All Right. (3) The Speech on Democracy: in film epics there must always be a moment when some minor character bawls out all the aristocrats in the cast, telling them that some day The Peepul will rise up and smite them; this is to show that all the good people in

---

✒ One of Marchbanks' principal associations with the academic world was through his acquaintance with CHANDOS FRIBBLE, Ph.D. to the fourth power. Fribble was a Canadian example of that character familiar in Russian literature, the Perpetual Student; having achieved one Ph.D. he immediately set out on another, and as these projects can be extended to seven years he was, when Marchbanks first met him, already well-advanced in middle age. Student grants and Canada Council grants, though they do not provide an ample income, have about them a beautiful inevitability which endears them to the scholarly heart.

the film are democrats at heart, although they are dressed up like sixteenth-century Italians; the dramatic climaxes are often complicated by the fact that the demeanour and speech of the actors makes it impossible to tell who is an aristocrat and who is Little Joe. It is doubtful if the cause of democracy is served by these tirades, but audiences like them.

At the film I sat in front of a young man who was suffering from Teen-Ager's St. Vitus Dance, which caused him to kick the back of my seat so often and so rapidly that my head wobbled like a punching bag. Whenever the hero did anything of a spectacular nature he uttered cries like a horse in a burning stable. In spite of these annoyances I studied the piece intently. I recognized that my restless neighbour was, in the modern jargon, "empathizing."

Yours to command,
Samuel Marchbanks.

• To Gomeril Marchbanks, Esquire •

Dear Uncle Gomeril:

Have you ever thought of going into the pawnbroking business? The attractions of the business are many. First of all, you have a cosy little shop, very informal in character. Then you have a wonderfully assorted type of merchandise, with a bias in favour of old watches, rusty precision tools, musical instruments of the twangling and tootling varieties, telescopes, binoculars and military decorations. Just think of sitting in one's shop all day, peeping through the telescopes, polishing up the lodge rings, blowing the bugles, and listening to the cuckoo-clocks! And, from time to time, helping some poor needy soul with a generous loan of $2 on a bass clarinet which cost him $85 in 1917, and which you can sell for $45 any time. Oh, how delicious to be a pawnbroker, and be an Uncle to all the world!

Your affct. nephew,
Sam.

• To Amyas Pilgarlic, Esquire •

Dear Pil:

The closing of the universities has caused the usual number of charming young men and women, with the chalk of the lecture-room still in their hair, to visit me and offer to revolutionize my affairs through the exercise of their talents. When I say that I have no jobs for them they look at me with pity and disbelief. They know that I am lying, that I really have excellent jobs in my gift, but that I am afraid of their brilliance. They assure me that they do not want to work for me for long; they just want to learn the trade, and then pass on to better establishments than mine. The young women are sure that I have a prejudice against their sex; they are, they tell me, capable of doing anything that a man can do. I have no doubt of this, but I also know what that amounts to.

Last week I picked up a magazine which contained an article advising college graduates on — of all things — How To Choose A Boss. I should not have read it, for I knew in advance that it would give me the trembles, but I did. And it did. The perfect boss, it appears, is unlike me in every possible way. He is a jolly extrovert, with a guilty sense that he is not quite equal to his job, and with a fine understanding of the frailties of youth. He is also rather stupid, and it is easy to cozen him in the matter of pay and holidays. His temper is quick, but soon dies down. Working for this Dream Boss, it appears, is hardly work at all. It is a great big romp from morning till night.

Do I wish I were a Dream Boss? No. Depressing though it may seem, I am quite ready to go on being my curmudgeonly, reclusive, grudge-bearing, suspicious, happy self.

Nevertheless, the article depressed me. It is always depressing when one has to disappoint people's expectations.

Yours depressedly (though not
to any intolerable degree)
Sam.

• To Miss Minerva Hawser •

Dear Miss Hawser:

Your suggestion that a few people in Canada try to revive the lost art of letter-writing is a worthy one, and I am flattered that you should include me in your group. I am grateful for the copy of *The Maple Leaf Letter Writer* which you have sent me, and I have read it with great care. But there is one point on which I disagree with the book, and that is its insistence on absolutely conventional spelling. Although I am myself a fair speller, I have thought for some time that a reasonable amount of personal choice should be allowed in this matter. After all, the passion for spelling according to a dictionary is only about a hundred years old; every writer of any importance before that spelled a few words at least in his own way.

Only the other day I was looking at a book of letters from the seventeenth century, in which one writer expressed himself thus: "As for Mr. A——, I esteem him no better than a Pigg." Consider that word "Pigg." The extra "g" is not strictly necessary, but what power it gives to the word! How pig-like it makes poor Mr. A——! How vivid his swinishness becomes! And look at that capital "P." It seems to enrich the sentence by calling special attention to the most important word.

I am not a spelling reformer. I am a laissez-faire liberal in matters of spelling. I do not care that our present system of spelling wastes time and paper. I firmly believe that both time and paper are of less importance than the perfect expression of the writer's meaning. Anyone who thinks otherwise is a Pedantick Booby.

Yours for orthographicall freedom,
Samuel Marchbanks.

• To Amyas Pilgarlic, Esquire •

Dear Pil:

The Americans are a remarkable people, and I admire them quite a lot. But I never cease to be astonished at their powers of self-deception which are, like so many of their institutions, gigantic, colossal, mammoth, gargantuan, jumbo, atomic and merely large. Today I saw a book in a cigar store which was called *Ballet—The Emergence of an American Art*. Since when, I wonder, did ballet become an American art? During the past years a number of American dancers have, by dint of the whole-souled energy which characterizes their nation, learned to jump as high, and twiddle as dizzily as dancers in other lands, and undoubtedly they sweat and puff more while doing so. But because ballet has gained what may properly be called a toehold in the U.S.A., does that make it an American art? Ponder before replying.

It is always an interesting point in a nation's history when it becomes so great that it does not believe that anything has real existence outside itself. The Romans reached it. The British kept it up during most of the nineteenth century. Will Canada, I wonder, ever achieve this delightful form of insanity? Ponder well upon this.

Yours,
Sam.

· TO CHANDOS FRIBBLE, ESQUIRE ·

My dear Fribble:

You know everything; can you tell me when the last writer of religious tracts died? I assume that all of them are dead, for though I am constantly receiving tracts through the mails from people who are anxious about my soul, I have yet to read one which appears to have been written within this century.

Yesterday I received a fresh batch. One of them shows a picture of a business man (called "Mr. O. U. Foolish Man") confronted by the spectre of death in his office. He sits at a roll-top desk, on the top of which are two large bags marked "$"; he wears a white vest and at his feet is a spittoon. Now, Fribble, let us apply Sherlock Holmes' methods to this picture; the roll-top desk, the white vest and the spittoon all place it in the nineteenth century; what business man uses such trumpery now? They all sit at steel desks and spit in the bottom drawer of the filing cabinet.

Another tract in this bunch — there were seven altogether — is called *My Experience With The Tobacco Habit*. It begins with this information: "I was a slave to tobacco for twenty years; Mother and Father used tobacco and I had the poison in my blood; Mother found me with her snuff box, when I was about eight years old." Later he says that he would pick up used quids of chewing tobacco from the street and chew them.

The last woman I know of who took snuff was my great-grandmother, who was born in 1800 and who lived to be eighty-seven; she did not chew it; she sniffed it. As for chewing tobacco, the habit has completely vanished from all settlements where civilization has a firm hold. Obviously this tract was written not less than sixty years ago.

Is no strong, new generation of tract-writers coming up to continue the work? Or will this remarkable literary form continue to rely on its past glories? Here is a meaty subject for research, Fribble.

Your admirer and crony,
S. Marchbanks.

• THE CURSE STRIKES •

A WOKE UNABLE to move, for I had fallen victim to the Curse of the Marchbanks, which is Lumbago; it runs in our family as haemophilia runs among the Bourbons. My grandfather, who was a deeply religious man and a great student of Holy Writ, identified it as the third claw of the Beast described in Revelation. After much moaning, snorting and shrieking, and with the aid of three completely new oaths which came to me in flashes of inspiration, I rolled from my couch and huddled on my clothes. One of my legs appeared to have shortened by six inches, and my axis was eighteen degrees out of plumb, but I could walk, after a fashion, and in this pitiable state I went about my day's work. To some I was an object of sly mockery; to others my condition was a matter for a deep and unnecessary concern, for Lumbago never killed anybody, though it has sometimes driven its victims to acts of violence. It is a treacherous and feline ill, for at times it seems to abate, and then returns with renewed malignity. Asked by a friend to describe it, I racked my brains, and then said that it felt like being stabbed in the small of the back with an old-fashioned carpet-stretcher.

• . . . AND CONTINUES •

*T*HE TROUBLE WITH Lumbago (or, to be more accurate, one of the contributory troubles) is that it rouses incredulity in people. "You've never got Lumbago!" they say, just after you have told them precisely that. Then they either laugh, which is cruel, or put on an expression that conveys their thought that you are prematurely old, which is worse. But anybody can get Lumbago, if they go about it the right way. A baby in its cradle could have it, if it was in a draught, or a bit damp, which a baby may so easily be. Lumbago, like a toothache, is one of the ailments that mankind refuses to take seriously in other people *ƒ*. . . . My worst moment today was when I tried to carry a large parcel through a revolving door; to do this, with Lumbago, is to experience every degree of alarm, confusion, sudden pain and gross indignity.

• DELUSIONS OF AMIABILITY •

*A*TTENDED A REUNION at my old school, and met a lot of fellows I had not seen for a quarter of a century. I was astonished at the ravages which time had inflicted upon them in body, but even more by the tricks it had played with their memories. It was not a teetotal affair, and as the evening wore on dozens of them suffered acutely from Delusions of Amiability; that is to say, they remembered that I had been on much more intimate terms with them in the past than was ever really the case. I am cursed with a memory like an elephant, and I am particularly certain

---

ƒ No longer so; Lumbago, described as Lower Back Pain, is now a Status-Ailment, and to suffer from it is to be blessed with an unfailing excuse, and an unlimited source of anecdote and high-toned complaint.

that I know who have been my friends and who—to put it mildly —have not; no amount of the genial juice of the grain can disturb my accuracy in such matters. Some of them obviously thought I was somebody else, some very dear old friend whom they had loved as a brother; others knew who I was, but had forgotten that I was a cantankerous and mocking wretch; some had lost all grasp of reality, and were not sure who they were themselves, but knew that they had only one true friend, and he was Marchbanks. A fascinating, revealing, uproarious evening, any way I choose to think about it.

• COMMUNIQUÉ •
(Left by an Indian Runner)

To Big Chief Marchbanks:
How, Marchbanks!

In Ottawa now, Marchbanks. Got business with government. I see by papers some Québec Indian want government to give freedom back to Indians. No good. Indians got too much sense. Who wants to be free and work for government, anyway? Every place I look here I see sad face. Glasses. Bald spots. Government no job for happy man.

Indian here I used to know on reserve. He get ambition. Go to school. Everybody say smart Indian, give him chance. He work. And work. Now he got place in government. Work like devil. Got black hat. Got briefcase for carry sandwiches. On reserve his name Joe Halfwit. Now he called Mr. J. Frontal Lobotomy. Sad sight, Marchbanks. How again!

Osceola Thunderbelly,
Chief of the Crokinoles.

• AN ALIEN WORLD •

SOMETIMES I have the sensation of one who has survived from an earlier age into a strange and uncanny era. Rode downtown today with a lady whose small child was in the back seat. Suddenly the moppet set up a great hullabaloo, and cried "Look! Look!" (In cold fact it cried "Yook! Yook!" but I have no intention of falling into baby talk). What had excited it so much was the appearance of a horse—an ordinary draught-horse—on the street. Horses were as strange to that child as elephants. Its mother told me that the child was being taken to see—a camelopard? a unicorn? a hippogriff?—no, none of these things, but a Jersey cow which has become a celebrity, and travels around to collect money for charity. What kind of a world do I inhabit, in which horses and cows are exotic rarities, and the combustion engine, that uncanny and devilish device, is taken for granted by the smallest child? I do not greatly like animals, but I like to see them about, for I am an animal myself; the horse is my brother and the cow my sister. But by the Beard of the Prophet, the combustion engine is no relative of mine, and a world where it is supreme will not tolerate me for long.

• THE ENEMY WITHIN •

*A*GREED WITH a man with whom I fell into conversation that it is, upon the whole, a bad thing to keep your temper at all times. Psychologists talk a good deal nowadays about something which they call "repressed hostility," but which an old psychologist who used to do washing for my mother called "bottled-up mad." She had a great deal of mad herself, which she rarely troubled to bottle, but when she did make the effort the vile substance could be seen mounting inside her, like mercury in a thermometer. It was said of Mary, Queen of Scots, that when she drank wine it could be seen bubbling down her lovely, transparent throat, like suds in a sink; the washerwoman's mad worked the other way rising from her bosom, up her neck, and rushing to the top of her head. Then she would unbottle some of it, at the top of her voice. But my friend and I decided that repressed hostility created tension, which led to ugly illnesses. It is better to beat up your wife, or strike your little ones with a chair, than run such a risk. Bottled-up mad is probably at the root of many of the world's baffling diseases.

• THE WEAKER SEX •

*R*EAD AN ARTICLE in a woman's magazine today called *How to Keep Your Husband From Dying of Heart Failure*. It was a sensible, well-written piece, pointing out that women are far less prone to heart injuries than men, and that women therefore should take on any heavy physical work that has to be done around a house, such as moving the furnace from one side of the cellar to another, or putting the car up on blocks for the winter. It included many anecdotes of poor, overdriven men who had been literally pushed into the Great Void by women who were afraid of such trifling tasks as carrying barrels of apples upstairs, or changing a tire on a truck. This strengthens a belief which I have long cherished, that in a few centuries women will be the larger, stronger sex, admired for their biceps and superfluous hair, and that men will be their toys and domestic comforters, exciting tenderness in the female breast by their small feet, pretty soft hands, and general helplessness. I do not think I have a heart, for I have never been able to locate my pulse, or any other symptom of a circulatory system, but I am willing to share any of the benefits of male delicacy.

• TO MISS NANCY FRISGIG •

Charming Nancy:

Of course you will get parking tickets if you leave a sports-car with a mink coat in it double-parked for two hours; only soft-drink trucks are permitted such liberties. And it is hopeless to try your charms on the police; they are the kind of men Cromwell used to recruit for his Ironsides, and to them feminine charm is as piffle before the wind.

In the more advanced portions of society it is now freely admitted that the man who stays at home while the woman goes out to win the bread is not a Big Flabby Lout but the Jewel of the Harem, and must be cherished.

My dentist, who is a man of wide and principally sad experience, tells me that he has professionally attended soldiers, sailors, hardrock miners, tax-collectors, and other nerveless and fearless people, and that they all bear pain like heroes; the exceptions are policemen, who are as sensitive as children to a touch of the drill.

So don't try to charm them. Pay your fine, shout, "Yah, who's chicken at the dentist?", put your foot on the accelerator and get away.

Subversively,
Sam.

• To Apollo Fishorn, Esquire •

Dear Mr. Fishorn:

You want to be a Canadian playwright, and ask me for advice as to how to set about it. Well, Fishorn, the first thing you had better acquaint yourself with is the physical conditions of the Canadian theatre. Every great drama, as you know, has been shaped by its playhouse. The Greek drama gained grandeur from its marble outdoor theatres; the Elizabethan drama was given fluidity by the extreme adaptability of the Elizabethan playhouse stage; French classical drama took its formal tone from its exquisite, candle-lit theatres. You see what I mean.

Now what is the Canadian playhouse? Nine times out of ten, Fishorn, it is a school hall, smelling of chalk and kids, and decorated in the Early Concrete style. The stage is a small raised room at one end. And I mean room. If you step into the wings suddenly you will fracture your nose against the wall. There is no place for storing scenery, no place for the actors to dress, and the lighting is designed to warm the stage but not to illuminate it.

Write your plays, then, for such a stage. Do not demand any processions of elephants, or dances by the maidens of the Caliph's harem. Keep away from sunsets and storms at sea. Place as many scenes as you can in cellars and kindred spots. And don't have more than three characters on the stage at one time, or the weakest of them is sure to be nudged into the audience. ✒

Farewell, and good luck to you,
S. Marchbanks.

• TO SAMUEL MARCHBANKS, ESQUIRE •

Dear Mr. Marchbanks:

Capital news, Mr. Marchbanks, sir! At last we see our way clear to bring your case against Richard Dandiprat to court. I fear that perhaps the proceedings may not be precisely as you have envisioned them in your layman's imagination. You have asserted that Mr. Dandiprat, with malice aforethought, induced a skunk to enter your car, and there to comport itself in such a manner as to constitute a nuisance. But as you appear to have lost all the documents which establish you as owner of the car our case breaks down at that point. We can only bring action against Dandiprat on charges of having behaved with cruelty toward a skunk, by incarcerating it in a stationary vehicle without food or water. You enter the case only as undoubted owner of the garage in which the car stood at the time. If the defence should claim that you were negligent in not locking the garage you may be censured by the judge, but I doubt if you will be asked to share Dandiprat's fine.

If we are very fortunate we may be able to get this case on the docket for the Autumn Assizes; otherwise it will hold over until Spring. The law is a dreadful engine, Mr. Marchbanks, and when set in motion it moves with frightening speed.

Yours in high glee,
Mordecai Mouseman,
(for Mouseman, Mouseman and Forcemeat).

✒ This was written before the Stratford Shakespearean Festival brought new life and hope to the Canadian theatre. Since 1953 several provincial governments have caused to be erected gigantic structures suitable for monster conventions, political rallies and other such functions, and at one end of the auditorium there is a stage so huge that the Decline and

• Captive Audience •

RECEIVED A LETTER from a wretch who is obviously suffering from a bad case of Stenographer Fever. This disease, which is well known in business circles but unaccountably ignored by medical science, is a condition in which a man dictates letters to impress his stenographer, rather than the true recipient of his message. His letter becomes rhetorical and hectoring in tone. He tends to call his correspondent by name several times, thus; —"Now, Mr. Marchbanks, as you are no doubt well aware, it is not my custom to mince words with such a man as you, Mr. Marchbanks, seem to be...."—generally I deal with such letters by replying in this strain:—"Samuel Marchbanks has received your note. His answer is No." ... No man, we are told, is a hero to his valet, but the world of business abounds with men who wish to be heroes to their stenographers ⫽ and to this end they soar and bombinate, keeping an appreciative eye on the Captive Audience on the other side of the desk.

• To Raymond Cataplasm, M.D., F.R.C.P. •

Dear Dr. Cataplasm:

I have just had a brilliant idea which, if you can make it practical, will revolutionize medical science. I am, as you know, of Celtic

---

Fall of the Roman Empire might be mounted on it, with the original cast; these are just as unsuitable for any rational drama as the midget stages of which Marchbanks complains.

⫽ A stenographer was a woman who performed the duties now expected of an Executive Assistant, though unlike the EA the stenographer could frequently write shorthand and do neat typing. Many Executive Assistants, these days, seem to be drawn from the ranks of those who respond cheerfully to the advertisements that are seen in the subway, which read, "F u kn rd ths u kn gt a gd jb n rn bg mny." It was not thus that Sir Isaac Pitman conceived of his system of phonology in 1837, nor yet John Robert Gregg his cursive shorthand in 1888. What happens if you gt a gd jb and your boss dictates a word like tetramethyldiamidobenzhydrols?

ancestry, and I have for many years been fascinated by the institution of the Sin Eater, once so popular in Wales and its border country. At every funeral there attended some old man who, at the proper time, accepted across the body of the corpse a piece of cake, a cup of wine, and a small piece of money; he ate these —not the money, of course—saying before everyone present that he took upon him the sins of the dead person, whose soul was then free to go to Heaven without any burden upon it.

Could not medical skill arrange for someone, to be called the Fat Eater, to undertake a similar service for people whose metabolism disposes them to put on excess weight? As the stout party sat down to meals he could hand a few victuals across the table to the Fat Eater, on the understanding that the latter would take upon himself any poundage which might result from his feeding. And thus, while the employer had the fun of the food, the Fat Eater would take on the burden of the weight.

Like all great ideas, this is essentially simple. It just needs a little working out, which I am sure you can manage easily.

Your perennial patient,
Samuel Marchbanks.

• TO AMYAS PILGARLIC, ESQUIRE •

Dear Pil:

I attended an admirable concert recently and enjoyed myself very much, but whenever the singer was about to tackle a song in a foreign language I would cast my eyes at the translation of the words which was included in my program, and would see something like this: "Beautiful lips, shuffling to and fro with indecision, why don't you render me the delicious happiness to say yes, again yes, oh yes, lips, hurry up lips, yes, yes." I am no great hand at understanding German and Italian, but I venture to say that the words of the songs were on a slightly higher literary level than the translations indicated.

Do you suppose that in Italy and Germany songs in English are translated in the same way for concert audiences? If so, I can imagine

Drink To Me Only With Thine Eyes working out something like this: "Let us agree, when drinking, to employ the eyeballs only; similarly with kisses; I sent you some flowers recently and you sent them back after breathing on them; they are still alive but are impregnated with your personal odour."

Could UNESCO do anything about this confusing question of translating songs?

Your crony,
Sam.

• To Haubergeon Hydra, Esquire •

Dear Mr. Hydra:

There is a matter of some delicacy which I feel should be brought to your notice, as Deputy Expediter of the Plan for the Beautification of the Dominion Capital. I had occasion to visit Ottawa recently, and as I entered the city by train, and again as I left it, I was painfully struck by its resemblance to a foreign capital which I shall only describe as M-sc-w.

Pause, Mr. Hydra, before you put the R.C.M.P. to work to investigate me. I mean no disloyalty. Quite otherwise. This re-semblance grieved me more than I can say, and I would like it to be minimized. I am sure that it has not come to your personal attention because, like all Civil Servants, you rarely leave the capital, and when you do you take a sack full of papers to work at on the train, and never look out of the window. Consequently you have never been struck, as I was, by the resemblance of Parliament Hill to the Kr-ml-n. Those spires surrounded by grey mist, that air of brooding secrecy, that sense of doom—oh, Hydra, they won't do at all! They give quite the wrong impression.

Do you think that in beautifying the capital you could alter all its architecture to something jollier—something more suggestive of democracy at work? Could the spires be swelled out a little, so that they became domes? Or perhaps the spires could be sawed off at the roots? For I assure you, sir, that those spires, rising above the low skyline of Hull, give quite the wrong impression to the visitor.

Yours for democratic architecture,
S. Marchbanks.

• TO SAMUEL MARCHBANKS, ESQUIRE •

Dear Marchbanks:

This lawsuit you are bringing against me is getting to be a nuisance. I only put the skunk in your car for a joke. Have you no sense of humour?

I'll tell you what I'll do. You like pictures, I believe. If you will tell your lawyers to drop the case I'll give you a picture my Aunt Bessie brought back from her tour of Italy before Great War I. I think she said it was Venus Rising from the Sea, by Botticelli. The family have always called it The Stark Tart, and we keep it in the attic. I believe it is the original, but maybe it is just a copy. Anyhow, it looks like the kind of thing you would like. It is a little stained by damp, but otherwise all right.

If this isn't generosity, I don't know what you could call it.

Yours fraternally,
Dick Dandiprat.

• TO RICHARD DANDIPRAT, ESQUIRE •

Presumptuous Dandiprat:

I would call it gross impudence, and an attempt to clog the mighty engine of justice. Keep your foreign pornography, wretch, to comfort you in prison.

Disdainfully,
Marchbanks.

In one important respect, however, Ottawa will not be confused with Moscow. Ottawa is, on a yearly average, colder and boasts

• To Amyas Pilgarlic, Esquire •

Dear Pil:

Last week I was bidden to a graduation banquet where a large number of students — after consuming the tomato soup, green peas and deliquescent ice cream which are obligatory at such orgies — listened to speeches of good advice from their elders, and made a few speeches themselves.

What particularly impressed me was that the elders who spoke all assured the young people that they were going out into a World of Chaos, and the young people all agreed with them.

This moved me to ponder that I was born into a world of chaos — the chaos of the moment being the First World War. My childhood was passed amidst the chaos of the Post War World, and then came the chaos of the Depression; this, in time, gave way to the chaos of the Second World War, and now I wallow in the chaos of the Atomic Age. This is a pretty good record for one life — chaos every minute.

In spite of all this chaos, however, most people seem to lead humdrum lives, and badly want livening up. Do you think we should organize a Chaos-of-the-Month Club, guaranteeing to supply all members with something really unnerving every thirty days? For I greatly fear that most of those students, rushing eagerly out into the world of chaos, are going to find that their particular part of it quickly becomes a deadly routine.

Yours for more varied chaos,
Sam.

• To Samuel Marchbanks, Esquire •

Esteemed Sir:

The costs of pursuing your case against Richard Dandiprat, Esquire are mounting. As you know, there are many charges involved in

---

the distinction of being the coldest capital city in the world. Scientists deny, however, that this is caused by the frost emanating from the Rideau Club.

legal proceedings apart from the charge brought in court. (Ha, ha: a legal jest, Mr. Marchbanks, and a great favourite with Mr. Mouseman, senior; pardon me for bringing it up but I could not help myself.) There is the cost, for instance, of having all the relevant documents copied in octuplicate. You may say that there were no relevant documents in your case, but you would be wrong; we have created several. That is part of the service a lawyer offers his client. And there are carrying charges, as well; these are the fees required to induce your lawyer to carry your case in his head; these are utterly indispensable. And there are incidental charges; for instance during the typing of some documents related to your case a typewriter ribbon frayed away to a juiceless shoestring; there was nothing to be done but to replace it, the first time this has been necessary since the purchase of the machine in 1907.

We never plague our clients for money, but we suggest to you that we do not live upon air, though we have been known to live upon heirs. (I crave forgiveness, sir; another pleasantry of the elder Mr. Mouseman; it slipped out, somehow.) A little something to be going on with would be a lovely midsummer surprise for

Yours faithfully,
Mordecai Mouseman,
(for Mouseman, Mouseman and Forcemeat).

• LAST ENCHANTMENTS OF THE MIDDLE AGE •

*T*O THE MOVIES, to see *Ivanhoe*, and enjoyed it thoroughly. It departs a good deal from the novel, but I am not one to complain of that, for Scott always put enough plot in a single book to last Hollywood for a year. Athelstane of Coningsburgh was cut out entirely, but I did not miss him; King Richard was trimmed to a mere sliver, but what remained was satisfactorily Lion-Hearted. The only change I deplored was in the death of Brian de Bois Guilbert; in the film he and Ivanhoe fought to the death with a Boppeur de la Tête (a chain with a spiky ball on the end) and a Hacqueur du Corps (a fire axe); my studies in mediaeval armoury enabled me to recognize these at once. But in the book Brian died in the most dramatic way possible; he simply exploded, a victim of the contending passions of love and hate, and died one of the most interesting psychological deaths in all literature. George Sanders is an excellent actor, with a vast repertory of sneers and leers, and he could have given us the biggest death-scene since Jumbo was hit by a train at St. Thomas. But Hollywood still fears these subtleties, and the final battle reminded me of one of my enraged assaults upon the furnace at the Towers.

• COMMUNIQUÉ •
(Wrapped 'round a stone and thrown through my window)

To Big Chief Marchbanks:
How, Marchbanks!

I lucky Indian, Marchbanks. Why? I tell. Last week Chief Fishbone-in-Throat die. Young man, Marchbanks. Only 102. Once I nearly marry his daughter, Princess Blocked Drain. Now Fishbone dead, Ottawa want succession duties. They take wigwam, take wampum, take truss off corpse. Bury Fishbone all busted. Now Blocked Drain poor woman. Owe Ottawa money. She offer Ottawa corpse of Fishbone but Ottawa refused because of rupture. Only want fancy corpse. I lucky Indian, Marchbanks. If I married Blocked Drain might have to work too, now. Instead I got job on roads. Wave red flag. Authority, Marchbanks.

How again,
Osceola Thunderbelly,
Chief of the Crokinoles.

• INFORMATION SCORNED •

TO THE MOVIES and sat first of all behind a small boy whose hair had obviously been cut at home; the poor child looked as though an Indian had begun to scalp him, but had been called out on strike when half done. Behind me sat a woman with a package of sticky popcorn; I did not much mind her noisy champings, but it bothered me that she dropped a lot of the goodies on the floor, and they rolled down under my feet and gave me a sense of treading on broken eggs. So I moved, and found myself behind two girls, both at the very pinnacle of romantic yearning.

The film, however, seemed to be beyond their modest intellectual grasp; it was about a period of history before the advent of the combustion engine, and everybody went everywhere on horses or behind horses. At one point a lady entered a room and said that she must stay a while because a shoe had been lost. The girls whispered busily between them, and then agreed that she must be crazy, as she was wearing both her shoes, as any fool could plainly see. I leaned forward helpfully, "Her horse lost a shoe, poppets," I said. They viewed me with the scorn of youth. "Drop dead, Gramps," said one of them; "since when did horses wear shoes?" Since when, indeed?

• UNEARNED INCOME •

HAVE BEEN LOOKING over the questions the census-taker will ask me. One of them is an enquiry as to how much money I earned last year. The answer to this will be, "about $125." Of course I had more money than this, but I didn't earn it. The Government itself says that I didn't. For I get my living as a writer, and the Government makes it very clear in its Income Tax forms that what a writer gets is Investment Income, comparable to the guilty gold which the Idle Rich derive from their holdings in Stocks and Shares. The census-taker will stare about him in amazement, his eye straying from the rich tapestries upon my walls to the priceless products of old Persian looms beneath his feet; as I scratch a match upon a rare piece of cloisonné, and scissor a chunk out of an early Picasso in order to mend a hole in my shoe, he will scratch his head and wonder how I came by such Byzantine luxury without earning it. But if my Government says that I do not earn my money, I am not the kind of saucy fellow who will suggest that they do my job, and see if it feels like work. No, no! I am behind my Government one hundred per cent, and when it says my labour is idleness, I knock my head upon the floor and cry Selah!

The Canadian Government has somewhat moderated its attitude toward authors since this was written, but Haubergeon Hydra is unshaken in his opinion that writing is not work unless it takes the form of

• To the Rev. Simon Goaste, B.D. •

Dear Pastor:

Don't you think it is high time that the Americans had their own translation of the Bible? Recently I saw Cecil B. deMille's film of *Samson and Delilah*, and afterward I re-read the story as it is written in *Judges 13-16*; it was clear to me what deMille had gone through, trying to turn Samson and Delilah into good, respectable Americans.

Consider: in the Bible version Samson carelessly allowed twenty years to pass between his strangling of the lion and his adventure with Delilah. Such a lapse of time would have made him at least forty when the film ended—practically an old man by Hollywood reckoning. In a new translation this period of time could be tactfully left out. And it is recorded also that Samson had an adventure with a lady about whose virtue the Scriptures, in their coarse way, leave no doubt. In fact, it appears that Samson was not A Nice Clean American Boy but a rowdy old delinquent. This blot on his character could be glossed over in a new translation, as it was in the movie. And there is also the flat statement that Samson set fire to the tails of a lot of foxes; the S.P.C.A. would certainly not have tolerated that if it had been shown in the film.

What the U.S.A. needs is a translation of the Bible all its own. It is now the dominant Western power, and should avail itself of the traditional privilege of a dominant power to impose its religion, or its version of an existing religion, upon the rest of the world. There is much in the Bible that is undemocratic and un-American. Indeed,

---

a speech for the Minister or a feasibility study. The agonized solicitation of the imagination that is so familiar to poets and novelists is known to him and his kind only when they are looking for a place to impose a new tax. Perhaps for those who are not familiar with government phraseology it should be explained that a feasibility study is a document prepared at great cost and expenditure of time to enable a public or private body to do something they have decided to do anyhow, by showing that it is possible, which they knew to begin with. But it creates delay, and generates jobs, and is therefore dear to the business and bureaucratic heart.

I put it to you that the implication that the Supreme Being was not democratically elected to that position casts grave doubts upon the moral magnitude and spiritual significance of the Constitution. It is time to abandon the King James Version, with its seventeenth-century cast of thought and its strongly English slant, and to adopt something more in keeping with the Gospel according to Washington. /

Your expectant parishioner,
Samuel Marchbanks.

• To Samuel Marchbanks, Esquire •

Dear Sam:

The other day I was looking at the Modern Library edition of Boswell's *Life of Dr. Samuel Johnson,* and in the Preface it was said that the inclusion of that book in that particular library of reprints awarded it "an accolade of modernity."

What a base passion our age has for pretending that whatever is good is necessarily "modern." What a depraved appetite we have for mere contemporaneity! How old Samuel Johnson would have snorted at the idea that a classic — particularly a classic about himself — was in some way ennobled by being declared the contemporary of the Wettums Doll, sliced, wrapped bread, and the singing telegram! This is an age without humility.

Your aggrieved
Amyas Pilgarlic.

• To Mervyn Noseigh, M.A. •

Dear Mr. Noseigh:

I am enchanted by the thought that you wish to do a full-scale Ph.D. thesis on my work. Of course I recognize your name imme-

---

/ *Several versions of Holy Writ are now available in mail-order cat-*
alogue prose, suitable for those who do not know what a shepherd

diately as that of the writer of essays already famous in the very littlest magazines:

Oh Marmee, What Big Teeth You Have:A Study of the pre-Oedipal mother in the works of Louisa May Alcott— (Peewee Review: Vol. 1, pp. 23-47*)*

Withering Depths: A Study of womb-frustration in Emily Bronte — (Wee Wisdom: Vol. 1, pp. 22-46*)*

Codnipped: A Study of impotence-fantasy in the adventure novels of Robert Louis Stevenson— (Microscopic Quarterly: Vol. 1, pp. 24-48*)*

These splendid studies are daily reading in the Marchbanks household. I cannot wait to see what you will make of me.

Tremulously yours,
Samuel Marchbanks.

• TO HAUBERGEON HYDRA, ESQUIRE •

Dear Mr. Hydra:

Enclosed find a cheque for $2.16; this, added to the $11.26 already deducted from my salary in weekly portions by my employers, completes the full sum of $13.42, the total of my Income Tax for the past year. It is also, if you care, almost an exact quarter of my yearly earnings, and I hope that you, as Deputy Confiscator-general, will take the utmost care of it.

Are you aware, sir, that when Captain Cook went to Australia in 1770 one of his men pointed to a kangaroo, and said, "What is it?" A native, standing by, said, "Kan g'aroo," meaning "I don't understand you." But the sailor thought that it was the name of the beast, and it has stuck to this day.

Now a similar error occurred when Jacques Cartier first set foot on the soil of our country. "What do you call this place?" he cried

---

is, or even what a sheep is, and who would change their butcher if he attempted to sell them veal from a fatted calf. When religion abandons poetic utterance it cuts its own throat.

to a native. "Canada," cried the Indian in return, and Cartier took it for the country's name. But the Indian—one of the Crokinole tribe—actually said in the remarkably economical language of his people, "Take my advice, gentlemen, and go back where you came from; the taxes here are well-nigh insupportable." That is what Canada really means, but the time for turning back has passed.

And so, Mr. Hydra, as you press my $13.42 into the hand of a career diplomat who is going to fly round the world in order to see whether it is round or merely egg-shaped, or as you send it to a Western wheat-grower who needs it to enable him to go to California for the winter, remember how hard I had to work to earn it.

Yours maliciously and grudgingly,
Marchbanks the Tax-Serf.

• MONOTONY OF DIET •

*T*HIS EVENING to the movies and saw *Fabiola*, an Italian film about the goings-on of Christians under the Caesars—in this case the Emperor Constantine. It concluded with a grand mass martyrdom in which, at a rough guess, eight or ten thousand head of Christians were fed to a total count of six lions. Afterward I consulted Gibbon's *Decline and Fall of the Roman Empire*, in which he says he can find no record of more than ten Christians being turned off at a time, so I dismissed *Fabiolà* as what Gibbon himself calls "holy romance." But the statistics and dietetics of the film still bother me, for even the most anti-clerical lion must weary of an unrelieved diet of Christians, consumed under circumstances of hustle and bustle. *

• PRIMEVAL FILM •

*T*O THE MOVIES, to see Charlie Chaplin and Marie Dressler in *Tilly's Punctured Romance*, which they made in 1913. In my younger days I was an ardent follower of Charlie,

---

How many modern Christians would face even a middle-sized dog in defence of their faith?

but as I watched this relic from the Old Red Sandstone Period of the cinematic art, I realized that time had bathed the humour of another day in a golden but untruthful light. It was the most restless film I have seen in years. Nobody stood up if he could possibly fall down. Nobody fell down without at once leaping to his feet in order to fall down again. Nobody entered a door without slapping somebody else in the face with it. Food was never eaten, it existed only to be thrown. Liquid was not taken into the mouth in order to be swallowed, but only that it might be squirted into somebody else's face. The usual method of attracting a lady's attention was to kick her; she invariably responded with a blow. The life of man in the comedies of the silent films was solitary, poor, nasty, brutish and short. And viewed from this distance it does not appear to have been especially funny, at that.

• To Mrs. Kedijah Scissorbill •

Respected but Unloved Madam:

Walking along the street today I passed an organ-grinder; I gave him ten cents. I write to you of this because you are a dominating figure in many charities, and I often receive unpleasantly mimeographed, badly worded letters signed with a facsimile of your niggling signature, asking me for money. These letters always stress the deserving nature of the cause, and the care with which the money is administered by a staff of competent, well-paid officials. I usually respond to your letters with a donation, for your causes are genuinely good, and I am sure that you use the money wisely. Nevertheless, my heart does not go with them. My heart was with the organ-grinder's ten cents, even though he was unable to give me a slip entitling me to deduct my gift from taxable income.

Charity is infinitely better conducted nowadays than it was a century ago. It is thorough, economical, informed—everything but charitable. It does incalculable good to the receivers; it does nothing whatever to the givers—the answerers of form letters who never see the objects of their benevolence. For there is no merit in giving money, if one has it: the merit is in the charitable impulse and the cleansing of the spirit which compassion brings.

Modern charity is wonderful for the receivers, but it is useless to the givers. And I remind you that they also have souls to save. Charity is something greater than organized pillaging of the haves on behalf of the have-nots.

Yours with qualified approval,
Samuel Marchbanks.

• To Samuel Marchbanks, Esquire •

Honoured Sir:

Unexpected tidings, Mr. Marchbanks, sir. Your case against Richard Dandiprat will not come before the Autumn Assizes as we had planned. This is the result of a legal complication of a type incomprehensible to the lay mind, but I will try to explain it.

The papers in the case went, as usual, to Mr. Mouseman, Senior, for his consideration before they were taken to the court house. Knowing that the case would be tried before Mr. Justice Gripple —an old law-school companion of Mr. Mouseman's—he made a pencilled notation on the document giving notice of the case, which said: "Don't let this come up any day when Old Gripple has lost heavily at bridge the night before. You know that he really needs a murder or a rape case on such days as a relief for his spleen." This was intended as a private direction to the sheriff, but some foolish clerk transcribed it on a document which reached Mr. Justice Gripple himself. He said several things which convinced our firm that it would be better to ask for a delay, and bring the case up again in the Spring, when we are confident that Mr. Justice Gripple will be in another part of the Province.

Oh, the law, the law! What a fascinating study it is, Mr. Marchbanks. You laymen cannot comprehend the subtle psychological elements which may sway the judgement of the courts! But patience —patience must be the watchword of the successful litigant.

Yours with infinite patience,
Mordecai Mouseman,
(for Mouseman, Mouseman and Forcemeat).

• TO MERVYN NOSEIGH, M.A. •

Dear Mr. Noseigh:

I am overjoyed by the news that you have really decided to do a Ph.D. thesis on my work, and am especially tickled by your title — *Skunk's Misery to Toronto: a study of spiritual degeneration in the work of Samuel Marchbanks*. The questions you ask fill me with delightful new importance. Number 7 (a) for example: "What were the first books you remember reading and what influence do you consider that they have had on your later style and symbological system?"

The first books I remember reading were called *Mother Hubbard's House Party*, and *Chuck and Cooney Caught in the Corn*; the first of these was about a Christmas party assembled by Mother Hubbard (a kind of Magna Mater or Demeter-figure, as I now realize) at which Jack and Jill, Mary Mary Quite Contrary, Tom Tom the Piper's Son, Georgy Porgy, Little Jack Horner and Little BoPeep acted out, in a high mimesis, various pseudo-Arcadian romances, culminating in a mass bedding at the end of the day. Although the writer had badly botched this conclusion, I assume that the Primal Scene was enacted by all these characters in turn, in every conceivable combination, under the obscene prompting of Mother Hubbard, who had assumed a Hecate-identity with the coming of darkness. I now realize that the book was a pseudonymous work by Frank Harris. *∮*

As for Chuck and Cooney, they appeared to be a woodchuck and a raccoon who were surprised by a farmer in his corncrib, and escaped by a narrow margin, but I am aware that it was a thinly-disguised fable of race-hatred, because Cooney was the stupid one and got into all the serious trouble.

All my subsequent work has drawn heavily on these sources, accounting for the ugly undertone on which you comment so

---

∮ Frank Harris (1856-1931) was a greatly gifted but not wholly trustworthy writer and editor whose chief work, My Life and Loves *(1925) remains a genuine eye-popper even in these days of demanding pornography.*

frankly. Please tell me more. There is nothing that flatters an author so much as having his work explained to him by a graduate student who brings a modern, critically-trained intellect to bear upon it. I can hardly wait for the next instalment.

Eagerly yours,
Samuel Marchbanks.

• FOG-DENSITY •

*P*ICKED UP A magazine this afternoon and read an article by a man who had appointed himself an expert upon what he called the "fog-density" of authors — meaning the difficulty which they presented to the average reader. He did not reveal all his secrets, but one way in which he measures this quality is to count the number of three-syllable words in every hundred words of a writer's prose. If they are frequent, fog-density is high. I suppose I present a considerable fog-density to some of my readers, but I don't care; who wants to be understood by everybody? I like long and unusual words, and anybody who does not share my taste is not compelled to read me. Policemen and politicians are under some obligation to make themselves comprehensible to the intellectually stunted, but not I. Let my prose be tenebrous and rebarbative; let my pennyworth of thought be muffled in gorgeous habiliments; lovers of Basic English will look to me in vain.

• LET US BE PATIENT •

*T*HE FAILURE OF yet another Canadian play on Broadway was attributed to many things, but I think it was owing to the simple fact that nobody is interested in Canadians except, very occasionally, other Canadians. Nations enjoy spells of popularity in the theatre and elsewhere; they become fashionable for no reason that I can discover. For centuries, for instance, nobody was interested in Scotsmen; they were regarded simply as hairy fellows who spoke faulty English. But during the nineteenth century plays about Scots, books about them, jokes about them and indeed everything about them sprang into a new popularity. We are beginning to tire of them now, but Irishmen, Armenians, and Scandinavians have become objects of popular interest. As yet the world does not think that Canadians are interesting; we stand where the Scotch stood before the Big Bagpipe Boom of the Victorian Era, and the period of 1900-1920, when Sir James Barrie persuaded the world that, appearances to the contrary, all Scots were delightful fellows with the souls of little children. Canada's day will come, no doubt, but we may have to wait a few centuries for it. ✒

• SABBATH MUSINGS •

*S*AT BY MY WINDOW, and as the church bells rang and people hastened past my door with their prayerbooks and hymnals in their hands, I pondered upon the secrets of the human heart. Do people go to church in Chalk River, I wondered, and in Los Alamos? And if they do so, do they try to square it with the Almighty that they are engaged in making the most devilish engines of destruction that the world has ever known? We are

---

It may be that Canada's day has come already, for during the 1984 visit of Her Majesty the Queen to this country the extreme dullness of its people was a matter of frequent comment in the British press, and Her Majesty was elaborately pitied by journalists (who normally seek to expose her to ridicule) for having to mix with such a pack of Airedales. We were said to be even duller than the Swiss, without the compensating factors of being very rich and self-preservative. We would be wise to accept this humbly. After all, are we to dispute the judgement of a nation that boasts the pulsing night-life of Tunbridge Wells or the fine-honed intellectual cut-and-thrust of a cocktail party in Peebles? No, let us develop our dullness so that when Hamlet's father's Ghost speaks of the dullness of the fat weed that rots itself in ease on Lethe wharf, the thoughts of audiences everywhere fly to Canada and whispers are heard: "Compared with a Canadian that fat weed looks like a veritable Bob Hope!" To be world's champion at anything, even dullness, is a form of distinction. Our real character —witty, ebullient, laughter-loving—doesn't matter: it's the publicity that counts.

assured, of course, that atomic power will do great things for the world at peace, but we never hear anything specific except what it will do for the world at war. Do the wives of atomic scientists worry about hats and social prestige? Did the wife of Dr. Faustus fret about what to do with the leftovers of yesterday's dinner while the Doctor was in his study chatting with the Devil? The answer to all these questions, I have no doubt, is Yes.

• CANADIAN SHIBBOLETH •

*W*AS AT A PARTY where a merry fellow — a Ph.D. and much respected in academic circles — was tormenting an Australian lady about the accent he believed to be characteristic of her native land. "I can always tell an Aussie by the way they say 'stewed fruit'," he declared, and then went on saying "stewed fruit" very comically, as well as he could through his laughter. "Please say 'wash and curl the hair of the squirrel'," said the Australian lady, and the savant obligingly said, "Worsh 'n currl the haira the squrrl." "That is how I always know a Canadian," said she, and he was not pleased. But there is something about a Canadian which compels him, however much education and sophistication he may have attained in other realms, to preserve intact the accent in which his barefoot old granny used to curse the timber wolves that raged around her cabin. It is one of the last areas in which illiteracy is equated with integrity.

• COMMUNIQUÉ •
(dropped down my chimney)

To Big Chief Marchbanks:
How, Marchbanks!

Meet fellow on park bench yesterday. Bum, Marchbanks. He awful fat. I got to get rid of this fat, he say. Why, I say. Fat not healthy, he say. All doctors say fat make you die young. First I got to get money to eat, he say, then I got to go on diet. You got fat head, I say. Look at bear. Bear awful fat. Bear healthy, too. Bear healthier than any doctor. Skinny doctor meet fat bear, bear win every time.

You poor ignorant Indian, he say. You know nothing about modern science. I know bears, I say.

Not in jail yet, Marchbanks. Winter come soon. How can I get in jail?

How again,
Osceola Thunderbelly,
Chief of the Crokinoles.

• CHURCH ECONOMICS •

*A*TTENDED AN ENTERTAINMENT in a church hall this evening, and during the intervals some little girls sold fudge in aid of their Sunday School. They handed over a large sack of first-class fudge in return for ten cents, and this struck me as typical church economics, for there was at least twenty cents' worth of delicious fattening sweetmeat in each bag. If these little girls had business instincts, they would reckon their overhead, time, cartage to the church, and materials, and would then sell the fudge at thirty-five cents a bag; but as no one could then afford to eat it, they would lobby for a government subsidy, which would pay them twenty cents on each bag of fudge, allowing them to sell for fifteen cents. As the fudge would still sell very well at that price, there would soon be a glutted market, and they would get the government to buy their surplus fudge at the full retail price, and sell it to Europe for ten cents a bag. However, I did not explain these things to them, but contented myself with buying two bags of bargain fudge, and stealing another, which somebody, in the seat in front of mine, left behind them at the end of the entertainment.

• TO AMYAS PILGARLIC, ESQUIRE •

Dear Pil:

It is a bit thick, your rebuke to me for believing in ghosts, calling them "superstitions unbecoming a scientific age." If there is one lesson science impresses on us all, it is surely that *nothing* is incredible.

Haven't you heard about "neutrinos"? Apparently there are such things—little doodads of which *sixty billion* penetrate each square inch of our bodies *every second* and go on their way having done no harm whatever. But nobody has so far suggested that the neutrinos are, in their way, unaware of us. I put it to you that to a neutrino you and I probably seem like ghosts. And I put it to you also that we may, in our turn, be as neutrinos to other beings, whizzing in and about them without much awareness, but with an occasional intuition that things are not quite as simple as even our five wits lead us to suppose.

Multiply my bulk in square inches by sixty billion, and reflect that it is from amid that assemblage of unknown but active creatures that I now adjure you to bethink yourself, and stop talking nonsense. We are all much more ghostly than we know.

Your eerie comrade,
Samuel Marchbanks.

• TECHNICOLOR FLAUBERT •

*P*ICKED UP Gustave Flaubert's *Salammbo*, a book which I read as a schoolboy and looked upon with wry smiles even then, as it appears to me to be written in Technicolor; however, as I read it in translation I would be wise to keep quiet, for any Frenchman can shout me down. But the tone of the book is exhausting; nobody ever says "Giddap" to a horse; they always "urge it forward with a hoarse cry." Nobody "looks" at a woman; he "devours her with his eyes." I prefer a quieter life. . . . *Salammbo* suggests that medical practice in ancient Carthage was on an equally irrational footing with war and the pursuit of love. One remedy which is described is "the blood of a black dog slaughtered by barren women on a winter's night among the ruins of a tomb"; a druggist who had filled a few prescriptions like that in the course of a day might well think of going into some other business. . . . However, *Salammbo* is enthralling, in its strange way, and I read it for half an hour after lunch before I realized that I had work to do, and urged myself toward my desk with a hoarse cry, devouring several women with my eyes as I trudged through the snow. One of them was eyeing a black dog reflectively, and I concluded that she was at least on the Pill.

• To Haubergeon Hydra, Esquire •

Dear Mr. Hydra:

As a citizen and taxpayer of this country I write to you, as Deputy Guarantor of Tourist Attractions, to complain about our prairies: they are not as flat as I was led to believe. People have assured me for years that the prairie is as flat as a billiard table. This, sir, is a lie put out to attract tourists. It is not nearly so flat as that.

There is much talk of conservation these days, but very little action. Let us not lose our prairies. Tear down the farm-houses at once: nobody wants them: the farmers are all in California spending their wheat subsidy. And then put a fleet of steam rollers on the prairies and get those unsightly humps out of them. Keep at it until they are, as advertised, flat as a billiard table.

Your indignant taxpayer,
S. Marchbanks.

• To Amyas Pilgarlic, Esquire •

Dear Pil:

Since last I wrote to you I have gone through what is widely believed to be one of the most moving spiritual experiences a Canadian can sustain — a jaunt through the Rocky Mountains. I enjoyed it, but spiritually I am exactly where I was before. I have been pleased, diverted and surprised, but I am not one of those who finds a sight of the Rockies an equivalent for getting religion at a revival meeting.

To make a shameful confession, the Rockies put me in mind of nothing so much as as the first act of *Rose Marie*, a musical comedy of my younger days and the favourite theatre entertainment of his late Majesty, King George V. ∬ At any moment I expected a lovely

---

∬ Rose Marie *was a charming and tuneful operetta by Rudolf Friml and Herbert Stothart, first produced in New York in 1924. It exploited to the uttermost whatever was picturesque in Canada—Rockies,*

French-Canadian girl to leap on the observation car, saying, "You make ze marriage wiz me, no?" Or an Indian girl, more lithe and beautiful than any Indian girl has ever been, to begin a totem dance on the track. The scenery was right: only the actors were missing.

Upon arrival in Vancouver, the first thing to meet my eye was a notice, signed by the Chief of Police, warning me against confidence tricksters. It told me in detail how I might expect them to work. I would be approached, first of all, by someone who would try to make friends: this would be "The Steerer" who would eventually steer me to "The Spieler," who would sell me Stanley Park or the harbour at a bargain price. Not long after I had read this I was approached by a crafty-looking woman carrying a handful of pasteboards. "Juwanna buy four chances on the Legion car?" she cried, blocking my way. "Madam, you are wasting your time," said I; "I know you for what you are — a Steerer." She shrank away, muttering unpleasantly. Never let it be said that Marchbanks failed to heed a warning.

After lunch I wandered among the Chinese shops, and found one which sold a scent called "Girl Brand Florida Water." There is a simplicity about that name which enchants me. In the same shop I saw the only piece of Chinese nude art that has ever come my way; the Chinese are believed not to care for representations of the nude: but this was plainly the result of Western influence; it was a Chinese girl, lightly draped, holding aloft a bunch of paper flowers. Her legs were short, her body long, and she seemed more amply endowed for sitting than Western standards of beauty per-

---

Mounties, girls with piquant French-Canadian accents, lithe Indian girls who could do the Totem Tom Tom dance to a pitch of delirious perfection, and an incorruptible young man with a big chin who won the heroine after fearful vicissitudes of fortune. For Canadian audiences it had only one grave fault. The final scene was laid on Parliament Hill, and in the background the Houses of Parliament were shown in the dusk, with lights twinkling in their windows; Canadians always greeted this scene with boos and hisses, for they knew that under every one of those lights Haubergeon Hydra, in one of his innumerable guises, was plotting a new tax.

mit. It was, I suppose, the kind of thing one finds in Chinese bachelor apartments, just as Occidental bachelors enrich their rooms with ash-trays held aloft by naked beauties in chrome, and drink beer from glasses into which libidinous pictures have been etched. East is East, and West is West, but bachelors are wistful rascals the world over.

Yours,
Sam.

• WHERE AM I? •

*W*AS DRIVING THROUGH the countryside today with some people who insisted upon frequent recourse to a road-map in order to discover, as they put it, "Just where they were." Reflected that for my part I generally have a pretty shrewd idea of just where I am; I am enclosed in the somewhat vulnerable fortress which is my body, and from that uneasy stronghold I make such sorties as I deem advisable into the realm about me. These people seemed to think that whizzing through space in a car really altered the universe for them, but they were wrong; each one remained right in the centre of his private universe, which is the only field of knowledge of which he has any direct experience.

• COMMUNIQUÉ •
(Shot through my window attached to an arrow)

To Big Chief Marchbanks:
How Marchbanks!

Good news, Marchbanks, I in jail now. Last week I try awful hard to get in jail. I throw brick at cop. He just wag finger and laugh. I call insult at mayor. He just lift hat. Getting near election time, Marchbanks. I write dirty word on City Hall. City Clerk come out and write "Ditto," under it. No hope, Marchbanks. Then one day cop look at me very queer. You pay your poll tax, he ask. No, I say, I never own no pole. Aha, he say, you got to pay poll tax. I never have no totem pole, I say. Sell 'um to tourist twenty year ago. Come along, he say, and we go to court. They find I owe

$3,000 back poll tax. Put me in jail. Ha ha. That great tax, March-banks. Friendly tax to poor Indian. All set for winter now. You got money? I not need money.

How again,
Osceola Thunderbelly,
Chief of the Crokinoles.

• TO HAUBERGEON HYDRA, ESQUIRE •

Dear Mr. Hydra:

I have been asked by several influential members of the Canadian Brotherhood of Snow Shovellers and Ploughmen to put their case to you as Pro. Tem. Sub-Re-Router of Labour, in order that you may draw it to the attention of the appropriate Minister. Here is our case in a nutshell:
(a) Some winters it snows a lot and we make money.
(b) Other winters it doesn't snow much and we don't make any money.
(c) We want a floor under snow. That is, in winter when the crop of snow is poor, we want the Government either to distribute false snow — salt, flour, Western wheat or something of that sort — so that we can shovel it and make money, OR —
(d) We want the Government to pay us for shovelling snow that isn't there, so we can make money.
You will see at once that this is in the latest economic trend and a good idea. See what you can do for us, like a good fellow, and some Christmas Santa may have something in his sack for a good Civil Servant.

Love and kisses from all us snowmen,
Samuel Marchbanks.

• TO SAMUEL MARCHBANKS, ESQUIRE •

My Dear Nephew:

Earlier this Summer your Uncle Gomeril and I observed our seventy-fifth wedding anniversary. You did not send a greeting card, for which abstention I thank you; we received several cards, all of a nauseating degree of sentimentality, bearing no conceivable relationship to the sort of domesticity your Uncle and I have waged during the past three-quarters of a century. You might, however, have sent a few flowers. Several people sent bouquets of what I learned as a girl to call "wind-flowers," but what people now call "everlastings." Whether this was intended as a delicate reference to the unusual durability of our match, or whether it was an ironical allusion to the hardy good health which we both enjoy I cannot determine.

We celebrated the occasion by visiting Niagara Falls for a few days, to rest and observe the great Natural Wonder. The Chamber of Commerce there offers a certificate of congratulation to all honeymoon couples, upon which appears a wish that their union may be as beautiful and enduring as the Falls itself. It occurred to me that the Falls is as much distinguished for its violence and its extreme dampness as for beauty and endurance, but as your Uncle and I completed our honeymoon and all that goes with it long ago this was a matter of merely academic concern to us.

We were, however, much affronted by the number of honeymooners who infested the place, wandering about hand in hand, wet smiles and goggling eyes proclaiming their condition for all the world to see. When your Uncle and I were married and went to the Shetlands on our wedding trip, we took great pains to look like a married couple of several years standing.

Perhaps we were foolish so to do, but I think that our reticence was preferable to the mawkish displays of unfledged connubiality which we observed at N.F.

We visited, among other places, a restaurant maintained by the Provincial Government, at which a bottle of wine cost almost twice as much as it does in a liquor store, also maintained by the Provincial Government. Your Uncle commented upon this in his accustomed ringing tones, but of what avail is it to protest against official extortion? Complaining about a government is, as Holy Writ tersely phrases it, kicking against the pricks.

Your affectionate aunt-by-marriage,
Bathsheba Marchbanks.

· To Genghis Marchbanks, Esquire ·

Dear Cousin Genghis:

I am terribly sorry that I was unable to be present at the Gala Opening of your new pawnshop. I understand that it was a wonderful affair, and distinguished by your own special brand of hospitality. Water ran like water, I am told, and guests who had brought their own sandwiches were permitted to eat them on the premises.

Let me deal with your last letter, before bringing up anything else. No, I do not want any binoculars at specially reduced prices, nor am I in the market for the telescope which you offer cheap. This is not for lack of goodwill. I admire telescopes, and would love to clap one to my eye, sailor-fashion, while taking a walk in the country, or even when attending the ballet; all a telescope does for me is to flatten my eyewinkers uncomfortably.

But I am in the market for a good concertina. Concertinas run in the Marchbanks family. Uncle Fortunatus plays one. I play one. And the other day I discovered our little niece Imoinda extracting the usual cow-stuck-in-a-swamp noises from a concertina which I discarded some years ago when I bought my super-Wheatstone. Can you find a nice instrument for Imoinda which some needy concertinist has hocked?

Your affectionate cousin,
Sam.

· To Miss Nancy Frisgig ·

Charming Nancy:

What is the greatest single beautifier available to womanhood? Is it a cream, or a top-dressing for the face, or a perfume which steals away the critical judgement of the beholder? No, poppet, it is shoes that fit.

How did I find this out? Well, yesterday I sat in a restaurant, munching a bowl of breakfast food — it was evening, but I practically live on breakfast food — when in came a young man with, obviously his Best Girl. She was stylishly dressed; her hair was nicely arranged, and she wore a few gew-gaws which indicated that she came from a home of some wealth and possibly even of cultivation. But her face was the mask of a Gorgon.

They sat down near me, and immediately, under the table, I saw her kick off her shoes. And at once her face melted into that expression—half Madonna, half Aphrodite—which reduces the male to a jelly. Beauty suffused her as though the moon had sailed from behind a cloud. She ordered a steak at $6.50, and a peck of lobster and a Baked Alaska to go with it, and her escort did not even notice. ∮ It was worth it, he seemed to think, to be the companion of that girl.

Now, Nancy, if that girl means to make the most of her considerable gifts, she must either go barefoot, or get the shoes she needs. And so I say to all her sex.

Yours with warmest admiration
down to the ankles,
Sam.

• To Samuel Marchbanks, Esquire •

Dear Cousin:

I have your letter, and as someone left half a sheet of paper in the pawnshop yesterday when they were pledging their diamonds, I take my pen in hand at once to reply. You should not speak so lightly of the concertina, Cousin. Are you not aware that there is quite a little body of music composed especially for it? Tchaikovsky arranged his second orchestral suite so that it might be played on four concertinas. Molique wrote a concerto for the concertina, as well as a sonata for concertina and piano. Regondi, too, wrote a

---

∮ These prices may provoke a smile. But in their day, when incomes
were lower, they were considered steep. Figures change: facts of life do not. The hopeful stoking of women by beglamoured men has always cost a lot of money. Older readers may be reminded of the brusque estimate of sexual enjoyment given by an eighteenth-century nobleman: "The pleasure is fleeting, the posture ridiculous, and the expense damnable!"

concerto for the instrument. Did you not know that the late Arthur Balfour was a most accomplished player, and a concertina was the solace of his few idle hours during his time in Parliament? I shall get one for little Imoinda, of course, but I entreat you to see that the child realizes that she handles a sensitive instrument, and not a toy.

Your reproachful kinsman,
Genghis Marchbanks.

• TO AMYAS PILGARLIC, ESQUIRE •

Dear Pil:

I was reading an interesting book the other day about the worship of the Bull-god, Minos, in early Crete. It appears that the High Priest had a golden head, like that of a bull, which he wore over

---

The words of Genghis Marchbanks should be heeded by the musical world; the concertina, invented in 1829 by Sir Charles Wheatstone, has been superseded by the piano-accordion, to which the concertina bears the same relationship as does the harpsichord to the piano. Works for concertina have been written by such composers as Piotr Ilyich Tchaikovsky (1840-93), a Russian civil servant with a turn for composition, by the violinist Wilhelm Bernard Molique (1802-69), and by Giulio Regondi (1822-72) of whom Grove's Dictionary of Music and Musicians *records that "the effect which he got out of so unpromising an instrument astonished the German critics." Quite apart from the musical pleasure provided by the concertina, there is the fun of seeing the thing squirm in the hands of the player. It was also played with taste and feeling by Arthur James Balfour (1848-1930) the statesman and philosopher who was Prime Minister of Britain 1902-06. British Prime Ministers in this century have often been musically gifted. David Lloyd George (1863-1945) sang splendidly, especially Welsh hymns; Richard George Edward Heath (1916) is a gifted orchestral and choral conductor, and your Editor has sung under his baton as a member of the Balliol College Choral Society, an experience to be cherished though not particularly for musical reasons. Do I digress? Yes, I do. Shut up.*

his own head when greeting visitors. He then removed it, and carried on conversation face to face. When he thought that the interview had gone on long enough or that he wanted his visitor to go, he put the bull's head back on again, in sign that the talk was over.

Don't you think that something of this kind could be worked out for people like myself, who never know how to bring an interview to a close? I don't suppose a gold bull's head would really do. It might seem a little eccentric and ostentatious. But a simple brass head, made in the shape of my own face, but stern and impassive, might be just the thing. Or, on second thoughts, better make it bronze. Brass has such a nasty smell, as anyone can learn by sniffing the bell of an old bugle.

There are for sale in joke shops rubber masks, which give one the appearance of a gorilla. I think I shall get one and try it out. If it works I shall get a bronze job done. Do you know of any good, cheap foundry which would undertake such a commission? ✒

Yours faithfully,
Sam.

• TO MERVYN NOSEIGH, M.A. •

Dear Mr. Noseigh:

When you put the question to me so baldly—"What led you to become a writer?"—I am momentarily nonplussed. On what level do you expect me to answer? The objective? If so, I became a writer because it looked like easy money. But that won't work well in your Ph.D. thesis, so let us try the subjective approach.

On this level, I became a writer because I suffered the early conditioning of the Unconscious that makes writers. That is to say, my Oedipus Complex was further complicated by the *Warmefläsche-reaktion.*

✒ There are now available rubber masks of U.S. Presidents, astonishingly lifelike, and Marchbanks always wears one on Hallowe'en; he likes to test how many of his fellow-Canadians fall down and grovel when confronted thus.

You know how this works. Think of the Infantile World as a Huge Bed; on one side lies Mum, on the other side lies Dad, and in the middle is Baby Bunting. The normal thing, of course, is for B.B. to work out his Oedipus Complex; he wants to kill Dad and mate with Mum — thereby fitting himself for some normal occupation like the Civil Service. But sometimes B.B., *for reasons still unknown to science*, turns from Mum and snuggles up to Dad who quite understandably shoves B.B. down to the bottom of the bed and warms his feet on him as if he were a hot-water bottle (or *Warmefläsche*). Thus, in the very dawn of his existence, B.B. acquires that down-trodden cast of mind that marks the writer.

Very often Dad kicks B.B. right out of bed onto the cold linoleum, bringing about that sense of Utter Rejection which turns B.B. into a critic.

I can hardly wait to read your thesis.

Reverently,
Samuel Marchbanks (your topic*).*

• THE UNIVERSAL FRIEND •

AS I STOOD on Yonge Street this afternoon, a man approached me with a happy smile. He stopped in front of me, rocked on his heels, puffed out a cloud of boozy breath and said, "Well, well, well!" As I am peculiarly attractive to persons in his condition, I feigned ignorance of his presence, but he came nearer, and peeped searchingly into my eyes. "Ain't goin' to speak t'an ole pal?" he said, coyly. "How do you do," I said, stiffly. "Cheest," said he, "I wouldna thought ole Jock would gimme the brushoff." "You are mistaken, my good fellow," said I. "Gwan," said he; "you're old Jock McGladdeny." "No," said I, firmly. He looked at me, and a gummy tear crept sluggishly down one cheek. "Ole Jock," said he, "an' he won't speak t'an ole pal." He took his cigar out of his mouth and prodded me with the wet end of it. "God love yuh, anyway, Jock," he said, and stumbled on, and as he receded I heard him murmur, "Old Jock a Judas; Cheest!". . . I wonder why I am so often mistaken for somebody else, especially by drunks? Do my features in some mysterious way suggest a Universal Friend — a man whom everybody, at some time or other, has known? This is a cross I bear with very ill grace.

• DIET SADISM •

I HAVE BEEN READING a lot of books about dieting, for my physician has spoken prayerfully to me on this subject. What annoys me about diet books is that they are written either by people who are funny, or people who are angry. The funny ones think it is the most hilarious thing in the world to be compelled to eat less than one wants, of foods that one would not ordinarily choose; they write as though a diet were a huge joke. The angry ones are worse: they threaten the dieter with quick and unpleasant death if he doesn't lose his excess weight, and they speak scornfully of the kind of life (cocktails and two-helpings-of-everything) which makes diets necessary. Both kinds of writers are crypto-Calvinists who have an addiction to gelatin in food; everything they recommend seems to contain either lettuce or gelatin. Now it so happens that an uncle of mine, Bellerophon Marchbanks, has devoted his life to the manufacture of gelatin and also of glue, and I cannot separate the two in my mind. Gelatin in moderation I accept; unlimited gelatin turns me cold and shaky to begin, and then produces the effect anyone could foresee as proceeding from a diet of glue — anyone but a doctor, that's to say.

• THE MEASURED STEP •

A FEW WEEKS AGO I bought myself a toy — a pedometer, which measures how far I walk when I am wearing it. Apparently I don't walk very much. I have always assumed that in the course of any ordinary day's work I walked four or five miles, but according to the pedometer an eighth of a mile is nearer the correct figure. The only time the pedometer gets much of a workout is when I am cutting my lawn, and then the miles tick up at a surprising rate. The instrument is worn on the right leg, and it has a psychological effect; it makes me stamp with that leg to make sure that the dial registers properly, and I am developing a gait like the Giant Blunderbore, or possibly Peg-Leg Pete the Pirate. The pedometer cheats, too; when I am riding in a car it registers a step whenever the car goes over a bump; on a long journey I can cover as much as a quarter of a mile, according to the pedometer, although I have not exerted myself in the least. I have no desire to clock astonishing scores on this gadget; I merely want to know if I do much walking. I am disappointed by what it tells me, but at least I am now in a position to lure other people to boast of the walking they do in an ordinary day's work, so that I may contradict them, and gain face as a statistician.

• To Samuel Marchbanks, Esquire •

Dear Sir:

It comes to our ears from a professional source that you are bringing suit against your neighbour, Richard Dandiprat, whom you accuse of imprisoning a skunk (*Mephitis Canadensis*) in your motor car, with resultant damage to same.

We learn also that the success of your suit is jeopardized by your inability to bring forward a single witness who saw Dandiprat commit this misdemeanour.

May we offer our services? For a modest fee we can provide witnesses who will give your case all the corroboration which it needs, ensuring your success. We feel that three capable witnesses (two men and a woman) would amply meet your requirements, and we will provide these for five hundred dollars and expenses. You will agree that this is a ridiculously low sum, and it is only because we work on a very large scale that we are able to make this very special price. All correspondence strictly confidential.

Yours, etc.
False Witness, Inc.

Telegraphic Address:
Ananias

• To Mordecai Mouseman, Esquire •

Dear Mouseman:

I enclose a letter which I have received from a firm that seems to have just what we want. The trial draws near — at least I hope it does, for it is now almost a year since Dandiprat ruined my car — and I will not tolerate any fumbling. I want Dandiprat to get at least two years hard labour. We want witnesses; these people have them. Will you attend to the matter?

Yours,
Samuel Marchbanks.

• To Samuel Marchbanks, Esquire •

Dear Mr. Marchbanks:

Oh, Mr. Marchbanks, sir! Oh, unhappiest of our clients!! Oh, luckless litigant!!! How often have I not counselled you against taking any step without consulting your lawyer; how often has not our senior partner, Mr. Jabez Mouseman (now, alack, prone upon a bed of pain — shingles, I grieve to say) given you the same tried and true advice? Tell me — though I dread the answer, knowing your fiery and impetuous nature — have you given any money to False Witness, Inc.? For if you have, all is lost indeed!

Understand, my dear sir, that not only do you sully the whole fabric of British justice by suggesting that we employ these people; you gravely endanger your case, as well. The fabric of British justice has been sullied, and dry-cleaned, many times; like an Oriental rug, it shows only the very largest stains; but there is not a judge on the bench in this country who does not know every employee of False Witness, Inc., intimately. For years they have paraded in and out of the witness boxes of Canada dropping the wigs, false whiskers, wooden legs and other unconvincing paraphernalia with which they seek to disguise themselves, and their appearance is now a signal for derisive laughter in every court in the land.

False Witness, Inc. employs all the Canadian actors who are so bad that they cannot even get jobs with CBC-TV. Far better no witness than a False Witness.

I am shocked, sir, that you should think a firm such as ours would lend itself to underhand practice. We rely entirely upon the probity of the court, and the forensic brilliance of our barrister, Mr. Cicero Forcemeat. You will understand the unique distinction attaching to Mr. Forcemeat when I tell you that he is one of the half-dozen lawyers in the country who is not a Q.C.

And if we feel that the support of expert testimony is required, we know where to get it without resort to the broken-down dialect comedians who work for False Witness, Inc.

Yours chidingly,
Mordecai Mouseman,
(for Mouseman, Mouseman and Forcemeat).

• FRIGID BOON •

THE MODERN ENTHUSIASM for the deep-freeze interests me, but I am not in the forefront of the movement, for I have observed that quite a lot of frozen food has a taste of brown paper, and is not always completely unfrozen. I satisfied my appetite for snow and ice when I was a boy. But I feel that the real possibilities of the deep-freeze technique have not been explored. If it can halt decay and arrest all bodily processes, why can the machine not be used as a baby-tender? Consider: a weekend is being planned, and parents are wondering what they can do with the infant; aha! pop it in the deep-freeze, and thaw it out on Monday morning, unharmed and the better for a thorough rest. Junior is behaving badly at school; the family psychiatrist says that he is going through "a phase"; put him in the deep-freeze until the phase has run its course. An expectant mother, who adores the memory of Queen Victoria, is told that her offspring will be born about May 10th; she deep-freezes herself until midnight, May 23rd, and little Victoria Alexandrina makes her debut, (perhaps a little stiff and blue) on the great Queen's birthday. Deep-freezing may prove the boon of the age.

• Pangs Of Leisure •

*F*OR THE FIRST TIME in several weeks I found myself this afternoon without anything to do. Of late I have suffered from congestion of the calendar; every hour of every day has been painfully crammed with duties and obligations. This afternoon I was free — free as a bird. But like a bewildered prisoner suddenly ejected from his dungeon I did not know how to use my liberty. I tried the TV, but the reception was terrible. I composed myself for a nap in my chair, but every five minutes or so I would leap up, wide awake, shouting, "All right! Don't strike me! I'll do it at once," — a horrible reflection on my life for the past six weeks. I tried a few light household tasks, but they were like work, and I wanted to avoid work. I thought of going for a walk, but the outer world was an indecisive mess of hail, snow, rain and fog. I paced up and down, pretending that I was thinking, but soon tired of it. By four o'clock I was almost frantic with leisure; if I did not find some pleasant way of loafing soon, my afternoon would be gone. And sure enough, it did go, and the jaws of duty closed on me again. Oh, the pity of it!

• Communiqué •
(discovered in entrails of a wild duck, written on birchbark)

To Big Chief Marchbanks:
How Marchbanks!

This one hell country, Marchbanks. Look at weather. Every Fall people say to me how about Winter? And I say long Winter or short Winter if bears go to sleep or sit up till maybe Christmas. This year my best bear that I trust nearly twenty year go to sleep awful early. He sound asleep right after hunting season. So I say to everybody long hard Winter cause bear asleep. But no hard Winter come. So I go to bear nest and look inside. Bear sound asleep. What hell, I think. Then I see bottle in bear paw. Grab bottle. It say sleeping pills on outside, Marchbanks. Bear steal bottle from some big city hunter, busy fellow can't sleep without pills. Bear

eat every pill. Bear sleep like dead. I wish big city hunter stay out
of woods. They ruin woods and weather forecast business for good
Indian.

How again,
Osceola Thunderbelly,
Chief of the Crokinoles.

• COMMUNIQUÉ •
(scrawled in chalk on my front door)

To Big Chief Marchbanks:
How, Marchbanks!

In awful trouble, Marchbanks. Winter come soon. I got to get in
jail. Been out two week now. No jail, no winter home. Two day
ago I get drunk. Sick on cop. He mad. Ha, I think; jail for sure.
But no. He take pants to cleaner and make me work cutting wood
to pay for clean pants. Yesterday I throw brick at cop. Hit him
hard. He jump. Ha, I think; jail now. But he say thanks pal; ser-
geant coming and you just wake me up in time. This one hell
country, Marchbanks. Cops all too mean to put poor Indian in jail.

How again,
Osceola Thunderbelly,
Chief of the Crokinoles.

• REMOVAL OF COUSINS •

*L*ISTENED TO A FAMILY discussion among some people
who were trying to decide the relationship to themselves
of the children of a brother of their grandfather's second wife. It
was perfectly clear to me, but they made a sad hash of it. The
Welsh and the Scots are the only people who really understand
the fine points of relationship, and I think that the Welsh have a
slight edge on the Scots in this matter. Indeed, I have given some
thought to writing a book on the subject with a special Appendix

dealing with the Removal of Cousins. The number of people, apparently well-educated and intelligent, who cannot distinguish between a Second Cousin and a First Cousin Once Removed, is staggering and reflects unpleasantly on our educational system. What these poor softies do when they get into the flood-tide of genealogy, with Intermarriage of Cousins and Collateral Cousinship In The Second Generation, I dread to imagine.

• CRITICS CRITICIZED •

*I*ALWAYS READ newspaper criticisms of concerts I have attended, but often I wonder if the critic and I can have been at the same affair. It is not their discontent that puzzles me; tastes differ, and after all a critic's stock-in-trade is a finer sensibility than that of the vulgar herd. And I make allowances for the fact that going to concerts is work for a critic, and there are plenty of people who have lost all love for the work by which they get their bread. No, it is the way most of them write that stuns me. They attempt to deal with the performances of artists who have spent not less than ten years acquiring insight and a formidable technique, in a maimed and cretinous prose which could not possibly give anybody any impression except one of confusion and depleted vitality. They are poor grammarians, and their vocabularies are tawdry. It is hard enough to interpret one art in terms of another under the best of circumstances, but when the critic has not understood that writing also is an art, his criticism becomes embarrassing self-portraiture.

• RESTAURANT COWARDICE •

*W*HAT IS WRONG with me? I seem to be the sort of man whom waiters immediately put at a table near the kitchen, which smells of other people's food, or in a draught, or too near the orchestra, or someplace where nobody wants to sit. If anything is spilled, it is mine; if anything spilled is scraped up from the floor, and served with carpet-fluff in it, it is mine. Am I so broken a creature that I fear to make a row in a restaurant? Well, all the evidence points in that direction. I am even so base that I lack the courage to refuse when the waiter suggests that I eat something which I do not want. This evening, for instance, I was thus dragooned into eating a Greek sweetmeat called Baclava; it tasted like a Bible printed on India paper which had been thoroughly soaked in honey, and took just as long to eat. When I had chewed my way down to Revelation the waiter asked me if I had enjoyed it and I, spiritless wretch, managed to nod. /

• TO THE REV. SIMON GOASTE, B.D. •

Dear Rector:

I suppose you have observed, in the course of your professional duties, the sad decline of literary exuberance in the writing of epitaphs? The modern epitaph is hardly worthy of the name, when one compares it with the great epitaph-writing of the eighteenth century.

Because I do not wish to be slighted on my tombstone, I am sending to you herewith my own epitaph, in order that you may circumvent any of my descendants or executors who want to do the thing on the cheap after I am gone.

Normally a fearless, not to say aggressive, creature, Marchbanks has a dread of waiters which he explains thus: in the Good Old Days, waiters were professionals—elderly men with bad feet, misanthropic expressions, and dress suits of incalculable antiquity. Nowadays waiters are likely to be very young, and of both sexes; they are obstreperously cheerful, give advice unasked about the food and slap it down on the table with the words "There y'go!" whereas the waiters of old said "Monsieur est servi" or even "Gott sei dank, der Tisch ist gedeckt!" Modern waiters are great sloppers of wine. BUT—and this is the point—modern waiters will not be waiters long; they are simply filling in between jobs, or as a relief from a university career; they are judges' daughters, authors not yet discovered, actors of a talent to make Olivier blench. You never know where you will meet them again, so it is best to tip heavily and keep your mouth shut.

(The Full Armorial Bearings of the Marchbanks Family)

Beneath this stone
Lies all that was Mortal
Of one
Who, in this transitory Life
Seemed to sum up in himself all those
Virtues
Which we are taught to admire
but which, alas,
We rarely see in action.

Pause, Passer-By and Ponder:

This man, beside an ample fortune for
Those Left to Mourn Him
Leaves a sum in trust to provide
Every child in this Parish
With copies of his own works
Durably bound in waterproof material,
As well as a medal bearing the impress of his
Noble Countenance
on the front, and on its rear
These Words:
"For Memorial Purposes only:
Not Negotiable as Currency."

Drop a Tear and Pass On
Drawing Such Consolation As You Can
From the indisputable fact
that
We Shall Not Look Upon His Like Again.

There. I think that covers the ground pretty thoroughly, and
will gladden the heart of the stonemason, if not of my relatives.
Oh yes, and on the top of the stone, please, an effigy of my own
head, with the left eyelid drooping slightly, as though in salute to
the living.

Yours cheerily,
Samuel Marchbanks.

• To Samuel Marchbanks, Esquire •

Dear Neighbour:

Aw, gee, I never thought you would mind me playing the hi-fi with my windows open! Aw, heck, I never thought you would resent a little thing like that skunk getting into your car! Not that I admit I did it. My lawyers told me that I shouldn't. But I never thought you'd go to court about it. Gee, Marchbanks, you're a cranky guy! Gee, haven't you any spirit of give and take?

I'm just sick about the whole thing, and so is Lambie-Pie. She says you're the worst crab in the world, but we ought to try to be friends with you because we're neighbours, and after all, even you are human. She says we got to extend the Right Hand of Fellowship. Consider it extended. How about it, Marchbanks, old pal? By the way, I borrowed your lawn-mower last month when you were away. I accidentally ran it over a big bolt somebody dropped on my lawn. I'll bring it back just as soon as it is fixed. Or would you rather have it fixed to suit yourself?

Yours repentantly,
Dick Dandiprat.

• To Richard Dandiprat •

Unspeakable Dandiprat:

I take note that you have extended the Right Hand of Fellowship. I have examined it. Take it back and wash it.

My legal action against you continues according to plan. I shall also sue you for the damage to my lawn-mower.

You may inform Lambie-Pie (whom I take to be your consort) that I am not human. I sprang, full-grown, from a riven oak one midnight many years ago.

Yours in a very limited sense,
Samuel Marchbanks.

• To Samuel Marchbanks, Esquire •

Dear Marchbanks:

Will you lend me your Santa Claus costume? I want it for the annual party of the Rowanis Club, of which I am Grand Exalted Merry-maker this year. We are having a Christmas celebration, and I thought it would be an original idea if I dressed up as S.C. and gave everybody presents containing sneeze powder, white mice, dribble glasses and etc.

I hope you are not brooding about that little matter of the skunk? We have led the lawyers a fine dance, haven't we? Ha ha! Still, we are both men of the world, eh Marchbanks?

Will you send the S.C. suit to the cleaners right away, so that I can pick it up next week? I want to look well at the party, and those suits get pretty dirty when they are not taken care of.

Your neighbour,
Dick Dandiprat.

• To Mouseman, Mouseman and Forcemeat •

Dear Mr. Mouseman:

I am going out of my mind! That misbegotten ruffian Dandiprat has just written me a letter in which he virtually confesses that he put the skunk in my car!

Now Mouseman, what can you do to Dandiprat? Don't talk to me about the gallows; it is too good for him. Is there a thumb-screw anywhere that we can borrow? Or what about the Chinese water torture? Should I ask my laundry man if he will co-operate? Or what do you say to Mussolini's merry prank with a quart of castor oil? I warn you, Mouseman, if I do not have revenge I shall drown in my own gall! Get to work at once.

Yours furiously,
S. Marchbanks.

· EPIDERMIS ·

A MEDICAL ACQUAINTANCE mentioned idly that you can tell a good deal about the age of a human being by pinching the skin on the backs of the hands; according as it retains the shape of the pinch, the patient is advanced in decay. Spent much of the day pinching the skin on the backs of my hands, which snapped back into place very quickly at some points, and at others remained obstinately curled up. From this I conclude that my skin reflects the character of my opinions, some of which are young and fresh, and others far gone in senility.

· FASHION IN KISSES ·

T O THE MOVIES, and as I sat through a double feature I was interested to observe that the audible kiss has come back into fashion. When the first talking pictures appeared, kisses were all of the silent variety; it was just then that silent plumbing made its first appearance, and there may have been some connection. But now the shadow-folk of Hollywood kiss with a noise like a cow pulling its foot out of deep mud. In my younger days there were two types of kiss: the Romantic Kiss was for private use and was as silent as the grave; the Courtesy Kiss, bestowed upon aunts, cousins and the like was noisy and wet, generally removing two square inches of mauve face powder. A visiting aunt, having been welcomed by two or three nephews, needed substantial repairs. The Romantic Kiss also involved closing the eyes, to indicate extreme depth of feeling, though it often occurred to me that if one cannot see what one is kissing, a pretty girl and a kid glove of good quality are completely indistinguishable.

· CUT-RATE AUTOGRAPHS ·

H AD AN OPPORTUNITY to examine a collection of autographs, and wondered once again what makes people collect them. The futility of collecting scraps of paper upon which people have scribbled (autograph-collecting) seems to me to be exceeded only by the futility of collecting scraps of paper which people have licked (stamp-collecting). There is a certain interest, perhaps, in the manner in which a great man signs his name, though not much. I would be delighted to own a page of manuscript written by Ben Jonson or Cardinal Bembo, for both were masterly calligraphers; but letters from most modern authors and statesmen are mere scribbles. In childhood most of us have a spell during which we carefully collect the autographs of our families, the milkman, the baker and the laundry man; then we lose the album. But I am surprised whenever I am reminded that the craze continues into adult life, and that great sums of money are spent on signatures of writers, musicians, criminals, politicians, and the like. I have a little skill in forgery, and I am thinking of going into a business where I shall undertake to provide a good facsimile of anybody's signature for twenty-five cents. Thus, for a modest sum, the eager collector will be able to get some rare items.

• VALIANT FOR TRUTH •

*R*ECEIVED A LETTER from a cow, or it may simply have been from somebody who takes orders from a cow; I couldn't quite make out. It appears that when I made public my intention of keeping a cow in my cellar I suggested that cows shed their horns annually; the letter denied this. It is possible, though improbable, that I am wrong. I am not sure that I would know a cow if I met one. A certain cloudiness of vision, caused by long hours poring over the Scriptures, makes it impossible for me to identify an animal or even a human being at a distance of more than five feet. The cows which Santa Claus employs to draw his sleigh certainly have horns, for I have seen pictures of them. But if cows do not shed their horns, how comes it that cow horns are so plentiful? Cow horns are used to make horn-rimmed spectacles, snuff boxes for Scotsmen, powder-horns for outlaws, inkhorns for scholars, horns for automobiles, and for a variety of purposes. Am I expected to believe that all these horns come from dead cows and represent a lifetime of patient horn-growing? No, no, I am not so foolish as that. Until I am shown otherwise I shall believe that cows shed their horns each Spring.

• TO SAMUEL MARCHBANKS, ESQUIRE •

Dear and Valued Customer:

With a sensation of sick shock we find that you have not yet been in to do your Xmas shopping. Already the best of our stock is picked over and unless you hurry! Hurry!! HURRY!!! you will miss out on the finest array of Xmas yummies of all kinds that it has ever been our privilege and pleasure to stock.

Everything that you could possibly wish to give to a relative is to be found in our Pharmacy Department, and may be purchased by presenting a doctor's prescription. Many goods in this line may be secured by signing a simple statement that you want to poison a dog.

In our Jewellery displays we have every sort of simulated gem with which husband or lover could wish to simulate affection.

In our Gigantic Kiddyland we have no less than three Santa Clauses, which avoids much of the queuing to shake hands with the genial saint which has caused irritation among busy tots at past Christmases.

You owe it to yourself to do your Christmas shopping RIGHT NOW. Stop owing it to yourself. Owe it to us.

J. Button Hook
(For the Bon Ton Elite Shoppery).

• TO RAYMOND CATAPLASM, M.D., F.R.C.P. •

Dear Dr. Cataplasm:

The other day I read the autobiography of an Armenian gentleman named Nubar Gulbenkian; he hopes to live as long as his grandfather, who died at the age of 106. The book described this ancient's meals in detail. Two facts about them impressed me; each meal (he ate four times a day) took forty-five minutes; each meal ended with a plate of Turkish sweets.

I have never taken forty-five minutes to eat a meal in my life. I can eat eight courses in fifteen minutes. ∮ Can it be that I eat too fast for long life and health?

I detest Turkish sweets. They appear to me to be made of raw mutton fat into which low-caste Turks have ground caraway seeds by rubbing it between the soles of their feet.

However, Gulbenkian eats slowly and he eats nasty things, and he expects to achieve a great age. Pehaps you would like to quote his example to a few patients who are not so hasty and fastidious as,

Your perennial patient,
Samuel Marchbanks.

• TO AMYAS PILGARLIC, ESQUIRE •

Dear Pil:

A few days ago I visited Toyland, as I do every year, just to see how the Christmas Racket is getting along. Toyland is as hot as

---

∮ *Marchbanks is assured by Dr. H.W. Davenport, author of* Physiology of the Digestive Tract *(4th edition, 1977), that it is perfectly all right to gobble; food, however hustled into the hopper, will be mashed, melted and reduced to a nutritious goo once it is in the works. The late Queen Mary (1867-1953) was a notable gobbler. In royal circles the etiquette is that once the highest-ranking person at table has ceased to eat, the dishes are removed and a new course served, and it was said that the meagre appearance of the late Queen's entourage was caused by the fact that they never had a chance to get more than a couple of mouthfuls before the Queen gave the slight nod that signalled the snatchingaway of their loaded plates. Many of them had to eat biscuits in their bedrooms in order to keep body and soul together. There used to be a very fine rose named "Queen Mary" that was described in some nursery catalogues as "a gross feeder" until a complaint from the Daughters of the Empire brought about a more delicate wording.*

ever; the temperature was not a smidgeon under 90 degrees F. Most of the customers, like myself, wore full Winter outdoor dress, and were suffering hideously. The only really comfortable people appeared to be the gnomes and elves who were helping Santa; these were young women ranging from the toothsome to the merely wholesome, dressed in shirts and very short shorts. This association between Santa Claus and the female underpinning fascinated me; Santa was there for the children, but the gnomes were there for the fathers—in a very limited sense, of course.

Santa himself, beneath his paint and ample white beard, seemed to be about twenty-five; when children approached him his eyes rolled in an agonized fashion that betrayed the youthful bachelor. A photographer was on the spot, assisted by a leggy female gnome, taking pictures of every tot with Santa. This impressed me as a fine stroke of commercial whimsy, and I started up the runway myself. "Where you goin'?" said a blonde gnome with a large bust, catching me by the arm. "To have my picture taken with Santa," said I. "It's just for the kids," said she, trembling a little and looking for the manager. "I am a child at heart, gnome," said I. But she had pressed a button in the wall beside her, and at this moment a store detective appeared, wearing the insensitive expression of his kind. "What gives?" said he. "This character wants to go up the runway with the kids," said the gnome. "Oh, one of them sex-monsters, eh?" said the detective, closing one eye in a menacing fashion. For a moment I feared that I might have to spend Christmas in jail with my friend Osceola Thunderbelly. But I talked my way out of it, and as I hastened away the detective gave the gnome a slap on the podex which was probably mere brotherly goodwill. Christmas is becoming a terribly complicated season, full of mixed and mistaken motives. ✒

Yours, still blushing at the shame of it,
Sam.

✒ Children, following the example of their mothers, are beginning to assert their rights, or what in their wild imaginings they believe to

• To Raymond Cataplasm, M.D., F.R.C.P. •

Dear Dr. Cataplasm:

It was most kind of you to send me a Christmas card. It is a beautiful thing, and I shall probably have it framed. By the way, what is it? I did not know that you were interested in modern art.

Yours gratefully,
S. Marchbanks.

P.S. How foolish of me! I have been looking at your card upside down. Of course it is a lovely photograph of autumn colours.

S.M.

• To Samuel Marchbanks, Esquire •

Dear Mr. Marchbanks:

Through some oversight my secretary has sent you a coloured transparency representing a drunkard's liver, in mistake for a Christmas card. If you will return it, a card showing myself and Mrs. Cataplasm on the verandah of our Summer home will be sent to you at once.

Yours sincerely,
Raymond Cataplasm.

---

be their rights. An instance has been recorded in the U.S.A. of a child divorcing its parents for neglect, which is probably sufficient grounds, but where will it lead when more advanced tots have taken up the notion? The idea of having to pay alimony to an estranged child strikes terror into the parental breast (one male, two female). Children are becoming a luxury beyond the reach of all but the affluent. What has become of the Old-Fashioned Child that slept on straw and was grateful for a bowl of table-leavings once a day? The Family Unit totters!

· To Mrs. Kedijah Scissorbill ·

Dear Mrs. Scissorbill:

Because I am a great admirer of novelty in any form, I write to congratulate you on your most successful performance as Santa Claus at the Christmas party which your club, The Militant Female Society, gave for the Misbegotten Orphans.

As you said in your speech to the Orphans, there is no reason whatever why Santa Claus should not be a woman. And I thought your costume and makeup excellent. It was a fine idea to wear your own abundant grey hair, loose and hanging down your back. This made up for the lack of the long beard which we associate with S. Claus. I think you would be wise another time to put some fire-proofing on your hair; I observed one well-developed male orphan, with quite a moustache, testing it with his cigarette-lighter. I think, too, that your pince-nez, and the natural austerity of your countenance, gave Santa an authority he sometimes lacks.

Altogether, it was a triumph, and I expect that the craze for female Santas will sweep the country.

Yours respectfully,
Samuel Marchbanks.

· Christmas Eve ·

*F*INISHED MY CHRISTMAS shopping. True, I finished it three weeks ago, but it is a job which I find requires finishing more than once. At the end of November I fought, bit and clawed my way through the shops, battling with savage women and bitten in the leg by cannibal children, and gathered enough assorted rubbish to fill, as I thought, my Christmas needs. But in the light of Christmas Week it has proved to be too little; my bosom is inflated, nigh to bursting, with Brotherly Love and eggnog, and today I sallied forth to shop again. The shops were almost empty, and although the clerks were a little vague and tended to hiccup when asked questions, I achieved my wishes in a short time and hurried home to decorate my tree. Preparatory to this task I nogged a couple of dozen eggs, and when visitors dropped in I was able to offer them a drink of the plushy, caressing fluid which does so much to take the bitterness out of Christmas. . . . I have made my own angel for the top of the Christmas tree. As a delineator of the female form I tend to express myself in unmistakable terms; I like even an angel to appear as if she had some fun in her. In consequence my angel looks a little like Diana of the Ephesians, what with eggnog and one thing and another.

• COMMUNIQUÉ •
(by ordinary surface mail but unstamped)

To Big Chief Marchbanks:
How, Marchbanks!

This one hell country, Marchbanks. No place for honest man. Listen. Last week I no money. Christmas come. I good Indian, Marchbanks. Baptized lots of times. Want to do right by Gitche Manitou on he birthday. Want for buy case lilac hair juice for drink Gitche Manitou health on birthday. No money. Every place Christmas shopper. All spend. All sad face. All think selfs happy. So I think I sell Christmas trees. One place I see plenty little trees. All blue. I get hatchet and cut down four. Then woman come to door of house. She say what I do? I say cut Christmas trees. Thief, she say — awful loud voice, Marchbanks, for skinny woman — I call cops. You cut my blue spruce. I grab trees. I run. Soon cops come in white car. ⨍ Hey you, say cops. What you do in white car, I say. Sell ice cream, maybe. Ha! Joke, Marchbanks. Cops mad. So mad they get out of car. That awful mad for cop, Marchbanks. Take me police court. Little fellow at desk he say I been drinking. How I drink, I say, with no money. Little fellow belch. He been drinking Marchbanks. I smell. Jail ten days he say, and belch again. I

⨍ *The police, at this time, travelled in white cars, and were uneasy when they had to leave them, as they had become fixed in a sitting posture. It was later that the black-and-white car, called a Holstein by the derisive taxpayers, came into use.*

belch too, for show polite, Indian style. Another ten days for contempt, he say. This one hell country, Marchbanks.

Osceola Thunderbelly,
Chief of the Crokinoles.

• TO AMYAS PILGARLIC, ESQUIRE •

Dear Pil:

On Christmas Eve it is surely not indiscreet of me to confide the secrets of my Christmas List to you. As I told you earlier, I am giving Canadiana this year. Here is the list:

Uncle Fortunatus: an old drum, almost certainly used by troops in the 1837 Rebellion. Both heads are gone, but can be easily replaced. All the decoration and regimental ornament have been worn, or rusted, away, but a skilful restorer could put them back again if we knew what they were. Spiteful people say it is an old cheese-box, but I have the true collector's flair, and know it is a drum. Uncle will love it.

Brother Fairchild: an old Quebec heater, almost certainly the one around which the Fathers of Confederation sat when planning the future of this great Dominion. Who can say what historic spit may not cling to it? It is, in the truest sense, a shrine. As a stove, of course, it has seen its best days. Fairchild will be delighted.

Cousin Genghis: a flag, used by a militia regiment which set out to quell the Riel Rebellion, but was detained in one of the bars in Toronto. It is a most interesting piece of work, which shows signs of having been an Orange Lodge banner before it was converted to its later purpose. It is rather stained with something which might be blood, though an analytical chemist says it still smells of whisky. Genghis will be ecstatic.

Nephew Gobemouche: a stamp used by a Member of Parliament in mailing a letter from the Parliament Buildings. Such stamps are exceedingly rare, and a few philatelists deny that any genuine examples are in existence. I happen to know, however, that on September 12, 1896, the franking-machine was out of order for a few hours, and free stamps were given to members at the Parliamentary Post Office. Gobemouche will be tearful with pleasure.

Nephew Belial: a horn from Laura Secord's famous cow. When blown it emits a musty smell but no sound. Belial will be livid.

And as for you, my dear friend—but no; you must wait until tomorrow to see what I have sent you.

A Merry Christmas!
Sam.

• To Samuel Marchbanks, Esquire •

(Written on a card bearing the message "A Merry Christmas and Good Wishes for 1949": the date has been altered in pencil to the current year.)

Dear Nephew:

Thank you for your thoughtful present. I opened it, as you suggested, as soon as it arrived, and a prettier parcel of soap I have never seen. I shall distribute new cakes on Christmas morning to the whole household. Your notion of a cake of soap fashioned in the likeness of an Aberdeen terrier for your Uncle Gomeril will flatter his Scottish susceptibilities.

I already have quite a number of gifts to be returned and exchanged as soon as the shops open after Christmas. Someone has thoughtlessly sent your Uncle a dressing-gown in the tartan of a clan from which the Marchbanks have been estranged for over three hundred years. He very sensibly asks what need he has of even an acceptable dressing-gown? He never wears one, and goes to his bath lightly wrapped in an old copy of the Toronto *Globe*, the Scotsman's friend.

Your affct. aunt,
Bathsheba Marchbanks.

• To Samuel Marchbanks, Esquire •

(Written on an expensive but aesthetically reprehensible card which reveals a robin sitting on a bare branch, with a twig of holly in its beak; the bird's eye is a black bead, and the holly berries are red beads, cleverly glued to the paper. Spelled out in twigs of holly and mistletoe is the message: "Just the Old, Old Wish.")

Dear Mr. Marchbanks:

I had hoped that this seasonable greeting might come from Mrs. Wittol as well as myself, but she has been absent from home for several days. I have not heard from her, but last night a man's voice on the phone made some very insulting remarks to me, and I thought I recognized her hiccup among the background noises.

Yours regretfully,
Waghorn Wittol.

• To Samuel Marchbanks, Esquire •

(Written upon a card which bears a portrait of Santa Claus, wearing an expression possible only to one drunk, or mad; realism has been added to the picture by a feather, glued on to represent the Saint's beard.)

At this gladsome tide I and Lambie-Pie hasten to freely offer yet once again the right hand of fellowship which you have so often spurned. As the angel's message of Peace on Earth, Goodwill Toward Men rings round the sad old world, I beseech you to drop your legal action against me for hiding a skunk in your car, and as Ye Goode Shippe NEW YEAR sets forth into uncharted seas of Time let the olive branch, symbol of neighbourly amity, wave freely from the poop.

Your repentant neighbour,
Dick Dandiprat.

• TO RAYMOND CATAPLASM, M.D., F.R.C.P. •

(On a Greetings Telegram)

HAVE BEGUN FESTIVITIES EARLIER THAN EXPECTED
STOP HASTEN WITH STOMACH PUMP STOP THINK
SELF POISONED THREE DINNERS STILL TO GO STOP
MERRY CHRISTMAS STOP

Marchbanks.

• TO GENGHIS MARCHBANKS, ESQUIRE •

My Dear Cousin:

I really think your terms are ungenerous, considering the season
of the year. If, as you suggest, I bring all the unwanted Christmas
presents I receive to your pawnshop, I shall expect more than a
mere one-third of their ordinary retail price. I hate to say it, Genghis, but I do not consider that you are showing the Christmas
Spirit. You can skin the public, if you like, but you ought to draw
the line at skinning a relative.

Yours reproachfully,
S.M.

---

*Younger readers may wonder what a telegram was. Long ago it
was possible to send messages by an electric or magnetic transmit-
ter, publicly owned and operated for the public convenience; wires charged
with electric current connected all centres of civilization—even quite mini-
mal civilization—and messages were conveyed along them by breaking
the circuit with a key which indicated letters according to an understood
code, devised by Samuel Finley Breese Morse (1791-1892); such messages
might be delivered to the recipient within an hour of being dispatched
and were a great convenience to everyone. Special forms, handsomely
printed, called Greetings Telegrams, were available for all great festival
occasions. There were even Singing Telegrams, delivered by a youth who*

· TO SAMUEL MARCHBANKS, ESQUIRE ·

My very dear Mr. Marchbanks:

It has never been the custom of Mouseman, Mouseman and Force-meat to send out greeting cards at the Festive Season; to a firm as old as ours such conduct would seem flashy. We do, however, send letters bearing good wishes to our more valued clients, of whom you, my dear sir, are not the least.

All of the firm are, I am happy to say, well. The life of our senior partner, Mr. Jabez Mouseman, has been considerably brightened since he began—through what scientific accident we know not—to receive television programs on his hearing-aid. When reception is particularly strong phantoms of charming young women in low-cut evening gowns may be seen to move gracefully across his shirt-bosom; at first Mr. Jabez thought himself beset by evil spirits, but now he spends many hours each day happily regarding himself in the mirror.

Mr. Cicero Forcemeat, is, as always, in rude health and his power-ful voice—that boon of the successful advocate—is, if anything, stronger than before. His peroration in a divorce case last week cracked a chandelier in the court-room.

I am as always in good health and beg to subscribe myself, dear Mr. Marchbanks, with no legal qualification whatever, your ser-vant and sincere well-wisher,

Mordecai Mouseman,
(For Mouseman, Mouseman and Forcemeat).

---

warbled a tuneful message at your very door. But in the Atomic Age, when we are able to put men on the Moon and otherwise astonish ourselves, the telegram has fallen into such disarray that to send one is to court service even worse than that of the postal system, once another source of pride and convenience.

• TO SAMUEL MARCHBANKS, ESQUIRE •

Dear Sir:

This department finds that in computing your Income Tax for 1948 you neglected to mention that when you addressed the Ladies' Arts and Letters Club of Pelvis, Sask., in that year you were treated by the committee to a dinner which cost seventy-five cents. This constitutes hidden income, and you must pay tax amounting to sixty-seven cents, plus extra tax for late payment, amounting to nine cents, making seventy-six cents in all, within ten days or we shall pursue you with the full rigour of the law.

This Department has received a card from you bearing Christmas Greetings. We are returning the card which is the wrong size for our files, and enclose herewith proper forms for the expression of this wish, to be completed in triplicate, and returned at once.

Yours, but not as much as you are ours,
Haubergeon Hydra.

• TO SAMUEL MARCHBANKS, ESQUIRE •

(A greeting card, obviously homemade, to which has been glued a snapshot of a stringy female of cheerful aspect, nursing what looks like a very old floor mop.)

Yuletide Greetings from self and dearest Fido.

Minerva Hawser.

• TO BIG CHIEF MARCHBANKS •

(An exceedingly dirty and crumpled picture of an ample lady of brilliant complexion, showing a lot of leg, and smoking a cigar.)

How, Marchbanks:

Find this picture in top of cigar box. Make a nice card for you. All us fellows in jail send you happy wishes. Warden promise good

Christmas in jail. Chicken and mince pie. No women, he say. We need women. You got any women?

Osceola Thunderbelly,
Chief of the Crokinoles.

• TO MISS MINERVA HAWSER •

Dear Miss Hawser:

Thank you for your letter; if you really want my old Christmas cards, you can have them; your idea of cutting them up into bits and distributing them for use as confetti at the weddings of the Underprivileged seems to me to be an excellent one, and an accurate reflection of your kindly and ingenious nature. My cards may be a disappointment to you. They were classifiable under the following heads:

Ghastly Good Taste: plain white cards made of hard stuff like the icing of a Christmas cake, with an engraved greeting on them; indistinguishable from old-fashioned death notices.

Art Drearies: designed by people who are determined to get away from conventional Christmas colours and designs; they are usually executed in shades suggesting cheese mould. Some are religious, in a strictly "God-is-dead" sense.

Stark Realism: cards to which snapshots of the senders have been pasted, showing them at their worst, and often in company with dead fish, half-dead dogs, and the like.

Canadian Art: showing the same French-Canadian farmer, driving the same sleigh through the same bluish snow, but in slightly different stages of his progress toward a village consisting of a Church and three huts.

Phoney Mediaeval: showing people eating and drinking and playing oversize guitars, and looking cleaner and healthier than was likely in the Middle Ages.

Unspeakables: on which a reindeer with a red nose is depicted.

I sent cards in all these forms myself, for there was nothing else to be had. But I really long for a decent old-fashioned Christmas card, with the Virgin and Child on it, and Santa Claus and his reindeer, and a robin with a twig of holly in its beak, and some mica clinging to it to simulate snow, and a really compendious and warm-hearted greeting in the manner of G.K. Chesterton:

> Here's for a bursting Yuletide
> To my friends wherever they be!
> With boozing and stuffing
> And praying and puffing
> All under the Evergreen Tree!

Yours sincerely,
Samuel Marchbanks.

• COMMUNIQUÉ •
(delivered by a Police car, envelope stamped OFFICIAL)

To Big Chief Marchbanks:
How, Marchbanks!

Us fellows in jail fix New Year Dance. Ball and Chain Ball, we call it. We got no women, so no dance. We got no booze, so no drink. We got no money, so no gamble. But we got peace and plenty dirty story. You want ticket? Fight cop. He give you ticket.

Osceola Thunderbelly,
Chief of the Crokinoles.

• NO ROAST OX, THANKS •

NEW YEAR'S DAY, and I hail the onset of another year by eating more than I should but not quite so much as I want. I yearn for the spacious days of the Middle Ages, when cooking was cooking. Those were the days when the lord of the manor was faced, at dinner, with a whole ox into which was stuffed a whole boar, into which was stuffed a lamb, into which was stuffed a hare, into which was stuffed a pheasant. When he had settled this difficult problem in carving, the lord ate the pheasant, and threw the wrappings to the scurvy knaves and lubberly churls who composed his household, and set to work on a venison pie and five or six pounds of mincemeat encased in marchpane. Only, if I had lived in the Middle Ages, I would undoubtedly have been a lubberly churl—or at best Pynne-Heade, the household jester—and would have had to eat over-cooked ox, swilled down with the water in which the mead-horns had been washed. I have no illusions about the glory of my ancestry. So I dismissed my dream of mediaeval gluttony, and picked at a few pounds of turkey and ham, and washed it all down with liquids so innocent that even the Government puts its stamp upon them.

• LET THE EAR JUDGE •

SOMEBODY IN THE States, I see, has conceived the notion of recording classics of literature on long-playing records. After listening to such a recording it would no longer be necessary to go through the fatigue of reading the *Iliad*, the *Odyssey*, *Paradise Lost*, the *Divine Comedy*, or any other exhausting work. It must be said for such a scheme that it would restore the ear as the first judge of poetry, and expose that false judge, the eye. But I doubt if many people would hear the great works often enough to get near the root of them.

• COMMUNIQUÉ •
(Delivered by carrion crow)

To Big Chief Marchbanks:
How, Marchbanks!

Everybody in jail crazy, Marchbanks. Jail doctor bring old white squaw see us jail prisoners today. She squint at me through glasses. You got any sociable diseases, she say. Sure, I say. You want be sociable? How much you spend? Don't know what she mean. Think

she mean party. Everybody holler at me. Doctor tell Turkey ✒
turn hose on me. This one hell country, Marchbanks.

How again,
Osceola Thunderbelly,
Chief of the Crokinoles.

• REPULSIVE LITTLE STRANGER •

*W*HILE HANGING ABOUT a friend's house I picked up a
book called *The Culture of the Abdomen*. It proved to be a
gloomy work, holding out little hope for the future of Western
Civilization unless we immediately get our abdomens into a condition resembling that of the Maoris and South Sea Islanders. These
people, it appears, do elaborate dances in which no part of them
moves but their abdomens. I don't know that I would care to see
the National Ballet go over to this technique, but apparently it is
wonderful for the tripes.... Even a mediocre writer may create
one golden phrase, and the author of this book achieved it in the
following sentence: "Upon many a death certificate we read the
words Heart Failure, but we know that Fat and Gas are the parents of Heart Failure." What a magically repulsive picture this calls
up! Fat, the loathsome Slob-Mate, is approached by Gas, the fluttering, elusive, faintly-squealing Spectre-Bride, who whispers,
"Honey, there's going to be a Little Stranger soon—little H.F.,
that we've always dreamed of!" And then—BANG!

✒ *After long cogitation I think that Thunderbelly must use this word to*
mean Turnkey, the prison guard who has charge of the keys. Com-
plete scholarly scruple, however, moves me to say that the word is used in
the underworld to mean an instrument which, inserted in a keyhole, will
turn a key which has been left in a door, and considering the company he
kept, we must assume that Thunderbelly was aware of this meaning. The
word was also at one time used to identify the instrument used by a den-
tist to extract a tooth, by twisting, but as Thunderbelly neglected his teeth
he was probably not aware of this. I think I have now covered the schol-
arly ground in this explanation.

• Sancta Simplicitas •

*A*FTER A LONGISH CHAT with some children today, I reflected that the child's attitude toward humour differs sharply from that of the adult. In the world of mature people a joke is funny once, and should never be repeated in the same company. But children, having decided that a joke is funny, go on repeating it, laughing more loudly each time, until they collapse in hysteria. The mental age of a man might be gauged by observing how often he can laugh at the same joke.

• King of the Beasts at Lunch •

*T*O AN EXCELLENT film about Africa, with some of the best pictures of wild animals that I have even seen. I was particularly interested in close-ups of a group of lions eating a zebra. Now I was brought up on picture books which insisted that the lion was a noble beast, that killed its prey with a single violent blow, and then stood upon the fallen carcass for a time, roaring; when it had thus worked up an appetite it tore off a leg, devoured it in lonely splendour and rushed off for further spectacular mischief. But here was a picture of five or six lions, all pushing and shoving like human beings, gobbling the guts of the zebra; there was no roaring, no defiance and no loneliness. One lion lay on its side near the feast, gorged and apparently slightly drunk. Vultures stood nearby, like waiters hoping to clear away the dirty plates. The lions ate messily, dropping bits and slobbering on their fronts. It seems that life in the jungle is rather more like life at a short-order lunch wagon than I had supposed. I do not know whether to be pleased or not.

• To Haubergeon Hydra, Esquire •

Dear Mr. Hydra:

I thought that you might like to know that I don't believe the Old Age Pension should be increased. Old age is too delightful and dangerous a state to require a pension. Old people are usually very happy, and they are also subversive and a Bad Example. Let me tell you what I know.

Last Saturday I went to a nearby school for boys to watch their annual cadet inspection. I well remember when I was a schoolboy what an agony these affairs were. For weeks beforehand we marched till our legs were stiff; a sergeant-major with an immense stomach rudely urged us to suck in our non-existent stomachs; we polished our buttons till all the brass was worn off them; we polished our boots inside and out; we learned to march slowly, quickly, and imperceptibly; we learned to perform complex quadrilles when other boys shouted hoarse and imcomprehensible words. And when The Day came, in an agony of fear we performed these feats, believing that we had the admiration and enthralled attention of our elders. We didn't know whether they admired us or not; our collars were so tight that we were bereft of the senses of sight and hearing. But we believed that they did.

Last Saturday I found out what really went on among the onlookers. While the boys marched, yelled, stamped and drove themselves toward hysterics their elders jabbered among themselves, laughed, averted their eyes from the sweating heroes and occasionally said, "Aren't the little boys sweet?" Some of those boys, Mr. Hydra, were daily shavers and not in the least sweet. And who were the worst offenders in this respect? Who mumbled trivialities during the General Salute? Who turned their backs and sniggered at private jokes while The Colours were being marched past? The Old, Mr. Hydra. The happy, carefree, irreverent, unpatriotic Old.

Don't raise their pensions until they smarten up, and show a suitable respect for the Young.

Yours from the philosophical
eminence of Middle Life,
Samuel Marchbanks.

• To Raymond Cataplasm, M.D., F.R.C.P. •

Dear Dr. Cataplasm:

A physician who writes for the papers says that a slow heartbeat is a good thing. This is just what I have been saying for years, but nobody will listen. You doctors are really the most self-sufficient tribe!

What animals live longest? Those with the slowest heartbeat. I have no figures handy, but I remember hunting them up once in a medical book. An elephant lives to a great age, and its heart beats about forty-five times a minute. A tortoise, if my memory serves me aright, has a heartbeat of approximately twenty-two thumps a minute. When you get down to really long-lived animals, like crocodiles, the beat is likely to be two or three times a minute. And I once pressed my ear to a parrot's bosom (getting badly scratched for my pains) and I couldn't hear any heartbeat at all.

Don't you think you could extend your patients' lives indefinitely, and make your fortune and ruin the insurance companies, simply by giving your patients some simple drug to slow down their hearts to the speed of a crocodile's?

Your perennial patient,
Samuel Marchbanks.

• To Samuel Marchbanks, Esquire •

Dear Marchbanks:

I can't go on like this! It half-kills me to live near a man who hates me the way you do! My lawyers say that if you take that case to court it might cost me my shirt, even if I win. I'm sorry I put the skunk in your car. Honest, Marchbanks!

So here's what I'll do. I'll sell you my car, at a sacrifice. It is a Pierce Arrow 1923, and I'll let you have it for $1,500 cash.

I can't say fairer than that, can I?

Your despondent neighbour,
Dick Dandiprat.

• TO RICHARD DANDIPRAT •

Abhorred Dandiprat:

The jaws of our irresistible legal system are closing upon you. It will be my pleasure, when the jaws open, to pick you out of their teeth.

Yours with demoniacal laughter,
Marchbanks.

• BABIES AND THE ADULT MALE •

*A*CROSS THE STREET from my workroom window is an apartment which has a baywindow at my level; during the past few weeks a baby has been making regular appearances there, so that the doings in the street below may entertain it. I judge that it is a male baby, and it is a fine, large child, with a solemn and philosophical countenance. The baby views the street and I view the baby. I like babies, under special circumstances, and by a lucky chance the relationship between me and this particular baby perfectly fulfils all my conditions. I can see it, but I cannot hear it; I can admire its winning ways, and laugh indulgently when it topples over, but it is not near enough to wet me; when it wants anything, a pair of hands appear from behind it with the desired object. This is ideal, and I am thinking of putting this baby in my will. I believe that if the truth were known, my attitude toward this baby is that of most adult males; men like children, but they do not like them to be too close. Some barrier — as for instance a wide street, filled with traffic — between a man and a baby, acts as a powerful stimulant to affection between them.

• THE MAGIC OF LATIN •

*A*MONG THE TOOLS of my trade I possess a number of books of quotations, most of which bear titles such as *Familiar Quotations, Quotations The Whole World Loves,* and the like. The only honestly named one is *The Oxford Dictionary of Quota-*

tions. The fact is that no great fat thick book of quotations can be called "familiar"; very few people can identify more than a dozen of them. Furthermore there are hundreds of quotations in such books which I solemnly swear are not familiar to anybody. The fake profundities of dead politicians, the treacly outpourings of fifth-rate poets, the moonlit nonsense of minor essayists — this junk makes up the bulk of most quotation books. I like Mencken's book of quotations because it is full of sin and impudence and does not pretend to be familiar; I like the Oxford book because it is unashamedly highbrow and contains a great many quotations in Latin. But the "familiar" nonsense I scorn. I love Latin quotations. I suspect that nobody ever said anything in Latin which was above the level of barber shop philosophy, but it has a wondrous sonority.

• TO SAMUEL MARCHBANKS, ESQUIRE •

Dear Mr. Marchbanks:

I write to enlist your support and membership in the Canadian Laudable Litter League which I am forming. Do you realize, sir, that every day thousands of pounds — nay, tons — of material of one sort and another which should be returned to the soil of our country is burned, or washed down our waterways to the sea, never to be recovered? Vital vitamins, irreplaceable minerals and animal and vegetable matter of all kinds are wasted this way. The time has come to Call a Halt.

During the Summer I have been doing my bit to preserve what is Canada's for Canada. Whenever I have been on a picnic I have taken care to throw my hard-boiled eggshell back on the land, to preserve minerals. I have thrown my banana skins and other peelings into farmers' fields, to put vitamins back into the soil. When others have gathered up their waste paper, I have left it to blow where the wind listeth, for it came from the soil and should return whence it came.

Each member of the Laudable Litter League pledges himself never again to give his garbage to a wasteful urban collector, for burning; instead he takes it into the country (preferably in the dark of the moon, as this is the time approved by our hero, the late Rudolf

Steiner ∥) and throws it into the field of some farmer whose soil appears to be impoverished. This should be done by stealth, for the League seeks no credit for its good work.

Begging you to become an honorary L.L.D. (Laudable Litter Distributor) at once, I remain,

Yours literally,
Minerva Hawser.

• TO HAUBERGEON HYDRA, ESQUIRE •

Dear Mr. Hydra:

As I have written to you so often in tones of complaint, it gives me particular pleasure to pay you a compliment on the agreeable manners of the men who deal with immigration on the international bridges at Niagara Falls. As Overseer of Conduct for Civil Servants I thought that you would like to hear about this. During the past month I have had some work to do in Niagara Falls, Canada, but I was living with friends in Niagara Falls, U.S.A., and I used the bridges a good deal.

Each time I crossed I answered much the same questions. "Where were you born?" "Skunk's Misery, Ontario," I would reply, in an accent which I acquired abroad, and which has at various times caused me to be taken for an Englishman, an Irishman, a Scotsman, and a native of the Scilly Isles. This accent, and an appearance which suggests an archimandrite of the Greek Orthodox Church, sometimes throws doubt on my Skunk's Misery origin. But I was always believed. Then, after a few more queries about my sex life and financial status, I would be passed through, with bows and cries of "Huzza for Marchbanks!" If I had any luggage the Customs men would finger it delicately, compliment me on the neat-

---

∥ *Rudolf Steiner (1861–1925) was an Austrian social philosopher, who became a Theosophist and then founded the Anthroposophical movement; his doctrines combined excellent common sense, forgotten folk-knowledge, and woozy speculation in a bewildering gallimaufry.*

ness of my packing and the exquisite taste which I showed in choosing socks and underpants, and wave me on.

The bridge attendants have a sterner side, however, as I saw on my last journey across the bridge. The man who came after me was elderly, with flowing white hair and a goatee — obviously a Southern Colonel. "Have you anything to declare?" asked the Canadian Immigration man. "I declare it's a mighty hot day, suh!" said the Colonel. As I drove away he was dragged into the Customs House and the thud of cudgels on pulpy flesh mingled with screams in a Southern accent rent the air. Presumably he was suspected of importing a joke, which would of course have been intolerable to our local funnymen, completely upsetting the economy of their trade.

Yours loyally,
Samuel Marchbanks.

• TO CHANDOS FRIBBLE, ESQUIRE •

Esteemed Fribble:

I want you to look into a curious psychological twist which has recently become observable in advertisements for cars. One of these (I need not specify the maker's name) shows a young man who is about to kiss a very pretty girl, but turns his head at the vital moment to look at a passing car. The second shows a young man in the act of telling a charming girl that he loves her hair, her eyes, and her father's new car. The third shows a young couple doting upon — a baby? each other? — no, upon a bright, shiny car.

Now, Fribble, it looks to me as though the North American male were beginning to exalt motor cars to the position in his esteem once held by women. This is dangerous, and I would like to find out how far it has gone. For if this trend continues the day is not far off when the American male will mate, not with a woman, but with his car, and the result of this union will probably be a winsome, cuddly little motorcycle.

Yours in alarm,
Samuel Marchbanks.

• MUSICAL PUZZLER •

*M*INGLED WITH some musical people today, almost on terms of equality. I like musical people but I am always astonished by the dogmatic quality of their statements, especially when they are young. For instance, a young lady who was probably about nineteen asserted this afternoon that J.S. Bach had embraced the whole scope of human feeling in his music in a manner more sublime than that of any other composer. I could not permit this to pass. "Where does Bach make even a passable stab at an expression of romantic love?" I asked her, and she could not answer. And truly old Bach, who had two wives and twenty children, had not much to say about this important matter; the majesty of his harmony and the remorseless deedle-doodle of his counterpoint were not geared for it, and in this sphere such lesser creatures as Puccini beat him hollow. The young woman took her revenge by behaving toward me as if I had no soul, which was typically feminine, and pained me not at all. I have quite a large soul — a number ten.

• SCENTING AN AUDIENCE •

*I*N A WEAK MOMENT some months ago I agreed to talk to a women's club today. I am a hardy optimist; when people ask me to make speeches several months before the appointed time I often accept, stupidly thinking that in the interval something will happen to prevent me from making good my promise. But the fateful day always comes, and there I am, on my feet, clutching my notes, with despair in my heart. An audience entirely of men is bad enough, but an audience entirely of women is as frightening as a battery of machine guns. There is one thing about female audiences, though — they have a delicious smell. Powder, expensive textiles and scent — all favourite sniffs of mine — combine to make them more glorious than a June garden. I am sure not one of these ladies today was wearing any scent below the rank of Chanel Number Five, and I thought I detected several twenty-five-dollars-an-ounce whiffs, ✒ for they were wealthy women, knee-deep in good works. So I inhaled deeply and gave tongue. Audiences of men smell of cigars, whisky and shoe-polish, which inspires me with solemn and world-shaking thoughts, unsuitable for the more delicate intellects of women.

• THE INIQUITY OF FREE BOOKS •

THERE IS A GREAT rejoicing in some parts of Ontario because the provincial government has decided to give free school-books to children, but I am not among the merrymakers. I am a writer of books myself, and any move which inculcates in children the idea that books are things you get for nothing excites my implacable enmity. There are too many free books already, in public libraries and other institutions primarily designed to rob authors of their livelihood. A pox on the memory of Andrew Carnegie and his misplaced benevolence! There are in Canada, by actual count, 528 people who buy books for their own use; an author may count on these people buying a copy of any book he writes. There are 6,417,333 people who are on friendly terms with the 528, and they all borrow their copies of new books, read them, and then write to the author, pointing out typographical errors, plagiarisms from Holy Writ, faulty economics, and other blemishes. If the Ontario Government is going to teach children that books drop from Heaven, or are supplied from the public purse, like wheat subsidies, the profession of letters in Canada will drop below that of the nightsoil removers. ✒

✒ The editor feels obliged to explain, for younger readers, that the cost of living—and especially of elegant living—has risen vertiginously since Marchbanks wrote these words. Twenty-five dollars for an ounce of perfume! Nowadays it costs $125 merely to smell the wrist of the elegant creature who sells perfumes, and vouchsafes you a maddening sniff, warmed by her person, before demanding a price that cracks the plastic on your credit card.

✒ Attempts are being made to do something for authors by establishing a Public Lending Right, which would provide the originators of

· To the Rev. Simon Goaste, B.D. ·

Dear Rector:

Can you tell me why it is that so many brides insist on having the Bridal Chorus from Wagner's *Lohengrin* played as they stumble up the aisle at their weddings? It seems to me to be a singularly ill-chosen piece of music for such an occasion.

Consider the story of the opera: Elsa, a silly girl, has got herself into a mess; a young man comes along and very competently gets her out of it; he marries her, on the understanding that she will never ask his name or whence he comes; but Elsa and her relatives nag him insufferably until he can bear it no more, and leaves her. The lesson of the whole opera is that nosiness is a first-class way to break up a marriage, and Wagner, who was married to one of the great snoops of his time, knew what he was talking about. ⟋ Why is it that girls want this prelude to a strikingly unfortunate marriage played at their weddings?

I have often wondered what happened to Elsa after Lohengrin ran away. My guess is that she set up in business as a Wronged Wife, forgot completely her part in breaking up her marriage, and passed her time very pleasantly at tea parties, warning younger women that Men Are Not To Be Trusted. What are your views?

Faithfully,
S. Marchbanks.

---

works of literature, or some facsimile thereof, with a fee whenever their books were borrowed from a Public Library. But as the establishment of the scheme is firmly in the hands of Haubergeon Hydra and a coven of librarians, the outlook is not rosy.

⟋ *Richard Wagner (1813–83) was a musical genius of the first order, but a whimsical fellow and never more so than when he lured Cosima, the wife of his friend and supporter Hans Guido von Bulow (1830–94) to desert her husband's bed and board and become his mistress, thereby creating one of the Great Messes of Musical History. Cosima was the daughter of Franz Liszt and accustomed to domestic dishevelment, and she*

512

• To Raymond Cataplasm, M.D., F.R.C.P. •

Dear Dr. Cataplasm:

I was at a party recently where a lady was explaining a new medical theory to me, in which she said that her husband (who is a physician) is keenly interested. The nubbin of the theory is that placid and careful living is just as aging as rowdy living if you make a habit of it, and that the human metabolism needs frequent shocks, just to keep it on its toes, so to speak. For this reason everybody should take care to overeat grossly every now and then, or get drunk or run a mile, or chop a cord of wood. Anything will do, so long as it is something to which the body is unaccustomed.

I have been testing this notion myself. You know that I will do anything to further the ends of science. I overate as much as possible all during the Christmas season, and washed the food down with strong waters. Result: except for a slight feeling of otherworldliness before breakfast I felt fine, and my metabolism chugged away like a Coin Wash. But during the past week I have run to and from my office, carrying a heavily-weighted briefcase, four times each day. Result: my metabolism has seized up, my circulation is at a standstill, and I see everything upside down unless I keep a firm hold on the top of my head.

Undoubtedly there is a great lesson for science in this. Perhaps you will explain to me what it is. Meanwhile I am going to lie down.

Your perennial patient,

SAMUEL MARCHBANKS.

---

survived it all triumphantly, living until 1930 when she died at the age of ninety-two. Her Diaries, in two volumes, extend from 1869 until 1883 and they give us a chilling sense of the constant surveillance under which Wagner lived. As Robert Louis Stevenson feelingly remarked, "To marry is to domesticate the Recording Angel."

• To Amyas Pilgarlic, Esquire •

Dear Pil:

Last night I was at the movies, and as usual it was necessary to sit through a good deal of rather depressing stuff before we were allowed to see the film which had really brought us to the theatre. *ƒ* Among these shorts (Why do you suppose they call them shorts? Surely shortness is a comparative thing? Judged by the anguish of spirit they induced, these affairs were immeasurably long) but as I was saying, among these shorts was one in which the audience was asked to join in the singing of popular gems of modern minstrelsy. But the audience refrained from doing so, and sat in a glum and resentful silence until the short had dragged out its weary length.

This is a hopeful sign. Human beings are refusing to be cajoled into doing silly things by machines, and by celluloid shadows. For a group of people to sing because a movie machine asks them to do so is just nonsense, and they know it.

Mark my words, the revolution of Man against Machine is close at hand, and when it comes we shall see the end of that era which historians are already referring to in learned works as The Age of Boloney.

Adieu,
Sam.

• A Bore in Training •

*T*ALKING TO A young man I realized, with a shock, that in fifteen years he would be a bore. The young are never bores, though they are often boring, particularly when they talk about themselves. But it does not lie in the power of youth to be a

---

ƒ This material, called "shorts," might be a travelogue about the habits of beastly foreigners, or a gem from the National Film Board, probably called How The Pussy Willows Got Their Fur Coats.

self-sustaining, day-in-and-day-out bore; a man must be at least thirty-five before he can manage that. Youth has a buoyance, a resiliency, which makes it impossible for the young to keep to that dead-level which is the very heart and essence of the bore's craft. The spirits of youth keep bobbing up and down; a bore must be steady as a rock. The eye of youth sometimes lightens; the eye of the bore is glazed with the film of stupidity. There are gloomy bores, and agreeable bores, and eager bores and stuffy bores, but once they have set their course and determined their character, they do not change.... This young man, however, was in strict training to become an agreeable bore, and as he seemed naturally gifted in that respect he may achieve his aim before thirty-five, and become one of the youngest bores in Canadian history.

• LILLIPUT •

SOME CHILDREN I know were showing me a doll's house which they had been given at Christmas. It was a spacious and pleasant dwelling which, on the human scale, could not be built for less than $80,000 at present costs. ∬ I should judge that some doll of the junior executive class lived in it. Like so many doll's houses, it lacked a staircase; dolls are used to being heaved from one floor to another. It was fully, though conventionally, furnished, and over the mantel in the drawing-room was that picture "The Boyhood of Raleigh" which suggested to me that the dolls were rather old-fashioned and romantic in their tastes, in spite of the modernity of some of their furniture. I envied the father-doll the neatness of his garage; mine, which doubles as toolshed, is a sorry thing beside it. The dolls had a remarkably nice bathroom, too, quite unlike the cornery afterthought at Marchbanks Towers. I enquired whether the dolls owned or rented, and was told that they were owners; roughly I computed their land-tax, school-tax and improvements tax, and decided that these dolls were not the

---

∬ *Nowadays, in the Age of the Minibuck, it would be more like $250,000.*

sort of people I would be asked to dine with, if some sudden shrinkage should whisk me into their world.

• CANADIAN CAUTION •

*I*T IS WRONG to say that Canadians have no distinctive national characteristics; what about our national custom of Keeping Down With the Joneses? In other countries people keep up with the Joneses; they vie with one another in the acquirement of showy and prestige-giving possessions. But the crafty Canadian always wants his neighbours to think that he has less money than he really has. He underdresses, for the possession of more than two suits might suggest affluence and a desire to seem glorious in the eyes of men. His wife probably has a fur coat, but she wears it to do the shopping, and to sweep off the stoop, so that it is really just a hard-wearing overall, and not a token of wealth. He eats good food, but he likes it to be disguised, so that even the tooth-test sometimes fails to reveal how good it is. It is only when he goes on a holiday to the U.S.A. that he splurges, takes suites in hotels, gives huge tips to hirelings, and drinks pearls dissolved in wine. At home he likes the neighbours to think that he is just keeping out of jail. Surely this is a striking and unusual national attitude?

• FRANKNESS DEPLORED •

*T*HERE ARE TOO MANY people in the world who think that frankness is an excuse for anything; so long as a man is frank and sincere, say they, he may talk as he likes. They also cling to the stupid and mistaken notion that people like and admire frankness and respond well to it. For instance, I was standing on a street-corner today, when a man in a windbreaker approached me and said: "Lookit, I'm goin' to give you no bull; I wanta get a coupla beers; will you gimme the money?" I looked deep into his eyes, and in low, thrilling voice I said "No.". . . Now if he had given me some bull — some richly ornamented tale of pov-

erty, of undeserved ill-fortune, of being robbed while on some errand
of mercy — anything in fact which would have revealed a spark of
imagination in him, I would have given him a small sum, knowing
full well that it would be spent on beer. But to ask me, flatly and
baldly, for money to buy beer —! Is that the way to appeal to a
Welshman, a lover of the spoken word and the gem-encrusted lie?
No, no. Let such ruffians beg beer-money from those who admire
frankness. Anybody who wants a quarter from me must first produce a quarter's worth of fascinating bull.

• FOOLISH CONTEMPORANEITY •

*I*N A NEWS VENDOR'S today I noticed a pile of books with
bright covers, which proved to be such titles as Dreiser's
Sister Carrie, and Romain's *Jean Christophe*. Wondering idly how
such long books were crammed into such a small space I picked
one up and found that it was marked "abridged for the Modern
Reader." Laughed out loud, and a few people stared at me, as if I
were mad. But I was delighted by the shoddy flattery of that word
"modern." It implied that the modern reader was a very busy fellow,
who had no time to be bothered with the windy nonsense even of
first-rate authors; he had to have everything boiled down for him,
so that he could gulp the essence in an evening's reading. The real
fact of the matter is that many modern readers are pin-headed
neurotics, who have not the staying power to read a great book at
full length. They must have it cut so that they can read all the bits
which describe how the heroine went to bed, and with whom, and
any murders which may creep into the tale. Beyond that, they
can't understand and don't care. Modern reader! Pah!

• TO HAUBERGEON HYDRA, ESQUIRE •

Dear Mr. Hydra:

I see that Parliament is much concerned about the quality of modern Canadianism. Apparently it is not Canadian enough — there
are still big lumps of British Influence and Colonial Inferiority Com-

plex swimming around in it. May I make a suggestion to you as Deputy Assistant Sterilizer of Canadian Patriotism?

We need bigger and better Canadian heroes. We have the raw material, but we must work on it. You know how Canada hates anything raw. We have heroes, but we have not yet blown them up to full heroic stature.

Look at what has been done in the States with Washington, Lincoln, Barbara Frietchie and others. Unpromising material to begin with. Just men and women. But by the use of gas and mirrors they have been given heroic stature. Think what that story about the Cherry Tree has done for Washington! We couldn't copy it, of course, for in Canada we still admire people who cut down trees, and could not see any particular nobility in admitting to such an action. In Canada, a tree is still looked upon as a Big Weed, to be hoiked up or chopped down, or mutilated with impunity. But there are other stories which we could bend to our use, and I submit the following examples for your consideration.

Sir John and the Spider

One day our Great National Hero, Sir John A. Macdonald, sat disconsolately in his lawyer's office in Kingston. Try as he might, he could not get the Canadian provinces to confederate. They simply wouldn't. As he sat, his eyes were attracted by a little spider which was trying to climb up a piece of string (or whatever that stuff is that spiders extrude so unpleasantly from their stomachs). He paid no attention, for spiders were then, as now, part of the standard furnishings of all lawyers' offices in Canada.

Up the spider climbed, and down it fell. Sir John's left eyelid twitched. Again the spider tried to climb the string, but again it fell with an arachnidal curse. And a third time it struggled up the string, and immediately set to work to gobble up a juicy fly.

Sir John was now fully awake. "By George!" he cried (referring to George Brown of the Toronto *Globe*, and thus uttering a terrible Conservative curse) "shall yonder foolish insect put me to shame? I too shall strive, and strive again, until there is a Federal Government in Canada, gobbling up the richest flies the land affords!"

And hastily taking a drink of soda water (of which he was inordinately fond) he rushed out and confederated Canada in a twinkling.

MORAL: Never sweep your office.

Laurier and the Teakettle

One day Sir Wilfrid Laurier sat by the hearth in his parents' home, musing and pondering in French (though being completely bilingual, he could just as easily have done it in English). Beside him, on the hob, the kettle bubbled. "Etre, ou non être?" mused Sir Wilfrid; "c'est la question." (This splendid line was later incorporated into the film of *Hamlet*, but it lost a great deal in translation.) "Blubbety-blub!" mused the kettle, in kettle-language. "Qu'est-ce que c'est que vous avez dit?" asked Sir Wilfrid. "Bloop!" said the kettle.

In that instant Sir Wilfrid conceived the whole theory of the steam-engine, and would have built a railway to the Yukon if the Senate had not vetoed the idea.

MORAL: The Senate should be reformed so as to consist entirely of the Cabinet.

Laura's Jewels

The constant companions of the great and good Laura Secord were her cows. Indeed, it was a cow that overheard the American officers planning their wicked attack upon Colonel Fitzgibbon's troops, and warned Laura. The story that she herself listened at the keyhole is a vicious canard. Being immovably upright, she could not stoop to a keyhole.

One day she was entertaining a purse-proud friend who boasted immoderately of her riches and her articles of personal adornment. "And will you not show me your jewels, Mrs. Secord?" said she.

Smiling enigmatically Laura called her cows to her. She put her arms around each brown neck, drawing the wet noses close to her own. "These are my jewels," said she, with well-nigh unbearable simplicity.

MORAL: The cream of the cream can get along without diamonds, even of the first water.

There you have it Mr. Hydra. Fill our children up with that sort of thing, and in no time their patriotism will have surpassed even our most unreasonable expectations.

Yours for an aggressively Canadian Canada,
Samuel Marchbanks.

• TO SAMUEL MARCHBANKS, ESQUIRE •

Honoured Sir:

On behalf of our client, Mr. Richard Dandiprat, we write to ask if it would not be possible to settle your difference with him in some amicable way which does not involve court procedure. Lawsuits among neighbours are to be avoided whenever possible, as we are sure you will agree. We learn to our amazement and chagrin that Mr. Dandiprat has written letters to you in which he virtually confesses it was he who imprisoned a skunk in your car while you were abroad. This was indiscreet, but Mr. Dandiprat is a man of lovable and open nature and concealment is distasteful to him.

We venture to suggest that if you care to pay some small sum — we suggest $2,500 — to Mr. Dandiprat as recompense for all the mental distress which your threatened lawsuit has cost him, the matter can be closed with good will on both sides.

Yours in a spirit of neighbourly forgiveness,
Jasper Raven,
(For Raven and Craven, Solicitors).

• TO RAVEN AND CRAVEN •

Sirs:

So, you are crawling, are you? Whining for mercy, eh? No, no, gentlemen, I intend to roast your client, Dandiprat, before the fire of enraged public opinion. To your roost, Raven! To your lair, Craven, lest you perish with Dandiprat in the whirlwind of my wrath!

Yours in triumph,
Samuel Marchbanks.

• TO SAMUEL MARCHBANKS ESQUIRE •

Honoured, Esteemed—nay, Beloved Sir:

Oh, Mr. Marchbanks, what a bitter tale I have to tell! Last Autumn, with Hallowe'en approaching, we sent two or three of our secretarial staff into the cellar to bring up the base-burner which heats our office in the Winter months. Hallowe'en is, as you know, a festival dear to the hearts of lawyers, and Mr. Jabez Mouseman loves to see the flames flickering behind the little mica windows in the stove when the great day dawns. The girls got the stove into the office, and with some difficulty they set it up, and fitted the stovepipes into the wall. But when it came time to light the fire, ah, then—. You know how impatient the old are, Mr. Marchbanks. My dear father, Mr. Jabez Mouseman, seized what he imagined to be some valueless material from a filing cabinet, and lit the fire. Unlucky fate guided his hand. It was your file, and all the evidence, so carefully piled up, and all the incriminating letters from Dandiprat are gone.

But the law is not without resource, sir. We shall rewrite all the documents, from memory, as soon as possible. We shall even provide facsimiles of the signatures. In the end the evidence will be better than ever. But for a law-term or two we shall be wise to allow the case to drift along without too much activity.

Yours in sorrow,
Mordecai Mouseman,
(for Mouseman, Mouseman and Forcemeat).

P.S.: The cost of restoring the evidence will add considerably to your legal expenditures, but Let Right Be Done is the motto of our firm.

• THE RULING PASSION •

I WAS INTRODUCED to a lady this evening who said, "Well, and do you still do any writing on the side?" I simpered and said, "Oh, a little, you know," for I was so thunderstruck that I could not collect my wits in time to make a proper rejoinder. But I made a speech to her in my head, afterward, which ran thus: "Woman, for almost all of my adult life I have lived by the pen, with some assistance from the typewriter and the printing press. I do not write "on the side" as you insultingly suggest. I write morning, noon and night. When I am not actually engaged in the physical act of writing I am thinking about writing—my own and other people's. Writing is my business and my pleasure, my cross and my salvation, my joy and my sorrow." But it would have been foolish to say this aloud. There are many millions of people who think that writing, and painting, and music are things which their practitioners pick up in an idle hour; they have no conception of the demands these apparently trivial pastimes make upon those who are committed to them. Such people live in a world which is as strange to me as the Mountains of the Moon.

• POSTURE PROBLEM •

I OBSERVE WITH no enthusiasm it is National Posture Week in the U.S.A.; thank Heaven this heathen festival is not being observed in Canada. When I was a boy we were taught that the only proper posture for the body was that of a sentry at attention—eyes glazed, chest bursting, shoulders under the ears, toes curled and chin digging into the Adam's apple. Later this position was somewhat relaxed, and it was admitted that it was sometimes permissible to touch the heels to the ground. Recently a scientist who had done a lot of work with monkeys has said that a relaxed posture, leaning forward and ambling like a gorilla, is the best and most natural for man. So confused am I by these changes that I have developed my own posture, which has two phases— standing up and lying down. I cannot sit. I lie in chairs on the back of my neck, allowing gravity to drag my vital organs toward the floor. When I stand, I lose height at the rate of about two inches every hour. In the morning, when I am thoroughly uncoiled, I am six feet tall; if my day involves much standing, I am five feet tall by lunchtime, four feet six inches by dinner, and go to bed a midget. Posture is a word I prefer not to use in connection with myself.

• To Samuel Marchbanks, Esquire •

Dear Mr. Marchbanks:

I have just finished reading a book by the eminent child-psychologist, Dr. Blutwurst Susskind, in which he makes it clear that what children want more than anything in the world is parental love. It is this desire, he says, which makes children ask questions at inconvenient times, wake their parents up early in the mornings, kick them on the shins, and in general behave in a way which thoughtless parents call "making a nuisance of themselves." Dr. Susskind says that an eager child should never be rebuffed. The parents should say: "I love you dearly, but I haven't time to attend to you now," or something of the sort.

Now I have a scheme which I would like you, as an internationally known lover of children, to assist me in popularizing. It is based upon the old system of Sunday School cards which you will remember: a child got a small card for each visit to S.S.; when it had ten small cards it could exchange them for a large card; when it had ten large cards it could get a Bible. Now my idea is that a parent should have a stock of cards saying: "Love you dearly; busy now," which it could hand to the child which interrupted at an inconvenient moment. Ten cards could be exchanged for a large card saying: "Dote upon you madly; go away." Ten of these large cards could be exchanged for a visit to the circus, a picnic, a soda-guzzle or some similar treat.

The cards, I feel, could most effectively be sold through the Home and School Clubs; the whole scheme could be financed for a beggarly $100,000 and it is for this laughable sum that I confidently turn to you.

Yours with complete confidence,
Minerva Hawser.

• To Chandos Fribble, Esquire •

Worthy Fribble:

It is indeed good news that you intend to prepare a thesis on the Rights of Women in Canada. I shall await the appearance of the Fribble Report with keen expectation. Is it true that the French translation is to be called, with greater frankness, *L'Amour en Canada*?

Meanwhile, let me report for you a curious conversation I heard the other night, when I attended an entertainment where a great many adolescents were present. Behind me sat a boy and a girl, both about fifteen.

> BOY: (Laughing at one of his own jokes) "G'wan, cut out that laffin'."
>
> GIRL: "Gee, I can't. You got me laffin' so's I can't stop."
>
> BOY: (delighted) "Cut it out, I tell yuh. Everybody's lookin' at yuh."
>
> GIRL: (trying to stifle mirth) "Fsssst! Splut! Eeeeeeeek!"
>
> BOY: (transported) "Cut it out! Cut it out!"
>
> GIRL: "Gee I can't! Not if you're gonna say funny things like that!"
>
> BOY: "Juh want me to take yuh out in the hall and slap yuh around? That'll stopyuh!"
>
> GIRL: (ecstatic at the idea) "Aw, yer killin' me! Fsssst!"

Here, I think we have a fairly typical pattern of Canadian sexual behaviour. The male, having subdued the female by his superior intellectual power, dominates and even threatens her. This produces in her a mounting physical and psychological pleasure, like the rising of steam in a boiler. This psychological pressure causes her to kick the back of my seat in an irregular rhythm, similar to the mating-dance of the Whooping Crane. It is this sort of thing that makes Canada the Amorist's Paradise it is.

I shall inform you of any other interesting manifestations of the biological urge which may come under my eye.

Scientifically yours,
Marchbanks.

• TO DIONYSUS FISHORN, ESQUIRE. • *f*

Dear Mr. Fishorn:

No, I will not support your application for a Canada Council grant to enable you to write your novel. I know nothing about you, but I know a good deal about novels, and you are on the wrong track.

You say you want money to be "free of care" for a year, so that you can "create," and you speak of going to Mexico, to live cheaply and avoid distraction. Fishorn, I fear that your fictional abilities have spilled over from your work into your life. You see yourself in some lovely, unspoiled part of Mexico, where you will stroll out of your study onto the patio after a day's "creation," to gaze at the sunset and get into the cheap booze; your wife will admire you extravagantly and marvel that you ever condescended to marry such a workaday person as herself; the villagers will speak of you with awe as El Escritor, and will pump your beautiful servant Ramona for news of your wondrous doings; you will go down into the very depths of Hell in your creative frenzies, but you will emerge, scorched and ennobled, in time for publication, translation into all known languages, and the Nobel Prize.

DIONYSUS FISHORN, brother of Apollo Fishorn the playwright, did not follow Marchbanks' advice but has made for himself a distinguished career as a Misunderstood Genius. His five novels, every one written on a grant of some kind, from somebody-or-other (gratefully acknowledged in the introductory pages of each book) have sold, in all, slightly under 10,000 copies, have not adventured beyond the confines of Canada, and are to be found, in almost mint condition, in the larger public libraries. However, he has been a boon to young academics, who write articles about his symbolism, his symbology and even his symbiosis, and quarrel delightedly about him in the university quarterlies. They are agreed on one thing: he beats the socks off writers who are more widely read, and this is the sort of publicity that keeps the grants coming.

Ah, Fishorn, would that it were so! But take the advice of an old hand: you won't write any better in Mexico than in Tin Cup, B.C., and unless you are wafted into a small, specially favoured group of the insane, you will never be free from care. So get to work, toiling in the bank or wherever it is by day, and serving the Triple Goodness at night and on weekends. Art is long, and grants are but yearly, so forget about them. A writer should not take handouts from anybody, even his country. /

Benevolently but uncompromisingly,
Samuel Marchbanks.

• DREAM MAIDENS •

SAW A MOTOR-BICYCLE parked in the street today, and on its wind-screen were several alluring pictures of girls, one of whom wore what appeared to be a scanty outfit of leopardskin underwear; she stretched her arms above her head (presumably in order to give greater freedom to her considerable bosom) and carried a banner upon which was written "If you don't see what you want, ask for it." As I looked, the owner came out of a house, mounted the machine, kicked it fiercely in the slats several times, and at last goaded it into action. He was a smallish, mousey fellow with rimless glasses, and did not look to me as though his acquaintance included any girls who wore leopard next their skins. And it has been my usual experience that all those wildly improbable girls who exist only in the minds of artists appeal chiefly to young men who either know no girls at all, or know only girls of a mousiness

---

What, no grants? Marchbanks has always maintained that a writer should have a job that brings him an income apart from his writing. If he cannot manage that, he should take care to be born into a family that can make him an allowance, or leave him some money. Samuel Johnson was able to take a pension from his government without feeling obliged to show unseemly gratitude, but Johnsons are few. Grants to authors are best confined to those who, by reason of age or misfortune, must have them, and public subventions are best confined to the performers, rather than the originators, of works of art.

equal to their own. Pin-up girls are dreams, and dreams unlikely to come true. And a good thing, perhaps, for what would the average young man do with a girl who never put on her clothes and whose bosom accounted for one-third of her total weight?

• FEATHERED FUTURITY •

I SEE BY THE PAPER that Rhythmic Arithmetic has been abandoned in the schools. I never understood what it was, though much time was wasted by adult educators explaining it to me, and I never met a child who could explain it. But I have long recognized that I have no mathematical facility whatever. Plato, who was a brainy fellow, said that "innocent, light-minded men who know no mathematics will become birds after death"; I rather look forward to being a bird, and taking a bird's revenge on all my enemies. Plato also thought that men who had no philosophy would become animals after death; really stupid people would continue their existence as fish; "cowardly and unrighteous men," he asserted, would find that in the next world they had been turned into women. Plato had a poor opinion of women, which would make life difficult for him if he were born again in this century; he also thought little of the professional educators of his day, an attitude which would make it utterly impossible for him to get a certificate to teach in a one-room country school in Twentieth-Century Canada.

Plato would no doubt say that the Nine Muses are all women, and that should be enough for them. But in the present day, when equality is the watchword of all truly advanced thinkers, Marchbanks thinks it is altogether too much for them, and that four-and-a-half Muses should at once be redefined as men. If halving a Muse proves difficult, perhaps one Muse might be classed as of indeterminate sex, and Urania, Muse of celestial phenomena and astronomy would split nicely down the middle.

• WORD OF HORROR •

*W*AS TALKING TO a musical person who informed me that a celebrated pianist would "concertize" in Toronto next month. This remark nearly caused me to swallow my pipe, for though I have seen the vile word "concertize" in print for several years this was the first time I had ever heard anyone use it in conversation. I was taken aback as if my hostess had said, "Won't you climax your meal with another cup of coffee?" Such words fill me with an urge to seize the person who uses them in a commando grip and twist him (more often the offender is a she) until I have broken every bone. Then their broken-boned walking would be appropriate to their broken-boned speech. O Mighty Music! Did David concertize before Saul, or Bach before Frederick the Great? Did Beethoven concertize? (In the time, of course, when they were not composerizing.) No, apes and dung-beetles, they PLAYED!

• SUPER-BOY •

*T*O A CONCERT given by a group of choir boys from Vienna. It was an admirable evening's entertainment, which was more than I had expected for I am not an enthusiastic admirer of the Human Boy. In my reckoning boys range from Good Boys —that is, boys who can pass the Towers without upsetting garbage cans and throwing rubbish on the lawn—to the lowest dregs of humanity, depraved slubberdegullions who do the above things, and worse. But these Viennese boys were quite unusual in several respects: they were clean; they were well-behaved; their hair was brushed; they looked as though they might be trusted with whole rows of garbage cans. . . . This was the first time I have ever heard choir boys who were not trained in the English tradition of fruity hooting; an English choir boy sounds like a lovesick owl, and although it is a pretty sound it moves me to a gentle melancholy—a kind of Sunday-night-and-another-week's-work-starts-tomorrow feeling. . . . Sometimes people say to me: Were you never a boy yourself, Mr. Marchbanks? Answer: Yes, for several years I was a noble, dutiful, clean, respectful Super-Boy.

• COMMUNIQUÉ •

(dropped at my door by an escaped prisoner)

To Big Chief Marchbanks:
How, Marchbanks!

You got any old magazines, Marchbanks? Magazines in jail awful. Sent here after long hard life in dentist office. All girl pictures got bustles. Educated fellow in jail read story out loud other day. Good story about detective. Name Sherlock Holmes. Magazine say this first story about him ever. But last page gone. Doctor leave magazine bundle here yesterday. Magazine all about how have babies. We know that already. Anyway that squaw work. You got magazines tell us what we don't know?

Osceola Thunderbelly,
Chief of the Crokinoles.

• THE PAST REARRANGED •

I WAS LOOKING at some records today, belonging to a friend who collects oddities for the gramophone, and was interested in a series called *Immortal Voices and History Making Events*. It was an odd jumble, but I found a record of Sarah Bernhardt reciting a Prayer for Our Enemies, and put it on. Amid the rustling and scratching inseparable from old recordings there was barely audible a passionate, female voice, speaking—or to be exact, howling—in French. In the descriptive note which went with the thing Sarah Bernhardt was described as "a great lady of the American stage," and thus France was robbed of one of its glories. The U.S.A. and the U.S.S.R. between them are dividing not only the earth, but the past thereof.

• ORGY •

*T*O A MOVIE called *Faust and the Devil*, made in Italy, which I enjoyed greatly, and particularly an Orgy scene, where Faust made genteel and ineffective plays for several girls in filmy frocks. The Devil, meanwhile, sat at a table loaded with goodies, but ate nothing save a few grapes. Watching his weight, I suppose. Have not seen an Orgy in a movie since the days of the silent film; they often had Orgies, and they always took the form of a light meal, eaten in the company of jolly girls in peek-a-boo nighties. I have never been at an Orgy, though I suppose my garbage this morning filled the neighbourhood with dark suspicion.

• LIFE AND ART •

*T*O OTTAWA TO ATTEND a performance of a play by my old friend Apollo Fishorn, the Canadian playwright. Fishorn got on the train at Smith's Falls, with a live hen in a net, and a basket of fresh eggs, which he said he was taking to the actors, who appreciate these little comforts from the farm. He also had a carpetbag with a bad catch, which kept falling open and revealing the sorriest pair of pyjamas I have ever seen. . . . I liked the play, but joining a party of knowledgeable persons in the lobby at one of the intervals, I learned that there was too much talk in it, and not enough action. Now this puzzles me. There are only a very few kinds of action which can be shown on the stage. Love is a great theme of playwrights, but if they try to develop it as action rather than as talk, the censor cracks down. ✏ Murder is good, but

---

✏ *Or did, but nowadays Censors are an endangered species and their mating grounds (very secret) have to be protected from predators whose battle-cry is Show All and Say All. Of course literary artists have always shown all and said all, but not in the bleak terms the enthusiasts demand. To call up in the reader's mind some shadow or dim vision of an erotic act or scene is to do him an inestimable favour and the best writers have always been dab hands at it. Yes, even the great Victorians if you read them sensitively. But there are many people who, unless all the heat and sweat and smell o' the drink is set down in detail, feel nothing and what they feel when they get their desire will not please them long; for with pornography, as with brandy, the draught must be ever stronger if it is to produce an effect.*

if you murder more than one person an act, people think you are trying to be Shakespeare, and complain. I mentioned this criticism to Fishorn, and he sighed, and said: "Yes, but life is 99 per cent talk. Look at the people who want more action in my play; what are they doing? Talking! What are you doing? Talking!" And sure enough when I caught sight of myself in a mirror, he was right.

• DOGS ON THE UP-AND-UP •

*F*OR YEARS PEOPLE have belaboured me about what they consider to be my disrelish for dogs; not only do they love dogs — I must love them too. But recently a philosopher friend (well, as much a friend as any real philosopher ever permits himself to be, for fear of accidents) took up the fight. "Dogs relate us to the chthonic realm," said he, "and without some measure of chthonicity you are an imperfect human being." He thought to bamboozle me with his fancy Greek word, but I already knew it, and what is more, I pronounce the initial "ch" which is more than he could do because he always has catarrh. It just means "of the lower world," and the lower world is much in fashion these days. But I know dogs. They are aware that they belong to a lower world, and are trying to improve themselves by begging upper-world food, lolling in upper-world chairs, and snuffling wetly at upper-world ankles (from which they proceed upward until outraged modesty demands that I give them a kick in the slats). Dogs are trying to take over, and I know it. Not that a dogocracy could be much worse than what we have now.

• BLESS YOU •

*S*INCE CHILDHOOD'S happy hour I have been the possessor of a particularly loud sneeze. It is not the loudest in the world; an Irishman I have known for many years has a supersneeze which he heralds with a plaintive cry, somewhat like that of an epileptic just before a seizure, and beside him I am but a child in sternutation. / But I am a pretty good sneezer, and kindly people say "God bless you" in awed voices, after they have crawled from under the tables where they have taken shelter. This custom of blessing a sneezer is said to have originated with Saint Gregory the Great, though the Romans said "Absit Omen," which is as near as a Roman ever got to blessing anybody. My Jewish friends, of course, say "Gesundheit" and one of them explained to me that it is an old Jewish belief, traceable to the *Cabbala*, that when a man sneezes his soul flies out of his mouth for an instant (presumably on an elastic) and in that fateful twinkling a demon may rush into his body, cut the elastic, and take charge. I know a good many people whose general hatefulness, contrariety and all-round objectionableness may well be the result of a sneeze during which the blessing was forgotten.

• TO MERVYN NOSEIGH, M.A. •

Dear Mr. Noseigh:

No no; I am not in the least offended by your letter asking about my sex life. I fully realize that no study of an author, living or dead, is of any value without this sort of saucy exploration. And my disenchantment has undoubtedly had more effect on literature than anything since Henry James had his mysterious misadventure. /

Like every Canadian of my generation, I picked up my knowledge of Sex in the gutter. I well remember the day I did so. There

---

/ *This was the late Sir Tyrone Guthrie (1900–1970) whose sneeze was known to bring down plaster in rooms of spacious dimensions, and frequently stopped theatrical performances in full spate.*

/ *When a very young man Henry James (1843–1916) suffered what he described as "a horrid even if an obscure hurt" which his biographer, Leon Edel, has been unable to identify more accurately. But it looks as if it was something that kept him pretty much out of the toils of women, whom he was therefore able to observe with a clear eye, and embody in some of the finest and most searching portraits of their sex in literature.*

it was, a torn scrap of print, fluttering on the very edge of a man-hole. I picked it up, and studied it with care. So far as I could make out, much of it was in foreign languages — squiggly scripts that meant nothing to me; but there was a little left of the English section, and from it I discerned that headaches, a furred tongue, and occasional spots before the eyes were signs of — the fragment was torn at that point, but it was obviously Sex.

From that time forward I made discreet enquiries of every attractive girl I met about her headaches; they never had any. Once I reached a point of intimacy where I was able to ask a marvellous girl to show me her tongue; it was as clean as could be, so obviously I had been misled about her feelings for me, and broke off the affair with a heavy heart.

Years later I discovered that what I had found in the gutter was part of the literature that comes wrapped around bottles of Eno's Fruit Salts.

Such are the tragedies that maim the lives of millions.

Yours in total disillusion,
Samuel Marchbanks.

• TO CHANDOS FRIBBLE, ESQUIRE •

Dear Fribble:

During the last few days I have received a horrifying number of invitations and supplications from people who want me to join or support something new. They all appear to want to create something which has never been known on earth before. But not me. I am sick of novelties — or what pass for novelties among easily satisfied people. And for that reason I am organizing a one-man *Society for the Resurrection and Preservation of Words which Have Been Permitted to Lapse into Unmerited Disuse.* Let's deal with something old, for a change.

There are many such words, and from time to time I may issue bulletins about them. But for the time being these will do:

(1) HUZZA: an excellent word which has been dropped in favour of "hurrah." But huzza has a nice, genteel air about it; it expresses

enthusiasm, but not too much. It is the ideal word to use when, for instance, somebody suggests that you go for a good long tramp in the country, just as you have settled down for a nap in your chair. It is a good word to shout, in a well-controlled voice, when unpopular officials pass you in a procession. My typewriter ribbon has just broken, and luckily I have another, which I shall have to put in the machine myself, getting my hands dirty and abrading my temper. Huzza!

(2) HOSANNA: another useful word of praise, expressing goodwill without overdoing it. It has hardly been used in ordinary speech since the following dirty limerick was current, around 1905:

> There was a young maiden named Anna
> Who sang as a High Church soprana;
>   When she fell in the aisle
>   The Dean said with a smile,
> "We have heard, now we see, your hosanna!"

(3) HEYDAY: the dictionary calls this "an exclamation of gaiety or surprise." Yes, but not of ecstatic gaiety or complete surprise. This seems to me to be just the word to use when unwrapping a gift of handkerchiefs, which has been presented to you by somebody who always give you handkerchiefs.

Words for the expression of limited emotion are not common in our language. The three I have listed above should not be allowed to die, and so far as I am concerned, they shan't.

Yours,
Samuel Marchbanks.

• TO SAMUEL MARCHBANKS, ESQUIRE •

Dear Mr. Marchbanks:

It is with a heavy heart, Mr. Marchbanks, sir, that I write to tell you that your lawsuit against Richard Dandiprat finally came to court on Tuesday last, and that you have lost it. It was a most unhappy chance that brought a case of such delicacy to the attention of the judge the day after his birthday. His Honour had obviously been keeping the festival in the great tradition, and as soon as he took his place on the bench it was plain that his mind was occupied with old, unhappy, far-off things. Our Mr. Cicero Forcemeat was also somewhat indisposed, having been called to the bar repeatedly the day before; the lustre of his eloquence was, shall we say, dimmed. Dandiprat's lawyers, Craven and Raven, were in like case, and the court presented an hapless picture. Nobody could hear anybody else; everybody was drinking bromoseltzer; the janitor had neglected to turn on the heat. The trial occupied precisely seven and one-half minutes. The judge was annoyed that you were not present, and has fined you $100 for contempt of court. ¶ This, with the costs of the suit, will amount to a rather larger figure than you have probably anticipated. But without the Unforeseen, Mr. Marchbanks, life would be intolerable and the law would be an exact science, instead of the tantalizing jade that she is.

A complete statement is enclosed, and prompt payment will be appreciated by

Your most faithful,
Mordecai Mouseman,
(for Mouseman, Mouseman and Forcemeat).

¶ Marchbanks was also unlucky in his judge, who was none other than the renowned Mr. Justice Sucklethug, known to the criminal world as Ol' Daddy. Sucklethug believed implicitly in the goodness and perfectability of mankind, and to him felons and even murderers were lost lambs, unfairly persecuted by society. He was deeply prejudiced against all prosecutors, including the Crown itself, and was famous for the light sentences he imposed upon criminals of the deepest dye. "Go, and sin no more," he would say to the prisoner, when dismissing him, and when the prisoner turned up after having sinned again, Sucklethug would be moved to tears by his plight. It is small wonder that he was all for Dandiprat and trampled Marchbanks beneath his feet. It is widely predicted that when Sucklethug dies, his monument will be erected by the Mafia itself, and will excel even that "statue in pure gold" which commemorated the romance of Romeo and Juliet.

• TO SAMUEL MARCHBANKS, ESQUIRE •

Well, Sammy Old Pal:

The trial is now over, and no hard feelings, eh? All good pals as before. Drop in any time, and bring your own bottle with you. Like I say to the Little Woman — "No use getting mad at March-banks; it takes all kinds to make a world; so let's be big about this thing, Goo-Ball, and forgive him for all the hard things he has thought about us; after all, like the fellow says, he's probably an eight-ulcer man in a four-ulcer job."

By the way, one day when you were out I borrowed your wheel-barrow, and it just came apart in my hands. You can have the pieces back any time, but you'd be better off to get a new one.

All the best for neighbourly relations,
Dick Dandiprat.

• TO MERVYN NOSEIGH, M.A. •

Dear Mr. Noseigh:

Your last question is a humdinger. "When did you first decide to be a humorist; who were your chief humorous influences; how do you define humour?" — you ask, just like that.

I never decided to be a humorist; if I am one, I was born one, but I have never really given the matter much thought. I was once given a medal for humour, but it makes me nervous; I have tried to lose it, but I am too superstitious to throw it away. Men who bother their heads too much about being something particular — a Humorist, or a Philosopher, or a Social Being, or a Scientist, or a Humanist, or whatever — quickly cease to be men and become animated attitudes.

I suppose some of the humorists I have read have influenced me, because I think of them with affection, but never as people to be copied. I have read others, greatly praised as funny-men, who simply disgusted me. If I had to name a favourite, I suppose it would have to be François Rabelais, but I do not give him my whole heart; he had a golden touch with giants and pedants, but he thought ignobly of women.

Don't you know what humour is? Universities re-define wit and satire every few years; surely it is time they nailed down humour for us? I don't know what it is, though I suspect that it is an attribute of everything, and the substance of nothing, so if I had to define a sense of humour I would say it lay in the perception of shadows.

Sorry to be so disappointing,
Samuel Marchbanks.

• TO MRS. KEDIJAH SCISSORBILL •

Madam:

So you are astonished that a man of my apparent good sense should believe in Astrology, are you? My good woman, if you knew more of my history, you would be astonished that my good sense is still apparent.

You have heard of the Wandering Jew, who roams the earth till Judgement Day? I am his cousin, the Wandering Celt, and my branch of the family is the elder. Therefore I have a had good deal of experience in belief.

In my early days I was invited by learned men to believe in the Triple Goddess, and a very good goddess she was. But when I was Christianized I was commanded to believe in a Trinity that was also a Unity, and a goddess who looked and behaved remarkably like my Triple Goddess, though I was assured she was somebody much more up-to-date and important. Then a man named Calvin demanded that I believe in Strength through Misery, and I did till a man named Wesley told me to believe in Personal Revelation and Ecstasy, and I did. During a brief spell in New England Emerson told me to believe in a Unity that had nothing to do with a Trinity, and was itself of doubtful existence, and I did. But then I was told by people calling themselves scientists to believe in Phrenology, Animal Magnetism, the Germ Theory, Psycho-Analysis, Sociology, Relativity, Atomic Energy, Space Travel, God-is-Dead, Quasars, Spiral Time and so many new faiths that I could not keep up with them, though I tried.

Until I wearied and went back to the Triple Goddess, with Astrology thrown in for fun.

Because as a Celt, you see, I am at once credulous of everything and sceptical of everything, and not a whole-hogger, who rushes from the Mother of God to Mary Baker Eddy, and from her to LSD, expecting some revelation that will settle everything. I don't want everything settled. I enjoy the mess.

So with all the fiery planets opposed to Uranus I am

Yours sincerely,
Samuel Marchbanks.

• VAIN BOAST •

*T*HERE CAN BE no doubt that future historians will look upon this present age as an Age of Decline. True, it will have its glories, and may be referred to in histories of philosophy and humanism as the Age of Marchbanks, but it is scarcely possible for a single man to redeem a whole era. Today, for instance, I found myself in the company of several men of business, and they were boasting, which is no cause for surprise. But of what were they boasting? They were blowing, to my grief and astonishment, about the rate of Income Tax they paid. "Fifty per cent of all I make goes in Income Tax," cried one. "Laughable pauper!" cried another, "I have paid sixty-five per cent for years!" "To the House of Refuge with you!" cried still a third, and revealed that he keeps only fifteen per cent of what he makes. When all men have left to be proud of is the poor moiety which the tax-gatherers leave them of their wealth, a greater decline than that of Imperial Rome is far advanced. Mark the words of Marchbanks the Prophet.

• COMMUNIQUÉ •
(delivered by a Dove with an olive twig in its beak)

To Big Chief Marchbanks:
How, Marchbanks!

Not out of jail yet, Marchbanks. This awful late Spring. No want freedom. Want jail. So when day come for let me out I kick Turkey awful hard when he inspecting beds. What for you kick me, he say. Seat your pants awful shiny, I say. Dazzle my eyes. Make me think sunrise. I kick for do Sun Dance. Ha, ha. Joke Marchbanks. Turkey get red neck. O, he say, funny fellow huh. Yes, I say. So he say I get no time off for good conduct and have to stay in jail another week. This good, Marchbanks. Maybe Spring in one more week. This awful snow remind me poem my grandmother Old Nokomis teach me.

> March winds
> And April showers
> Always a month late
> In this damn country of ours.

Nokomis fine poet, eh Marchbanks?

How again,
Osceola Thunderbelly,
Chief of the Crokinoles.

Alas, this was the last message to reach Marchbanks from his old friend. A few days afterward, Thunderbelly died in jail. The warden, writing to Marchbanks, identified his illness as "psoriasis of the liver."

L'envoi

*O*F COURSE such a book as this must have an *envoi* in which the author takes farewell of his work, and begs the public to accept it in a kindly spirit. It is simply a matter of literary good manners. I—Davies—would be glad to write it myself in the tone of gentle regret which is thought proper to an *envoi*, speaking of the happy relationship between its contents (portions of which have been known to the public since 1947) and the Reader, and bespeaking his goodwill for this new and (because of my labours as editor and explainer) greatly improved version. But ever at my back I hear, Sam's noisy yammering, loud and clear.

"Author?" he shrieks. "Author! Are you attempting to palm yourself off as the *author* of this florilegium of *my* work? You have nipped and tucked and stuck in footnotes as if the Reader were imbecilic, but you have originated nothing. *I* am the author—the sole begetter—of this volume unless the word author has suddenly become synonymous with hack-editor. If there is any envoying to be done I shall do it myself. So, Davies, stand aside; and Reader, hang on to your hat!

"I say as Walt Whitman (not a bad fellow, though a noisy writer) said—

> ...this is no book,
> Who touches this touches a man

—and that man is myself, Samuel Marchbanks. Of course Davies has done some editorial work, and very lucky he is (poor daub) to be associated with me. But let us have no misunderstanding about who is the real writer. Davies never had an original idea in his life that I did not hiss into his ear."

Can I deny it? Not with a clear conscience. Marchbanks and I have struggled through a literary life like two men in a three-legged race. And as anyone who has ever run a three-legged race knows, the only way to manage is to keep thrusting the two linked legs forward, leaving the two single legs to catch up as best they may.

To put it more elegantly, one of us is the writer and the other is the *Doppelgänger*, and who is to say which is which? As Marchbanks put it when I met him for drinks at the Crank and Schizoid, we are *The Canadian Brothers*, and like those far-off Corsican Brothers we are seemingly individual but mystically united, forever.

So, hand in hand, me bowing gracefully with my free hand on my heart, and Marchbanks exhorting and haranguing to the last, we bid you, our Reader

FAREWELL